To Govern the Devil in Hell

To GOVERN the DEVIL in HELL

THE POLITICAL CRISIS IN TERRITORIAL KANSAS

PEARL T. PONCE

NIU Press *DeKalb, IL*

© 2014 by Northern Illinois University Press
Published by the Northern Illinois University Press, DeKalb, Illinois 60115

All Rights Reserved
Design by Shaun Allshouse

Library of Congress Cataloging-in-Publication Data
Ponce, Pearl T.
To govern the devil in hell : the political crisis in territorial Kansas / Pearl T. Ponce.
    pages cm
Includes bibliographical references and index.
ISBN 978-0-87580-486-6 (cloth) — ISBN 978-0-87580-706-5 (pbk.) — ISBN 978-1-60909-159-0 (e-book)
1. Kansas—Politics and government—1854–1861. 2. Kansas—History—1854–1861. I. Title.
F685.P66 2014
978.1'02—dc23
2014002303

Table of Contents

Acknowledgments vii

Introduction 3

1—Jupiter's Gift: *The Creation of Kansas Territory* 9

2—Territorial Politics and the Struggle for Party Supremacy, 1854–1855 39

3—Kansas in 1856: *The Escalating Conflict* 73

4—Congress and the Kansas Issue in 1856 99

5—The 1856 Presidential Campaign and Kansas as a Party Issue 130

6—Pledges and Principles: *Buchanan, Walker, and Kansas in 1857* 148

7—"The Noise of Democracy": *The Struggle over the Lecompton Constitution in Congress and Kansas* 175

Conclusion—"To the Stars through Difficulty" 198

    Appendix A—*Kansas-Nebraska Vote in the Senate (March 3, 1854)* 215
    Appendix B—*Senate Results by Section and Party* 217
    Appendix C—*Final Kansas-Nebraska Vote in the House (May 22, 1854)* 219
    Appendix D—*House Results by Section and Party* 227
    Appendix E—*House Results by State* 229
    Appendix F—*Kansas Contested Delegate Election: Comparison of Vote to Oust Whitfield and to Seat Reeder (August 4, 1856) with Vote to Authorize a Special Investigating Committee (March 19, 1856)* 239
    Notes 245
    Bibliography 289
    Index 309

Acknowledgments

I would like to acknowledge the historians who have shaped my education: the late Richard Harrison at Pomona College; John Lewis Gaddis and Steven Miner at Ohio University; and the late William Gienapp at Harvard University. In addition, I greatly appreciate the funding I received throughout my training, in particular at Ohio University where I was a Contemporary History Institute Fellow and at Harvard University where I was a Prize Fellow. At all three institutions, I was fortunate to be in the company of marvelous professors and dynamic colleagues. In particular, I especially would like to recognize the cohort at the Contemporary History Institute, especially Ruud van Dijk and Steve Taaffe, and my fellow tutors at Pforzheimer House, Harvard University, especially Elisabeth Guzman, John Yee and Mia Chung-Yee, Dayle Delancey, and David Bear.

Research for this book was facilitated by various grants. Thanks to the National Endowment for the Humanities, I spent five weeks in Nashville learning more about the South in Don Doyle's Summer Seminar for College and University Teachers on "Faulkner and Southern History." A Gilder Lehrman Fellowship allowed me to spend several weeks immersed in the Gilder Lehrman Collection at the New-York Historical Society. California State University provided a Summer Research Fellowship while travel funds in the History Department paid for a number of research trips, including significant ones to archives in Kansas, Pennsylvania, New York, Connecticut, and Washington. Finally, at Ithaca College, I received a Summer Research Grant and multiple grants from the Center for Faculty Research and Development which provided time off from teaching to focus on my scholarship. Furthermore, an Academic Project Grant paid for a research trip to St. Louis while my funding through the History Department and the Dean's Office in the School of Humanities and Sciences paid for several trips to Kansas.

Portions of this manuscript have been published before. I would like to thank Virgil Dean for his early encouragement of my work and for soliciting an article for the journal he edited. A condensed version of chapter six was published in *Kansas History: A Journal of the Central Plains*, vol. 27, n. 1–2 (Spring-Summer 2004). In addition, my article "Pledges and Principles: Buchanan, Walker, and Kansas in 1857" was subsequently reprinted in Virgil W. Dean, ed., *Kansas Territorial Reader* (Topeka: Kansas State Historical Society, 2005). A condensed version of chapter seven was published in Jonathan Earle and Diane Mutti Burke, eds., *Bleeding Kansas, Bleeding Missouri: The Long Civil War on the Border* (Lawrence: University Press of Kansas, 2013). I would especially like to thank Jonathan and Diane for inviting me to participate in the Border Wars Symposium in Lawrence, Kansas, in April 2011, and the Border Wars Conference in Kansas City, Missouri, in November 2011. I enjoyed contributing to the commemoration of the sesquicentennial of Kansas's admission to the Union and meeting my fellow specialists in the era. I greatly appreciate all of Jonathan's and Diane's hard work in organizing these events and editing the resultant book.

In finishing this book, I have incurred a great many debts. Thanks to all my friends and colleagues who read this work in its various incarnations. To all the research librarians and archivists with whom I worked, your dedication makes all historians' work, not just my own, possible. To the anonymous readers of the manuscript, I valued your insights, which guided me as I made my final revisions. Thank you to Silvana Siddali for introducing me to Mark Heineke, formerly of Northern Illinois University Press, who contracted my book. In ushering this to publication, I would like to thank everyone at the Press, especially Kenton Clymer, Interim Director; Linda Manning, Director; Susan Bean, Managing Editor; and Shaun Allhouse, Production Manager.

To close, I would like to acknowledge how much my professional life has been enriched through the relationships I developed on faculty at two institutions. I would like to thank my colleagues in the History Departments at California State University, San Bernardino, and especially at Ithaca College where I now teach. In particular, I wish to thank Kurt Graham, Brett Flehinger, Jennifer Germann, and Angela Branneman for their support and friendship. As always, I am grateful for my family, especially Florence and Lauren Ponce-Cornejo, Andres Cornejo, and Aurora Ponce. Finally, I would like to dedicate this book to the late William Fahey, William Gienapp, and Melecio Ponce. They remain greatly missed.

Introduction

"Govern Kansas in 1855 and '56! You might as well attempt to govern the devil in hell."[1] Although tinged with the bitter recognition of his own failures, former territorial governor Wilson Shannon's assertion does reflect the difficulties Kansas's executive teams faced when the typical settlement process disintegrated under the weight of political expediency. Better known as "Bleeding Kansas" in popular lore, antebellum Kansas continues to linger in our imagination as the subject of monographs, plays, poetry, songs, literature, and graphic novels. Concerned with explaining Kansas's strife, many historians have outlined the territorial struggle, especially the conflict between those for and against slavery, to answer the question of why Kansas was bleeding in the 1850s. Of equal importance, but far less illuminated, is the question of why the government, both local and national, allowed the violence to continue unstanched for so long. This question is fundamentally about governance—its existence, exercise, limits, and continuance—and it is why "Bleeding Kansas" and the answers its study holds still matter more than 150 years after its admission to the Union.

At the local level, Kansas suffered from an excess of governance because the official government had a shadow: an extralegal organization formed by ideologues who believed that the territorial government was illegitimate since it had been tainted at the moment of its creation. During the first two territorial elections in late 1854 and early 1855, proslavery activists from neighboring Missouri had violated the integrity of the ballot box. At the behest of national political figures, these men crossed the border, assaulting and intimidating voters at the polls. The territorial legislature they helped elect soon passed laws supporting the implantation of slavery in Kansas and curtailing traditional American rights such as freedom of speech, freedom of the press, and the right to sit on a jury. In the wake of such legislation, antislavery advocates became convinced that the territorial government was trying to eradicate them, not represent them. Believing their only recourse was to establish their own government, complete with a separate executive, legislature, and constitution, free-state partisans appealed to the national government for relief, specifically for immediate admission to the United States.

In part, the decision to create a shadow government stemmed from the conviction that outside interference had disenfranchised voters. Because it is the one branch of government that territorial residents elect, the legislature accrues even greater significance at a local level. But self-government in Kansas was also complicated by decisions made beyond its borders. In 1854 Congress passed the Kansas-Nebraska Act, which organized the territory under popular sovereignty and controversially overturned the Missouri Compromise. In 1820, during a crisis sparked by a movement to emancipate slaves in Missouri as a condition of its admission to the United States, Congress had forged a compromise whereby Missouri entered as a slave state, Maine entered as a free state, and the remaining Louisiana Purchase lands were divided so that slavery was prohibited from those lands above the latitude of Missouri's southern border and allowed below it. Thus for more than three decades, Americans expected this region would be free of slavery when organized. However, the Kansas-Nebraska Act allowed for the possibility that either or both territories could become slave states. Because of the sudden appearance of two territories (instead of one as in previous, failed bills), many observers believed the legislation was designed to ensure balance. Farther north, Nebraska would be free while Kansas, directly west of Missouri, would likely become a slave state.

In the best light, popular sovereignty is a tremendous expression of democracy, for who better to decide local institutions, namely slavery, than those affected? However, shortly after Kansas was opened to immigration, marred elections demonstrated that the territory's settlement would be atypical. The now politicized process meant that while a Kansas settler was easily identified, a bona fide settler was not, and suffrage rights were suddenly fraught with serious implications. Should a settler who claimed a homestead in Kansas, but lived a few miles away in Missouri while making improvements, be allowed to vote in Kansas? Should a settler whose travel to Kansas was sponsored by a New England political organization be enfranchised? What distinguishes a bona fide settler from someone tampering with the political process to further an ideological agenda? Should individuals without a genuine intention to settle be allowed to shape the future state's institutions? Such questions flummoxed authorities at both the local and national level.

With dueling governments in place and weighty decisions to be made, Kansas witnessed a flurry of self-government—the territory took census after census; held election after election; called convention after convention; and wrote constitution after constitution. In its seven years as a territory, Kansas sent Congress four constitutions in its premature efforts to become a state: the first, the Topeka Constitution, was written by the extralegal organization it was named after; the other three—the Lecompton, Leavenworth, and Wyandotte constitutions—were more traditionally constructed. These proceedings required constant organizing, debating, and canvassing, which served to keep the territory's political questions before all Kansans as well as their fellow Americans. By far the most significant question was whether Kansas would become a free or slave state, but that cannot be separated from the larger issue of whether territorial events compromised residents' self-determination. Were settlers freely able to exercise their rights? Did a constitution written on their behalf accurately represent their wishes? Would the federal government, either by acting or by failing to act, force its own agenda on settlers? This active experience in governance reflects the importance of agency in American democracy, but it nonetheless complicated efforts to ameliorate territorial tensions.

A rival government, repeated fraud at the polls, contested elections, and charges of illegitimacy and bias were only a few of the trials the executive teams in Kansas faced. Unfortunately for the territory and the presidents who appointed them, Kansas's myriad governors varied greatly in talent, efficacy, and nerve. And once skirmishing broke out between the two factions, an air of neutrality, a flair for diplomacy, a willingness to call for armed support, and an understanding of when to do so were sorely needed. However, an absence of these qualities and political pressure led to considerable turnover: from 1854 to 1861, the territory had six governors and another four acting governors. The continued instability in Kansas's top post illustrates the limits of territorial government: the nature of the violence and the seriousness of the questions at hand made it unlikely that Kansas's tribulations could be resolved locally.

If instability and personnel problems made a territorial solution doubtful, why was the Kansas issue, as it became known, not decisively settled nationally? Territorial Kansas was overseen by two presidents, Democrats Franklin Pierce and James Buchanan. Both men were Northerners with Southern proclivities when it came to their support of slavery; both men came of political age during an era when the spirit of compromise was seen as essential to preserving the Union; both men were badly damaged by Kansas events and, in turn, badly damaged their party with their Kansas-related decision making. But the greatest ordeal each man faced was of his own making: he became an activist instead of an advocate. As a result, they lost the air of impartiality without which they could not successfully intervene in the sectional conflict then coalescing in this one territory. Fellow Democrat Andrew Jackson had asserted that the president represented the will of the people but neither Pierce nor Buchanan was able to accurately identify what Kansans wanted, and so both continued to push policies that were increasingly untenable.

It can be argued, however, that responsibility for Kansas lay not in the White House, but in Congress. Indeed, Congress was beset by testimonials, memorials, letters, and petitions requesting action; in turn, that body generated thousands of pages about the troubles in Kansas. Yet solutions were in short supply despite ample opportunity to intervene, most notably each time a constitution arrived. Moreover, Congress had a responsibility to act in Kansas, for its decision to overturn the Missouri Compromise transformed a region that ought to have been free into a free-for-all instead. Finally, and perhaps most significantly, not quelling the fracas posed a severe risk. Since the Mexican-American War, popular sovereignty had gained traction precisely because it promised a straightforward solution to the disruptions created by expansion. By removing the slavery question from politicians and placing it in the hands of those most affected by the presence of slave labor, popular sovereignty promised to quiet the sectional storm, which extremists increasingly fueled. However, by not intervening soon enough, Congress allowed popular sovereignty to be perverted. There would be no other opportunities to demonstrate that this method could ameliorate the sectional conflict. But Congress could not effectively act during these critical years because of the uncertain power dynamic resulting from the collapse of the Second Party System, dominated by the Democratic and Whig parties, in the 1850s. Congress lacked the will to forge a compromise on Kansas, but even had that desire been there, there was insufficient party parity to form and support an acceptable solution.

Finally, while the chaos alone would have made governing Kansas difficult, this challenge was augmented by the sense of elevated stakes. The crisis of the Union, of which Kansas is an integral part, is also a question of governance—in this case, the continuance of a government dependent on balance and compromise for its success. One Kansas booster described the country's regions by writing, "The South is impulsive and enthusiastic, the North prudent and energetic; the South loves ease, enjoyment and leisure, the north loves enterprise, work and accumulation. Each has what the other wants, each requires the other to complete its attributes and supply its needs, and the harmonious blending of the two would make a grand and noble whole. Unfortunately, the South has one peculiarity which satisfies no want, which excites no sympathy in the North, and thus from the South comes the danger that menaces both."[2] Although this characterization is rife with stereotypes, the author captures the balance of the American system and the threat posed both by the South's devotion to slavery and growing Northern antagonism to that institution. Utah and New Mexico had been organized under popular sovereignty in the Compromise of 1850, but their settlement as a part of the Mexican cession was anomalous. Part of the nation since 1803, the organization of Kansas and Nebraska in 1854 dashed decades of expectation. Two years later, Kansas was more than a territory; it was a crossroads. Could the country agree on the place of slavery in the national fabric or would the American experiment in self-government end?

The meaning of Kansas was explored to great effect in 1856 when the territory was at its most violent and electoral politics condensed the issues into succinct slogans. But for many Americans, fatigue and frustration with the system were also evident. The Compromise of 1820 had lasted three decades; that of 1850, barely four years old and changing the rules, seemed to bring only vitriol and violence. When asked what the Whig Party intended to do, Ohio's Thomas Corwin explained that he expected they would "act as they always have, after the Democratic party may set the country on fire, they will come up with their fine compromises" and save the country, but he "for one, intend to let the fire rage. . . . I will do nothing—*nothing*. . . ."[3] Despite his defiant unwillingness to act, Corwin's sentiments reflect the expectation that sectional disputes could be defused through compromise. Although Corwin still identified himself as a Whig, his party had scattered; unable even to field a presidential candidate in 1856, the Whigs would not be saving the country. Instead, the Democrats and two parties new to presidential politics— the American (or Know-Nothing) and Republican parties—would bear the burden. Yet election results revealed that after a brief flare of success, the American Party was already on the wane. On the rise was a Republican Party focused on antislavery and on how Kansas demonstrated the depravity of the slavocracy, a favorite Republican epithet for the slave South. While victorious, the Democrats owed a debt to the three-way race but had earned four more years to quiet Kansas and contain the damage its instability inflicted on the body politic. The 1856 election was a transitional one—while the Second Party System had collapsed, it had not yet been replaced, and as Congress demonstrated, without parity compromises cannot be formed even when bloodshed demands it.

But events set in motion by the Kansas-Nebraska Act would be hard to arrest. In particular, the emotions on both sides of the conflict were stoked by fears of what Kansas represented. For Southerners, acceptance of a slave

Kansas would demonstrate the willingness of Northerners to respect their institutions. As Alabama's James Buford implored fellow Southerners, "The Crisis has arrived. The time has come for action—bold, determined action. Words will no longer do any good; we must have men in Kansas, and that by tens of thousands. A few will not answer. . . ."[4] For Northerners, the sudden opening of Kansas to slavery heralded the growing aggression of the South. "My country calls," Connecticut's Charles Whipple wrote, "and he that would refuse to obey the call that urges to arms the freemen of Kansas, is worse than a traitor. Life is sweet but Liberty sweeter. . . . . There is no alternative now, but to die an ignominious death, or fight as become freemen and if need be die as become men."[5] Whipple did not die that summer of 1856, but under his real name of Aaron D. Stevens, he would be executed in 1860 for his role in the raid on Harpers Ferry in the company of men who had exported the fight against slavery from Kansas to Virginia.

In stumping for the Democratic Party in 1856, former senator Robert Walker of Mississippi had observed that "popular revolutions are always sudden. The dark cloud is seen in the horizon; we hear the muttering thunder, nearer and nearer, louder, still louder, it rolls above us—then comes the lightening flash, the crash of the Union, and all is over. We will all then stand amid the ruins of the irrevocable past."[6] While Walker would be called to govern Kansas the following year, he could not offset this grim future either. One hundred fifty years after it joined the Union, Kansas remains compelling because it was an opportunity, but instead of a disaster averted or a lesson learned, in five years that storm Walker feared had arrived. In retrospect we recognize that the conflict in Kansas was a first draft for war, and the inability of the country's government, at either the local or national level, to solve it contributed to the deaths of six hundred thousand men who were willing to die for their beliefs. Although the more romantic story is the struggle for the fate of the country encapsulated in one small territory, one with clear antagonists and distilled ideas, at its heart, Kansas is also a story about the limits of governance and administration.

1

Jupiter's Gift

The Creation of Kansas Territory

At the dawn of the Thirty-third Congress, nine months into Franklin Pierce's presidency, Democrats seemed poised to fulfill their vision for the country. The election of 1852 had been a great victory as they regained the presidency by carrying all but four states. After several factions returned to the fold to ensure his election, the president hoped to fuse any remaining party cleavages. Nationally, the triumphant Pierce resolved to evade potentially debilitating fissures by having the executive and legislative branches steadfastly avoid reopening the slavery debate, a necessity as Democrats remained at odds over the Compromise of 1850, which had admitted California as a free state, established territorial governments in Utah and New Mexico under popular sovereignty (whereby territorial settlers would decide the slavery question), terminated the slave trade in Washington, and passed a fugitive slave act.

The party's 1852 platform had deplored the antislavery agitation that "ought not to be countenanced by any friend of our political institutions."[1] Official campaign materials depicted Pierce, a New Hampshire native, as a Union conservative impermeable to the antislavery agitation swirling throughout New England, a "statesman of practical sagacity—who loves his country as it is, and evolves good from things as they exist. . . ."[2] Many expected Pierce's March 1853 inaugural address to echo the platform's call for stability. Indeed, speaking of "an efficient discharge of duty," he pledged to adhere to the Compromise of 1850 and assured the nation that the 1820 Missouri Compromise also would be "unhesitatingly carried into effect." Because Pierce had promised that sectional conflicts would remain dormant, observers anticipated a term without slavery-based controversy.[3]

But appearances of stability were misleading—potentially devastating fault lines ran just under the surface of the Democratic Party and national politics, which would soon tear asunder the national fabric. The party's landslide electoral victory created the hubris of victory without a genuine mandate, owing more to a return to a "big tent" version of the party than to popular support for a coherent ideology. Selected on the fifty-ninth ballot, Pierce was nominated after more prominent men faltered due to mismanaged political alliances. Even his campaign biographer agreed "it would be a pretension . . . to assert that" Pierce was equal to those "distinguished men, whose claims, to use the customary phrase, had been rejected in favor of his own."[4] Further, the 1852 coalition required papering over significant party divisions, and a cohesive strategy remained unarticulated. Lacking his party's wholehearted endorsement, Pierce's ability to unite Democrats was unclear and was promptly undermined by competition for patronage positions worth more than 50 million dollars a year.[5]

This lucre was a source of dissension as Democrats disagreed over its distribution, and as a compromise candidate, the president proved equally drawn to compromise in managing the party. In New York, for instance, the party had long been wracked by factionalism. In 1847, Barnburners (Democrats and Free Soilers who favored the Wilmot Proviso) left the state convention when they were outvoted by conservatives (known as Hunkers). The party recognized both factions but demanded each support the 1848 presidential platform, which the Barnburners refused to do. When they were welcomed back in 1849, the Hunkers split into two groups: the Hards (or Hard-shells), who believed forgiveness had been extended too easily, and the Softs (or Soft-shells), who recognized the damage the split had caused and wanted to settle the issue. But in New York, Pierce divided the nine most lucrative positions equally among these three factions.[6] Rather than fuse the party together, Pierce's patronage policies, which rewarded free-soilers of questionable loyalty, emphasized the strains within it. His efforts to finesse such factions were not without their critics; *Putnam's Monthly* complained, "It is not the business of the chief magistrate of a great nation, to try to dance upon two cross wires; to come down from his lofty seat to adjust the brawls of street fighters, or to contrive plans for the artistic management of local jealousies and ambitions."[7] Another observer charged him with neglecting Union men, resulting in the absence of "that eagerness to defend Administration policy which is so necessary to Administration success." But perhaps party conflict was inevitable as returnees felt entitled to the spoils of victory while longtime loyalists saw themselves as worthier than fair-weather political allies, however useful they had been of late. Resentments among Democrats of all philosophies were well publicized, leading to the perception that the party was not as robust as their victory indicated.[8]

Without "the boldest and most decided action," Missouri judge Samuel Treat warned in mid-December, Pierce's administration and the fortunes of the party were doomed.[9] Resentments over the patronage struggle continued to reverberate; as the *New York Herald* reported soon after Congress convened in December 1853, the general feeling among party leaders did not favor the administration even though Democrats controlled Congress.[10] Lingering sectional distrust of a New England president contributed to the tension, as congressional Democrats were suspicious of Free Soilers popular in the region. "There is a general disposition," Democrat John Slidell (LA) remarked, "to give [Pierce] a fair and frank support [but] I do not believe that there is one man upon whose personal devotion he can count. . . . He is the 'de jure' not the 'de facto' head of the party."[11]

The Democrats benefited from an opposition in transition. The Whigs had experienced a contentious national convention (seven men declined the vice presidency) and their 1852 platform reaffirmed the Compromise of 1850, condemning agitation "as dangerous to our peace." Southern Whigs had insisted upon this plank, leaving Northern Whigs to be consoled by Winfield Scott's nomination, an unpopular choice in the South because he was connected to antislavery senator William Seward (NY). After the 1852 loss, their diminishing presence in the South, and the drift of Northern Whigs toward overt antislavery, the party was unlikely to maintain its unity.[12]

A third party, comprised of refugees from the Free Soil and Liberty parties and a few straying Whigs, ran as the Free Democrats in the 1852 election. Unlike the two established parties, their platform emphatically promised to parry slavery's burgeoning power: "to the persevering and importunate demands of the slave power for more slave states, new slave Territories, and the nationalization of slavery, our distinct and final answer is—no more slave States, no slave Territory, no nationalized slavery, and no national legislation for the extradition of slaves." The Free Democrats remained on the fringe garnering only 5 percent of the three million votes cast.[13] Nonetheless, their organization represented an alternative for disaffected Whigs and Democrats.

In addition, Pierce also faced a country still disconcerted by the Mexican-American War since management of the 500,000 square miles of land acquired in the 1848 Treaty of Guadalupe Hidalgo had not yet been resolved. In 1850, Senator Henry Clay's (KY) omnibus bill had failed, and the legislation passed in its place was merely a mirage, gained only after congressmen "intent on overcoming the crisis" accepted the piecemeal legislation.[14] Despite hopes that it would settle the slavery question, this compromise did not command the devotion inspired by earlier ones, a reflection, most likely, of the South's increasing insecurity. Moreover, such compromises were problematic, dependent upon an amorphous sense of honor for enforcement.

Despite Pierce's optimism, grumbling on both sides of the Mason-Dixon line about aspects of the Compromise that were unfair (the constraints placed upon slavery's expansion), were unjust (the Fugitive Slave Law), or hampered sectional goals (limits on the opportunities for both slave and free labor in the west), would prove premonitory. In many ways, the Compromise represented the worst kind of political marriage—one in which each side considered itself more moral in its views and more self-sacrificing than the other. Yet even aware of national discontent, few political observers would have selected Kansas as the catalyst for the turmoil that would augur civil war in the nation five years after territorial warfare commenced. In 1853, Kansas was merely part of the unorganized frontier and registered weakly if at all on the political radar. Yet this region possessed the dangerous combination of being vital to westward expansion while being disregarded (for many considered the region as fundamentally inhospitable to slave labor) as a potential slavery trouble spot.

The Transition from Nebraska to Kansas-Nebraska

Even after his presidential aspirations had been dashed, Senator Stephen Douglas (IL), chairman of the Committee on Territories, retained tremendous power. Before the congressional session, he downplayed his ambition, writing that since it was "in a distracted condition," the party "requires all our wisdom, freedom & energy to consolidate its power and perpetuate its principles."[15] But to unseat a Democratic incumbent, Douglas would need to increase his electoral capital with a significant legislative achievement.[16] Without pressing business, the time seemed propitious for a favorite project, construction of a Pacific railroad, to acquire the impetus that fruition demanded—organization of the interior.

Interest in Nebraska had increased since Utah's and New Mexico's organization. Local residents requested a territorial government in April 1852, as did a group in Missouri a few months later. Publicity increased after Thomas Jefferson Sutherland launched a newspaper campaign urging Nebraska's development.[17] In addition, Reverend Frederick Starr, writing as "Lynceus" in the late summer and fall of 1853, penned a series of letters on western issues. Focusing on slavery, Nebraska, and a Pacific railroad, he argued that because multiple territories aided the country by drawing off excess population, it was foolish to allow current territories to fill before authorizing new ones. An intriguing element of Starr's series was his examination of whether Missouri itself had violated the Missouri Compromise when it absorbed land bounded by the Platte and Kansas rivers in 1836. According to the 1820 legislation, this triangular region, located above the 36°30' line that formed Missouri's southern border, was free territory; however, Missouri acquired it and a previously free region now supported 4,500 slaves in violation of the compromise. Starr urged resolution of this ambiguity; otherwise, Southerners might establish slavery, only to discover years later the institution would be outlawed.[18]

In March 1853, Douglas's bill to organize Nebraska failed due to insufficient Southern support; only two senators from slave states, both from neighboring Missouri, had voted aye. Acquiring necessary Southern support would involve concessions to slavery, most likely reconsideration of congressional limits on expansion.[19] Before the new session commenced, Missouri's David Atchison, Senate president pro tempore, warned Douglas that he should resign his chairmanship if he again failed to pass a Nebraska bill, and three prominent Southern senators, Virginians James Mason and Robert Hunter and South Carolinian Andrew Butler, similarly pressed him. These four men were bound by friendship and a determination to push a Southern agenda in Congress; moreover, a shared residence transcended typical boardinghouse arrangements in the capital and cemented their ties such that they were known as "the F Street mess." Given their power—Mason chaired the Foreign Relations Committee; Hunter the Finance Committee; and Butler the Judiciary Committee—Douglas understood their support was critical.[20]

Ten years of frustration must have led him to the realization that continued western organization might involve reversing the Missouri Compromise, but Douglas was clearly reluctant to eliminate a demarcation that had contributed to 30 years of stability. In mid-December, describing himself as a "warm and zealous advocate" before a Missouri group organizing a pro-Nebraska convention, Douglas argued that continued territorial organization was locally "important and desirable," but preserving Pacific interests through removal of the tribal barrier and creation of a railroad reflective of "the spirit of this age" was a "national necessity." He denounced the agitation diverting the country from these goals and stated the need to support the Compromise of 1850.[21]

Drafting the Kansas-Nebraska Bill

On December 14, 1853, Senator Augustus Dodge (IA) introduced a copy of Douglas's previous bill creating the Nebraska territory, and Douglas reported the bill out of his committee three weeks later. Writing for the majority, he lauded the 1850 compromise measures for possessing the nation's confidence while removing the question of slavery from politics. The majority report also reviewed the 1850 debate over New Mexico's and Utah's organization. While the United States had absorbed these territories with Mexico's prohibition of slavery, Nebraska was part of the Louisiana Purchase. Although the 1820 provisions prohibited slavery above 36°30′, in 1850 Congress had debated whether it could legislate slavery in the territories and, according to Douglas, determined it could not. As such, "the 8th section of the act preparatory to the admission of Missouri is null and void...," and the committee would not affirm or repeal this section.[22] Initial response was routine. The *Washington Union* lauded the Nebraska bill for the "sound, national, Union-loving sentiments with which it abounds" as did the free soil *Albany Atlas*. The Whig *New York Tribune*, however, warned that while antislavery might be weak among politicians, the masses merely waited for "a practical demonstration of their power to show how firm is their attachment to the principles of freedom, and show how deeply they scorn the shallow fools, who have the impertinence to talk about 'crushing out' those principles."[23] Finally, the states' rights *Washington Sentinel* protested Douglas's prevarication, asking Congress to "*directly and positively*" repeal the relevant section.[24]

In Congress, Southern dissatisfaction mirrored that of the *Sentinel*—forbidden from extending slavery into Nebraska, they gained little from its organization. Philip Phillips (AL), a member of the House Committee on Territories, complained to Hunter that the bill was fatally flawed and informed Douglas that "repeal by implication was not allowed."[25] So pressed by Southerners, he adjusted his bill. On January 10, his revised report claimed a "clerical error" had eliminated the portion relating to slavery. The new section revealed that the "propositions and principles" of the Compromise of 1850, which allowed territorial residents to determine their institutions, were to be carried into "practical operation." But popular sovereignty remained controversial because Northerners believed a territorial legislature could establish or prohibit slavery at any time, while Southerners believed it could be done only in a state constitution. Southern ultras were only partially mollified by the explicit addition of this doctrine.[26]

Archibald Dixon (KY) claimed the bill was "deficient in one material respect" because it did not repeal the 1820 legislation. On January 16, he offered an amendment that citizens could take their slaves into the territories "as if the said act . . . had never been passed." But Dixon neglected to consult an astonished Douglas, who nonetheless soon adapted. Later that day, he invited Dixon for a carriage ride; by its end, he had incorporated this repeal.[27] However, he did so without consulting leading Democrats, including Senator Lewis Cass (MI), the party's 1848 presidential candidate and foremost proponent of popular sovereignty, who was livid about a bill he described as "fraught with infinite evil." He personally "begged" the president to steer clear and found a sympathetic audience in him and Secretary of State William Marcy.[28] The *Washington Union*, the administration organ whose editorials were often written by Attorney General Caleb Cushing, came out against Dixon's amendment on January 20, writing that "*Prudence, patriotism, devotion to the Union, the interests of the Democratic party*, all suggest that the public sentiment which now acquiesces cheerfully in the principles of the compromise of 1850 should not be inconsiderately disturbed. . . ." The following day, it condemned "partisan and uncalled attempts to stir up strife."[29]

The South, however, was more positive. The *Charleston Mercury* warmly reported that it would restore the region "to the position of equality in the Union." It did not expect a slave Nebraska, but appreciated "seeing a just principle of legislation established. . . ." Acknowledging Southern preference for repeal but hoping to influence its language, Pierce's cabinet drafted an alternative, which protected Southern rights by acknowledging property rights were only limited by the Constitution but stopped short of outright repeal. Representative John C. Breckinridge, a Kentucky Democrat, brought this alternative to Douglas and the F Street mess on January 21, but with a stronger version in hand, they would not agree. By Saturday night, Pierce realized that prominent Southern Democrats on whose goodwill he depended were committed to overt repeal.[30]

"With a good deal of trepidation" Pierce was persuaded and drafted the legislation. He wrote that the Missouri Compromise was "inoperative and void" but not repealed, likely the sole concession the president gained.[31] As a result, organization of Nebraska and Kansas became an administration measure. Pierce's involvement can plausibly be understood as either sincere support for legislation helpful to party and nation, or as a savvy move to prevent Douglas from emerging with all the credit, or perhaps both. If the measure failed, Douglas would shoulder the blame as the bill's originator; if successful, Pierce's contribution would neutralize it as a weapon in the race for the 1856 presidential nomination.

On January 23, Douglas reported a third version of his bill. In the president's language, the Compromise was declared lapsed; the "clerical error" section was dropped; and as rumored, the territory was divided: the region west of Iowa and Minnesota extending to the Canadian border became Nebraska, while Kansas was formed from the region west of

Missouri. Kansas's southern boundary was adjusted to the thirty-seventh parallel to leave Cherokee land intact. Now the *Washington Union* abruptly embraced the new bill and proclaimed that it removed all doubt about the intent of the Compromise of 1850.[32] In addition, the paper noted that this would be "a test of democratic orthodoxy."[33]

At Senator Salmon P. Chase's (OH) request, debate was postponed until January 30. On January 16, Senator Charles Sumner (MA) offered an amendment stating the Missouri Compromise would apply to Nebraska. A more important salvo came three days later when Free Soil members of Congress—Chase, Sumner, and Representatives Joshua R. Giddings (OH), Edward Wade (OH), Gerrit Smith (NY), and Alexander De Witt (MA)—released a tract arguing the bill violated a sacred compact between the sections. Given Chase's obvious familiarity with the bill, his request for a delay was revealed to be a strategic bid for time to organize a response. In *An Appeal of the Independent Democrats in Congress to the People of the United States: Shall Slavery be Permitted in Nebraska?*, these nominal Democrats condemned the bill as "a gross violation of a sacred pledge; as a criminal betrayal of precious rights; as part and parcel of an atrocious plot to exclude from a vast unoccupied region, immigrants from the Old World and free laborers from our own States, and convert it into a dreary region of despotism, inhabited by master and slaves." Heralding the Missouri Compromise as "inviolable American law," they relied on it to argue against extending slavery into Nebraska. They also refuted arguments that the Compromise of 1850 had affected the exclusion of slavery as it was relevant only to postwar circumstances.[34]

Echoing the Free Democratic platform that the "right of all men to the soil is as sacred as their right to life itself," the *Appeal* argued that white men should not have to toil next to slaves because "labor cannot be respected where any class of laborers is held in abject bondage." Moreover, opening the area to slavery would split the East from the developing West; by forcing commerce to pass through slave states, the entire country would be subjugated to its degradations. The appeal depicted an aggressive and depraved South powered by an immoral slave system, a threat so dire it demanded an immediate response. Claiming "the cause of human freedom is the cause of God," they pledged to "call on the people to come to the rescue of the country from the domination of slavery." By January 24, the day after Douglas's final report, the *Appeal* was widely circulated throughout the North, and the Senate debate promised a showdown over the primacy of the compromises of 1820 and 1850.[35]

The Senate Debate

With the controversy over missing sections, new amendments, and dissemination of the *Appeal*, the bill dominated discussion in Washington for a month before debate commenced. "The intense excitement and the groundswells of which we hear so much in certain quarters, are mere figments of a morbid and restless imagination," the *Annapolis State Capitol Gazette* commented. "The clarion tones and irresistible logic of Douglas, Cass, Atchison, and their noble compeers in both houses, will silence the croaking, carping, hypocritical enemies of popular sovereignty." Yet the excitement only intensified once Douglas took the floor on January 30. Enraged by Chase's disingenuous request for a delay, he indicted the tract's authors for slander and conduct unbecoming legislators. Given his maligning for "criminal betrayal," "bad faith," and "an atrocious plot against the cause of free government," he was rightfully indignant and charged these "pure, unmitigated, unadulterated abolitionists" with hypocrisy. But because the bill was based on sound principles, the *Appeal* would not sway the bill's supporters from their course. Speaking "with an energy and power ... that was manifested in a way unusual in the Senate," Douglas's performance delighted observers.[36]

Discomfited by the *Appeal's* discourse, the *Washington Union* justified Douglas's attack: "we doubt whether two senators ever received so terrific an excoriation in that chamber as that to which Messrs. Chase and Sumner were subjected on yesterday; and we are very sure that, when the speech of Judge Douglas is read, the judgment of the country will be deserved just such an exposure."[37] However Wade believed the danger the country faced justified the *Appeal's* rhetoric; even though they had been decried as "factionists," a majority of Americans opposed the bill.[38] But Senator Robert Toombs (GA) charged opponents with using "intimidation to effect their objects. We are invited to listen to the mutterings of the distant thunder of popular indignation (not yet audible) which is about to burst upon our ears, and we are warned of the earthquakes which are about to burst from under our feet." He dismissed this "melo-dramatic thunder" as lacking even novelty.[39]

Nonetheless, the bill's managers took the *Appeal* seriously and Douglas countered what he perceived as a campaign of misinformation designed to create fear. The *Concord* (NH) *State Capitol Reporter*, for example, supported the bill but published a guest editorial warning slavery would be established in Nebraska once Pierce signed it. Douglas chastised the paper for distorting the bill's meaning in a manner "so grossly and wickedly perverted and misrepresented, as to leave no doubt that the article was prepared by a deadly enemy, under the hypocritical guise of friendship...." He reiterated that the bill did not implement slavery but instead offered freedom of action and choice. Citing speeches by Whigs Edward Everett (MA), Truman Smith (CT), and George Badger (NC), Douglas argued that slavery could not thrive there, which made it a question solely of principle.[40]

The Senate was divided because support for popular sovereignty hinged on the perception of "territory." Should territorial residents be considered wards of the federal government residing in too embryonic a society to regulate themselves? Or were settlers as capable of decision making as they had been before relocation? Did a critical mass even exist to be governed? "Until society is formed, there is no need of laws...," Whig James Cooper (PA) emphasized. "When men are so far scattered over a country as scarcely to number a dozen to every hundred square miles, it can hardly be said they form a society at all...."[41] Given the sparseness of settlers, critics believed organization was being undertaken for other reasons, especially since Commissioner for Indian Affairs George Manypenny had dismissed newspaper accounts of a thriving territory in a fall report. Such claims were "destitute of truth" as "there was no settlement made in any part of Nebraska."[42] But while there may not have been formal settlements in the region, settlers had moved in.

Given Douglas's ambition, he had difficulty dodging charges that the bill derived more from political expediency than from concern for inhabitants. Five current territories rendered claims of urgency moot, and Truman Smith amused the chamber by describing Douglas's obsession. "The Senator from Illinois was the most prolific man he ever knew in getting Territories. [Laughter.] Every year he called attention of the Senate to the parturition of a Territory, and sometimes they come two at a time—[loud laughter]—and that too when he had a whole litter of them on hand. [Laughter.]" Douglas intentionally used "equivocal language," Smith charged, because "tenderfooted Democrats and Whigs" wanted to be able to swear they had not repealed the 1820 bill; without such sweetening, it would have swiftly died.[43]

Many Senators were unconcerned with any alleged inhabitants. By mid-February, as expected given his belief that popular sovereignty provided a middle ground, Cass had embraced the bill, no longer dismayed by its evil aspects. While the South wanted to prove that "*slavery is the best condition of human society*," the question was whether the federal government had the right to regulate the institution.[44] Cass's criticism dwindled to semantics ("superseded" defied logic), and Douglas gained his endorsement by simply clarifying that "by the use of the words 'superseded by,' I mean which was 'inconsistent with' the compromise of 1850."[45]

But determining this inconsistency was difficult. "I do not know whether it is constitutional, technically," Democrat Samuel Houston (TX) argued. "It is sufficient for me to know that it has stood for more than thirty years . . . and was never questioned until after the commencement of the present session of Congress."[46] However, most of the great "compromise" statesmen had since died, and newer senators seemingly lacked reverence for previous generations' achievements. As John Clayton (DE) stated, "I was not here, I did not give it my vote, and therefore I am not bound by it."[47] Ironically, Dixon's amendment dismantled the work of his predecessor, Henry Clay.

Almost every congressman entered a different history and constitutional interpretation into the record. For Southerners, the issues centered around the common-property doctrine, which held that the territories were not federal property but held in common by all the states. As such, it would be unconstitutional to prevent a citizen from taking his property into the territories. Perhaps constitutionally more significant, the United States could not delegate to a territory, a subordinate entity, any power (to outlaw slavery) that it itself did not have.[48] In addition, the Constitution only mentioned "territory or other property." Did the meaning alter if "territories" was at issue? William Pitt Fessenden (ME) did not think it was significant that the country only had one territory when the Constitution was ratified, but Cass countered that Congress could not make rules and regulations for the multiple territories as Fessenden claimed because the singular form of "Territory" in the Constitution referred to property, not an unborn state. The precedents were with Fessenden, but Cass's narrow, deconstructive argument illustrated the philosophical divide.[49]

As expected, Dixon's amendments prompted previously disinterested Southerners to embrace the new bill. On February 3, Toombs reported a Southern caucus had revealed that all the section's members would support the bill. He argued that repeal was proper because the South would not benefit otherwise. Furthermore, unlike the 1820 legislation, the Compromise of 1850 was accepted in the North and put into both parties' platforms, thus revealing "the almost universal sanction of the nation."[50] Butler agreed the Missouri Compromise was not a compact because sections could not enter into them. He supported the bill because it would "obliterate a line of geographical distinction, indicating, for the first time, that the federal States, by this line, had adverse as well as separate interests."[51] Echoing many of his messmate's arguments, Hunter asked, "How is a more perfect union to be formed if you have destroyed the existing equality of the States and substituted inequality?"[52] Both believed the Missouri Compromise hurt the South, but as Butler concluded, "a Wise man knows how to take advantage of circumstances."[53]

Although the *Albany Atlas* agreed that one Congress did not bind another, compacts nonetheless carried an obligation because of "the faith of pure public men who participate in it, and of the political parties who acquiesce in it, that the bargain will not be consummated on one side and repudiated on the other."[54] In two renowned speeches, opponents argued that the nation risked violating sacred pledges. This was "not merely the repeal of an existing law," Sumner argued, "but the infraction of solemn obligations originally proposed and assumed by the South, after a protracted and embittered contest, as a covenant of peace. . . ." But the 1850 acts did not address slavery within the territories; they merely stated that "when admitted as States, they shall be received 'with or without Slavery.' Here certainly can be no overthrow of an act of Congress which directly concerns a Territory *during its Territorial existence*."[55] In an equally riveting speech, Chase urged the nation to "maintain plighted faith" and disputed that the 1850 Congress had intended to abrogate the compact. He chided Douglas's tactics in achieving a repeal, telling him he should "do it openly—do it boldly. Repeal the Missouri prohibition. Repeal it by a direct vote. Do not repeal it by indirection. Do not 'declare' it 'inoperative,' 'because superseded by the principles of the legislation of 1850.'"[56] However, despite efforts to force a vote on outright repeal, Dixon's amendment survived.

The Kansas-Nebraska debates underscore that though beloved, the Union was but a confederacy at its heart. Many professed Unionists spoke of an idealized Union corrupted by the passage of time but weighed fidelity differently. Both sections considered elements like states' rights, honor, and pride, and should the Union no longer balance these elements, then separation remained an option. By the debate's end, Northerners were fatigued by Southern rights' rhetoric. Fessenden warned against the efficacy of threatening disunion for "if that is the only alternative to be considered, it ceases to be a very grave question for honorable men and freemen to decide."[57] Some like Wade believed disunion would come, for if this "act of perfidy" were passed, the Union could not survive ten years.[58]

Yet on May 4 the bill passed easily, 37 to 14, with only the Clayton amendment to restrict suffrage and territorial offices to citizens being added to the bill.[59] Douglas closed with a speech of such length that he would have exhausted his opponents into capitulation had there been enough of them. But the victory was so comfortable that the *New York Evening Post*, an antislavery, anti-Nebraska, Free Soil yet Democratic paper, mourned the opposition's ineptness. "But this humiliating spectacle—the more humiliating sight of the northern men who, prostrating themselves at the feet of the administration, and meekly taking on their dishonored shoulders the heavy burden of this wicked measure—all this does not prove that there is no North. It does, indeed, prove that there are white slaves—pitiable and despicable too—in Congress—whether or not there may hereafter be black slaves in Kansas and Nebraska."[60] But there were too few opponents to deflect Douglas, who reacted well even when caught off-guard. He incorporated the Dixon amendment and buttressed it with Pierce's approval to induce Democratic support; against the *Appeal*, he launched a varied and sustained counterattack through speeches, letters, and personal persuasion. A prolific Douglas wrote to protesters, clergy, newspaper editors, friends, and foes, explaining their flawed logic in often excruciating detail.[61] For his efforts, Douglas was widely excoriated throughout the North—he claimed he "could travel from Boston to Chicago by the light of my own effigy. . . ."[62]

Yet with his controlled and systematic management and Pierce's patronage to lure reluctant Democrats, only 5 of the 28 Democrats voting dissented. Four were Northerners: Henry Dodge and Isaac Walker of Wisconsin; Hannibal Hamlin of Maine; and Charles James of Rhode Island. Houston was the lone Southern Democrat to vote no, warning his colleagues that Northern Democrats would "be held to a strict account. They will have to answer for it."[63] However, the most striking division was among Whigs. Although the Northern vote was close, with 14 supporting it and 12 against it, as Appendices A and B reveal, all the yes votes came from Democrats—not a single Northern Whig supported it.[64]

In the South, Southerners overwhelmingly favored the bill. Of the 25 Southern votes, one member from each party voted against the bill. Both Houston and John Bell (TN) were members of the Committee on Territories who believed the bill threatened the Union. Houston admonished the South that it was "an eminently perilous measure," and refused to believe it was an administration measure, since Pierce had pledged to prevent agitation and this measure would "convulse the country from Maine to the Rio Grande."[65] While Bell's views were widely known and he had attended the Southern Whig caucus, he had not joined their advocacy, instead maintaining an ominous silence (which he later attributed to a reluctance to stand apart from his Southern brethren) until the final debate.[66] Bell placed the Union above sectional gains. These two anomalous Southern votes underscore party strengths and divisions. Northern Democrats favored the bill 14 to 4 while Southern Democrats favored the bill 14 to 1. However, the Whig vote analysis reveals serious strain. They were divided 9 to 7 along a sectional divide: Southerners cast all 9 yes votes while Northern Whigs cast 6 of the 7 no votes.

Faltering in the House

On January 31, Democrat William Richardson (IL), chairman of the Committee on Territories, reported a bill to organize Nebraska into the House of Representatives, but the committee vote (5 to 3) was far closer than in the Senate, and disagreements among committee members—complaints that it lacked the committee's general approval, requests for a popular sovereignty amendment by William English (IN), and objections from Whigs E. Wilder Farley (ME) and John Taylor (OH) over the lack of a formal minority report—were early indications the House might prove more difficult.[67]

Douglas described popular sovereignty as an American tradition giving territorial residents a legislative blank slate, land "in precisely the same condition as our ancestors found Plymouth rock—with no code of law, no system of political, civil, social, and domestic institutions, but with full power and authority" to write all necessary laws limited only by the Constitution.[68] Although settlers could decide on slavery, popular sovereignty was oddly limiting, giving inhabitants agency over this one question because, as Galusha Grow (PA) reminded them, residents did not select their government.[69] Moreover, "territorial sovereignty is a monstrosity, born of timidity and ambition," Thomas Hart Benton (MO) argued, "hatched into existence in the hot incubation of a presidential canvas and revolting to the beholders when first presented."[70] However, as in the Senate, other Southerners emphasized principle. Whig John Kerr (NC) professed not to care what Nebraska needed, but Northern statesmen "come and tender us our principle and form of government for the Territories—which are our common property—and we cannot refuse the offer."[71]

But the popular sovereignty the Senate proffered was limited because the Clayton amendment restricted suffrage and territorial offices to citizens and proved unpopular among congressmen accountable to voters. Democrat E.M. Chamberlain (IN) protested "legislating negro slaves into this Territory; and legislating Dutch and Irish emigrants out of it," warning of unleashed evils which would "spring like hydra heads" as the territories developed. In short, "in giving this measure to the Territories for the people," he argued, "you give them identically what Jupiter gave Pandora for her husband." The territories' large size required caution, because as George Simmons (NY) pointed out, if they became slave states, slavery would "form a cordon" around Northerners "on all our borders except Canada and the ocean."[72]

Democrat Preston Brooks (SC) noted the "army of speakers" whose views coalesced around four central themes: the exclusion of slavery from the territories; the 1820 legislation favoring one section over another; the "assumed antagonism" between free and slave labor and between immigrant labor and slave labor; and the "immorality and inexpediency" of slavery. While each had adherents, none outweighed principle. This bill was not about making slave states, but about carrying "out a good old republican principle, that the people shall decide for themselves the character of their municipal Government ... when they multiply into States, slavery or no slavery."[73]

Whig Theodore Hunt (LA) warned that the Missouri Compromise was a touchstone for America and that its repeal could lead to other such repeals, up to and including "that most glorious compromise, the Constitution of the United States." However, most Southerners disputed the existence of a sectional compact. If there was one, Alexander Stephens (GA) argued, it was solely between the government and Missouri, but that state "had no right to the territory outside of her limits." Samuel Smith (TN) congratulated Northerners who risked their seats to sustain "the Constitution and the rights of the States, a debt of gratitude which time will not enable it to pay." On the whole, however, Southern Democrats rallied around their Senate counterparts and downplayed the possibility of disunion. Instead, those "guided by religious fanaticism and fury" represented the actual threat. "The fanatics among you are sowing the wind," Lawrence Keitt (SC) warned, "and we must reap the tempest, which you moderates of the North will not be able to control."[74]

Democrat Samuel Bridges (PA) claimed dissent derived from abolitionists, sustained by a parasitic lecture circuit, who inflamed "the public mind." These agitators were "too indolent to procure a living by honest industry"; instead, they "traverse the country, sucking their existence from the people, and poisoning the public mind with their pernicious doctrines." Even given such propaganda, the bill could only be described as "startling." Moreover, as Democrat Reuben Fenton (NY) asserted, most Northerners were opposed to repeal and not all of them could be dismissed as abolitionists.[75] Moderate Northerners warned that its passage would be too costly and urged a delay. James Meacham (VT), for instance, argued that they should make it an issue in the next election and "see how many members will be returned in support of it."[76] This was especially vital because as Democrat Andrew Harlan (IN) stated, if voters had known national policy would be so radically modified, "Franklin Pierce would have been a private citizen, and the seats of the northern men who now tender this repeal would have been filled by others."[77] By making the fight now, Charles Skelton (NJ) promised the North would defend its rights "under the Union, and in the Union."[78]

But in preserving those rights, it was important not to trample on others. Whig Richard Yates (IL) warned against allowing "the tyranny of party" to "force this bill through this House, in violation of solemn compact, and against every principle of justice, right, and humanity." His colleague John Norton emphasized that "Peace is not peace that comes with injustice or dishonor," and urged Congress to allow the people to speak to the question at the ballot-box. "You might as well ask the sea to stand still as to ask the North to submit in silence to the repeal of the Missouri compromise," a third Illinois Whig, Elihu Washburne, echoed. Indeed, although Douglas led the charge in the Senate and Richardson did so in the House, their state's delegation was not united.[79]

The administration had expected opposition, but they were startled by the rough reception the New York Hards gave the bill. Their bitterness demonstrated that while Pierce wisely recognized the need to ameliorate that tension, his efforts had been for naught. "You must trim your sails to the Executive breeze, or you will be driven among the breakers; you must lose all independence, and submit to a dictation as impudent as it is overbearing . . . ," John Wheeler complained. But now the administration was "begging—BEGGING the Hards on this floor for their votes to aid in the passage of the Nebraska bill. *Where are their allies*—the Free-Soilers?" Democrat Rufus Peckam mocked administration attempts to whip members into line given its vacillation on the issue. Another New Yorker, Orsamus Matteson, a Whig this time, saw Pierce's decision to back the measure as evidence of desperation and asserted that the entire North would suffer from Douglas's misrepresentation of the section.[80]

On March 21, Richardson was finally ready to move the bill to a vote, but he needed to postpone the 18 bills ahead of it; if he could not, pro-Nebraska forces could fall back to the Senate bill, which awaited action. However, his plans immediately went awry when the House rejected his motion to convene into the Committee of the Whole. Immediately after, Democrat Alfred Edgerton (OH) ominously moved to consider the Senate bill with its unpalatable Clayton amendment. Since Edgerton was vehemently opposed to the bill, Richardson understood the opposition was trying to kill it, but the direction and method surprised the bill's managers.[81]

Francis Cutting, a New York Hard and a purported friend of the bill, moved to refer the Senate bill into the Committee of the Whole. Supporters immediately objected because the bill would be buried, but Cutting defended his motion as necessary for clarity—the Senate bill was flawed, "enveloped in a multitude of words, with sentences argumentative, sentences explanatory, and with a proviso in the bargain, whose chief merit, its author now supposes is, that it means nothing in the world. Plain men, who are not astute lawyers, become bewildered in the midst of this multitude of words and accumulation of sentences." The North needed more time to recognize its value.[82] Richardson objected that this was "killing it by indirection" and vainly tried to refer the bill to his committee, but the House sent it into the Committee of the Whole, 110 to 95.[83]

Cutting succeeded because even some of the bill's supporters agreed a delay would be advantageous. Whig John Franklin (MD) favored non-intervention, but did not believe that the Senate bill reflected that in its "mischievous form." Until the territorial legislature recognized slavery, the institution was in jeopardy because local judges could free fugitive slaves, and he urged fellow Southerners to "pause and deliberate." After the vote, Breckinridge's fury over this motion grew but he remained hopeful; it would pass because Cutting's methods "aroused the friends of the bill" and demonstrated "there are ninety-six men here who, if waked up by an alarm bell at night, would be ready to support the bill." For now, however, the committee of the whole had 50 other bills to consider. On March 23, the *Washington Union* reminded Democrats that since it was now an administration bill, its defeat was one for the administration as well. The *Union* blamed a coalition of Whigs and abolitionists for the bill's troubles, and did not recognize that although "THE ISSUE IS THUS MADE—THE TEST IS THUS APPLIED," House Democrats were uncooperative. As April came to a close, tensions were high and party relationships had deteriorated such that Cutting and Breckinridge planned to settle their disagreement with a duel.[84]

Opening "Pandora's Box of Evils": Reaction Outside Congress

On the night the Nebraska bill passed the Senate, Houston warned his colleagues that public reaction would mimic the uproar with which the Senate had greeted the bill. "We are told, to be sure, that there is no necessity for agitation, and that soon the public mind will be tranquil, and the country will be in a state of repose and quiet . . . ," he stated. "I cannot believe, from what we have witnessed here to-night, that this will be the exclusive arena for the exercise of human passions, and the expression of public opinion."[85] In January, the *Washington Union* dismissed abolitionism—"a formidable and dread monster of destruction" in 1852, it now had "dwindled down to a puny, sickly dwarf, whose feeble cry is scarce loud enough to attract the notice of the chance passerby his to miserable dwelling."[86] However, with news that the Nebraska bill relegated the Missouri Compromise to a mere relic, dissent flourished.

By mid-January, Chase and Sumner had prepared a strategy to sustain public pressure in the legislature: one senator would present a petition with the other delaying until the next day so that "the voices may be renewed, in secession. It will be for the people to enable us to present a petition each day."[87] The people responded and flooded Congress; soon others were transmitting evidence of the public mood. Wheeler (NY) presented a petition on "behalf of several thousand working-men and other citizens of this city" against repeal. Democrat George Kittredge (NH) presented another signed by 3,900 voters "respectfully and earnestly protesting against any repeal of the prohibition of slavery, upon the addition of slave territory to the Union, immediate or prospective, such as is proposed in the Nebraska bill of Senator Douglas." The outcry was such that members even presented resolutions with which they disagreed. Cutting, for example, presented a petition from a public meeting opposing the measure for fear that withholding it "might be attributed to motives very different from those that actuate me."[88]

Additionally, many Congressmen presented resolutions from their state legislatures that often included voting exhortations. Massachusetts' resolutions protested the "violation of plighted faith" in language deliberately echoing Sumner's speech warning "that, if we are to witness fresh scenes of sectional animosity and contention, the authors and supporters of the Nebraska bill must forever bear the responsibility, and be answerable for all the fearful consequences of so flagrant an act of injustice." Rhode Island, Maine, New York, and Wisconsin also issued resolutions against the bill. In the other five legislatures then in session, four were controlled by the Democratic Party. Pennsylvania, New Jersey, and California heatedly debated resolutions but issued none; in Ohio, the legislature tabled it to avoid dissension altogether. Illinois was the only Northern legislature to support the bill, but half the Democrats abstained from that vote.[89]

In the South, support was more forthcoming. Resolutions from Georgia protested Congress's restriction on the free movement of citizens and applauded the North for recognizing Southern rights. The legislature "had their confidence strengthened in the settled determination of that great body of the northern people to carry out in good faith those principles" contained in the Nebraska bill. Mississippi's issued a similar resolution against the unconstitutional exclusion of the South from the territories and requested their legislators' support. Louisiana expressed concern over Northern agitation but unanimously passed a resolution citing the bill's non-intervention principles for its support.[90]

Although in the minority, a few Southern voices rose against the bill. "Let the Nebraska bill be rejected to-morrow," the *New Orleans Bee* suggested, "and the south will sleep quite as sound at night as before."[91] In addition, former Virginia Congressman John Botts published a series of letters warning of the bill's hazards. Although advantageous in the short-term, he believed it was ultimately detrimental to Southern interests. "The South professes to despise Mr. Seward as its worst enemy," Botts wrote. "I tell the South, that every man who helps to destroy the Compromise of 1820, is unwittingly engaged in the service of Mr. Seward. He is uniting the North as one man on a sectional issue in which their pride and principle is as much involved as ours, and which will throw them all into the ranks of Mr. Seward. You will have no more national whiggery, no more national democracy. . . ." Botts described the Kansas-Nebraska Act as a "pandora's box of evils," but his position's unpopularity is underscored by the virulent reaction to his letters.[92]

Advocates across the country were concerned by the changes presaged by the bill, especially given the territories' size. Northerners feared inflicting "the evils of that cruel system" to a vast area previously reserved for freedom.[93] Moreover, if the South triumphed, 20 states might be carved from the vast territory, resulting in an "irrevocably fixed" Senate.[94] With the Missouri Compromise forcing Southerners to look southward toward Mexico and Cuba instead of westward, achieving congressional parity would be difficult if not impossible. Given the South's disadvantage in the House, popular sovereignty promised renewed life. Unless Southerners could carry their property into the territories, safe at least until a state constitution was written, "the Nebraska bill," the *Charleston Mercury* argued, "is a worthless and deceptive truce."[95]

In a race for Kansas and Nebraska territory, who would win? A cautious Botts desired expansion, but preferred to divide California and Texas into additional states rather than pursue uncertainty in new territories.[96] In *Appeal in Behalf of the Republic* Southerner W.B. Davis dismissed the bill as a scheme. Under the mirage of self-government and popular sovereignty, "the 15 Southern States will then be more *practically*, permanently and scientifically robbed of those two Southern Territories [Kansas and Nebraska]. . . ."[97] The *Macon Telegraph* similarly wondered, "What possible good can any bill assenting to and affirming this monstrous idea [squatter sovereignty], do the South, when the Freesoilers have any the start of us in populating the territory that may be in dispute."[98] However, like the *Charleston Mercury* most Southerners preferred to anticipate the best outcome.

An Appeal of the Independent Democrats had explicitly requested that religious leaders lead the opposition, for ministers and Christians to "protest, earnestly and emphatically . . . against this enormous crime."[99] The Society of Friends of Delaware, Pennsylvania, and New Jersey was just one of the many groups informing Congress it viewed the Nebraska bill "with deep regret and with unfeigned alarm. . . ." Although these petitioners regretted interfering with other states' rights, the repeal of the Missouri Compromise was "a violation of right and of faith, and destructive of that confidence and regard" which federal law should inspire.[100] In March, Whig William Appleton (MA) presented a petition with "upwards of three thousand signatures, which occupy two hundred and fifty feet of paper" from New England clergy opposing repeal.[101]

This religious response prompted wide concern in Congress as Douglas, Mason, Butler, and Stephens Adams (MS), among others, protested the impropriety of religious petition. Butler attacked those who "dared to quit the pulpit, and step into the political arena, and speak as the organs of Almighty God." Senate response was so vehement, 25 clergy from Chicago remonstrated the "want of courtesy and reverence towards man and God" exhibited. The sheer volume of religious petitions sparked a debate on religious interference in politics. While he did not dispute the right of private citizens to petition Congress, their constitutional rights "recedes and disappears," Douglas maintained, "when placed in subordination to the authority of a body of men, claiming, by virtue of their offices as ministers, to be a divinely-appointed institution for the declaration and enforcement of God's will on earth."[102]

In the pulpit as well as through petition, ministers proved equally voluble. Francis Wayland disputed Douglas's denial that he sought to overturn any compromises in a March sermon. "To suppose the universal agitation of this subject to be revived . . . without an assignable object, is to suppose men to act without motive; that is, to be either idiotic or insane."[103] This object was widely believed to be the extension of slavery into Nebraska and those who denied it were, as Reverend Heman Humphrey stated, either "unaccountedly demented or insincere." Despite their majority in the House, Northern help allowed Southerners to push back against liberty and extend slavery.[104] Ministers had been obliged to honor compromises that had "a paralyzing influence. They have formed a barrier around the evil which the friends of freedom have wished to overcome and kept them at bay." Indeed, while Northerners might have been united against slavery, many agreed that the "*bargain* of binding force, having been ratified by all concerned," allowed for no recourse to the status quo.[105] In repeated sermons, Northern ministers opposed the Kansas-Nebraska Act as a breach of faith. But this breach resulted not in disappointment or disbelief, but deliverance. Having been repulsed by slavery but constrained by the compact, ministers were now liberated to undertake the action they had yearned for.

Leonard Marsh was one of many who knew whom to blame for the Nebraska bill. "We have all been guilty together. We have all, for the sake of some present party interest, or party pride, or through dough-faced good nature played into the hand of the ever watchful and crafty slave-power."[106] Civil society would unite to offset the political establishment's failures. "Now we are at liberty—the other party having taken the impediments out of the way," Massachusetts minister J. Nelson said in compelling his church to action, "to array ourselves, not simply as we have hitherto done against the extension of Slavery, but to enter with the best influences we can command, political and moral, its very seats and strongholds, and to do all we can, by Christian means, and instrumentalities to destroy it." Not only was the Kansas-Nebraska bill "in the gravest sense revolutionary" in setting aside three decades of stability, but it demanded a revolutionary response as well.[107] Although the bill had not yet passed, the attempt to undo the Missouri Compromise demonstrated the South's true nature.[108] Such exhortation provided the impetus for the aid societies that would flourish in the North, sponsor settlers to Kansas, and provide the famous Beecher's Bibles (boxes filled with rifles instead of the eponymous bibles) to protect soldiers of freedom against the forces of slavery.

Resurrecting the Bill

Although Chase had celebrated the Nebraska bill's demise in late April, Douglas and the administration had not abandoned the struggle. A key player in drafting the bill, Breckinridge did not participate in the debates, being "too busy making a show of confidence by striding up and down the House lobby arm-in-arm with Douglas, helping to keep the wavering in line."[109] The administration had been leaning on rebellious members, focusing on Northerners who voted to refer the Senate bill to the Committee of the Whole. As an administration measure, the stakes increased, for opponents risked missing out on prestigious posts at Turin, Buenos Aires, Havana, Chile, and London that Pierce had at his disposal that spring. "All the methods of influence and intimidation which organizations, numbers, and patronage can supply are used without stint at the seat of government," the *New York Evening Post* reported, "to silence those who disapprove of the bill and engage the wavering to give its support."[110]

Finally, on May 8, Richardson was confident he had enough votes and moved the House into the committee of the whole, where in successive roll call votes, the membership uncovered the Nebraska bill. He succeeded because the anti-Nebraska forces' unity had begun to crumble under the administration's assault. In caucus the night before, the opposition had agreed not to vote so as to deny the House a quorum, but enough Democrats voted to defeat this strategy.[111] However, the anti-Nebraska forces regrouped and began a filibuster on May 11. "The minority tried and exhausted the physical endurance of the majority," the *New Orleans Picayune* reported, "and spent sixty hours in parliamentary devices for delay; motions to lay over, to amend, to postpone, &c., interspersed, at every possible opportunity, with motions to adjourn, taking the yeas and nays on every question."[112] The opposition tried to force a delay until May 16 when the Pacific Railroad bill was scheduled, and as it had precedence over the Nebraska bill, a delay would consign it to a quiet death on the speaker's table.

During this "remarkable and significant spectacle," Whig Emerson Ethridge (TN) urged Democrats to ponder how their actions violated national pledges and augmented sectionalism. "Had they not for a few days past been attempting to force upon an unwilling people a measure for which they had never asked?"[113] But the filibuster continued until Richardson managed an adjournment, during which he pressured Northern Democrats. By Monday, May 15, to the great fury of Northern Whigs, Richardson had convinced 19 anti-Nebraska Democrats that their resistance thwarted the will of the majority. With these additional votes, he acquired the two-thirds vote necessary to suspend the rules and open debate.[114]

Once debate commenced, opponents tried to kill the bill through amendment. John Eliot (MA) and Giddings and Lewis Campbell (OH) tried to limit the territories' ability to enter the Union with slavery, while Daniel Mace (IN) moved to allow the territorial legislature to establish or prohibit slavery at any time (the Senate had defeated Chase's similar amendment). Rufus Peckham (NY) advocated the organization of only one territory, while Samuel Walley (MA) suggested none. Samuel Parker (IN) wanted to move the Kansas border five degrees north to equalize the two territories' size, while Thomas Flagler (NY) wished to delay implementation until American Indian rights were protected.[115] Pro-Nebraska forces deflected all these efforts to amend or delay the bill.

Finally, in the afternoon session on May 22, Stephens trumped the opposition with a parliamentary tactic of his own. Once the House resolved into the Committee of the Whole, he moved to strike out the enacting clause of the Nebraska bill in order to vote. Under House rule 119, "a motion to strike out the enacting words of a bill shall have precedence of a motion to amend; and, if carried, it shall be considered equivalent to its rejection." Invoking this rule meant that the stream of amendments would cease and the House would be required to vote. Stephens expected the bill's supporters to vote down the motion, which would leave the chairman of the Committee on Territories free to offer his substitution (which Stephens wanted) as an amendment, thus allowing a direct vote. Completely caught off guard by this citing of rule 119, which the chair conceded was often violated, the bill's opponents were left blustering. Joseph Chandler (PA) cried out at the "wicked" move, complaining it allowed the majority to "ride rough-shod" over opponents who retained the right to amendment. "Amid great confusion" and the cries of Gilbert Dean (NY) that the minority would "oppose tyranny by revolution" by not voting, Edson Olds (OH), chair of the Committee of the Whole, ruled that a vote was required and it passed 103 to 2. After a recount mustered only 20 additional negative votes, appeals on the vote's propriety and efforts to force an adjournment all failed. Stephens had successfully cut off debate. Moving the House to a vote had been an enormous struggle—there had been 146 roll calls alone on the bill, and it squeaked by with only a 13-vote margin, 113 to 100. The contest was close and bitter partially because the pressure exerted on representatives was more intense as they considered the bill for a longer period while under the judgmental attention of their constituents.[116]

Democrats provided 88 percent of favorable votes (100 of 113), while providing only 46 of the 100 negative votes. Indiana and Pennsylvania gave the bill the most support, with 7 of the former's 10 Democrats and 11 of the latter's 26 Democrats voting yes. On the other hand, only 4 of Ohio's 12 Democrats voted for the bill. Despite the victory, the North as a whole revealed other disappointments, which warned of important divisions. In Connecticut and Maine, 3 of 4 Democrats cast no votes while 2 of 3 did so in New Hampshire. Moreover, in California, Massachusetts, Rhode Island, and Wisconsin, the entire Democratic slate voted against the bill. Finally, the bill passed without significant cooperation from the largest Democratic state. A full two-thirds of New York's 33 representatives were Democrats, but the administration garnered only 9 yes votes. While the *New Orleans Daily Picayune* believed this was a positive outcome "for the New York factions have acted for a year or two as though they thought nothing could be done in the Union until one or the other of them had been conciliated and enlisted," given Pierce's attention to appeasing them, it was disappointing. As Appendices A, B, and C reveal, of the 135 Northern legislators casting votes, 44 favored it and 91 were opposed. Eighty-eight Northern Democrats were evenly divided, while in the House, as in the Senate, Northern Whigs uniformly opposed the bill—all 42 rejected it.[117]

Although many Northern Democrats hesitated in the face of the overwhelmingly negative public sentiment, enough were willing to bend either to the Democratic will or their own greed to assure passage. Pierce worked his best asset—patronage—to coerce more than half the Democrats considered moderates on this measure to the administration's side.[118] Although Pierce swayed enough Democratic senators to assure passage, his reach failed in symbolic areas. Most damaging, he could not influence his own state's representatives: of the three, only Harry Hibbard complied. While Pierce pursued votes, the party published a pamphlet to rebut unfavorable press and redefine party policy. For instance, it derided Rhode Island's anti-Nebraska resolution "as hasty and inconsiderate; as an abandonment of strong constitutional and truly national ground; and as sectionalising the democratic party."[119] This pamphlet linked popular sovereignty to Cass and the 1848 presidential campaign. Given that that campaign had prompted a disastrous split in the party, one with which Pierce still contended, it might explain why the administration only partly united the party and why many rejected this new test of Democratic faith. As dissenter Wheeler stated, New York "hard-shells" had always been loyal and did not need to be tested.[120]

Among Southern Democrats support was strong. Of the 58 Southern Democrats, only two objected. The only Missouri representative to do so, Benton was serving a term in the House after a distinguished Senate career and could not be budged from his belief that the bill was too divisive. "I am a southern man," he declared, "but vote nationally on national questions."[121] Benton could not bring himself to declare the Missouri Compromise irrelevant since he had seen "the sacrifice of feeling or prejudice which was made, and the loss of popularity incurred, and how great the danger of the country from which it saved us. . . ."[122] The other Southern Democrat to vote against the bill was John Millson (VA), who favored self-government but believed adding more territories was unwise. As the United States already had 5 territories, he "was not willing to precipitate the formation of non-slaveholding communities, and force, by a hot bed process, their unnatural growth." Moreover, he shared Benton's concern for the 1820 boundary but whereas Benton sought to retain it, he disliked Congress's "timid declaration" to overturn it.[123]

Of the 78 Southern legislators voting, 69 favored the bill and only 9 voted against it. Of the 20 Southern Whigs who voted, 13 supported the bill and 7 opposed it. Of the Tennessee Whigs, 4 of the 6 followed Bell's lead and rejected the bill. The other 2 joined the Democrats in voting for it: both Charles Ready and Felix Zollicoffer were committed to ameliorating sectional inequality, but Ready emphasized the principle of popular sovereignty while Zollicoffer stressed the need to settle constitutional issues. North Carolina's Whigs were also divided. Richard Puryear and Sion Rogers voted against the bill, but John Kerr cast the anomalous Whig vote in his state, emphasizing the South's need to compete freely in the territories. Theodore

Hunt was the sole Whig in the Louisiana contingent and also cast the sole negative vote from his state, claiming the bill threatened national unity. In Georgia, Kentucky, and Missouri, 9 Whigs joined their Democratic colleagues to pass the bill.

In late May, Stephens confided to a friend that "the contest in the House was close and hot but we whipped the opposition out and carried the measure by 13 majority. The excitement has nearly all passed away. Nobody says anything now against it but the abolitionists. Let them howl on—'Tis their vocation.'"[124] But he was overly optimistic, for unexpected coalitions had formed that augured well for future antislavery achievements. Long an advocate of "moral revolution," radical Joshua Giddings was delighted that Seward, Wade, and Hamlin "came into the very position which they have so long condemned."[125] Similarly, Fessenden was undeterred by this recent defeat, for "a brighter day is dawning. The spirit of the North can do anything, if it will express itself. The day of flunkyism is, I trust, over, and if so, there is hope for the future."[126]

Back to the Senate

After receiving the House bill, the only substantive aspect of the debate centered on whether the Senate would accept the elimination of Clayton's nativist amendment. Clayton reminded his colleagues that "*the right to vote is the right to govern*" and principles established then would later affect the territories' state constitutions. Moreover, they could not ignore the 12,400 Germans, Irish, and other Europeans who had arrived on one day alone the previous week. However, most Senators were unwilling to risk the bill merely to restrict alien suffrage. George Jones (TN) changed his vote to protect the bill for this reason, worried that keeping it increased the likelihood the House would defeat it. Most accepted Jones's rationale, and only 7 of 48 members continued to support nativist efforts to limit suffrage.[127]

This final debate also revealed the strain this battle had inflicted on the Whigs. Forming one-third of the Senate, their cohesion was pivotal for party success, but Southern Whigs continued to squabble over the late January Southern caucus. They remained furious over Bell's dissent and charged him with betraying them, while an equally inflamed Bell denounced such an "infamous falsehood." Outside this sectional wrangling, Wade voiced the more worrisome development and claimed Northern Whigs could no longer associate politically with the Southern wing as "an impassable gulf separates us, and must hereafter separate us."[128]

In early April when the bill's fate in the lower chamber remained uncertain, Douglas confided to Howell Cobb that the struggle in the House for passage would be waged by the North and that "our Southern friends have only to stand firm and leave us of the North to fight."[129] This was astute, as sectional divisions in both chambers are the most striking aspect of the vote. However, a gulf widened across both parties and sections. "I accept it in behalf of the cause of freedom. We will engage in competition for the virgin soil of Kansas," Seward pledged, "and God give the victory to the side which is stronger in numbers as it is in right." Although Wade, Chase, Sumner, and Seward railed against the bill and in their more poetic moments alluded to the appropriateness of a forthcoming solar eclipse, it went quietly to the president when the opposition could not even gather enough votes to order yeas and nays.[130]

At end of May, Pierce signed a bill to organize two territories covering a vast area—the Territory of Kansas was 126,283 square miles while the Territory of Nebraska was twice that and included over twenty-seven Indian tribes whose relocation had been achieved only a decade earlier.[131] It eliminated the prohibition against slavery in favor of popular sovereignty and resolved that a territory's efforts to prohibit slavery were likely unconstitutional.[132] The bill represented the ultimate congressional slavery compromise—an agreement to deflect the decision to nascent states.

When Congress had convened in December, Charles Upham (MA) recalled that tranquility had prevailed in a legislature where "there was no North, no South, no East, but one undivided America." By May, however, "our harmony is turned into confusion, and a fatal paralysis has crippled our legislation."[133] The change stemmed from the debate's rhetoric as well as the bill's details. Advocates charged opponents with the classic insult of faction or demagoguery. Often an opponent was criticized for both their views and fellowship with abolitionists whose tactics had plagued many Congressional sessions. While Democrats withstood this pressure, repeated charges of factionalizing disappointed those who hoped to avoid damaging infighting. By insisting on a new test of party loyalty, Democrats risked destroying their already fragile unity, but this issue proved even more contentious and devastating for Whigs. The unity of Northern Whigs against the bill demonstrated a deep divide on slavery's expansion. In the South, where the Whig Party was already in decline, the Kansas-Nebraska bill might well have been designed to destroy them, and Bell warned, "as many of the Whigs of the South took the bait, it may have that effect."[134]

The 1854 Midterm Elections

After passage, many legislators confronted angry constituents, and those who deviated from state instructions faced angry legislatures too. On July 25, the General Assembly of Connecticut censured Isaac Toucey for disobeying them, but he defended his vote, stating that he could not cooperate with the assembly in its "legislative warfare against the Constitution and government of the country." He blamed their reaction on the "abolitionization" of the Whig Party, which would drive "patriotic union-loving citizens from its ranks."[135] In advance of the election, other congressmen like Gerrit Smith (NY) resigned after angry constituents blamed him for not actively blocking the legislation. The depth of Northern hostility—Smith voted against the bill and had a 25-year antislavery record but was nonetheless tarred as proslavery—emphasizes what a bellwether vote it proved to be.[136]

Although the Kansas-Nebraska Act was a Democratic victory, events in the spring indicated that passage would be costly. In March, Pierce's home state rebuffed Democrats and they lost control of the lower house. In April, both Rhode Island and Connecticut were lost to reform Whigs while Wisconsin and Michigan fell to various fusion groups (often a combination of antislavery Whigs, Know-Nothings, anti-Nebraska Democrats, and social reform groups, depending on the nature of the opposition beforehand). By August, Iowa had gone to an anti-Nebraska coalition, as Maine and Vermont did the following month. By the time November arrived, the loss of seven more states was in keeping with the reverses of the preceding eight months. Two years after Pierce's decisive victory, Democrats controlled only New Hampshire and California in the North and had lost two-thirds of congressional seats, while control of the House had swung to a new opposition.[137]

The bill's opponents were delighted. Democrat Daniel Mace (IN) claimed the public had condemned the bill, but the electoral results were not that clear. In Pennsylvania, supporters Asa Packer, Thomas Florence, and J. Glancy Jones were reelected, while opponents Augustus Drum and Isaac Heister were defeated. In Massachusetts, Whigs Samuel Crocker, Edward Dickinson, Thomas Eliot, John Goodrich, Charles Upham, Samuel Walley, and Tappan Wentworth were all swept aside despite their anti-Nebraska credentials. In New York, Reuben Fenton, George Hastings, and Charles Hughes were all defeated despite voting against the bill.[138] Nonetheless, the anti-Nebraska contingent preferred to believe that the people, as Congressman Henry Goodwin (NY) declared, had spoken and "everywhere the supporters of this measure were utterly overthrown and prostrated." Moreover, he was elated by the 117 antislavery representatives who had been reelected.[139] Indeed, if the outcome hinged on the Nebraska bill, then this was "the most formidable demonstration against the institution of slavery that has ever yet been exhibited" and, as the *Charleston Mercury* stated, seemed "distinctly to foreshadow one of two results; the dissolution of the Union, or the extinction of Slavery."[140]

Of greater concern, perhaps, was the performance of the Whigs. As the *Lynchburg Virginian* noted, there was not "a single northern whig of national reputation seeking to moderate the storm of fanaticism."[141] In June, a victorious Stephens had emphasized that although "the Southern Whigs must strike out a lead for themselves," they must avoid becoming a nominal party. "We want no sectional men or sectional issues. . . . Hundreds of thousands of Northern Whigs when they see that this is our fixed determination will abandon the Seward ranks of Antislavery agitators."[142] However, Northern Whigs found other homes in 1854. In the 33rd Congress, Massachusetts had the largest and strongest Whig contingent in the House, with 10 of 12 representatives. But all campaigning Whigs lost their seats to Know-Nothings. Although it was too early to determine the staying power of this new party, the Whigs were clearly in crisis.[143]

Conclusion

When the 33rd Congress convened in December 1853, prospects for the creation of two Western territories had been slim; yet within six months both Nebraska and Kansas were organized in concert with a repeal of the Missouri Compromise. Furthermore, this territorial organization had gone from a mere legislative gleam in Stephen Douglas's eye to a test of Democratic loyalty and party solidarity. Changes that his bill embraced would once have required a tremendous battle, yet in the Senate it proved to be more a matter of semantics than of philosophy. The House battle was marked by bitterness and hostility, but managers and supporters remained convinced the opposition was a fringe element powered by misguided politicians at odds with the majority. There is no evidence Douglas planned to overturn the Missouri Compromise nor that he expected to destabilize the nation by reviving the slavery question. A more likely explanation for his catastrophic miscalculation was the singular importance Douglas placed on organizing the West; he considered the interior as neither "Northern" or "Southern" but like his home state of Illinois, a product of the western frontier. Moreover, popular sovereignty added uncertainty and instability to the territorial system. Finally, the creation of Kansas Territory, a significant change, fed a widespread belief that Democrats wanted to ensure that the South would have a new slave state. Nonetheless, Douglas had an understandable naiveté about the commitment Americans would make to obtaining these territories for slavery or for freedom. What amounted to tunnel-vision, in conjunction with his belief that concerns about slavery were of secondary importance to other issues, led Douglas to underestimate national feeling on the question.[144]

Although the Kansas-Nebraska Act had concrete political ramifications, as the midterm election demonstrated, to focus solely on politicians obscures the larger picture of why the act moved beyond legislation to guerrilla warfare in the mid-1850s. The political transition at hand was not solely the transition from pre- to post-Missouri Compromise, but one from rhetoric to action on the part of non-abolitionists. The bill's supporters too easily dismissed public reaction as the usual fire and brimstone from ministers, not men of action, and familiar rhetoric from abolitionists who enjoyed fanning the flames of injustice, confident that abolitionist threats would once again prove impotent. The country had witnessed similar agitation in 1850, but after "two or three riots got up," Toombs noted, "the good sense, the patriotism, and the nationality of the people of the North came to the rescue." The reaction would not be any different four years later. "Senators may compose themselves; these are not the men either to get up or guide revolutions."[145] But others, better suited to revolution than mere congressmen, heeded the call of revolution and poured into the new territory, determined to mold it in their images of freedom.

The gulf between the politicians and the people proved as vast as the territory itself because a disjunction existed between the intent of the Kansas-Nebraska Act, as expressed by its authors, and the public's understanding of its goals. Supporters vehemently denied that the bill was designed to benefit slavery, especially since many Southerners argued slavery could not thrive in the region. However, given that slavery existed in nearby Missouri, antislavery activists refused to accept such reassurances and were suspicious about the decision to split the proposed Nebraska territory in two. Antislavery activists embraced absolutes in defining a new battle: Seward warned it was "an eternal struggle between Conservatism and Progress, between Truth and Error, between Right and Wrong."[146] Moreover, the Nebraska debate was infused by religious sentiment, which worried Southerners. "Political abolition is an element difficult to control," the *Lynchburg Virginian* noted, but "religious abolition is a powerful force whose destructive energy is the more dangerous from the very sincerity of its delusion."[147]

Although Douglas had been the engine behind passage, Pierce's contribution was equally pivotal. By expending patronage to assure passage, he became closely identified with the Kansas-Nebraska Act. Although the reasons for his party's defeat were then unclear, the damage to both parties was undeniably extensive. As Democrat Howell Cobb stated, "The Democratic party has been literally slaughtered in the Northern, Middle and Western States, whilst of the Whig party there is not left even a monumental remembrance. It is with the Democracy however that we have to deal, leaving 'the *whigs* to bury *the whigs*.'"[148] And in the opinions of most of the Democracy, dealing with the election's aftermath meant acknowledging Pierce's vulnerability. Although it is unlikely Pierce concurred, the remaining two years of his term would be complicated by the president's support for this legislation. In 1852, Pierce's campaign biography had assured Democrats that he would not engage in divisive measures "and if the work of antislavery agitation . . . must be done, let others do it."[149] The irony is that at the close of 1854, Pierce was instrumental in reinvigorating the debate, and in the eyes of some Northerners, the president came to symbolize Northern capitulation to the worst aspects of Southern aggression.

2

Territorial Politics and the Struggle for Party Supremacy, 1854–1855

The passage of the 1854 Kansas-Nebraska Act ushered in a new phase of territorial policy. Although the legislative debate had been contentious, settlement was expected to be routine because popular sovereignty would affect only the territories' constitutions. Frontier life was fraught with violence and uncertainty, but underpinned nonetheless by a political structure. However, unlike in previous territories where settlers requested organization, territorial status preceded settlement in Kansas. In 1854 perhaps seven hundred Americans lived at missions and trading posts while an equal number were posted at army forts; yet few were invested in local politics.[1] This absence of a unifying local political organization combined with popular sovereignty—a process now indelibly shaped by how a wide range of Americans reacted when Congress overturned the 1820 prohibition on slavery—to lead to chaos.

Sparsely populated by Americans, Indian tribes abounded; Kansas had approximately 17,000 American Indians, with the Osages (4,951), Pottawatomie (4,300), and Delaware (1,132) among the most populous tribes.[2] With the exception of the unincorporated land above Texas, these two territories contained all of what was commonly referred to as Indian territory.[3] Commissioner of Indian Affairs George Manypenny had secured treaties with half the tribes by 1853, but Congress had not ratified most of them (and two important ones remained unfinished) nor had provisions been made to protect Indian reserves or survey the territory.[4] Many tribes refused to relocate, an additional complication since their reserves frequently blocked desirable land; the Delaware land reserve, for instance, constrained settlement of the Kansas River Valley around Fort Leavenworth.[5] The Indian treaties obligated Congress to administer ceded lands for three years until publicly auctioned; however, relevant regulations remained unenforced. Thus when Congress opened Kansas Territory on May 30, 1854, not one acre of land was legally salable and almost one third, 15,230,430 acres bordering Missouri where most settlers would enter, was closed. Congress opened a land office in July and authorized surveys later that month, but the first contract was not awarded until November 2 and the first plats were not delivered until January 12. Congress thus extended preemption privileges to squatters on the unsurveyed public domain, but lagged behind the process of settlement.[6]

Although Franklin Pierce had declared the Kansas-Nebraska Act a party measure, typically presidents were not involved in territory creation; their role began with the selection of territorial officials. Territorial administration required a sizable bureaucracy, but no overall policy tied the various departments together. While the governor served as the focal point for executive policy, other federal, extraterritorial agents—including the Army, Indian agents, the surveyor-general, and government contractors (especially for postal delivery)—were active, but the lack of coordination among them was striking.[7] The Department of State exerted the most control, as it oversaw the governor, but the secretary of war directed the Army, the attorney general supervised federal judges, and the Treasury Department controlled salaries and expense accounts and supervised public construction.[8]

A minor political position, the territorial governorship offered prestige and upward political mobility with scant responsibility. A popular governor could use his visibility in local politics to gain a Senate appointment after statehood and thus acquire the influence and distinction lacking in a territorial post.[9] However, inadequate official salaries relative to the high cost of frontier living made the recruitment of quality men difficult. Nevertheless, it drew ambitious men because of opportunities for enrichment through establishing towns, infrastructures, and services. Like many patronage positions, the territorial post rewarded party men whose loyalty often outstripped their management skills. In fairness, however, the position rarely demanded genuine leadership. This was the president's most significant appointment in territorial affairs, and after the repeal of the Missouri Compromise, it assumed greater importance for residents and the Democratic Party's ability to gain ground in the West.

Given the vociferous debate on the Kansas-Nebraska bill and suspicions that Congress organized two territories to guarantee each section one new state, Pierce's nominations were designed to demonstrate neutrality and balance. And expectations for territorial officers were low—in reviewing possible appointments, the *New York Daily Tribune* merely asked the president to "get men who have back-bone, and won't cheat."[10] By choosing a Northern man for Kansas and a Southern man for Nebraska, the president hoped to defuse charges of predetermination.[11] For Kansas governor, Pierce selected Andrew H. Reeder of Pennsylvania after lobbying by two prominent Democrats from that state, Congressman Asa Packer and newspaper editor John W. Forney. But the *Daily Tribune* did not believe a Northern governor could counter the remaining staff's proslavery beliefs. Reviewing a list that included a Southern secretary, two judges, and a district attorney, "who does not see that there is foul play throughout and that 'Popular sovereignty' in Kansas is the sovereignty of the slaveholders' bowie-knife and revolver, beginning in usurpation, sustained by terror, and finally bolstered up by judicial perversion and subversion of law?"[12]

However displeased Northerners were with Reeder, Southerners, having wanted a Southern man, were even more so.[13] Despite reports of his indifference to slavery, privately Reeder was more supportive; considered "deeply sympathetic toward the South," he had backed popular sovereignty and allegedly expressed regret that he could not purchase slaves to bring to Kansas.[14] A lawyer, he was active in the state machine but lacked executive experience. Like most Democrats, Reeder shared an antipathy toward abolitionism and anticipated that any conflict would stem from zealous antislavery emigrants.[15] Confirmed by the Senate on June 30, Reeder took the oath of office a week later but remained in Washington at Pierce's request until Congress adjourned in August. Thus he did not arrive in the territory until October. While he tarried in the capital, settlement proceeded. In fact, it preceded passage of the organizing act. The Massachusetts Emigrant Aid Company acquired a charter two months beforehand, and on April 26, Eli Thayer had begun organizing emigrants.[16]

Despite Thayer's quick start, two factions had already settled with plans to organize a temporary government before the first Emigrant Aid Company party even arrived in the territory. The Actual Settler's Association of Kansas Territory was generally abolitionist, while the Wakarusa Association was comprised mainly of proslavery Missourians without claims in the area.[17] However, the Emigrant Aid Company (EAC), later reincorporated as the New England Emigrant Aid Company (NEEAC), was the most active. In a May 4 report, the company put forth its raison d'être: "to give confidence to settlers, by giving system to emigration. By dispelling the fears that Kanzas will be a slave state, the company will remove the only bar which now hinders its occupation by free settlers." It furnished tickets at reduced rates, assured that travelers would incur no other expenses, and although the NEAAC denied political tests, it offered settlers companions of a similar mindset.[18] During 1854, it sponsored 750 settlers. Most came from New England, a few others from Pennsylvania, Ohio, Wisconsin, and

Michigan.[19] During 1854–1855, the NEEAC sent 18 parties (1,240 settlers) to the territory.[20]

Closer to Kansas, other interested parties also sprang into action. Ten days after passage, a party of horsemen ferried across the Missouri River, announced slavery was instituted, and then rode back.[21] The ease of making a claim, which only required marking the property, led numerous Missourians to cross the border to "establish a sort of Missouri pre-emption upon all this region."[22] In meetings soon after, resolutions were passed urging slaveholders to introduce slaves to the territories as early as possible to reinforce a region that already had some, most notably at Shawnee Mission. In June, the *Platte County Argus* declared it intended to thwart northern aid societies' efforts, by force if necessary. Indeed, by June 8, the (Liberty, Missouri) *Democratic Platform* was pleased to discover emigration had already started and hoped the presence of slaves would force Northerners toward Nebraska.[23]

The well-publicized effort of Northern emigration societies prompted the formation of societies to thwart Kansas's settlement by those who would threaten slavery. On July 29, the Platte County Missouri Self-Defensive Association pledged its aid in removing settlers sponsored by eastern aid companies.[24] The tension between western Missourians and Northern emigrants traveling under the aid societies thus started almost immediately, and to emphasize this, the NEEAC collected two tracts, one pro- and one antislavery, as *Information for the People: Two Tracts of the Times*. The first, written by the association's chair, Benjamin Stringfellow, outlined its problems with aid societies and abolitionism: abolitionists were not true settlers but "really negro-thieves, their purpose not to procure a home in Kansas, but to drive slaveholders therefrom." Given that slaves in Weston had already been set free, Missourians had to defend themselves against settlers who were "not free-men, but paupers, who have sold themselves to Ely Thayer & Co., to do their masters' bidding." The Association stood ready to expel these abolitionists whenever Kansans asked. Finally, Stringfellow claimed that Kansas's geography made free labor too expensive to be profitable.[25]

The second tract, written by Daniel Goodloe, disputed the position that Kansas could only thrive with slavery. Identifying the level of internal improvements as a hallmark of progress, he noted that while Illinois had 1,262 miles of railroad and 100 miles of canals, Missouri had only 50 miles of track and none of canals despite being older. Cities and slavery could not thrive in tandem. "Why curse the virgin soil of Kansas with slavery?" Goodloe asked. "Is it not too plain, that the idea springs from mere passion, or sectional pride and jealousy? And must Kansas in all the elements of prosperity and civilization, be sacrificed to these passions?"[26]

Yet for some, Kansas provided an opportunity for social engineering. In *Kanzas and Nebraska*, Edward Everett Hale urged immigrants to plant themselves in Kansas before slaveholders could do so. Hale had never visited the territory but immediately recognized the possibility for abolitionist control. Written in August 1854, his book echoed themes from an earlier pamphlet, *How to Conquer Texas before Texas Conquers Us*.[27] In 1845, Hale argued a proslavery Texas was not foreordained. "May not the north pour down its hordes... and bear civilization, and Christianity and freedom into their recesses?"[28] Moreover, unlike Texas, Kansas was closer to friendly territories, and the intervening decade had produced an explosion in converts to the antislavery cause. Like Hale, many others believed Kansas's settlement would decide the slavery question and the territory's first fervent settlers' letters were printed in newspapers throughout the east. An antislavery activist who bought into the *Kansas Tribune*, Samuel Wood's letters to the *National Era* began soon after he left Ohio in June. By late August, his appeals became more strident and urgent in tone. "*Now* is the proper time—now is the time that the slaveholders are moving heaven and earth to establish slavery here; and now is the time, like men, we should meet them, and not, like cowards, cry 'Hush, be quiet; don't agitate the question *now*; wait til we are stronger.'"[29]

Even without the slavery issue, emigrants likely would have collided since land claims frequently led to strife. But the organized societies created additional resentment and hostility, which transcended typical frontier violence. By January 1855 two groups were arrayed as "sovereign squatters" against free-state "stock-jobbers and money-getters... covered from head to foot with the leprosy of materialism...."[30] That month a "Territorial Indignation Meeting" condemned Charles Robinson, the EAC's primary agent, for stealing timber and the company itself for "making a grand land speculation under the guise of making Kansas a free state."[31] Most settlers from Missouri were farmers while those from New England and the mid-Atlantic states were more diverse, including mechanics, artisans, and other professionals in addition to farmers.[32] With the added complication of politics, conflicts escalated beyond land and lifestyle.

The Governor Arrives

Although immigration under the aegis of organized societies proceeded apace, governmental functions evolved more slowly. Reeder's delay meant that by the time he arrived, settlers had already divided themselves into factions according to their business interests, which often dovetailed with their views on slavery. Given the heightened emotions elicited by the Kansas-Nebraska Act, a prudent executive would have ensured he was present to control partisan activists. More critically, Reeder inadvertently cast suspicions on his political leanings when he refused to attend a public dinner in his honor hosted by the Platte County Self-Defensive Association.[33] Without a strong governmental presence to mediate and provide structure, tensions grew.

Reeder delivered his inaugural address on October 7, promising to make Kansas "a country of law and order" and emphasizing the attributes of popular sovereignty under which residents would demonstrate their capacity for self-government. By voting, Kansans could "contribute to its permanency as a means of easy solution, for all future time, of a dangerous and exciting question in our National Councils."[34] After a short tour, the governor created election districts and set a territorial delegate election which, unlike elections for the legislature, did not require a census for November 29. The organizing act ordered the first delegate to hold his seat only for that one session.[35] Since the upcoming congressional session ended in March 1855, if they waited to hold both elections simultaneously, Kansans risked being unrepresented.[36] Thus, Reeder set the required census and registration of voters for February, delaying the territorial legislative elections until March as was his prerogative.

The territory's first elections were complicated by Congress's ambiguous residency requirements. The Kansas-Nebraska Act stated that all free white resident males 21 years and older could vote if they were citizens or had sworn to uphold the Constitution. However, Congress neglected to define what transformed someone present in the territory into an actual resident.[37] Did a settler have to be actively improving his land? Was it appropriate to make improvements while living across the river in established towns in other states? Was merely staking a claim sufficient?

The ramifications of these unanswered questions were immediately apparent. After Reeder set the delegate election, Senator David Atchison urged his state to blunt the anticipated participation of Northerners by voting. "Now if a set of fanatics and demagogues a thousand miles off could afford to advance their money and exert every nerve to abolitionize the Territory and exclude the slaveholder, when they have not the least personal interest," he asked, "what is your duty?" Much depended on the outcome and "should each county in the State of Missouri only do its duty, the question will be decided quietly and peaceably at the ballot-box."[38] Residents of Platte County called a meeting in Leavenworth and wrote a memorial addressing Reeder's decision to postpone legislative elections until March. In Nebraska,

Governor Francis Burt held both elections concurrently that fall; as a result, its first legislature convened before Kansas had even conducted its census. Proslavery settlers thus believed Reeder's delay cloaked a free-state bias by giving Northern settlers more time to emigrate.

On November 21, Reeder replied that he would resist outside interference.[39] "It may be," he wrote the Missouri memorialists, "very desirable for gentleman to live among the comforts of the States, with all the accumulated conveniences and luxuries of an old home, and make an occasional expedition into our Territory to arrange our affairs—instruct our people and public officers and control our government; but it does not suit *us*. . . ."[40] However apt, it was common to stake a claim by laying four logs in a rectangle before retreating to more comfortable surroundings while building a home. For many settlers, then, it made sense to stay a few miles across the border. Reeder correctly stated his responsibility to protect the territory, but his tone engendered hostility from a proslavery faction already distrustful of the new governor's motives and allegiance.

In the November 29 delegate election, Democrat and former Indian agent John Whitfield represented the proslavery faction, and with free-state strength diluted by two candidates, John A. Wakefield and Robert P. Flenneken (a Reeder protégé), his victory was decisive, culling 2,258 votes to his opponents' combined 553 votes. A total of 2,833 men of the 2,905 eligible voted, but district votes did not match census counts. For instance, 230 votes were recorded in district 11 although only 24 persons were eligible to vote. However, no one seriously contested this election.[41] The election did not draw large numbers of free-state participants, and even if all illegal votes were eliminated, Whitfield would still have won.[42] Free-state disinterest was attributed to various factors: poor communications under primitive conditions; the dispersal of settlements; the precedence of establishing claims over a one-issue election; or simply that "the brevity of the session prevented Republicans from making a contest."[43] Moreover, Whitfield's victory cannot be attributed solely to proslavery support, as he defended squatters' rights, supported preemption on Delaware trust lands, and left the slavery question to the people, positions that would have resonated for many settlers.[44] Despite a petition to set aside the vote, Reeder certified the election on December 5, and Whitfield took his seat in the House of Representatives two weeks later. Nonetheless, suspicions persisted that Reeder was antislavery and would "not lend himself to assist in carrying out the designs of the 'Squatter Sovereigns' of Missouri. . . ."[45] In early December, in fact, Atchison asked Pierce to remove Reeder for moving too slowly to assure slavery's triumph,[46] but Pierce supported his governor.

The Spring Scrimmage

Both factions learned lessons from this first election. Although victorious, the proslavery faction remained bitter about the delay because if Reeder had authorized both elections as Nebraska's governor had done, they would already control the legislature. The proslavery men planned to turn out in force on election day. As the *Weston Reporter* stated the day before, "Should the pro-slavery party fail in this contest, it will not be because Missouri has failed to do her duty to assist friends. It is a safe calculation that two thousand squatters have passed over into the promised land from this part of the state within four days."[47] Moreover, resentment toward abolitionism was growing. The *Leavenworth Kansas Herald* published an address to "Freemen of the West," setting the tone for proslavery activists. "We hate a deceiver. And a party, like this ragged, miserly, nigger-stealing crew, who skulk behind the name of Free State, we hold in meaner contempt than we do the immediate and avowed pupils of Lloyd Garrison."[48]

In February, Reeder ordered a registration of voters and completed the census for the March 30 election. The 1855 census revealed the dominance of Missouri settlers, but the 192 slaves were balanced by 151 free blacks. This scarcity of slave labor likely reflects the risks involved in transferring assets, which would lose their value should Kansas become a free state.[49] Kansans continued to take a broad view of the resident qualification Congress left undefined, but it was garnering notice. "Who shall be an actual resident of said Territory, and at what time?" asked Congressman Sion H. Rodgers (NC). "Why, unquestionably the language in the Nebraska bill means persons who shall be actual residents at the time of the holding of the first election in the Territory. . . . Was it [a change from typical settlement acts] because there were no people in the Territory of Nebraska at the time of the passage of the bill except Indians?"[50] However, the time for Congress to elucidate their understanding of eligible voters had passed.

Unlike the delegate election four months before, turnout on March 30 was considerable; in a territory with 2,905 eligible voters, 6,307 ballots were cast.[51] As the *Kansas Herald* reported, "The triumph of the pro-slavery party is complete and overwhelming. Come on, Southern men; bring your slaves and fill up the Territory. Kansas is saved."[52] Many residents were outraged, but a few were actually pleased by this ebullience. "So open, unblushing, and overwhelming was the demonstration," Robinson wrote, "that it defeated itself. . . . This was very satisfactory to the Free-State men, and most of them looked on without effort to prevent the illegal voting, except in a formal way by entering protest before the judges of election."[53] Even at such a pivotal moment, the propaganda value of being overrun was recognized by the faction that would use it so effectively in the years to come.

Perhaps fearing that some legislative seats would be set aside, proslavery forces soon circulated a handbill characterizing Reeder as "incompetent and unfit for the duties of his position," complete with an election scheduled to replace him.[54] Indeed, on April 16, Reeder cited voter irregularities to refuse election certificates for 4 of the 13 council seats and 13 of the 26 assembly seats, arranging to fill the vacated seats on May 22.[55] The following day, he left to brief Pierce and persuade him to dismiss the legislature. Motivated partially by the intense proslavery hostility against him since the election, Reeder was already moving away from his proslavery views.[56]

More voters cast ballots than were eligible, but much of the resultant tension derived from the uncertainty over who was entitled to vote. Both sides assumed fraud; each believed the other was sending voters not settlers to Kansas. Many Missourians embraced a generous definition of a settler. "If the very day of his returning is not fixed," Benjamin Stringfellow stated, "if he is uncertain, he is in the strictest law 'a resident' and 'an inhabitant.' By the Kansas act every man in the territory on the day of the election is a loyal voter if he has not fixed a day for his return to some other home."[57] Moreover, this confusion was compounded by the organizing act's statement that "every free white male inhabitant above the age of twenty-one years, who shall be an actual resident of said Territory" could vote as long as he was a citizen, had taken an oath to support the Constitution, and was not active in the military.[58] However, the act never defined an "actual" resident. Many claimed fraud, and violence at the polls was simply border life, as "Reeder knew them [the facts] perfectly when he opened the returns at Shawnee Mission in the presence of a gang of Missourians and two or three wagonloads of men from Lawrence armed to the teeth."[59]

After the election, both factions' sense that Kansas represented a national crossroads intensified. Writing to Senator Robert Hunter (VA), Atchison emphasized that Kansas was a zero-sum game the South must win: "We are playing for a mighty stake, if we win we carry slavery to the Pacific Ocean if we fail we lose Missouri, Arkansas, Texas and all the territories, the game must be played boldly."[60] If Kansas was not made safe for slavery, the possibilities of colonizing these territories would be gone; more importantly, without Kansas, slavery would be rolled back in states where it already existed. "You come to drive us and our 'peculiar' institution from Kansas," Atchison wrote Amos Lawrence, the treasurer of the NEEAC, that same month. "We do not intend, cost what it may, to be driven, or deprived of any of our rights."[61] As the proslavery men were gearing up, the free-state faction was also gathering their forces. Robinson asked Eli Thayer and Edward Everett Hale for arms three times in April before they were finally sent to the territory in boxes marked books.[62]

Moreover, both sides had secret societies of dubious efficacy. For instance, the 1855 signs for the Vigilance Club had an amusing reference to the administration: "sign—rub corner of eye with left little finger; answer—seize lower part of left ear with thumb and finger; password—have you heard the news from Washington? Anw—yes, with trembling."[63] But the administration had been oddly silent about the recent elections, due, the *Worcester Spy* charged, to the fact that "slavery, which is now the supreme power at Washington, strikes the Government blind and dumb with moral paralysis."[64] With Reeder off to Washington, the territory would soon discover whether its legislature would be sustained or repudiated.

On his way to the capital, Reeder gave an impromptu speech in his hometown of Easton that displeased both proslavery advocates and Pierce. He denounced the recent elections, claiming that "Kansas had been invaded by a regular organized army, armed to the teeth, who took possession of the ballot-boxes, and made a Legislature to suit the purpose of the Pro-Slavery party." Furthermore, he blamed Dr. John Stringfellow, senior editor of the *Squatter Sovereign*, for the situation, arguing that "it would never have existed had it not been for the course pursued by him in agitating the public mind." While indicting "border ruffians," Reeder overlooked the emigrant aid societies Democrats identified as the impetus behind territorial troubles. As the *New York Tribune* reported, he "denounced with bitterness the violence and force of the Missourians, but he wholly overlooked the conduct of the Massachusetts Abolitionists, on which the Missourians based their pleas of justification."[65]

While largely true, it was nonetheless unwise for Reeder to isolate the proslavery faction for condemnation, as he was already under siege. Not only was the administration displeased with the uproar over the elections, but Secretary of War Jefferson Davis and others in the executive branch believed he had taken advantage of his position by engaging in speculative dealings in Pawnee lands, unethical if not illegal actions.[66] During his initial tour of the territory, Reeder and two associate territorial judges, Saunders W. Johnston and Rush Elmore, expressed interest in purchasing land from a local tribe while at Fort Riley. Along with the fort's commander and other officers, they tried to use an unauthorized survey to adjust the reservation's boundaries to provide room for a future town named Pawnee.[67] In January, Reeder purchased the land, prompting John Butler Chapman, who had tried to purchase it himself, to complain to Superintendent of Indian Affairs George

Manypenny. Chapman accused Reeder of using public funds to underwrite the transaction by conducting private business during his fall tour. After Attorney General Caleb Cushing found the governor had violated "federal statute and departmental regulation," Pierce voided the contracts.[68]

During meetings in May, Reeder claimed the president had backed his policies despite complaining about his Easton speech. Even if Reeder accurately reported his support, Pierce was clearly unhappy about recent developments. The president "stated that this Kansas matter had given him more harassing anxiety than anything that had happened since the loss of his son; that it haunted him day and night, and was the great overshadowing trouble of his administration. He stated that the most pertinacious complaints of me had been made to him. . . ."[69] Members of the territorial legislature, for instance, complained Reeder was a "clog" that was "dragging heavily at its [the administration's] wheel."[70] According to Reeder, Pierce reasoned that perhaps "it would be unsafe for myself, and for the country" if he returned to Kansas.[71] A more sensitive man might have realized such comments and offers of a foreign mission were attempts to delicately remove him, but Reeder interpreted them favorably. Indeed, the president retained him although he warned the governor that his land speculations were a problem. Although he may merely have been dim, Reeder likely hoped Pierce would overlook these financial dealings and allow him to continue as governor, a necessity if he hoped to obtain national office.

After these meetings, Pierce outlined a letter for Reeder to fill in and sign, explaining his position on how the Kansas-Nebraska Act affected whether the territory would be slave or free. He asked Reeder to discuss the "interposition of Emigrant Aid Society to *force* a solution on one side" and the "reactionary interposition of citizens of Missouri to *force* a solution on the other side." Additionally, he inquired about Reeder's politics, "his purpose of just administration," and the "difficulty of suggestion any means by which the President can interpose in election. . . ."[72] Pierce also directed his cabinet to pursue the charges against Reeder. On June 11, the day before his scheduled return to Kansas, Secretary of State William Marcy asked the governor to explain his speculative practices, with the implication that an unsatisfactory answer would lead to his dismissal. Three days later, Cushing sent similar letters to Reeder's partners, Judges Johnston and Elmore.[73] If Pierce could not induce a resignation, he clearly intended to curtail Reeder's autonomy.

The president's concerns for Reeder's safety were prescient, as his Easton speech had proved equally unpopular within the territory as it had been within the White House. Enraged by the defamation, John Stringfellow assaulted Reeder on June 27, and he only escaped being shot because two proslavery officials restrained Stringfellow.[74] Reeder's impolitic speech would have other ramifications. As Stringfellow soon after became speaker of the territorial house, the upcoming legislative session promised to be contentious because an open breach now existed between the governor and the legislature.

The First Territorial Legislature Convenes

Located three miles from Westport, Missouri, Fort Leavenworth was the temporary seat of government and Reeder's official residence. But the governor ordered the legislature to convene at Pawnee, near Fort Riley, purportedly to remove it from local influences and take advantage of standing buildings.[75] In the fall of 1854, however, the secretary of war had expanded Fort Riley and absorbed Pawnee, ordering the buildings destroyed and settlers relocated. Although these orders were not completed until late the following summer, Davis's plans unequivocally rendered Pawnee a poor choice for the permanent seat of government.[76]

Given this situation and the administration's obvious displeasure, Reeder had to regain control of territorial matters. In opening the legislative session on July 2, he asked legislators to commence their duties "with pure hearts, tempered feelings, and sober judgments...." However, the legislature threw down the gauntlet by removing the free-state men elected in the special election and replacing them with the proslavery men originally elected in March. They were easily replaced because a free-state meeting in Lawrence had asked these legislators to "resign and repudiate the fraud." Martin F. Conway did so for the group in a letter that refused to recognize the legislature's legitimacy. When the free-state legislators were unseated and replaced, protests were entered into the record, but no other action was taken. However unfair, legislatures judged their members' credentials, and since the May victors were deemed to have been "irregularly elected," their removal was nominally justifiable. The proslavery legislature was unable to unseat one member who had been elected in March, but S.D. Houston eventually resigned as well, because to remain "was a condescension too inglorious for the spirit of an American freeman."[77]

Having eliminated all free-state members, the legislature turned to the issue of the seat of government. Declaring Pawnee too rustic (many legislators had to camp out), they passed a bill to relocate the seat of government to Shawnee Methodist Mission near Fort Leavenworth. The financially interested governor vetoed this bill, but the legislature overrode his veto and adjourned to the mission. Reeder loudly denounced the move from Pawnee as illegal, but the organizing act only required the legislature to meet on the day and place the governor appointed; it was not required to remain in said location thereafter.[78] Thus once called into session, the legislators could lawfully relocate.

Close to the Missouri border, Shawnee Mission had long kept slaves, and Thomas Johnson, its superintendent, was elected president of the first territorial council. While Reeder impotently condemned its relocation to Shawnee Mission, the legislature adopted Missouri's harsh slave code.[79] As one partisan noted, the legislature passed "enactments stripping the governor of almost every vestige of power, attempting even to deprive him of the privileges granted by the organic [organizing] act. They arrogated to themselves the appointment of all the territorial officers, and selected none but persons of their own class, and those who were known to be of the most ultra character."[80] This inflamed tensions as free-state loyalists disavowed the legislature and its laws as "bogus."[81]

The legislature overrode all the governor's vetoes, and the two branches of government soon came to an impasse. In a July 21 veto message, Reeder argued that because the move to Shawnee was illegal, all laws passed there were invalid and since he refused to sign any of them, henceforth, "we must act independently of each other."[82] In turn, the legislature ignored him, and despite Reeder's assertion that he could act independently, the governor was left adrift. "The unseating of the free-state men was palpably unlawful and unfair," wrote one sympathetic biographer who overlooked Reeder's silence on this point. "The Governor could not rule the territory without a legislature, and he could not govern it with the one he had. He found himself in the unhappy position of an executive who reigns but does not rule."[83] For a man already in a precarious position, this stalemate was untenable.

The resultant impasse ended when Pierce replaced Reeder with Wilson Shannon, George Manypenny's brother-in-law, the following month. Pierce had already made his decision when proslavery residents petitioned on July 27 for his removal. When rumors of his impending dismissal reached the territory on July 31, the legislature adjourned in celebration.[84] Pierce offered Reeder a graceful exit, but he refused reassignment and was fired on July 28, although official notice did not arrive until August 16. The official rationale for his dismissal was Reeder's inappropriate speculative ventures; but as most territorial residents engaged in similar activities, free-state partisans dismissed this as mere window dressing.[85] The governor's inability to manage the legislature or calm free-state partisans, combined with Pierce's displeasure, made removal inevitable. That he was removed so quickly was partially attributable to the proslavery faction's hostility, but it would not have been so damaging if Reeder had not left himself vulnerable to charges of financial misconduct.

After his removal, Reeder joined the free-state organization and ran for territorial delegate in alternative elections sponsored by the antislavery faction. By abandoning his proslavery background and party, Reeder was embraced by antislavery forces as a patriot, a man of conscience who had withstood party expectations.[86] Writing their father's biography in 1881, Reeder's children ascribed his conversion to the free-state movement to the greater economic rewards available, but also implied that the excesses of the proslavery faction drove Reeder to abandon his party, that it "caused him to think more deeply than before upon the moral aspects of that question; and it may be said that the pro-slavery zeal of western Missouri was the chief instrument for converting a Democratic Governor of Pennsylvania training and Southern sympathies into a warm and devoted friend of the slave. . . ."[87] Although Reeder had not demonstrated a deep philosophical immersion in these questions, he was aware of opportunities within the nascent free-state movement. There would be at least four prestigious positions available once Kansas became a state: governor, two senators, and one representative, and Robinson was the only clear leader. After his Easton speech and contretemps with the legislature, Reeder would not benefit politically if Kansas became a slave state. Moreover, a likely reluctance to return to a life of relative obscurity in Pennsylvania probably added to Reeder's willingness to throw in his lot with the developing free-state party.

Reeder's children also depicted his dismissal positively, characterizing it as a gift of freedom that allowed him to pursue his true feelings.[88] However, he did not crave the freedom of being stripped of his position, having declined reassignment in the spring and summer. Had he solely wanted freedom, Reeder could have resigned. It is more likely that he was reluctant to lose one prestigious position without securing another. As governor, he might have been able to strong-arm the legislature and oversee a free-state constitution, but it was unlikely. Still, if Reeder pursued this course, even failure and removal would transform him into a victim of the slave oligarchy.

That summer saw increasingly strident condemnation of Pierce in the free-state media, particularly for his inability to control fellow Democrat David Atchison. As a letter to the *Chicago Democratic Press* argued, "Our citizens have anxiously looked to the strong arm of Government for protection. But, Great God! that is on the side of oppression. . . ."[89] Reeder's removal galvanized local politics, and both factions formalized party structures. During May and June 1855, proslavery factions held meetings in Missouri to plan a July 12 convention, insist antislavery settlers go to Nebraska, and denounce congressional interference. This convention published an "Address to the People of the United States," reaffirming their belief that outside interference was at odds with the Kansas-Nebraska Act. They claimed Missouri had to protect itself because slave property worth 25 million dollars was threatened.[90] However, efforts to create a Democratic Party faltered. James Henry Lane, the former Indiana lieutenant-governor and congressman whose support for the Kansas-Nebraska bill had ended his career, came to Kansas, allegedly at the instigation of Senator Stephen Douglas (IL) and Pierce, to form "a new, Anti-Southern Democratic party on the platform of 1852." Although such a party was unlikely, the goal was probably to establish one more resistant to Southern demands. A week after his August 27 efforts floundered, Lane had abandoned the Democrats entirely to join the free-state party.[91]

For its part, the free-state movement resolved to put aside differences and focus on party formation. On July 17, Josiah Miller and R.G. Elliot, editors of the western-oriented *Kansas Free State*, called a small group together near the Kansas River (later called the Sandbank convention) to organize and adopt a broad antislavery platform.[92] The next step was the Big Springs Convention of September 5 and 6, which provided the first official break with the territorial government. The convention asserted that they found themselves "in an unparalleled and critical condition—deprived by superior force of the rights guaranteed by the Declaration of Independence, the Constitution of the United States, and the Kansas bill."[93] Proceedings reveal a strategy to subsume all issues except for disfranchisement, to "proffer an organization calculated to recover our dearest rights, and into which Democrats and Whigs, Native and Naturalized citizens may freely enter without any sacrifice of their respective political creeds, but without forcing them as a test upon others."[94] It dismissed the legislature as a "foreign body" and denied any duty to heed its laws. Instead, "every freeman amongst us is at full liberty, consistently with all his obligations as a citizen and a man, to defy and resist them, if he chooses to do so."[95] The center of the free-state strategy was repudiation of the territorial legislature, a decision made even before it had met in July because activists believed their laws would "crush us out" if recognized as legitimate.[96]

Moreover, at Big Springs partisans also established that Kansas would not provide a haven for free blacks even if it became a free state. According to John Speer, like many free-state partisans, he and Lane, just beginning his metamorphosis from devoted Democrat to radical Republican, were divided by their attitudes toward free blacks. Lane believed most people wanted to bar blacks from Kansas. Speer agreed but asserted that "such a clause in the constitution would defeat admission, and drive all sympathy with us from such men as Sumner, Wade, Wilson, Stevens and Chase, and utterly defeat the project." They agreed to make the black laws "a separate question, distinct from the constitution, to be voted on pro and con, and to be operative only as instructions to the first legislature, to be null and void afterwards." As 91 of 100 delegates voted to exclude free blacks, Speer saw this as an acceptably pragmatic decision. As the *Kansas Tribune* stated, "In essentials unity, in non-essentials charity."[97]

Thus the convention resolved to make "fair and reasonable provision" regarding the slaves already in the territory to "protect the masters against injustice and total loss."[98] Moreover they argued that "the best interests of Kansas require a population of free white men" and so they favored "stringent laws excluding all negroes, bond or free, from the Territory."[99] The more radical men understood such pragmatism but were unhappy about being made into hypocrites, as this ban made them antiblack as well as antislavery. The *Herald of Freedom*, for instance, disliked being put in "a position which will require us to stultify ourself [sic], or give the lie to our entire past history."[100] The convention brought radical fears to pass, a move abolitionists saw as a moral decline in favor of self-interest. As a Leavenworth correspondent wrote to the *Herald of Freedom*, "I have no particular love for the black man, but I do loathe and detest oppression; and as to being enslaved myself, and bearing the taunts and sneers, and submit to the outrages which have been practised on our people in Kansas, and all because we loved freedom and hated slavery *I will not*."[101] This greater interest in one's own oppression did not surprise die-hard abolitionists such as William Lloyd Garrison, the influential editor of *The Liberator*. Earlier in the summer, he had distinguished between mere opportunists and true believers. Although he believed most emigrants wanted a free Kansas, they had "not gone to Kansas to be martyrs in the cause of the enslaved negro, nor to sacrifice their chances for a homestead on the altar of principle, but to find a comfortable home for themselves and their children."[102]

Indeed, settlers echoed Garrison's viewpoint: "The community here are very nearly united on the free-state question. But the majority would dislike and resent being called abolitionists . . . ," John Everett wrote. "They have a strong instinct against slavery, do not want it about them, but lack the strong moral sense of its injustice which we feel."[103] This distinction was important locally because of the proslavery faction's animus against abolitionists. For instance, Atchison distinguished between free soil activists and abolitionists. "I respect a man who is willing to overthrow our government,—involve the United States with each other in civil war,—that African slavery may be abolished.... The term 'free-soiler' is far more odious to me than 'abolitionist.' The one implies something of honesty; the other all of knavery and hypocrisy...."[104] The convention nominated Reeder as territorial delegate and planned to meet in Topeka on September 19 and 20.

The free-state activity of men previously tied to the Democratic Party flummoxed many observers. While Reeder simply looked like an opportunist, others' transformations were more confounding. As late as June 27, for example, Lane recognized the legislature's validity, in part because he wanted a divorce. Nonetheless, once he embraced the cause he did so wholeheartedly, allegedly proposing to "'settle the vexed question and save Kansas from further outrage' by a battle between one hundred slave-holders, including Senator Atchison, and one hundred free-state men, including himself, to be fought in the presence of twelve United States Senators and twelve members of the House of Representatives!"[105] While the free-state party welcomed his oratorical skill, they remained wary. "He is riding & lecturing night & day ... & yet he is a pro-slavery man at heart. I have heard him say that he looked upon a slave, as he did upon a horse—merely as property."[106] While men like Robinson had always been antislavery, Lane and Reeder exemplify the fluidity of Kansas's politics during late summer 1855.

Shannon's Deal: Dual October Elections and the Topeka Movement

In replacing Reeder, Pierce had turned to a prominent Democrat with state, national, and international experience. Wilson Shannon of Ohio had served the party as governor, senator, and foreign minister. Moreover, he had recently demonstrated his loyalty by voting for the Kansas-Nebraska Act, a vote that had prompted many congressmen like him to retire rather than stand for reelection. This decision made Shannon available for immediate deployment to Kansas.[107] Prior to his Senate term, he had been governor but resigned in April 1844 to become minister to Mexico. He was less successful in this post; his "lack of tact in communicating with the Mexican Government" led to a quick recall in March 1845.[108] Shannon cannot be held responsible for the war that broke out with Mexico soon after, of course, but this diplomatic experience augured poorly for success in Kansas. At a time when the territorial government required strong leadership and discretion, Pierce selected the experienced Shannon, but his efficacy while acquiring this experience was questionable. Yet most proslavery advocates were pleased as Shannon "hates abolitionism as bad as I do," George W. Clarke wrote. "He came here intending to throw all his influence for our success and went to work openly and above board with us—he had the confidence of the entire pro-slavery party."[109] However, skeptics saw evidence of Pierce's free-state leanings in this appointment: "He has all along done everything in his power to bring it in as a free state and but for his natural deficiency of intellectual calibre on this and all other matters he would have succeeded. . . . If he had been with us he would after Reeder's treachery have appointed Atchison or Whitfield."[110]

Shannon arrived in Kansas to discover that the breach between the two factions had only grown. He took his oath of office on September 7, two days after the Big Springs convention and two weeks before the Topeka meeting where free-state activists solidified their position. The convention issued a "People's Proclamation" outlining the depredations against them. A "Constitutional Proclamation" defended their decision to pursue admission given that the organizing act did not anticipate "an emergency like ours." Thus, it urged writing a constitution, adopting a bill of rights, and organizing a state government. They assured residents that this path had been "adopted after mature deliberation" and that Kansans were "fully alive to the importance of the step they are about to take, in disenthralling themselves from the slavery which is now fettering them. . . ."[111]

The legislature scheduled an October 1 election for territorial delegate and Whitfield once again decisively won, garnering 2,721 votes to a scattering of 17 votes for other candidates in an election boycotted by the free-state party.[112] On October 9, directly defying local government, the free-state party elected Reeder for the same position (no doubt hoping to capitalize on his status as a rebuffed governor) and a week later, elected delegates to a constitutional convention to be held in Topeka on October 23.

Against this backdrop, immigration continued. One free-state settler from Rhode Island believed the political troubles emanating from the "*sham legislature* and the border ruffians under Atchison and Stringfellow" was slowing immigration, but that their cause would prevail. "People need not fear to come to Kanzas [for] the *Missouri* laws are a *dead letter* to Kanzas freemen, their hirelings *dare* not enforce them," Thomas Wells wrote. "There are eight free state men to two . . . and the ratio is constantly increasing in favor of freedom *Kanzas must* and *will be free.*"[113] Indeed, while organization increased some settlers' confidence, others worried about decisions being made under the free-state banner. In October, Charles Stearn warned Senator Charles Sumner (MA), one of Kansas's greatest supporters, that the Topeka government did not necessarily represent the people.

There had been inadequate debate over important issues and the people "go for the project simply because they are told it is the only remedy for their troubles. They are sick of anarchy, & hail with delight, the idea however deleterious [?] it may be, of sustaining the resolution of a sovereign state to the other states of the Union."[114]

Despite Stearn's doubts, the unauthorized October elections commenced the first part of a two-pronged strategy to press free-state views before Congress. First, the Topeka government would challenge the territorial government's legitimacy by contesting Whitfield's October reelection as delegate and proving the legislature's illegality. On October 16, Reeder informed Whitfield of his challenge and of free-state claims of rampant electoral fraud. Whitfield viewed this as the bitter fruit of Reeder's removal from office and maintained the latter's election was a mockery. He dismissed the contention that his own election was backed by illegal election law and emphasized that only the courts could invalidate federal law.[115]

The Topeka group wagered that a successful challenge would result in the repudiation of both Whitfield and the entire territorial political organization. This was crucial to the second part of the Topeka strategy: admission of Kansas as a free state under a constitution they had written. Although statehood after only 18 months was premature, the movement hoped to demonstrate that territorial citizens were so endangered that only immediate statehood could save them. Moreover, they believed the large anti-Nebraska contingent elected to Congress in 1854 would support this strategy.

The Topeka Constitution addressed the major issues of the free-state party. It included a bill of rights that outlawed slavery (unless as a criminal sentence) in section VI. In response to the legislative assembly laws, section XI stated that "every citizen may freely speak, write and publish his sentiments on all subjects." Voting included all white males and "civilized" male Indians over the age of 21 who had spent 6 months in territory and 30 days in the county in which they would vote. Finally, neither a new constitutional convention nor an amendment could be initiated before 1865.[116] On October 26, in a vote that illustrates the factional divide, delegates failed to strike the word *white* from the constitution 7 to 25. Although observers saw a North-South schism most clearly, an East-West one was also evident, most clearly in attitudes toward the land. "The Western men, notwithstanding their positive enmity to slavery," editor John Speer reported, "were generally in favor of a law prohibiting negroes, bond or free, from settling in the country; and some of them went so far as to say, if they must have negroes among them, they wanted slaves."[117] This could cost the constitution outside support, but it was accepted 1,731 to

46, and in a December referendum, free-state residents ordered their legislature to exclude free blacks from Kansas by a vote of 1,287 to 453.[118]

The proslavery Law and Order Party evolved more slowly. Organization began in October and proslavery adherents convened in Leavenworth on November 14. Territorial officials were actively involved, as Shannon presided over the convention and Surveyor-General John Calhoun, Territorial Secretary Daniel Woodson, and Chief Justice Samuel Lecompte participated.[119] In addition, the governor opened the convention by stating "the President is behind you."[120] Such overt ties ensured that the close connection between the administration and the proslavery faction continued.

Despite Whitfield's election, proslavery advocates felt pressured by the organizing free-state party and ongoing northern immigration. Southern emigrants had been slow to come to Kansas, perhaps lulled into complacency by the active Missouri contingent and confident that their proximity would secure Kansas without other Southern help. "Alabama and Georgia may hold public meetings, and resolve to sustain the slaveholders in Missouri in making Kansas a slave state," the *St. Louis Intelligencer* wrote. "But their resolutions comprise all their aid—which is not 'material' enough for the crisis. When slaveholders of Alabama and Georgia Emigrate, they go to Louisiana, Arkansas, and Texas. They do not come with their slaves to Missouri or to Kansas."[121]

Atchison warned Southerners that "the prosperity or the ruin of the whole South depends on the Kansas struggle."[122] Finally, the Kansas Emigrant Society of Missouri published an appeal throughout the South acknowledging that their state could "no longer stand up single-handed, the lone champion of the South, against the myrmidons of the North. It requires no foresight to perceive that if the 'higher law' men succeed in this crusade, it will be but the beginning of a war upon the institutions of the South, which will continue until slavery shall cease to exist in any of the states or the Union is dissolved."[123] Jefferson Buford of Alabama heard this plea. In November 1855 his call for three hundred "industrious, sober, discreet, reliable men capable of bearing arms, not prone to use them wickedly or unnecessarily, but will to protect their sections in every real emergency" was reprinted in Southern newspapers. Buford promised settlers a 40-acre homestead with more acreage allotted for any ministers, mechanics, or those with mill or agricultural equipment. Buford funded his expedition with $20,000 of his own money, raised by auctioning his slaves, and pledged that for every $50 given, he would provide one bona fide Kansas settler.[124]

The Wakarusa War

Shannon's misfortunes began ten weeks after he took office when proslavery Franklin N. Coleman killed antislavery Charles W. Dow on November 21 and set off a chain of events known as the "Wakarusa War." Despite opposing political views, the two men were at odds over property, not philosophy. Their conflict had grown over the fall such that Coleman believed he was in danger. "It was also reported to me, some four days previous to my reencounter with Dow, that he (Dow) had declared that 'he would beat my d——d brains out, if I went into the grove, on my own claim, to cut timber.'"[125] Sheriff Samuel Jones of Douglas County called a posse to arrest Jacob Branson, Dow's roommate, for threatening a neighbor, and set off for Lecompton. However, Dow's free-state friends liberated Branson from custody. As his rescue interfered with official business, Jones informed Shannon that "an open rebellion" existed and requested three thousand men to recapture Branson.

Shannon agreed that a response was necessary but deemed Jones's request excessive. He ordered General Hiram Strickler of Douglas County and Major General William P. Richardson of the northern division of territorial militia to arrest Branson and his liberators.[126] He urged caution and ordered Jones not to deliver the writs until he arrived with federal troops. Although Jones had been reinforced, Shannon told the sheriff to use the fewest men necessary.[127] He informed Pierce that Strickler and Richardson could gather between five and eight hundred men to protect Jones in executing his office. Shannon contacted Strickler because the southern division of the territorial militia had not been organized; he later wrote the president that the only forces available to him were those who volunteered to help Richardson or Strickler. The lack of a territorial militia increased the likelihood of violence because only those men most motivated by partisan feeling were likely to respond to a call for aid.[128]

In his report, Shannon characterized Branson's rescue as an egregious rebuff of territorial authority. "If the lives and property of unoffending citizens of the Territory cannot be protected by law, there is an end to practical government, and it becomes a useless formality."[129] He believed the territory could descend into civil war at any time as "we are standing on a volcano; the upheavings and agitations beneath, we feel, and no one can tell the hour when an eruption may take place."[130] Thus motivated to control such border skirmishes, the governor asked citizens to support the law and ordered the county's district attorney to arrest those who helped Branson evade it.[131] The free-state organization had forced his hand; otherwise he would face the "disgraceful alternative of surrendering the Territorial government into the hands of an armed and lawless mob."[132]

Jones appealed to Shannon for authorization since "if I am to wait for the government troops, more than two-thirds of the men now here will go away, very much dissatisfied. They are leaving hourly as it is. I do not, by any means, wish to violate your orders, but I really believe that if I have a sufficient force, it would be better to make the demand."[133] However, Shannon delayed. As Jones's posse grew outside of Lawrence, free-state men within the town similarly gathered their forces.

Shannon went to Lawrence expecting that Colonel Edwin V. Sumner, in command at Fort Leavenworth, would join him. However, after agreeing to do so, Sumner decided to await formal orders from the Department of War. As he wrote on December 7, "The more I reflect upon it, the more I am convinced that I ought not to interpose my command between the two hostile parties in this Territory until I receive orders from the Government. . . . If you find those people bent on attacking the town, I would respectfully suggest that they might be induced to pause for a time on being told the orders of the General Government were expected. . . ."[134] When Shannon arrived he found three to four hundred poorly armed men arrayed against approximately six hundred well-armed men fortified within Lawrence in place of Sumner's expected troops. Moreover, once this disparity became known, men rushed over from Missouri and enrolled in Jones's posse.[135] Believing these new arrivals worsened an already strained dynamic and forced his hand, Shannon again asked Sumner for support, but no response was immediately forthcoming. After being told that no one on Jones's warrants was present, he concluded that ordering Jones, Richardson, and Strickler to disband would lead "undisciplined" Missouri men to riot. This tense standoff was resolved without bloodshed when Shannon negotiated a peace treaty with 13 men from each faction.[136]

Although he averted a battle, Shannon's treaty officially recognized the nascent free-state organization—making them party to this agreement legitimized them. The treaty stated that there had been "a misunderstanding" which threatened "civil strife and bloodshed" and absolved Lawrence residents of complicity in Branson's rescue. But Shannon's concessions were more significant: the Lawrence group agreed to help execute any warrants, provided those arrested appeared before a district judge and were granted bail; he would "use his influence" to secure payment for damages inflicted by Jones or his posse; that he had not, nor would he ever, call on citizens of other states for aid; that he "has not any authority or legal power to do so"; and finally, that "we do not herein express any opinion as to the validity of the enactments of the Territorial Legislature."[137]

The folly of thus restricting his gubernatorial authority was compounded the following day when reports from Lawrence indicated Shannon had attended a "convivial party" where he was "entertained by the citizens of both sexes." Afterwards Shannon signed a statement authorizing Robinson and Lane to use their forces to preserve the peace and protect people and property in Lawrence "as in your judgment shall best secure that end." Shannon claimed this agreement applied to that night only, as Robinson and Lane had told him they were under attack and wanted to defend their homes: "With this view, *amid an excited throng, in a small and crowded apartment, and without any critical examination of the paper* which Dr. Robinson had just written, I signed it; but it was distinctly understood that it had no application to anything but the threatened attack on Lawrence that night." Shannon later claimed he was betrayed by "tricksters" and had pursued "too pacific a course" in trying to save Lawrence "from destruction and their citizens from a bloody fight."[138]

Proslavery advocate George Clarke acknowledged that with Shannon's treaty "we lost ground—but it can be regained in the Spring." He criticized Shannon for lacking the nerve to press the proslavery advantage. "Hearing them express a determination not to submit to 'compromise' but to 'have a fight any where'—he became alarmed at the storm he had raised—his inauguration was fired with the horror of a 'massacre' which would shock the world . . . and that he would be responsible for all the consequences—from that moment he began to feel from his high position. His whole study became to avert a collision. . . ."[139] Shannon was aware of such dissatisfaction but believed the situation was too precarious to rely on the militia. Thus he asked Pierce for authority to call on federal forces since any violence was likely to be "sudden, and before orders can be obtained from Washington the crisis will have passed."[140]

Free-staters regarded Shannon as too proslavery and blamed him for allowing an extremist to control the militia since Jones clearly interpreted a "mandate to restore order" more broadly than Shannon had intended.[141] Although the governor averted any loss of life, he inadvertently aided the nascent free-state movement by imparting legitimacy on its leaders with his treaty.[142] Doing so concerned anti-Topeka members of Congress for as Representative John Bingham (OH) stated, "It is the only treaty that I know of, which has been negotiated within the memory of man, where there was but one sovereign party assenting to it."[143] It elevated the free-state party to an equal partner in territorial affairs when it was still unclear whether free-state efforts to create an alternative government would succeed.

Conclusion

The first 18 months of territorial administration in Kansas represented a series of missed opportunities for Pierce. He had bungled his initial policy by appointing an unknown entity as governor. Although Pennsylvania was a critical state in presidential politics and Reeder was vouchsafed by well-known men, he lacked executive experience. The position of territorial governor had not previously demanded men of vision and strength, but the vitriol of the Kansas-Nebraska debates ought to have alerted the administration of potential trouble. Certainly the emigration societies organizing in the spring and vehement editorials about the necessity of winning Kansas were omens of a difficult settlement.

Pierce cannot be blamed for failing to foresee Reeder's defection to the free-state cause—despite their subsequent dismay, even Reeder's critics considered him a loyal party man when appointed, "a national man then, whatever he may have become now" the *New York Tribune* acknowledged.[144] Given Pierce's criteria for selecting the governors of Nebraska and Kansas, he likely believed Reeder would support the party. But Reeder's failure to protest the unseating of free-state men in July 1855 reflects his character. He only repudiated the legislature once its move from Pawnee negated his financial plans. The eagerness with which the free-state men embraced Reeder is mystifying and can only be attributed to their desire for a national figure to personify the cause. In 1855, Lane had national standing but was a neophyte in the movement, having been a member for only a few weeks, while other prominent actors were too closely identified with the EAC to garner widespread support.

Pierce would later compare the orderly government established in Nebraska, whose first legislature met more than a month before Reeder began the first census, with the developing chaos in Kansas. Pierce condemned Reeder for his late arrival and for allowing his personal schemes to distract him from his responsibilities. However, Pierce was culpable as well. Although he was not aware initially of Reeder's malfeasance, he could have fired him in May 1855. Moreover, while it was already too late to expunge the mishandled elections, had Pierce forced Reeder out at that time, a governor without open hostility toward the proslavery party might have managed the legislature's excesses more firmly. At the very least, the Pawnee fiasco would not have occurred. Although the free-state argument centered on illegal voting and the expulsion of free-state members from the legislature, its relocation helped justify their revolutionary organization. Pierce's first governor represented his first Kansas failure as well, but given his May 1855 meetings and indications that Reeder was not taking his precarious position seriously, the president should have had his replacement, one with the necessary character to assert control, ready to go. Instead, the violence increased and the difficulties of the first territorial administration merely previewed the upheaval to come.

Shannon had the experience Reeder lacked but had not demonstrated any leadership gifts in previous posts. He became governor at a difficult time—the free-state party already planned to repudiate the territorial government—but his obvious bias added to his difficulties. His speech before the "Law and Order" convention of November 1855 indicating administration support inspired little confidence among the free-state faction. Although the Democratic Party wanted Kansas to be a Democratic state, questions of slavery aside, Shannon's responsibilities demanded if not actual neutrality at least its appearance.

The Wakarusa War represents a turning point in the conflict. Although arms had been brandished with impunity at election time, this was the first time a genuine battle seemed imminent. In rallying free-state forces in Lawrence, Robinson had told them that "this is the last struggle between freedom and slavery and we must not flatter ourselves that it will be trivial or short."[145] The clash, which ended the year, was Shannon's first test and its failure provides the key to understanding his future problems. He was too easily manipulated, first by Jones and more infamously by Robinson and Lane. However, Shannon also exhibited extremely poor judgment. Despite the gravity of the situation and a desire to avoid bloodshed, he ought not to have signed any agreements recognizing or favoring the free-state faction. The "Wakarusa War" did not warrant a treaty. Under his gubernatorial authority, Shannon ought to have ordered the Lawrence men to stand down and Jones's posse to disperse. But once Sumner failed to show, Shannon was badly rattled and could not recover his equilibrium.

At the same time, however, the Wakarusa War revealed weakness in the administration's territorial policy. The militia was completely unreliable and motivated by partisanship. In the absence of military support, the governor needed reliable backup. Shannon had tried to contact Pierce early in the imbroglio but telegraph lines were down. Sumner assured Shannon of his support but opted to await official orders. Even after Pierce informed Shannon that he would order Sumner to deploy troops to Lawrence, Sumner delayed until he received the secretary of war's official order, which was slow to arrive. By December 1855, it was evident that popular sovereignty had broken down in Kansas and the local opposition presented a serious threat to the local government. If territorial disagreements were going to assume a martial aspect, the administration needed a strategy in place so that the governor understood his options, knew what Washington was likely to sustain, and would be supported by federal troops if necessary. In the wake of the Wakarusa War, the ease with which the administration could adjust to the changed situation in the territory would determine how comfortably it could meet future challenges.

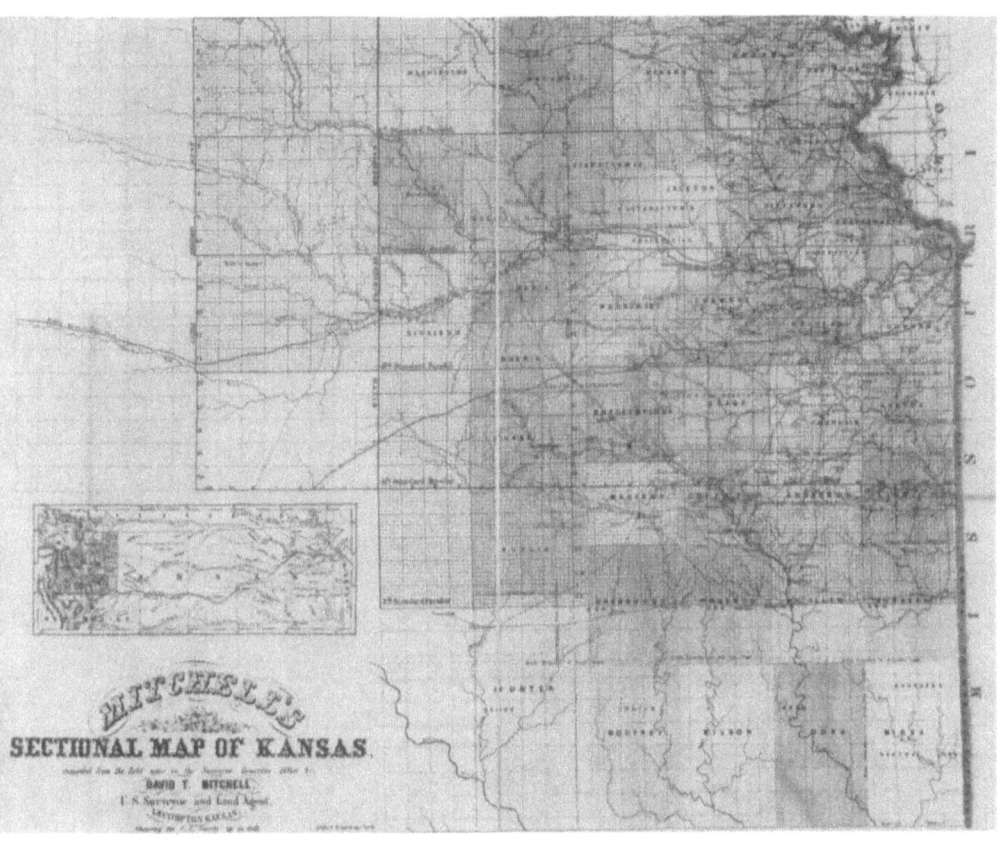

David T. Mitchell, 1859. The Library of Congress, Geography and Map Division.

President Franklin Pierce. Lithograph by N. Currier, Library of Congress, Prints and Photographs Division, LC-USZC2-2424.

This drawing of voting in Kickapoo in 1855 by Frank Beard appeared in Albert Richardson, *Beyond the Mississippi: From the Great River to the Great Ocean* (1869). Courtesy of the Kansas State Historical Society.

Seated in the front row are the members of the Howard Committee: Democrat Mordecai Oliver (MO), Republican William Howard (MI), and Republican John Sherman (OH). Courtesy of the Kansas State Historical Society.

The Ruins of Lawrence. This image of Lawrence after the sack of 1856 appeared in the September 19, 1863 edition of *Harper's Weekly*. The Library of Congress, Prints and Photographs Division, LC-USZ62-132750

Andrew Reeder, the first territorial governor of Kansas, left the Democratic Party and joined the free-state movement. Courtesy of the Kansas State Historical Society.

Territorial Delegate John Whitfield. In 1856, the House of Representatives unseated Kansas Territorial Delegate John W. Whitfield over concerns about the integrity of Kansas elections. The Library of Congress, Prints and Photographs Division, LC-USZ62-84335.

Guarding Free-State Prisoners, Lecompton, K.T. This illustration of federal troops guarding free-state prisoners near Lecompton in the summer of 1856 appeared in *Frank Leslie's Illustrated Newspaper*, October 4, 1856. Courtesy of the Kansas State Historical Society.

The Democratic Platform. This political cartoon by Louis Maurer emphasizes how Southern interests drove the Democratic Party during the presidential campaign of 1856. The party's nominee, James Buchanan, is depicted as a mere platform to support slaveholders' interests. The Library of Congress, Prints and Photographs Division, LC-USZ62-10359.

President James Buchanan, from a Matthew Brady daguerreotype. The Library of Congress, Prints and Photographs Division, LC-BH82101-6628.

Governor Robert Walker broke with the Buchanan administration over the Lecompton Constitution. Courtesy of the Kansas State Historical Society.

This ink drawing clearly illustrates the unpopularity of the Lecompton Constitution with its depiction of the devil introducing slavery into what had been a free settlement of Kansas. Courtesy of the Library of Congress, LC-DIG-ppmsca-23095.

3

Kansas in 1856
The Escalating Conflict

After the Wakarusa War, Governor Wilson Shannon left Kansas to consult with the president. Soon after, Franklin Pierce issued two statements detailing the difficulties in Kansas Territory. On January 24, 1856, he asked Congress to adopt the necessary legislation that "the grave exigencies of the case appear to require" and explained how the territory had become mired in conflict. Specifically, he focused on former governor Andrew H. Reeder's actions and the contributing factor of the emigrant aid societies. Condemning Reeder for "maladministration," he also blamed "pernicious agitation" for prompting "the unjustifiable interference" of non-Kansans. Pierce acknowledged the voting process had been marred by illegalities, but Reeder had declared the legislators "duly elected," and the organizing act allowed the legislature's relocation; furthermore, if relocating was illegal, Reeder had done so twice—from Leavenworth to Shawnee Mission and then again to Pawnee. Furthermore, the president drew attention to the unprecedented, extralegal election of Reeder as territorial delegate and the Topeka government's drafting of a constitution, warning that these actions could become "treasonable insurrection." Pierce emphasized that other methods of protest, such as elections and repeal (both "more prompt and effective then illegal violence"), were available. Without decisive action, the territorial conflict would become violent. As such, Congress should enable a constitutional convention for when Kansas had the requisite population and appropriate funds to meet expenses incurred in ensuring public order.[1]

On February 11, Pierce issued a proclamation against outside interference, asking those "engaged in unlawful combinations against constituted authority" to withdraw. He stressed that popular sovereignty undergirded American institutions and should warfare arise, it would be between the government and its lawless opponents. Territorial residents needed to adhere to local law or federal troops would subdue them. Pierce authorized

Shannon to call upon the federal troops commanded by Colonel Edwin V. Sumner, commander of Fort Leavenworth, to suppress "insurrectionary combinations or armed resistance to the execution of the law."[2]

Reeder had asked friends to impress upon Pierce the necessity of presidential intervention, but the resultant February proclamation was not to his liking. "That document is just the low contemptible trickstering affair which [one] might expect from Pierce. . . ."[3] According to the *New York Times*, Pierce's "manifesto" was "a declaration of war"[4] against Kansans that left the free-state faction concerned about a possible military response. Yet both sides realized caution was necessary. NEEAC Treasurer Amos Lawrence warned Charles Robinson that he should not "resist any legal representative of the U. States, nor allow our people to do it,"[5] as he was worried that armed resistance would discredit the movement. On the other hand, proslavery partisans were pleased by the president's tone. Former Missouri senator David Atchison wrote Secretary of War Jefferson Davis of his "great satisfaction" but warned Pierce needed "the assistance of the 'border *Ruffians*.'"[6]

Pierce's statements reflected the administration's increasing attacks on the aid societies, but subscriptions to the Emigrant Aid Company surged that spring.[7] And while the president's removal of Reeder was decisive, Republicans were displeased with his successor. Senator Henry Wilson (MA) upbraided Shannon, attributing the territory's woes to his "gross intoxication" and blamed the administration for bringing "the nation to the perilous edge of civil strife." Kansas needed a "prudent, judicious, sagacious statesman—a man of individual honor and personal character, in whom the people can place the fullest confidence. Wilson Shannon is not that man."[8] On the other hand, Republican Senator John Hale (NH) lamented Shannon's confirmation for "if this issue is to come, the President had better send out as Governor of Kansas a real fire-eating slaveholder. . . . Let him send such a man as that, and let the issue—if he is determined to make it—come."[9] Representing states with high emigration to Kansas, both Wilson and Hale monitored territorial events. But the president sustained Shannon and believed his proclamations and exhortations to Congress for relief were sufficient executive action.

Despite warnings from Washington that their efforts would cause Pierce to stubbornly support the territorial government, the Topeka contingent moved forward.[10] Certainly, Kansas activists were determined to present their struggle on the national stage. As one free-state man wrote his wife, "We intend to start a State Government at all hazards. If we are not admitted we shall have to fight and hard too but we are ready. . . ."[11] The organization had been gathering steam since the previous fall: they ratified their constitution on December 16, 1855; a week later a caucus nominated state officers; on January 15, they elected Robinson governor and Mark Delahey representative. Although unsanctioned, Robinson embraced the title and the Topeka "government" commenced.[12]

On March 4, this extralegal organization met for a ten-day session and the legislature selected Andrew Reeder and James Lane as senators-elect. Their most significant achievement was drafting a memorial to Congress petitioning for admission under their constitution. They argued that the legislature had usurped a power granted by the organizing act to the governor alone, rendering its removal from Pawnee to Shawnee Mission illegal and its very existence nullified. The memorialists believed themselves so vulnerable that their only protection was with statehood. Although only seventeen hundred voters ratified the constitution, they claimed "the people" had sanctioned it and ascribed the paucity of votes to the destruction of ballot boxes.[13] The legislature adjourned until July 4, convinced that powerful friends in Washington would forward their agenda.

Perceiving an increasing threat, the proslavery party was frustrated. Atchison had urged Missourians to vote in the first two elections but wanted an even stronger response. "I say, prepare yourselves. Go over there. Send your young men, and if they attempt to drive you out, damn them, drive them out. Fifty of you with your shotguns are worth 250 of them with their Sharps rifles. Get ready, arm yourselves, for if they abolitionize Kansas you lose $100,000,000 of your property. I am satisfied I can justify every act of yours before God and a jury."[14] Much of Atchison's ire stemmed from disbelief that free-state men dared defy the authorities. Without a doubt, organizing a shadow government violated both the spirit and letter of territorial law. "The Abolitionists go on in their work of Treason," Pottawatomie Indian Agent George W. Clarke argued. "They have elected their state officers, and say that if Congress do not admit them as a State they will go on without admission, and send their Congressional delegation to Washington from year to year— and agitate, while at the same time they will rule this Territory and 'wipe out' Slavery."[15] Faced with such defiance, proslavery activists found the lack of support for themselves and the territorial government incomprehensible.

Believing a sympathetic administration backed them, the proslavery faction must have assumed that the governors sent by Pierce would be more cooperative than they proved to be. Reeder had been a severe disappointment and now had unfathomably transitioned from disgraced executive to free-state standard-bearer. Then Shannon faltered when presented with an opportunity to strike against the free-state faction at Wakarusa. Given that Southern efforts to acquire Kansas for slavery fell short of Northern energy, numbers, and propaganda, the proslavery faction felt abandoned. "Unfortunately *our* friends are doing but little—Here, we are but few and poor—we have neither time or money to spare over what little we do contribute—we have not the aid of organized societies in the South—their counsel or advice—but we are a determined set," Clarke wrote.[16] Although the proslavery forces were buoyed by Pierce's messages, the continuing evolution and augmenting strength of the free-state movement was worrisome.

The Topeka government's extralegal status was a local irritant, but once Congress received its constitution, it became a national dilemma as well. While the free-state transgression was clear, proslavery partisans also flaunted the law, and some argued that had they not controlled the legislature, they too would have set up an alternative government. Moreover, as tensions increased, some pressed an even greater commitment. "To those who have qualms of conscience as to violating law, State or national, say, the time has come when such imposition must be disregarded," former Missouri attorney general Benjamin Stringfellow, brother of the speaker of the territorial legislature, urged. "As your rights and property are endangered, I advise one and all to enter every election district in Kansas . . . and vote at the point of bowie-knife and revolver. . . . . It is enough that the slaveholding interest wills it, from which there is no appeal."[17]

On April 4, Robinson criticized Pierce's January dismissal of the Topeka movement, arguing that the president had misunderstood their organization. The president's annual message had argued that rejecting a state because of its constitution would result in two hostile confederations, each trying to drive the other from the territory. From this, Robinson inferred that Pierce, in fact, supported the Topeka government's right to exist. The official territorial government was "an instrument of oppression and tyranny unequaled in the history of our Republic" because the legislature had arranged that "no man shall vote in any election who will not bow the knee to the dark image of Slavery" that led to widespread disenfranchisement. Since the organizing act gave the territorial legislature sole authority to decide voter qualifications, there was no "hope for relief."[18]

Moving against the Free-state Faction in Lawrence

Shannon watched these spring events with alarm, but assured Secretary of State William Marcy that both sides had calmed down and opposition would be confined to "legal and peaceful means."[19] By April 27, however, he reported increased resistance to territorial laws. In particular, the governor worried about Samuel Wood's return to Lawrence. Robinson welcomed Wood despite two outstanding warrants against him (for larceny and assisting in Branson's rescue). On April 23, Douglas County Sheriff Samuel Jones arrested Wood in Lawrence, but a free-state group rescued him. A deputized Jones returned with a military posse under Lieutenant James McIntosh's command and served a few warrants, but could not find Wood. While he was camping overnight in Lawrence, an unknown assailant shot Jones, leading McIntosh to request reinforcements. Given that shots had been discharged from various locations, it was believed an assassin targeted Jones.[20] Although the sheriff was widely despised, Shannon defended his character, assuring Marcy that Jones was "a high-minded, honorable, and brave man" whose attempted assassination further inflamed tensions.[21]

The conflict over the government's ability to execute territorial law intensified the following month when Chief Justice Samuel Lecompte opened the spring session of the United States District Court. On May 5, he instructed a Douglas County grand jury that territorial laws represented federal authority and resistance to them was treason. Regarding charges of aiding and abetting, Lecompte stated that the jury must "still find bills for constructive treason, as the courts have decided that to constitute treason the blow need not be struck, but only the *intention* be made evident."[22]

At this tense time, national politics intruded. After two months of disarray, the House of Representatives had finally organized itself, electing Nathaniel Banks, a member of the opposition, as speaker under a plurality vote. Thus able to control the agenda, the opposition ably agitated the Kansas issue, and on March 19, the House authorized a select committee, comprised of two Northerners, Republicans William A. Howard (MI) and John Sherman (OH), and one Southerner, Democrat Mordecai Oliver (MO), to investigate Kansas's controversial elections. Just before the Douglas Country grand jury began deliberating, the Congressional Special Investigating Committee, known as the Howard Committee after its chair, opened hearings in Lawrence on April 18.[23] "Those men were sent there to enter into an important investigation of the difficulty in Kansas," one contemporary account charged, "but came very short of it by countenancing resistance to the law, and inflaming the populace to open rebellion."[24] The committee lent the Topeka government legitimacy, and its majority report provided over a thousand pages of antislavery propaganda, which ensured Kansas remained before the nation.[25]

While Reeder was before the committee on May 7, United States Marshal Israel B. Donelson served him a subpoena to testify before the grand jury. However, Reeder refused the subpoena by claiming congressional immunity as Kansas's territorial delegate and was sustained by Howard and Sherman. Donelson next sent deputy W.P. Fain to serve Reeder for contempt of court, but again he refused, to the general approbation of Lawrence citizens.[26] Soon after, however, Reeder fled Kansas.

On May 10, the grand jury issued treason indictments against Robinson, Lane, Reeder, George W. Brown (editor of the *Herald of Freedom*), Gaius Jenkins, George W. Deitzler, George W. Smith, and Samuel N. Wood for usurpation of office and declared the Free State Hotel, the *Herald of Freedom*, and the *Kansas Free State* be "abated as nuisances."[27] These indictments and Reeder's refusal to cooperate proved a turning point. In updating an absent wife as to events since Jones was shot, free-state settler Jonas Colburn wrote that they had been intending to fight, gathering "evidence against them that we might prove that we were justified in killing them. But when they tried to arrest Senator Reeder, we saw it would not do to resist them for they had warrants from the United States Court and the Mob were organized by the United States Marshall and if we whipped them, which we could do and not half try, we should have to whip the United States which we could not do. . . ."[28] Because Lawrence residents had supported Reeder in rebuffing federal authority, Donelson called for a posse.

Fearing the posse was a cover for nefarious activity, a committee of Lawrence residents asked Colonel Sumner for protection,[29] which reveals local confusion over federal troops and how they could be used. Most likely they hoped to find Sumner sufficiently sympathetic to defend Lawrence against the growing posse, but he responded that the governor ordered troop deployment. They then asked Shannon for protection, but he refused to disband the posse on May 12, noting that "so long as they keep up a military or armed organization to resist the territorial laws and the officers charged with their execution, I shall not interpose to save them from the legitimate consequences of their illegal acts."[30] Lawrence residents grew more fearful, aware that he was unlikely to interfere.

Shannon, however, remained confused about his own authority. "The governor," wrote Sumner, "is evidently desirous of availing himself of the regular troops as the only means of preserving peace, but he does not think proper to assume the responsibility of *controlling* them under civil officers by taking it upon himself to decide what kind of posse they shall use, and consequently they are made up of partisans, and if they do not bring about a serious collision it will be because both parties have a wholesome fear of each other." Sumner believed the two forces would collide because the posses were composed primarily of partisans.[31] He warned Shannon that trouble was brewing and placing forces between Lawrence and Lecompton would help.³² When consulted, the president stressed that while Shannon had to enforce territorial law, he could only do so after actual resistance. He approved Sumner's suggestion as "wise and prudent," but was concerned by reports the marshal had gathered a posse at Lecompton. Given Sumner's proximity, Pierce believed it unnecessary.³³

On May 21, McIntosh warned Sumner about the threat. Five to seven hundred men were arrayed outside Lawrence, delaying and disarming travelers, taking prisoners, and impressing their horses. The Free-State Hotel and the printing presses were at risk because the marshal would be unable to control these men.³⁴ As they had in December, the Lawrence group attempted to negotiate, citing their status as "order-loving and law-abiding citizens." Donelson disputed this characterization because this same group had "made such hostile demonstrations that the deputy thought he and his small posse would endanger their lives" if they served Reeder the subpoena. In fact, residents were well armed and well fortified, engaged in military maneuvers, and "openly defy the laws and officers thereof"; indeed, the most recent demonstration of their peaceful nature had been the attempted assassination of Jones.³⁵ Although he had not been consulted beforehand, Shannon supported efforts to deliver the indictments.³⁶ After a few more days during which forces on both sides grew, Fain entered Lawrence on May 23, served the warrants, and withdrew, and Donelson then disbanded the posse.

Jones immediately called the same men into a new posse and entered Lawrence. They destroyed the hotel and both presses, setting fire to Robinson's home and vandalizing the town.³⁷ Although the grand jury had authorized this destruction, Shannon believed it stemmed from the proslavery faction's "deep and settled conviction" that it was endangered by "those who refuse obedience to the laws [who] held their Sharps rifles, artillery, and munitions of war" and were allowed to maintain a "fort, arsenal, and barracks."³⁸ Jones was not authorized to act on these legal writs, but the dual role of many participants led to considerable confusion. As the sheriff of Douglas County, the federal court had occasionally deputized Jones. Here, however, Jones acted solely as a county official since he had not been authorized to enforce these federal writs.³⁹

The sack of Lawrence discomfited the Pierce administration, contributed additional evidence that Shannon could not control the proslavery faction with whom he was friendly, and provided a propaganda boon for the Republican Party. In its appeal for aid from Illinois supporters, one organization described "bands of heartless desperadoes, bearing arms by the authority of the United States, paid from their treasury, directed by officials chosen by the executive to drive out and plunder our sisters and their little ones, slaying unarmed men and trampling under foot freedom of speech and of the press."[40] Condemnation fell upon Pierce and the Democrats, and the repercussion of the Lawrence debacle extended far beyond the events of that day as sympathetic newspapers carried wildly embellished accounts that contributed significantly to the notoriety of the territory's mythic "border ruffian." Increasingly hostile to the thriving free-state propaganda, proslavery advocates were satisfied by the presses' destruction.

Three days later, abolitionist John Brown led a small party to Pottawatomie Creek, 40 miles south of Lawrence, and killed 5 proslavery settlers in cold blood.[41] Unlike the coverage of the sack of Lawrence, many newspapers dismissed initial reports, and it was widely believed the victims had been shot in the midst of heinous crimes against antislavery settlers.[42] Although both factions officially condemned Brown's actions, renewed violence erupted and Sumner blamed Shannon. "From present appearances," he warned Adjutant General Samuel Cooper on May 28, "it looks very much like running into a guerrilla warfare. If the matter had been taken in hand at an earlier day, as I earnestly advised the Governor, the whole disturbance would have been suppressed without bloodshed."[43] Although like most military men Sumner believed early intervention was key to controlling conflict,[44] he had been reluctant to act, most notably in December, but also in Lawrence when he insisted federal forces not be deployed until after territorial authorities had been resisted. As such, federal intervention would occur only after the two factions actually collided.

The Repercussions of Lawrence

After treason charges were issued in early May, the arrests of free-state leaders (such as Robinson's dramatic capture in Missouri on May 10 and his subsequent extradition) were staggered, but cumulatively caused considerable embarrassment.[45] The men were kept in "The Pavilion," a row of tents near Lecompton for much of the summer since treason charges do not allow bail, and at least one was happy with his situation. "The prospects of Kansas were never brighter to me than at present," wrote one detainee, "with our presses destroyed, our principal citizens fugitives and outlaws, else deprived of their freedom."[46] The free-state men were imprisoned until late September, and propagandists productively used this to impress upon outsiders that the territory lacked law.

After the events in Lawrence and Pottawatomie, disorder reigned. Free-state activists focused their wrath on the militia and blamed the governor for not controlling them. Shannon's refusal to intervene in Lawrence and his continued support of Jones strained the already tenuous relationship between the territorial government and the free-state faction.[47] But the governor was trying to control volunteer forces. He stationed troops throughout the territory, ordered a disarmament of the militias, and warned that any notices ordering residents to move out of the territory would be regarded as violations of law designed to incite violence.[48] On June 4, he detailed these orders and asked Kansans for their help in "preserving the peace, repressing violence, and in bringing offenders to justice, and in maintaining the supremacy of law."[49] Despite Shannon's executive proclamations for all forces to disband, tensions had grown too much to easily control the volunteer forces, and the militias were slow to obey.[50]

Concerned about "confused and contradictory reports" detailing "scenes of disorder and violence," Pierce ordered Shannon to "maintain the laws firmly and impartially and take care that no good citizen has just ground to complain of the want of protection." His dispatch underscores the difficulties of distance. He was angry that neither Sumner nor Shannon had acknowledged his May 23 telegraphs, and chastised Shannon that he ought to have been advised if authorized forces were insufficient.[51] On June 27, Pierce placed Brevet Brigadier General Persifor Smith, the commander of the Army of the West and a friend from the Mexican War, in charge of territorial forces. By doing so, he tried to distinguish between military and political objectives. Secretary of War Davis cautioned Smith to tread carefully, to "abstain from encroaching in any degree upon the proper sphere of civil authorities, ... avoid any conflict between the civil and military power."[52]

Settlers viewed the federal military with deep suspicion. That summer, for instance, one resident complained about two companies that passed through his neighborhood headed for Fort Leavenworth. "The Soldiers came without our request," antislavery John Everett protested, "and went away just in the only time they were at all wanted. They seem to be only efficient when on the side of the Missourians."[53] The free-state faction did not distinguish between forces, believing that the territorial militia and federal troops were both against them. While the territorial administration was seen as proslavery, federal troops ought at least to display greater neutrality and defend them against raiding Missourians. The change from Sumner to Smith did not persuade many settlers they would have greater protection, as "it matters not who has that post so long as Frank Pierce is Commander in Chief. I should not lose 10 sec. of sleep if I should hear any night at bed time that *that* man or demon or whatever he be had been assassinated."[54] The military policy in the territory had engendered bitterness and anger toward the federal government.

Shannon warned Pierce that continued immigration contributed to the violence and undermined his policies, but "if the influences outside of the Territory would cease to act, and let us alone to manage our own affairs, I would guarantee order and quiet in the Territory in ten days, through the agency alone of the United States troops."[55] Both sides wished for peace but a few within the territory assisted by outsiders wished to incite a civil war. While Shannon assured Pierce his policies were working, skirmishes between the two factions acquired a more martial character that summer. In truth, without a strong executive, the presence of well-armed, enthusiastic, and determined partisans meant peace might require martial law. According to Lt. Col. Philip Cooke, commander of Fort Riley, the chaos attracted bandits whose unrelated robberies and murders complicated matters.[56]

That summer, the question of how to help Kansans split supporters. The aid societies were not as radical as men on the ground. Of those delegates who spoke at a Cleveland convention of state aid societies on June 20 and 21, many urged restraint, emphasizing the continued importance of settlement; one New Yorker, for instance, believed the infusion of five thousand free-state settlers would turn the tide because of their moral influence, while an Ohio partisan advocated fighting with "*bread and beef*, rather than rifles and powder." However, such peaceful options were countered by Kansans. Reeder, for instance, warned moderates not to believe that territorial accounts were mere propaganda for "there was so much exaggeration in the acts themselves, that there was no room for exaggeration in their detail." Kansas was "a contest for an empire, almost for a continent," since the area beyond the territory was large enough for six Pennsylvania-sized states.[57]

But the various state emigrant aid societies did agree to an address that sounded a common theme, that Kansans were being abandoned and left with just one choice. Because those levers of government designed to protect the citizenry had been "converted into one mighty, potent engine of oppression," settlers had to rely on "that law which is deeply engraven by the finger of *God* upon the hearts of all his creatures, the *universal law of self-defence*."[58] Delegates wanted five thousand men to emigrate but that would require one million dollars.[59] The convention, which adjourned and reconvened in Buffalo in July, closed by resolving "that the federal administration instead of protecting Kansas is the great upholder of the oppressions and outrages which she suffers."[60]

Free-state observers awaited word on Congress's reception of their petitions. Most watched the Toombs Bill (a Senate solution providing for a census, an electoral commission to ensure fair voting, and a new constitutional convention) with apprehension because its passage boded ill for their strategy. "If Douglas's bill [the Toombs bill] should become law, another just such an invasion would take place as have taken place, although perhaps more cunningly contrived. We should have thousands of Missourians among us on sham claims. . . ."[61] Antislavery activists feared the president would be biased when selecting the five commissioners.[62] The convention of Kansas Aid Societies had also passed a resolution condemning the Toombs Bill as "deceptive and fraudulent . . . , and leaves the great wrongs of Kansas unredressed, with liberty crushed out . . ." and "is only designed to make Kansas a slave state."[63] Pierce tried to sway critics by confiding to Amos Lawrence, a longtime friend and ardent free stater, names of potential commissioners. In turn, Lawrence leaked these names to Congressman Solomon Haven (NY) so he could persuade other members, but the bill failed.[64]

For the Topeka government, summer events further justified their "rebellion" and efforts to build the parallel state infrastructure continued. On July 3, George Smith reassured free-state supporters gathered apprehensively outside Topeka the day before the free-state legislature would convene that the injustices inflicted by territorial authorities justified their course. "You have a Constitutional right to meet as a Legislature, complete the State organization and pass all laws necessary to the successful administration of Justice and the Federal Government has no authority to interfere with you in the exercise of this right; Should it do so, it becomes a tyrannical usurpation of power and resistance on your part becomes justifiable self-defense."[65] But Sumner arrived the next day accompanied by federal troops. According to free-state reports, he merely told legislators he would not arrest them if they dispersed, news that was "received with three cheers for Col. Sumner, three for Gov. Robinson and three groans for Frank Pierce."[66] Despite earlier declarations that they would resist federal officers if any collision arose *during* meetings of the state organization, they dispersed without a confrontation.[67] The representatives were satisfied that if Kansas were not admitted by beginning of the year, "we shall declare our Independence and start on our own hook."[68]

The Topeka government walked a fine line that summer. The sack of Lawrence garnered enormous sympathy, but territorial battles could not imperil efforts in Washington. Thomas Webb, secretary of the New England Emigrant Aid Company, was concerned about Lane's plan for an "Army of the North" to engage territorial forces. "We are struggling against odds at Washington to have something accomplished prior to the adjournment advantageous to Kansas, and our imprisoned friends," Webb wrote. "Should Lane foolishly come in collision with the U.S. forces, the act would be charged upon us however earnestly we might deprecate the whole affair; and vain would it be for us to endeavor to get any measure through Congress. I think Lane's whole proceedings thus far have been ill judged, ill timed, and ill managed."[69] Similarly, in mid-August Robinson wrote that it was "easy to commence operations, but difficult to stop at the right time & in the right way." He urged James Blood and William Hutchison, who oversaw a number of proslavery prisoners captured during late summer skirmishes, to behave "*honestly*" though he did commiserate. "If your prisoners cannot be proved to be guilty of *murder* you will hardly be justified in taking life *after* surrender. It is sometimes unfortunate that some people live to surrender, but if they do, then we must take the course that highminded gentlemen would take, with a world to scrutinize every act...."[70]

Given the disasters of the previous nine months, many expected Pierce to dismiss Shannon. In late June, settlers had "various reports—that Shannon has been removed, that Col. Sumner is at the head of affairs, and that the Territory is now under Marshall law, but do not know what to believe."[71] Nonetheless, Shannon continued negotiating a peace between the warring factions. In August, Lane's men robbed and burned the postmaster's house in Franklin, Missouri, allegedly to acquire arms. A proslavery party led by Henry Titus captured those involved, but were in turn captured by a Lawrence company; in the subsequent battle, two proslavery and one antislavery partisans were killed.[72] Shannon's "Second Treaty of Lawrence" released 15 free-state prisoners, returned a howitzer seized in May in exchange for the release of Titus's group, and agreed that "no more arrests should be made of free-state people under territorial laws."[73] If these events were reported accurately, Shannon had reached the end of his dubious efficacy, demonstrating yet again his malleability and susceptibility to free-state manipulation. Soon after, the long-swirling rumors reached the governor, who resigned immediately because "without the moral power which official station confers, and being destitute of any adequate military force to preserve the peace," he was "unwilling to perform."[74] With his abrupt resignation on August 18, Territorial Secretary Daniel Woodson became acting governor. A "zealous Democrat," he fanned the flames of discord, declaring the territory "to be in a state of open insurrection and rebellion" and "infested with large bodies of armed men."[75]

Woodson asked Colonel Philip St. George Cooke to go to Topeka, disarm and arrest the insurrectionists, and level their fortifications, but Cooke refused. "If the army be useless in the present unhappy crisis, it is because in our constitution and law civil war was not foreseen, nor the contingency of a systematic resistance by the people to their governments of their own creation, and which, at short intervals, they may either correct or change." Resistance to territorial law had to precede the deployment of forces; without it, his request was a call "to make war upon the town of Topeka," and neither his orders nor the Constitution authorized such action.[76]

Although biased, Woodson nonetheless had a point when he rebuffed a free-state request for protection in September. "It is passing strange," he wrote, "that those who have thus defied the Territorial laws and who have thus attempted to subvert by force and violence the existing Government of the Territory, should at this time, as if oblivious of their fatally lawless conduct, apply to those very laws and the very Government they have been and are still seeking to subvert by force and violence, for protection." That was only available to "peaceable, law-abiding citizens."[77] This question—of how to deal with those resisting territorial laws—led to tension between the administration and settlers, for one person's warriors for justice and freedom were another's "paid adventurers and jesuitical hordes of northern abolitionism."[78]

In Woodson, Smith saw the problems which could arise if an activist acting governor was allowed to gather the proslavery men milling about Lecompton into a legally constituted militia. "It is a gross absurdity to pretend that the men brought in here lately are *bona fide* settlers; they are hired and paid to get possession of the country, but the result will be a national calamity."[79] Smith attributed Kansas's troubles to the existence of four factions: the territorial government; the Topeka organization; Atchison's Missouri faction; and a fourth group of "idle men congregated from various parts, who assume to arrest, punish, exile and even kill, all those whom they assume to be bad citizens."[80] The conflict between the two factions was serious enough without adding marauders and an eager ideologue to the mix.

After the sack of Lawrence and the Pottawatomie massacre, fighting broke out at Black Jack, Fort Franklin, Fort Saunders, and Fort Titus among others, but local observers stressed the greater culpability of the proslavery faction precisely because they had governmental support. Free-state incursions, especially those of John Brown, whose most ardent supporters continued to justify his actions late into the century, received extensive popular support and newspaper coverage.[81] The military skirmishes that transformed the territory into bleeding Kansas were not as deadly as propaganda would indicate. One Kansas newspaper later recalled the results of the civil war as such: "Killed: 0; Wounded, contusion of the nose: 2; Missing: 0; Captured: 3; Frightened: 5,718."[82] Although this makes light of the conflict, it speaks to a larger truth: few died at the hands of their enemies. In 1856, there were 38 political deaths, by far the greatest of any territorial year and more than double the total political killings of the remaining 5 years. However, these deaths are dwarfed by the over 500 killed in California the previous year and the 1,200 who died in San Francisco alone from 1850 to 1853.[83] Nonetheless, most combatants fervently defended their beliefs, and their attitude transcended these tallies. "Judged by the number of men engaged and the number of casualties, it was petty warfare indeed," historian Samuel Johnson wrote, "but judged by its consequences, it was far more important than many a conflict waged on a much grander scale. The strength of the 'armies' was numbered in dozens, not thousands, and the 'battles' were the merest skirmishes, often only minutes in duration.... And petty as it may appear, this was real war. The combatants grappled in deadly earnest. The tiny armies marched, entrenched, and battled in mortal combat; guerrillas plundered; towns were sacked; prisoners were taken and exchanged."[84]

Shannon's tenure coincided with the presidential campaign. The turmoil damaged Pierce for he "did not choose to stop the invasion when it first began! He knew it all, but could not spare the sacrifice of life and property in sight of the Cincinnati Convention!"[85] Critics linked his inaction to an overwhelming desire for a second term. By June, however, the party had discarded Pierce, "the present President having lost prestige so dreadful that he was the very first struck from the list!"[86] Yet Kansas would dominate the campaign. "Has the Government no power to make peace in Kansas, and to protect citizens there under the organic law of the Territory?" asked Republican Congressman Anson Burlingame (MA). "She throws the responsibility upon this Administration, and holds it accountable; and so will the people at the polls next November."[87] The military skirmishes injured the Democratic Party and these difficulties were reflected in the congressional session. As a result of the Howard Committee's report, the House rejected John Whitfield as territorial delegate, accepted the Topeka Constitution, and tried to force Pierce to withdraw federal troops from Kansas by withholding appropriations.[88] In this atmosphere, the Democratic Party had to suppress the Kansas tumult.

The Arrival of a Competent Governor

After Reeder's dismissal, proslavery advocates unsuccessfully urged Woodson's elevation to governor. Since he had previously been passed over, the proslavery faction looked elsewhere and, emulating the free-state strategy, selected Democrat John Calhoun, the surveyor-general for Kansas and Nebraska, as their governor. In an address signed by prominent proslavery activists, they expressed their wish for an executive who "would not be prejudiced or misled by the falsehoods which have been so systematically fabricated against us. . . . We cannot hazard a second edition of imbecility or corruption."[89] However, Pierce disappointed them yet again when he selected John Geary, a Pennsylvania Democrat, to replace Shannon.

With his third choice, the president finally selected a man with backbone and experience. Active in territorial California—*alcalde* of San Francisco in 1843, postmaster in 1848, and mayor in 1850—Geary was considered a "territorial expert" familiar with frontier conditions, whom Pierce had initially approached about replacing Brigham Young in Utah. Moreover, his proslavery credentials were clear: after returning from California, he had used slave labor for mining in Virginia. He arrived in Kansas on September 9 accompanied by rumors that Pierce had endowed him with "greater discretionary powers" than his predecessors. Although Reeder and Shannon had been ignominiously shunted aside, Geary was confident of Pierce's full support.[90]

But because Woodson had extended territorial authority to men "of the most atrocious character," the new governor found matters worse than he had anticipated. "I find that I have not simply to contend against bands of armed ruffians and brigands, whose sole aid and end is assassination and robbery, infatuated adherents and advocates of conflicting political sentiments and local institutions, and evil-disposed persons actuated by a desire to obtain elevated positions," Geary complained, "but worst of all, against the influence of men who have been placed in authority, and have employed all the destructive agents around them to promote their own personal interests, at the sacrifice of every just, honorable and lawful consideration."[91] Such men controlled Leavenworth while Lane was fortified at Lawrence. It "can be no worse," he concluded.[92]

In his inaugural address on September 11, Geary reassured Kansans that he desired "to know no party, no section, no North, no South, no East, no West; nothing but Kansas and my country."[93] He urged Kansans to "banish outside influence and prove ourselves worthy of self-government," asking residents to recognize that unpopular laws could be remedied by peaceful means; to focus on developing Kansas's infrastructure; and finally, "to make our territory the sanctuary of those cherished principles which protect the inalienable rights of the individual, and elevate states in their sovereign capacity." Popular sovereignty was best expressed when the people demonstrated their capacity to govern themselves and decide their institutions. Geary closed by asking residents to adhere to the laws no matter their grievances.[94]

Secretary Marcy's instructions to the new governor were simple: maintain the peace and punish violence, and his "energy and discretion" would work with Smith's "capacity, decision, and coolness of character" to "prevent or suppress all attempts to kindle civil war. . . ."[95] Thus, after using his inaugural to set a tone, Geary carefully disconnected the tenuous political situation from over-armed citizens. He insisted that laws that authorized the chief of the militia to defend Kansas infringed on his own power and involved the "Territory in war."[96] He issued two proclamations to discourage armed conflict: the first stated that volunteer militias lacked federal authorization and were no longer needed; the second called for free male citizens to enlist in a territorial militia.[97] Moreover, believing that Shannon relied too much on federal troops to execute routine paperwork, he warned Donelson that troops could no longer be used to discharge warrants to avoid interjecting the military into civilian matters.[98] Despite strict instructions regarding the military, Geary had considerable latitude in forming policy, as Marcy had written that the "exigencies of affairs . . . on the spot" could better indicate how to fulfill administration goals than his directives.[99] The challenge of combining strong expectations with specific instructions in one area and wide latitude in all others would soon come to light. After the disastrous Reeder and Shannon administrations, Pierce tried to enforce a hard line but lacked the initiative and insight to effectively oversee territorial affairs.

The free-state faction viewed Geary with suspicion, concerned that yet another national Democrat would be proslavery. Thus the governor faced a skeptical audience when he spoke in Topeka on September 22. *Herald of Freedom* editor George Brown had urged him to "seek an acquaintance with *all* parties . . . and then give us such relief as will be effective in laying the foundations of a great and prosperous State . . . ,"[100] but the free-state men were as truculent as Geary expected. They "informed me that they were not bound to obey my instructions, as there was another government, and another Governor in Kansas, to whom only they owed fealty. . . ."[101] The governor believed his predecessors' weaknesses had encouraged such boldness, but both forceful and fair, Geary acquired their cooperation without resort to treaties. However, the free-state men would not disavow their alternative government.[102]

The record reveals Geary to be a serious, focused executive armed with a multifaceted approach to calm territorial tensions. After addressing the immediate problems presented by the militias and the free-state faction, he embarked upon a three-week tour to understand Kansas, which informed his views.[103] Geary returned convinced that "large discretionary power" was necessary to ensure "order and the protection of life, liberty, and property" because the distance from Washington slowed communications when conditions demanded swift action.[104] He also sought help in ameliorating contributing aggravations. The eastern border, for instance, provided a haven for proslavery activists, and so he asked Missouri governor Sterling Price for assistance and commended him on the patriotism of his state's citizens, noting that a group intent on destroying Lawrence had complied with a request to disband.[105] But such cooperation was anomalous, and the problems on the border persisted. Geary informed Price "that roving bands of murderers, incendiaries and robbers, have been in the habit of stealing the horses, burning the houses, and murdering the citizens of this Territory, and then retiring with their spoils and crimes into your state."[106] He asked him to declare he would not tolerate such activities or grant refuge to such men. Governor Price also helped keep the Missouri River open to immigration that fall, helping dampen free-state criticism on this issue.

Geary also ordered mayors to fall in line with administration policy. He ordered the suspension of liquor sales because he believed public drunkenness contributed to territorial problems; moreover, frequent imbibing often rendered troops "almost unfitted for duty." In locales like Lecompton where the mayor moved too slowly, Geary sent troops to close saloons operating without proper licenses.[107] He also castigated Leavenworth mayor William E. Murphy for allowing the harassment of antislavery citizens and warned that if Murphy did not disband the so-called "Regulators," he would dispatch troops to assure their safety.[108] A chastened Murphy promptly responded that troops were unnecessary; however, despite his best efforts (suspect due to the town's proslavery bent), he had been unable to identify any "Regulators."[109]

Murphy's letters reveal the difficulties of asking loyal Democrats to tolerate and protect those whom they considered traitors. "When I see men aiming direct blows at the glorious Constitution of our common country," Murphy wrote, "and hear them denouncing ... true northern democrats for upholding the constitutional rights of every section of our Union, I am not surprised to hear them express themselves in opposition to the statute laws of Kansas, and I feel forced to view them as maniacs, and look upon them more in sorrow than in anger." Murphy stated it was the policy of the "law and order" party to protect even those who denounced territorial laws.[110]

With these actions, Geary notified Kansans that he was less malleable than Reeder and Shannon. Indeed, the new governor was pleased with the subsequent calm but was not so sanguine that he was ready to dispense with the military. In September, he mulled that "it seems impossible that after a few bold strokes only a continuous peace could be established after so long and serious a conflict."[111] Elections elicited numerous offers from both sides to "help" protect ballot boxes. Geary declined one such offer, writing to Henry Clay Pate, a free-state activist and correspondent for the *St. Louis Republican*, that while he appreciated the offer he had "already anticipated problems and directed troops."[112] By September 30, the governor confidently reported that tranquility prevailed, a condition that at least one antislavery partisan mourned: "Only just at this moment things look discouragingly safe, and the men are beginning to fear marching in without a decent excuse for firing anything at anybody.[113] The peace held and in November General Smith reported that life was now routine—farms were once again cultivated and travelers were able to move about "unarmed and secure."[114]

Because the territory had opened for settlement so far in advance of any infrastructure, many settlers were left adrift when they arrived. Conditions were far harsher than most had prepared for, and Geary blamed the aid societies for so zealously encouraging settlement. "Very many persons are induced to come out here, under flattering promises which are never fulfilled; and having neither money to purchase, food or clothing, nor trades or occupations at which to earn an honest livelihood, are driven to the necessity of becoming either paupers or thieves; and such are the unfortunate men who have aided materially in filling up the measure of crimes that have so seriously effected the prosperity of Kansas."[115] Settlers found conditions difficult, especially the drought of the first winter and spring, which also led to higher transportation costs in navigating the Missouri River.[116] However, whereas Pierce focused on political problems, Geary had to contend with the social ramifications of displaced settlers.

He also had to determine who were bona fide settlers. On October 1, for instance, the governor met with a small group planning to escort a settlers' party armed with weapons for protection and hunting. After asking if they were part of Lane's "Army of the North," Geary provided a letter stating that they should travel undisturbed by troops.[117] Eleven days later, however, Deputy Marshal William Preston reported that this group was "equipped with munitions of war."[118] Indeed, with solely seven families among them, the party carried "3 boxes of navy revolver pistols, all new; 4 boxes fixed ball cartridges; 1 bag caps; small lot of rifle cartridges; 1 box, 10 sharps rifles; 145 breach-loading muskets; 85 percussion muskets; 115 bayonets; 61 common sabres; 17 kegs of powder, 61 Dragoon saddles; 1 drum."[119] Even given perceived threats, this was excessive for peaceful immigrants.

In addition, Geary tackled the judiciary, a branch of the territorial government frequently decried as excessively proslavery. In late September, he complained to Judges Sterling G. Cato and Samuel D. Lecompte that he had found Kansas "in a state of insurrection, business paralised, operation of the courts suspended, and the civil administration of the government inoperative and seemingly useless," with residents complaining about their "alleged neglect of duty, party bias, and criminal complicity with a state of affairs which resulted in a contempt of all authority."[120] Claiming his efficiency depended on how his subordinates carried out their duties, Geary sent the justices a questionnaire.[121] Fortified by numerous complaints, he demanded descriptions of their duties and districts; frequency of court sessions; number of bills presented and indictments issued; and number of convictions for which crimes.

Chief Justice Lecompte was affronted by the request, but not by the charge of party bias since every man "has a 'party bias.' I am proud of mine. It has from my first manhood to this day, placed me in the ranks of the democratic party." By placing his defense within party parameters, Lecompte subtly reminded Geary that as a fellow Democrat, the governor had a responsibility to establish the party in Kansas while denying that his participation in local organizations affected his judgment. Lecompte was especially offended by the implication that the judiciary was subordinate to the executive.[122] But Geary placed the need to inculcate the populace's trust above hurt feelings or party goals and Lecompte's "injudicious actions" endangered his plans for peace.[123] Unable to reach an accommodation with Lecompte, Geary insisted on his removal; an obstructionist chief justice vulnerable to charges of partiality would hamper his own neutrality.

Unlike Geary, free-state observers recognized his dangerous path. "Self-conceited man, he has taken the responsibility to suspend Judge Lecompte and Marshall Donelson and does not know," Jonas Colburn wrote, "that he stands over a Magazine of Pro-Slavery wrath that may explode at any moment."[124] Pierce rebuked Geary for exceeding his authority in issuing a warrant to rearrest a suspect which had "embarrassed the matter," but agreed to remove Lecompte on "grounds of *public policy*" while urging him to get along with Cato, whom he praised as an able, learned man.[125] Pierce also removed Donelson and Clark, to the displeasure of many proslavery activists. "My opinion of him [the governor], and I told my friends so from the first, is that he is a doublefaced Free-soiler," Axalla Hoole wrote. "I have never had much faith in Pennsylvania politicians, *Buchanan not excepted*. Geary is an energetic Gov., but I believe that he is working for the Free-soil party here."[126]

Others believed anti-Geary feeling intensified after the presidential election; while he could not affiliate openly with the proslavery faction during the election, with James Buchanan safely elected he was free to show his true sympathies. "They say the show of moderation to the free state people before the presidential election was a political necessity, to carry Pennsylvania and Indiana; but now he should throw off the mask and openly show the proslavery colors."[127] If proslavery partisans believed party success required restraint, once the threat of a Republican White House passed, they could press their advantage and had little patience for waffling. And they were right to be concerned—by election time, Geary was reputedly on "intimate terms" with Robinson and Samuel Pomeroy and was developing an admission plan that would combine the free-state platform with himself, an administration Democrat, as governor.[128] According to Robinson, Geary agreed to push for admission under the Topeka Constitution in exchange for the governorship of the new state.[129]

More concrete evidence of a shifting policy is found in Geary's reports to the president. In one, he tried to educate Pierce about Kansas's true condition, claiming that the persecution against the antislavery group "was not exceeded by that of the early christians."[130] He tried to correct the popular misperception that eastern extremists were responsible for the turmoil of 1856. "From the most reliable information," Geary reported, "I am satisfied that there was a settled determination in *high quarters* to make this a Slave State *at all hazards*, that policy as communicated to agents here, and that most of the public officers sent here, were secured for its success." As a result, Northerners were "told that this soil, which previous to the repeal of the Missouri Compromise was devoted to freedom, did not belong to such as them, and *that they must settle in Nebraska*. These immigrants, *highly conservative* in their character, excited by this injust treatment, wrote back to their friends in the North and thus by a little indiscretion on the part of zealous persons in Missouri, a spark was ignited which nearly set the whole Country in a flame."[131] Geary's experiences had affected his perceptions of why Kansas had become so chaotic and led to increasing sympathy with the free-state faction. However, like many Democrats outside the territory, Pierce could not view abolitionists with any favor or sympathy.

Certainly Geary's efforts to remove Lecompte and other proslavery officials he deemed excessively partisan demonstrated his growing efforts to limit proslavery influence. He assured Pierce that the removal of Donelson, Lecompte, and Clark had been well received and further urged him to remove Woodson, District Attorney A.J. Isaacs, and John Calhoun, characterizing them as "prominent actors in this fearful tragedy and willing tools to carry out this wicked policy. *They have, therefore, destroyed their public usefulness*, and their removal would be hailed with a tumult of joy by the entire population."[132] Geary knew the president was in a delicate position, but relied on Pierce's desire to leave office with an improved public image.[133]

Writing to the president in late December, Geary attributed his difficulties to a conspiracy to deprive him of reliable intelligence. "The Country should know ... that the censure which had been heaped upon your administration from mismanagement in Kansas affairs is not attributable, but is the consequence of criminal complicity of public officers, some of whom you have removed the moment you were clearly satisfied of their true position."[134] Given the politicized atmosphere, it is doubtful that Pierce expected strict neutrality from these Democrats, but he certainly must have expected professional conduct, and many of those Geary named had crossed over into partisan politics without regard to their positions. Despite the governor's success in quieting the territory and Pierce's status as a lame duck, Republicans continued to criticize the administration's territorial policy. That same month, Congressman William Cumback (IN) argued that Pierce had transformed himself into an "arch-agitator" by denying his own responsibility and deflecting blame upon Congress for the trouble miring the country.[135] Pierce's antagonism toward abolitionism had always been strong, but fueled by such comments and Republicans' legislative agenda, it increased over the year, and Geary's efforts to elucidate the free-state view would not change the president's mind at this late date.

Although Pierce removed Lecompte, the contretemps with the chief justice haunted Geary throughout the winter and revealed the administration's pandering to outside interests. The president nominated C.O. Harrison of Kentucky for chief justice but failed to officially revoke Lecompte's appointment, which allowed the Senate to avoid action.[136] In the meantime, Lecompte protested his removal and counted powerful congressmen among his supporters. Senator Robert Toombs (VA), for instance, insisted Pierce had removed Lecompte because he could not be "intimidated or seduced" and wanted to impeach Geary for this transgression.[137] In December, Lecompte defended his judicial decisions in a public letter; his state's senator, James A. Pearce (MD), approached the secretary of state, who forwarded the letter to the governor in February 1857 demanding an explanation. Having already expressed regrets for the "collision," Geary refused Marcy's request and complained to his brother that the South wanted him fired "for they are determined to make Kansas as 'a slave state *in* or *out* of the Union.'"[138] He renewed efforts to publish his executive minutes, believing it would garner more public support. Both Lecompte's and Geary's efforts underscore how often internal administrative issues were subsumed by proslavery pressures.

In January 1857 Geary turned to the legislature, hoping his neutrality could influence them where Reeder's antagonism and Shannon's pandering had failed. In addressing a joint session, Geary tried to arouse a sense of patriotism among legislators, asking them to reconsider some of their laws and emphasizing their greater responsibility to the territory. As Senator William Bigler (PA) had written the governor after the election, "Nothing could go farther to reconcile the people of the north than a measure of that kind & no single act could take from the demagogues of the Republican party so much of this political capital."[139] Geary followed his advice before the legislature and condemned laws designed to intimidate voters, such as the use of test oaths, and actions "well calculated to incite terrorism," such as ordering militia training on election day. Moreover, the most reprehensible statutes had not been enforced, but damaged the body's reputation and ought to be repealed. Together, they could start anew. "Let the past which few men can review with satisfaction, be forgotten," Geary urged. "Let us not deal in criminations and recriminations; but, as far as possible, let us make restitution and offer regrets for past excesses."[140] That same day, however, Geary complained to Pierce that local partisans were undermining him, trying "to create the impression that the existing peace is entirely illusive and without solid foundation."[141] Like most Democrats, Geary arrived in Kansas with little patience for abolitionism. By the time the legislature convened, however, he equally disdained proslavery officials. Unlike the reasoned tones of his legislative address, Geary's private observations were antagonistic toward the body, believing them beyond rehabilitation. "The 'bloody Legislature' of Kansas is now in Session. They find they have some nerve to deal with this time in their Executive, and although they are a set of conspirators and Southern disunionists, I think I am safe in assuring you that this will be about their last effort."[142]

In the final months of Geary's administration, both factions continued to organize. The free-state legislature met at Topeka early in January and sent Congress a memorial. Their leaders were arrested on usurpation of office charges and released on bail, but the district attorney entered *nolle prosequies*, declaring before a judge the intent not to prosecute, and so they were not brought to trial.[143] Similarly, on January 12, a law-and-order convention drew almost all members of the territorial legislature under the banner of the "National Democratic party of Kansas Territory." Geary's private secretary John Gihon claimed they hoped to attract Washington's attention by adopting the Cincinnati Platform. However, the proslavery legislative assembly passed a resolution stating that since their party was tied to the union, it was "the duty of the proslavery party, the union-loving men of Kansas Territory, to know but one issue, SLAVERY, and that any party making or attempting to make any other, IS AND SHOULD BE HELD, AS AN ALLY OF ABOLITIONISM AND DISUNIONISM." The party offered Geary a senatorship in exchange for his support, but he declined.[144]

Geary tried to block the legislature's move toward statehood in February 1857. The territory was too embryonic for statehood, indebted with no land titles and no public buildings, and "just emerging from the disastrous effects of a bitter civil feud; it seems unwise for a few thousand people, scarcely sufficient to make a good county, to discard the protecting and fostering care of a government, ready to assist us with her treasures and to protect us with her armies."[145] He vetoed the convention bill because it was premature, there was too much opposition, and it did not provide for a public vote.[146] At this time, Geary needed to remain in Pierce's good graces without alienating Buchanan. Managing the legislature under such conditions proved impossible, as he could not derail their plans and his veto did not impress the president-elect.[147]

Geary expected to remain governor after Buchanan's inaugural. After all, he had a four-year appointment, and although none of his predecessors had survived even two years, as a Pennsylvania Democrat whose program of peace had contributed to his election, Geary optimistically believed his compatriot would retain him, especially given Buchanan's laudatory November 1856 speech. "We shall hear no more shrieks for her unhappy destiny," Buchanan had stated; instead, under Geary and Smith, Kansans would be able to "decide the question of slavery for themselves, and then slide gracefully into the Union and become one of the sisters in our great Confederacy."[148] In February, Geary laid the groundwork for his retention by blaming extremists and emphasizing that the tenuous peace required a firm hand and governmental support because "there are men here, urged on by others at a distance, who are determined to play a desperate game, and accomplish immensely important measures involving the peace of the country, if not the preservation of the Union with a high and reckless hand."[149] He assured Buchanan of his indifference on the slavery question and offered to continue the "sacrifices I have hourly to undergo for my country's good."[150]

In deference to the new president, Geary tendered his resignation, and his tenure ended quietly and abruptly when it was accepted.[151] In his farewell address at Lecompton on March 12, 1857, Geary graciously ignored Buchanan's slight and blamed his departure on the tremendous pressure of his position and its toll on his health and wallet.[152] He disputed that personal ambition had driven him for "those who have attributed my labors to a desire for gubernatorial or senatorial honors, were and are themselves the aspirants for those high trusts and powers, and foolishly imagined that I stood between them and the consummation of their ambitious designs and high-towering hopes."[153] He remained sanguine about assessments of his administration. "That I have met with opposition and even bitter vituperation and vindictive malice is no matter for astonishment. No man has ever yet held an important or responsible post in our own or any other country and escaped censure."[154]

Conclusion

Unlike Reeder, Shannon was unable to rehabilitate himself after his governorship ended. He was portrayed in the press as "fit only for the vilest uses ... who had held many offices and disgraced them all; ... a low, profane, drunken, gambling wretch, whose long-indulged vices, as well as his original incompetence and incurable ignorance, made him the mere instrument of villains more energetic than himself."[155] Although overly harsh, even the biography prepared for the Kansas State Historical Society portrays Shannon as a bumbling bureaucrat. In assessing his administration, it excused him for having too trusting a character: "He was sympathetic and confiding in his nature. Hence he was not unfrequently misled by wrong information and great exaggeration of fact, constantly presented to him."[156] Given the critical presidential election, Pierce was forced to remove Shannon if only to stem the negative criticism flowing from the Republican Party.

He proved to be a faithful party man but was undone by his responsibilities as commander-in-chief of the militia. In fairness, the need to design a military policy against residents of an American territory was a new and unwelcome innovation disorienting all involved. The growing unrest was one of the greater problems confronting the executive branch locally and in Washington. To whom could governors apply to protect civilians? Normally, local militias provided support, but in Kansas these were highly politicized and therefore unreliable. Western troops had mostly been involved in territorial affairs when they protected immigrants against American Indians, and they were unaccustomed to refereeing between conflicting settler groups. Davis addressed this anomaly when he ordered Sumner and Cooke to aid Shannon in suppressing insurrections or armed resistance to local law and indicated each was to "avail yourself of the first opportunity to return with your command to the more grateful and prouder service of the soldier—that of common defence."[157] On the whole, he was firmly against quartering troops in Kansas, believing "that if the people were fit to form and maintain a state and take their place as equals in the union, they would not require troops in their midst."[158] In issuing instructions to Persifor E. Smith, commander of the Department of the West, Davis stressed awareness of "the peculiar conditions of affairs in Kansas" and reminded him to carefully distinguish between civil and military authorities.[159]

Shannon would later recall his difficulties with some humor: "Govern Kansas in 1855 and '56! You might as well attempt to govern the devil in hell."[160] He was correct in perceiving the precariousness of his situation. He had to contend with a shadow government and political violence. However, he lacked both the administrative skill and the guise of neutrality to work productively with both factions. Slavery could only be successfully implanted in Kansas if popular sovereignty was seen to have provided a fair opportunity for freedom to be victorious as well. Shannon could not control Sheriff Jones, was wary of commanding the militia, and did not inspire confidence among free-state settlers because of his proslavery affiliation. Given the territory's instability, executive stability was of utmost importance. Although Reeder's incompetence and rejection of the Democratic Party were unexpected, once it became necessary to replace him, how to proceed was very much in Pierce's hands. Often, the second choice is most critical, but in appointing Shannon, he selected a man with experience but lacking tact. Instead of improving the situation, Shannon blundered into mistake after mistake and oversaw the seminal events that earned the territory its "Bleeding Kansas" sobriquet. However, Pierce can be credited with bypassing Woodson for the second time after Shannon's resignation in favor of an untainted administrator.

Unlike his predecessors, Geary immediately took control and demonstrated that a competent governor could dampen the turmoil. As Persifor Smith told him, "I thank God sincerely that the administration of affairs here is fallen into your hands & thus the frauds of one, the imbecility of another & the narrow self-interests of a third [Woodson] have been replaced by the honest, manly energy of a patriot who has the capacity & will to do all for his country."[161] Indeed, in doing his all, Geary tried to serve the territory in every capacity. Barely a month into his administration, the governor informed Marcy that he was taking a "small body of men to the southern portion of the territory, in pursuit of a gang of thieves who are said to be pillaging that region."[162] While Pierce and Marcy had granted Geary wide latitude, it is difficult to imagine this was his proper role. His multifaceted approach to achieving peace succeeded, but he was brought down by forces outside his control and by his overly ambitious approach. Although Geary arrived with Pierce's full support, that support withered under proslavery criticisms. Ultimately, he grew extremely resentful toward Pierce and Marcy, believing "the Gen. Government has not sustained according to promises. . . ."[163] Achieving his objectives when the executive department overseeing him seemed more biased than popular sovereignty required was difficult. Pierce seemed to favor the establishment of a slave state but would not force the issue, most likely because he believed the territory was naturally inclined toward slavery and thus his intervention was not required.

Moreover, while Geary was the most capable administrator Kansas had seen, his efficacy came at a cost. Within two weeks of his arrival, Marcy had to warn him that while the administration supported his efforts to ensure peace, there were limits: "To the troops in service, military law can properly be applied, but you have not the power to proclaim martial law; you must get along without doing so."[164] Most contemporary sources comment on Geary's ego; indeed his supreme self-confidence gave him an inflated sense of his own importance. This is most clearly evident in his clash with Lecompte. Geary correctly insisted that the territorial judiciary function impartially, but he erred in communicating these concerns. Moreover, his insistence that he was the sole authority, when in fact he was one part of the territorial administration, led even so interested a party in Lecompte's removal as the *Herald of Freedom* to express concerns over Geary's "excessive powers."[165] Ultimately, Geary's lack of finesse in dealing with Kansas's factions stranded him without any territorial support, and in Kansas this was unsustainable.

4

Congress and the Kansas Issue in 1856

The Constitution endowed the legislative branch with control over the nation's growth process by assigning Congress the power to create territories and admit states. Additionally, the Senate's review of presidential appointments checked the executive's power in the territories. As the new country developed, Congress exerted significant leverage within this sphere by deciding under what conditions territorial status and admission were warranted.[1] When Kansas and Nebraska were organized in 1854, the country was nearing a decade of active continental expansion and the Union was burgeoning with recent admissions. In 1845, both Florida and Texas had become states, followed by Iowa in 1846, Wisconsin in 1848, and California in 1850. Oregon was organized as a territory in 1848, and Utah and New Mexico were organized under the Compromise of 1850, which had also admitted California. In terms of policy, Congress isolated each territory, never enacting statutory legislation applicable to all; instead, relevant legislation was passed anew and limited to the specified territory.[2] Thus Congress allowed some regions to languish in territorial limbo while welcoming others, which had not been territories beforehand, to statehood. Such autonomy reserved judgment to the legislative branch, but the absence of established regulations could also lead to disorder, a result most fully realized when the issue of Kansas's admission arose during the 34th Congress.

With the territory open in advance of settlement, the delay in implementing land policy contributed to the disordered nature of settlement under popular sovereignty. "In an unoccupied Territory, where the lands have not been surveyed, and where there were no marks or lines to indicate the boundaries of sections and quarter-sections, and where no legal title could be had until after the surveys would be made," Senator Stephen Douglas (IL) argued, "disputes, quarrels, violence, and bloodshed might have been expected as the natural and inevitable consequences of such extraordinary systems of emigration. . . ."[3] While Douglas, who was so instrumental in organizing western territories, saw the resultant upheaval in Kansas as inevitable, he failed to take responsibility for pushing territorial organization in advance of settlers' demands for recognition. During the typical course of settlement, usually over more than a decade, Congress established local government with an organizing act, consented to presidential appointments, and accepted a constitution. However, the chaotic situation in Kansas spilled into legislative affairs far more than expected. Amid an intensifying rhetorical war, routine matters such as seating territorial delegates or debating the territorial constitution acquired greater significance.

In concert with the 1856 presidential campaign, maneuvering for which had begun the previous fall, Republican senator William Seward (NY) indicted both the president and Congress for their inaction in Kansas in widely circulated speeches. Another influential Republican, Charles Sumner (MA), garnered attention with similar speeches charging the administration with abandoning Kansas under the rubric of "popular rights."[4] Many Kansans considered both men special friends and their speeches raised expectations. "What will you do for us in Congress?" Lydia Hall wrote Sumner on January 27, 1856. "We trust you will do a great deal. Don't we deserve it?"[5] The Topeka government's plans rested on the assumption that a sympathetic legislature, when apprised of the true nature of territorial events and arrayed against an indifferent executive, would wholeheartedly support Kansas's immediate admission. Republican campaign speeches that fall had laid the necessary foundation for this strategy. The party identified itself as the savior of Kansas and, after charging both Congress and the president with "dereliction," was poised to take advantage of the administration's 1855 blunders in the upcoming legislative session.[6]

The organization of the extralegal Topeka government and Governor Wilson Shannon's territorial travails weighed heavily on President Franklin Pierce. During the fall 1855 elections, his administration reeled from charges that its policies exacerbated tensions without providing succor. Believing the Constitution limited executive action, Pierce had hesitated to intervene, but this reluctance ebbed as the military was drawn into the conflict in December. With the Wakarusa War and Shannon's insistence that federal troops were needed to maintain control, Pierce became more proactive; but congressional support was uncertain. Although the Senate was Democratic, his policies, especially regarding patronage, had alienated many party members. Even with few committed supporters in the Senate, it was far more sympathetic to the administration than was the House of Representatives, where affiliations of Whigs, Republicans, and Americans who comprised the opposition remained fluid and whose ability to function as a united front was unclear. The two-month delay in organizing the House beset the administration, especially as legislation to address the worsening territorial situation that winter was delayed due to this internal disarray. When the House finally organized itself in February, the administration was dealt a severe setback. Through a political miscalculation, Democrats were outmaneuvered and helped elect Nathaniel Banks, a Republican-Know-Nothing, as Speaker.[7] Given that one partisan called Banks's election "the first victory which the north has won over the South since 1808, when the slave trade with Africa was abolished,"[8] there was no doubt that antislavery members would set an agenda at odds with administration goals.

On January 24, Pierce offered Congress suggestions on how they might ameliorate the Kansas conflict. Whereas Nebraska had convened its first legislature on January 16, 1855, Kansas had not done so for another six months. The president blamed former governor Andrew Reeder for this delay, despite the fact that he remained in Washington until Congress adjourned at Pierce's request. Nonetheless, Reeder's October arrival, six months after his appointment, left the territory "without any legislative authority, without local law, and, of course without the ordinary guaranties of peace and public order" for more than a year after its creation. While Pierce recognized the role of outside interference, he reserved his greatest condemnation for Reeder: "[I]nstead of exercising constant vigilance and putting forth all his energies to prevent or counteract the tendencies to illegality . . . ," he had been "diverted from official obligations by other objects, and himself set an example of the violation of law" that led to his removal.[9]

Pierce acknowledged the electoral irregularities of the previous year's elections but believed the time to address them had passed, especially since Reeder had verified the results. Now, contrary to that recognition, the free-state party had "elected" a delegate. The president argued that their creation of an alternative government was of a "revolutionary character" and unjustified given the constitutional remedies available. Not only were these "more prompt and effective than illegal violence," they had to "be scrupulously guarded; this great prerogative of popular sovereignty sacredly respected." If the Topeka group resisted local or federal authority, their actions would become "treasonable insurrection." In such an event, Pierce would call upon federal forces, state militias, or naval forces to ensure faithful execution of federal laws. Fearing more violence, the president asked Congress to authorize a constitutional convention once the territory had sufficient residents for admission. Although it appeared that Kansas might not attract enough residents for some time, Pierce likely believed the promise of a convention would be a salve and allow the territory to focus on the future. Finally, he requested a special appropriation to meet any expenses incurred while maintaining public order.[10]

This request for legislative action demonstrates Pierce's belief that Congress was responsible for the developing conflict. It also implies the president could no longer control events on his own. With the admitted failures of the first territorial administration and the possibility that Shannon would deploy federal troops against residents, Pierce asked the legislature to intervene in territorial affairs beyond its normal scope. It is doubtful, however, that he expected Congress to involve itself to the extent it did, much less to interfere with his ability to deploy federal troops. Pierce's preferences for congressional action were simple—a convention and additional funding—but Reeder's claim to John Whitfield's delegate seat and the likelihood that the Topeka Constitution would be introduced complicated the situation. Nonetheless, for pushing a territory into existence prematurely—and then allowing the settlement mechanism (however well intentioned an expression of democracy popular sovereignty represented) to devolve into chaos—the legislative branch had much for which to repent when it convened in December 1855.

The Whitfield-Reeder Territorial Delegate Quandary and the Howard Committee

The position of territorial delegate was established early in the nation's legislative history when the Southwest of the River Ohio Territory dispatched a representative to Congress in 1794. This unique position offered a symbolic presence to an entity lacking national representation. For potential delegates, this attractive opportunity offered "the same franking privileges and the same pay" as a representative with few attendant responsibilities. Territorial delegates typically functioned as a clearinghouse for "special petitions and memorials," prompting scant debate and even less notice.[11]

The territorial delegate assumed greater importance during the 34th Congress. Although the Senate organized itself on December 5, 1855, the bitter speaker contest delayed business in the House until February 8. After swearing in its membership, the House turned to the delegates; when Democrat and former Pottawatomie Indian agent John W. Whitfield was called to represent Kansas, an informal protest was raised. Congressman Lewis D. Campbell (OH) cited the delay in organization for not pressing his objection harder as doing so would only "confuse and embarrass us further." Galusha Grow (PA) stated that accepting Whitfield's credentials was premature but settled for drawing attention to a potential problem. Despite these informal objections, Whitfield took his place as Kansas's delegate.[12]

Disputed elections were routinely brought before the House; in this session, objections were lodged over elections in Maine, Louisiana, Nebraska, and New Mexico. All contested elections were referred to the Committee of Elections, a nine-member committee dominated by Northerners.[13] Whitfield's situation differed from the others' in that his challenger was not a disappointed candidate. An incumbent who had first won his seat in 1854, Whitfield was returned after running unopposed in the October 1, 1855 territorial election and arrived in Washington with papers certified by the legislature. On the other hand, his challenger came before the House as a disgraced former governor claiming victory in an unsanctioned election. While it was easy to dismiss Reeder as grasping for renewed prominence, the two October elections revealed internal confusion even if only one election was authorized. Although the House unquestionably judges members' credentials, in deciding who the legitimate Kansas delegate was, it accepted a role in the dispute between the territorial government and its extralegal challenger. How it decided the matter would indicate where its sympathies lay in an increasingly volatile and polarizing debate.

In a memorial addressed to the House, Reeder argued that Whitfield should be dismissed because neither the law nor the people supported him. The memorial summarized the free-state position: the legislature was illegitimate because it had not been elected by bona fide residents. In denying basic civil and political rights to residents, the territorial legislature was unrepublican. Since Whitfield had been elected under laws passed by this illegitimate body, his election was invalid. Finally, Reeder's election had been supported by "the people" of Kansas as opposed to those of Missouri and was thus the only valid election. The Topeka organization focused on a power granted in the organizing act to the governor (determining the seat of government) and argued that the legislature had usurped this power when it convened at an unauthorized location. Thus "the legislature never had any legal existence, for nothing can be legal which is unconstitutional. . . ."[14] Because Reeder argued all territorial elections were invalid, the Committee of Elections asked for additional testimony before ruling. On February 19, John Hickman (PA) reported a resolution enabling the committee to send to Kansas for persons and papers to aid its investigation.

However, Reeder's actions in Kansas undermined his case. As governor, he had certified the March 1855 election returns and recognized the very legislature he now derided as illegal, a fact Alexander Stephens (GA), a minority member of the election committee, brought to the chamber's attention.[15]

John Phelps (MO) concurred, arguing that the incumbent Whitfield had previously been accepted under the same laws Reeder contested. Moreover, any legal questions were more appropriately handled in the courts. Phelps dismissed Reeder's supporters as traitors intent on overthrowing the territorial government. The Topeka organization's "farce of creating a government" was designed to supersede federal authority. Reeder was not an innocent victim; instead his group was recruiting troops from sympathetic state governments to use against the territorial legislature.[16] Opponents of the request for more information argued that both sides had committed "excesses" and denied the need to gather testimony from the distant territory. William Lake (MI) believed the outrages had been exaggerated, calling them caricatures: "If they [the free-state men] are the pusillanimous abject creatures that this picture would have us believe they are, interference is vain. The government did wrong to exchange the Indians who possess the country for such land. It was a bad trade." However, supporters claimed the excitement in Kansas rendered an investigation even more urgent, no doubt wishing to take advantage of a situation that placed the administration on the defensive. Yet, despite the clear value to the Republican Party of an investigation held in advance of the presidential election, this division reflected diverging reports coming out of Kansas.[17]

The resolution was returned for the committee to determine the extent of its authority and, on March 5, the committee issued its report. The following two weeks sparked a broad debate on the committee's goals. Opponents focused on two broad themes: the character of the contestant and the tactics of the opposition. Conversely, supporters embraced a wide interpretation of the issues at hand, focusing on internal conditions and the dangers faced by antislavery advocates.

William Boyce (SC) insisted that any investigation undertaken focus on whether Whitfield's election had been invalidated by the legislature's relocation to Shawnee Mission.[18] Phelps reminded legislators that the Kansas-Nebraska Act required the territorial legislature to convene at a location chosen by the governor, but did not prevent subsequent movement.[19] Moreover, territorial judges had validated the relocation.[20] A further complication in this contested election was that Whitfield had run unopposed, rendering any contention of fraud moot.[21] Few congressmen denied that irregularities and violence had occurred but characterized it as routine. "There has been no Legislature elected in our history where there has not been more or less of violence at the polls," Henry W. Davis (MD) argued. "The course of political life in this country is that of disturbance, turmoil, and collisions of fierce passions; but it is the paramount power of the people and their submission to the organized authorities, when a result is once brought about, that makes this grand organization the model of the world."[22] In this session, however, the free-state group did not follow precedence.

It was difficult for Whitfield's supporters to take Reeder seriously. "Upon the other side, you have the revolutionary, unlawful, outside, and unauthorized government to support and defend. In opposition stand the Senate, the Executive, the Judiciary, the American people—all on the side of law and order," argued Martin J. Crawford (GA).[23] Hendley S. Bennett (MS) charged the antislavery party with a provocative strategy, accusing them of encouraging "civil discord . . . you bid that revolution go on, instead of stretching out your arm and staying the desolation of civil war and the shedding of blood. . . ." Instead, their speeches encouraged revolution, all because of their opposition to the South's constitutional rights.[24] Thus the contested election was placed within the framework of a larger propaganda war, and the committee's request for wide discretion was portrayed as merely a new version of familiar agitation. Thomas L. Harris (IL) argued that the committee's proponents perceived the hollowness of Reeder's claim but wanted "to renew and increase the excitement in the country raised by false or exaggerated statements of the abolition press, of mobs, invasions, riots, and bloodshed perpetuated by the ruffians of Missouri upon the meek, pious, and puritanical people of Kansas."[25] Only by constructing a hagiography of the free-state side could antislavery advocates accomplish what they were unwilling to pursue within the bounds of territorial law.

Reeder's role in the elections was reviewed in efforts to defeat the resolution. If the former governor's charges of fraud were accurate, Stephens argued, his behavior constituted a more "flagrant and gross dereliction of duty than any public officer in the whole history of the country was ever guilty of."[26] His claim was also problematic: in a personal memorial, he simply informed Congress he was the true victor. But Kansans had not petitioned Congress for redress and Reeder's position was weak. As John Wright (TN) noted, while the former governor claimed to be elected, "he can produce no statute of Congress nor resolve of that body—no act of the Kansas Legislature nor resolve thereof, nor any other acknowledged legal authority or warrant, by virtue of which he claims to have been elected as a Delegate to Congress can be shown by him." To displace Whitfield in Reeder's favor would be the worst type of "squatter sovereignty."[27]

Investigation opponents also brought the president's message to the fore. Pierce had informed Congress about territorial developments, had suggested remedies, and had denounced and removed Reeder. Did Congress then need to conduct a thorough investigation?[28] The entire spectrum of territorial troubles was not before the House; only a contested election was at hand. While Kansas might warrant a wider investigation, John Millson (VA) believed it could be addressed in the usual manner.[29] Moreover, Mordecai Oliver (MO) believed the committee requested excessive powers to determine Whitfield's legitimacy.[30] As Boyce argued, perhaps the committee was instead trying "to inflame the public mind on this agitating question."[31] Many Southerners believed Republicans pursued this case for political capital because they recognized that Kansas was unlikely to become a slave state. "Leave Kansas to herself," Democrat William R. Smith (AL) urged his colleagues. "She will work out her own destiny. That Kansas will be a non-slaveholding State, the best-informed men of all parties believe."[32] Nonetheless, it was the House, not the Committee of Election, that would decide whether a larger investigation was warranted.

Many Congressmen charged Republicans with playing to the gallery. Millson protested against excessive emoting on the Northern side, arguing that it served no true purpose. "Is it that you have more sensibility than the men of the South, that you are excited while we are calm? Is it that you cling to your ancient principles with more fondness than we do? Or is it that you are jealous of our supposed triumph over you?" The question before the House was of "comparative insignificance," just one election in one territory.[33] Ultimately, Congress was not the proper forum for such an investigation. As Davis stated, "We are a political body. We are not a court."[34] However, his argument was specious. Congress judged its members' credentials, and while it was not authorized to investigate crimes, electoral fraud had always been a basis to deny a member a seat. Thus, the House could certainly decide the legitimacy of Whitfield's election. However, Reeder's claim to Whitfield's seat, even if vacated, was tenuous due to the illegality of his own election.

As a political body, however, the committee's supporters believed the Reeder-Whitfield contretemps was appropriately before the House. Indeed, they cast the investigation as necessary to preserve law and order, a rather ironic description given that in Kansas "law and order" had been adopted by the proslavery party. Nonetheless if the Topeka faction was to diminish Missouri's influence in Kansas, they needed to draw attention to the territory's electoral irregularities. As Israel Washburn (ME) stated, the House needed to be certain that "the law, rather than the resolutions of marauders, shall control its decisions." Supporters disputed any contentions that Reeder's former position ought to disqualify him. While Reeder may have acted foolishly, his actions paled in comparison to greater crimes.[35]

Reeder's defenders believed the question of how foreign (Missouri) interference had corrupted popular sovereignty was more significant. "Let the country know *who* is to blame for all this mischief, and *what* is the blame," argued George Dunn (IN). "Let us ascertain if the real evil is not in this new fledged eagle of liberty—this outside-popular sovereignty doctrine—this liberty-without-law theory, which is to take the place of our old well-considered and well-tried theory and practice of liberty under the law."[36] Moreover, because the dual elections raised concerns about residents' freedom of expression, Congress had to ensure Whitfield's election was legal. "Have the people of Kansas chosen the sitting Delegate, or have they been conquered by an invading army?" John Bingham (OH) asked. "Is the sitting Delegate here without the consent of the people, in violation of law and by the act of lawless invaders? Is he here by the decision of the sword and not of the ballot?"[37] Only a full investigation could determine why Kansas Territory had sent two delegates to Congress.

Republicans reminded Southerners that their power was waning. Opposition to the committee was perceived as an effort to conceal the region's reliance on undemocratic methods to acquire another slave state. However, "in excusing this invasion from Missouri—in attempting to hold on to an advantage obtained by force and fraud—you are setting an example which, in its ultimate consequences, may trample your rights under foot," John Sherman (OH) argued. "Until these wrongs are righted, you must expect northern men to unite to redress them."[38] Proponents believed the administration supported Southern efforts to bury the truth. William S. Damrell (MA) believed the administration's friends wanted "to cover up these frauds, and prevent the people of this nation from becoming acquainted with the facts in relation to these outrageous proceedings."[39] While Pierce advocated a constitutional convention to provide future relief, the opposition insisted an investigation must come first.

There is little doubt that investigation proponents had concerns beyond the legitimacy of Whitfield's election. Most speeches reveal that the contested election allowed Republicans to push their agenda. "We cannot, by our separate action, reach the root of this wide-spreading tree of wrong and iniquity in Kansas; but we can lop off a branch of that same tree, protruding into this House in the person of General Whitfield," Samuel Galloway (OH) argued. "If we cannot strike the axe at the root of the tree, we can withhold the nutritive *sap*, without which its vigor will decline, and thus at least partially teach the wrong-doers in Kansas that the 'way of the transgressor is hard,' and that justice, although it may linger, will yet have free course, and be glorified in the triumph of LAW AND ORDER."[40] While opponents decried the committee's charge as too far-reaching, proponents believed theirs was a quest for truth. William Cumback (IN) typified this stance: "Rather let me ask where is the man who will stand up in this Hall and say he will not vote for a full and free investigation of all the facts connected with this Kansas matter? . . . *Truth never shrinks from investigation.*"⁴¹ Cumback and others argued this position so strongly and colored opposing views so negatively, that a vote against an investigation seemingly indicated a preference for injustice and prevarication.

Despite concerns about the wide discretion demanded, on March 19 the House authorized a committee to investigate Kansas affairs 110 to 93. Because the Committee of Elections had other concerns, Banks pared the select committee to three: Republicans John Sherman (OH) and William A. Howard (MI) and Democrat Mordecai Oliver (MO), a recent defector from the Whig Party.⁴² The Howard Committee arrived in Kansas in April, spent two months recording testimony, and created tremendous excitement. Free-state supporters believed this committee's creation indicated the House accepted legislative responsibility for the territory. "I fear we shall see more troubled times yet, unless something effectual is done for us at the East," one antislavery activist had written. "Why does not the House of Representatives initiate something bold, decided and effectual and make their weight felt as it should be."⁴³ Forming this committee was indeed a bold act, and proslavery partisans worried about its interference when it presented its findings, a 1,206-page majority report supporting free-state accounts, on July 2. In the eyes of one bitter proslavery partisan, the committee was sent to Kansas to investigate, but instead "came very short of it by countenancing resistance to the law, and inflaming the populace to open rebellion."⁴⁴

The majority report argued that without the Kansas-Nebraska Act, Kansas would have been at peace. But the bill had renewed Southern hopes of extending slavery into a previously excluded area and intensified beliefs that Congress had abrogated a national compact. Missourians thus perceived free-state efforts as infringing their rights and became determined to save Kansas for slavery. "This unlawful interference has been continued in every important event in the history of the Territory; *every election* has been controlled not by the actual settlers, but by citizens of Missouri, . . . your Committee have been unable to find that any political power whatever, however unimportant, has been exercised by the people." The committee included data on all three territorial elections and determined each had been tainted by widespread fraud. Even the 1854 delegate election, in which fewer than half the settlers participated, had been marred by voter intimidation. Although Whitfield's victory over William P. Richardson was unaffected, the fraud "was a crime of great magnitude." Moreover, intimidation had affected the slate of electors—free-state candidates declined to run "because they were unwilling to run the risk of so unequal a contest, it being known that a great many were coming up from Missouri to vote." The committee asserted that genuine Kansas settlers had been prevented from voting, both because armed residents had been at the polls and because free-state men had not been, and thus Missouri residents had elected Kansas's legislature. "It is not to be tolerated, that a legislative body thus selected should assume or exercise any legislative functions; and their enactments should be regarded as null and void; nor should the question of its legal existence be determined by itself, as that would be allowing the criminal to judge of his own crime."[45] The majority report exonerated Reeder for certifying the legislature because the former governor had acted without sufficient knowledge of the extent of the fraud. With two of its three members being Republicans, the committee's free-state bias was clear, and they had partisan reasons to exonerate Reeder.

Finally, the report addressed Whitfield's October 1855 reelection: "it was manifest that from there being but one candidate—Gen. Whitfield—he must have received a majority of the votes cast" and acknowledged free-state men had made other electoral arrangements. Without, then, disputing Whitfield's election, the committee defended the free-state organization's actions, noting they had sent "a graphic and truthful memorial to Congress" beforehand. Moreover, the committee found "that every allegation in this memorial has been sustained by the testimony." The free-state men reflected "the will of the majority of the settlers" in organizing their own government, elections, and constitution. Moreover, the Topeka Constitution respected the "right of the people to assemble and express their political opinion in any form, whether by means of an election or a convention," and so the committee was unconcerned with greater legal issues. The free-state organization reflected the will of the people and so "these [actions] were not illegal."[46]

The majority report also harshly criticized the territorial judiciary, singling out Chief Justice Samuel Lecompte for participating in political meetings hostile to abolitionism. They decried territorial laws as direct transcriptions of Missouri statutes and emphasized the legislature's excesses, such as limiting jurors to those willing to swear allegiance to slavery. These explorations of Kansas law provided evidence of the depth of Missouri's interference. Although Missourians testified to the legitimacy of their land claims, complaints about eastern interference (specifically the Emigrant Aid Company's actions and Reeder's decision to postpone elections, which allowed immigrants from distant states time to arrive) were dismissed as unfounded and, according to the majority report, masked nefarious intentions.[47]

In conclusion, the majority report determined that armed Missourians had disenfranchised bona fide settlers, rendering every election void. Thus selected, the territorial legislature was illegal and their laws unenforceable. Therefore, Whitfield's election was invalid and "should be regarded only as the expression of the choice of those resident citizens who voted for him." While conceding that Reeder's election should be viewed similarly, the report concluded that he had the greater claim to the seat because he had received more votes in his October 9 election than Whitfield had received on October 1. Finally, the majority report stated that future territorial elections would require "a new census, a stringent and well-guarded election law, the selection of impartial Judges, and the presence of United States troops at every place of election." Until such a time, the Topeka government "embodies the will of a majority of the people."[48] In reaching these conclusions, Sherman and Howard had not adhered to rigorous evidentiary standards, entering rumors into the record and allowing testimony from individuals who had neither participated in the elections nor been in Kansas at that time.

Missouri's Mordecai Oliver, the committee's minority representative, complained the report was "*ex parte* and one-sided, but highly partisan in its character from beginning to end" and challenged its conclusions.[49] He protested the acceptance of hearsay and complained about the majority's shifting standards on acceptable testimony. For instance, according to the majority report, the committee only considered events occurring prior to its creation. However, testimony favorable to the free-state side (such as the tarring and feathering of Pardee Butler, which reflected poorly on proslavery men) was accepted while negative testimony about antislavery excesses (such as the Pottawatomie Massacre whose victims were proslavery and which occurred when the committee was in Kansas) was excluded.[50]

Oliver disputed the "broad and sweeping language" that described each election as unlawful, especially since the committee found that even if fraudulent votes were eliminated, sufficient legal votes had been cast for Whitfield to elect him in 1854. Using data tables provided by the majority, Oliver demonstrated that the free-state party was then too weak to elect a majority in either branch of the legislature even if every free-state vote was counted without question. Moreover, the committee neglected evidence of the growing strength of the proslavery party from November to March. A widespread relocation had transpired in Kansas during the three months between the initial election and the census of voters, but the committee dismissed any voter not living in the same location in February as an illegal November voter.[51]

Oliver defended his home state by emphasizing that weapons proliferated on both sides, and since secret societies arose soon after the 1854 legislation, fears of eastern interference were sensible. The majority report, for example, included the testimony of Daniel Mace (IN) regarding the creation of one such organization in the capital immediately after passage of the Kansas-Nebraska Act. As such, any organizations formed in his state were, Oliver asserted, created for "counteracting those organizations previously formed elsewhere." Although it was easy to argue that Missourians had been too aggressive, it was impossible to completely discount their reactions.[52]

Regarding the March elections, Oliver emphasized that the testimony derived from witnesses residing in districts where Reeder had set aside the results; thus those concerns had been addressed the previous year. Stressing the connection between eastern aid societies and the Big Springs Convention, he underscored witnesses' unreliability. One participant, for instance, described the convention, stating that "many of them [antislavery activists] told him they were making use of language that would make the pro-slavery party appear to the world more guilty than they in reality were. . . . Many told him, when called upon, they were willing to swear that thousands of Missourians came over and voted, although he saw none; but admitted to him that they saw no Missourians vote, nor did they know of any who did."[53] Oliver depicted the Topeka group as so committed to abolitionist goals, they would willingly lie to achieve their objectives.

In conclusion, Oliver argued that both Whitfield's and the legislators' elections were valid and the House could not justifiably invalidate the territorial government. Moreover, as Whitfield "received a large number of legal votes without opposition, he was duly elected as a delegate to this body, and is entitled to a seat on this floor as such." Even if the House believed each delegate-elect's support should be tallied, the majority had provided no evidence to prove that Reeder received a larger number of votes in his election than Whitfield had received in his own. Oliver denied that Reeder had a legal right to displace Whitfield, as his election was "the expression of a band of malcontents and revolutionists, and consequently should be wholly disregarded by the House."[54] Because of this, the House had no basis for vacating Whitfield's seat.

Nonetheless, after two weeks, the Committee of Elections resolved to replace Whitfield with Reeder. In the report accompanying the resolution, Washburn argued that in the absence of valid law, Whitfield's election was merely the personal preference of those voters who had selected him. Similarly, Reeder's claim reflected personal choice, but Washburn maintained it had greater validity since more voters preferred Reeder to Whitfield. "To deny to Kansas the right to be heard through the choice of its resident citizens, merely because that choice was manifest outside of legal forms, and necessarily so," Washburn argued, "because the law-making power was destroyed by foreign violence, is to deny to Kansas the right to be heard at all on the floor of the House." Given the territory's inability to elect anyone else—Whitfield would be returned if another election were held without changing the election mechanism—Washburn suggested Reeder serve as delegate until Congress could order new elections.[55]

On August 1, Whitfield defended himself by arguing that while elections were contested frequently, the House had changed the context unfairly and politicized the issue. His critics had tied Whitfield's repudiation to "their own political fortunes" and were trying to create sectional conflict to benefit the Republican Party. He claimed riots and other violence far exceeding Kansas events had occurred in many states without those elections being overturned. Moreover, characterizing all Missourians as "border ruffians" was unfair; they were involved in the territory because mutual interests transcended any border demarcation. Moreover, the Kansas-Nebraska Act had neglected to specify voter qualifications, making it difficult to prove that those with a Missouri connection were illegal voters. An impartial review of the facts was impossible, for as Whitfield noted, the majority report was so voluminous that no member could read it without forsaking all other duties.[56]

Whitfield asked the House to focus on two facts in deciding for him: first, he had run unopposed in October; second, protests began only after Reeder's removal from office. The investigation was thus connected to the opposition's desire to force "upon the country a sectional contest for the Presidency." In pursuit of a larger goal, he had been denied the opportunity to cross-examine witnesses, just one aspect of a poorly conducted investigation. The committee had been sent "with a drag-net, and fish up all the testimony they can find of any acts of riot or tumult, from the passage of the act to the present day, whether such acts be committed by residents or strangers; and all encouragements of acts of violence and disturbance; to gather up all the evidence of offensive conduct that scandal-mongers may choose to detail, and throw the reeking mass, thus fished up, before this House—and for what purpose? Can it be said, with any show of reason, law, or justice," Whitfield asked, "that I am responsible, civilly or criminally, for all and every act of violence committed in Kansas?" He implored the House to disregard all testimony not directly relevant to his election. Whitfield was unable to reconcile that he, the legally elected representative of Kansas, could be removed, "an act so at war with all that is republican in our institutions."[57]

Despite Whitfield's impassioned defense, on August 4 the House unseated him 110 to 92. However, a second resolution to seat Reeder failed 88 to 113 as the House instead ordered new elections to fill the vacated seat.[58] After five months of debate, the vote to unseat Whitfield mirrored the vote to authorize the Howard Committee almost exactly, as Appendix F demonstrates.[59] Of those voting to oust Whitfield, only three had voted against establishing the Howard Committee in March.[60] Of those voting to retain Whitfield, all 92 rejected Reeder as his replacement. Those 92 were joined by 21 Northerners to defeat the resolution; all 21 had voted to oust Whitfield.[61] These 21 members probably were uncomfortable with the flawed territorial elections but could not justify the Topeka government's radical course. Vacating the seat in this manner rendered Whitfield's election illegitimate due to widespread disenfranchisement but also rebuffed the free-state elections erected in opposition to the territorial government.[62]

The failure of months of investigations to significantly alter legislators' views support the contention that the investigation was designed to shape public opinion. Similarly, the wide discretion granted to the committee represents the House's prior partiality for the free-state cause. Rebuffing Whitfield despite his lawful credentials and accepting Reeder's views on territorial matters, despite his complicity in the disputed elections, underscores the opposition's commitment to making a stand in Kansas. Reeder was a weak foundation upon which to base the free-state case, and although he failed to become Kansas's delegate, the investigation's supporters accomplished other goals. Testimony of more than one thousand pages was a boon to the opposition and transformed Reeder from incompetent to hero. The most problematic aspect of Reeder's own case (his recognition of the allegedly illegitimate legislature) was reduced to a mere clerical function; moreover, the Topeka government's treasonous actions were now perceived as a heroic and democratic response to "ruffianism in Washington" and an illustration of the Federalists' argument that "in such emergencies 'forms ought to give way to substance.'"[63]

Toil and Trouble: The Calamitous Summer of 1856

The spring debate over the competing territorial delegates and the Howard Committee's investigation marked the beginning of a contentious summer. Other setbacks for the Democratic Party soon followed as May brought a public relations disaster: Democratic congressman Preston Brooks (SC) assaulted Republican senator Charles Sumner (MA) in chambers; proslavery forces had sacked Lawrence; and abolitionist John Brown led a retaliatory slaying of five proslavery men at Pottawatomie Creek. June brought accounts of intensifying skirmishes across the territory as each faction in turn captured and liberated "Old Sacramento," apparently the sole cannon in Kansas. July witnessed the use of federal troops to disperse the free-state legislature at Topeka while the "Army of the North" waited on the northern border to engage proslavery forces. August brought Governor Wilson Shannon's resignation, Acting Governor Daniel Woodson's proclamation of an "open rebellion," and continuing skirmishes. Full-scale engagements were averted only after federal troops dispersed the various militias. The situation continued to degenerate until a new governor, John W. Geary, implemented a multifaceted strategy to defuse territorial tensions. Amid this chaos, the ongoing special investigation and presidential campaign fueled politics in the capital as all parties were aware that Kansas policy would influence the upcoming elections. Aside from the delegate quandary, Congress confronted two major Kansas issues that summer—the fate of the Topeka Constitution and the military's role in the territory.

The Topeka Constitution

All spring, the issue of the free-state "government" had percolated through Congress. The president's January message revealed administration hopes that Congress would rebuff the Topeka Constitution in favor of a constitutional convention for the territory at some distant future. Aside from political questions, a more concrete concern involved the territory's suitability for statehood. Did Kansas have a sufficient population to support itself and warrant representation in the House? At what point could a territory meet the responsibilities of a state, including paying government expenses through tax collection? Speaking for the majority of the Committee on Territories, Grow enumerated these very responsibilities when the Topeka Constitution was presented in the House.

> While the capacity of men to govern themselves is the same, whether in a State or a Territory, their relations to the government are not the same, and it is no good cause of complaint that they must submit to all the conditions incident to their new and changed position. In the States they are members of an organized community which makes its own laws, elects its own rulers, and pays all the expenses thereof by levying and collecting its own taxes. The people of a Territory do none of the acts, either one of which is an indispensable requisite of popular sovereignty. So long as they are unable, for want of sufficient numbers and wealth, to support a State government, with all the tribunals necessary to secure life and property, they cannot exercise all the rights of an independent and sovereign people.[64]

The constitution's early submission brought these practical and political concerns to the foreground. Kansas was vaulting ahead of the anticipated schedule by submitting a constitution so early when it clearly lacked the requisite population, but it had predated many markers in its precocious career. In addition, there was no clear precedent as to when a territory should become a state or whether it needed congressional permission to commence the process. Not only had a constitution arrived before Kansas was even two years old, but it was brought forward by an extralegal group. However, the March vote to authorize the Howard Committee indicated that the House, at the least, was arrayed with the Topeka government in its interpretation of Kansas events.

As the leading territorial man in the Senate, Douglas was proprietary about popular sovereignty and took umbrage at the rising criticism about the developing chaos. He defended proslavery partisans against Pierce's January and February characterizations. He argued that the emigration of Northerners, especially that sponsored by the Emigrant Aid Company, was deliberate and aggressive—underwritten as it was by a "vast moneyed corporation for the purpose of controlling the domestic institutions of a distinct political community...."[65] Douglas depicted Missourians as so startled by antislavery hostility and scorn for their domestic institutions that their reactions were "natural and defensive." They moved into Kansas to protect "themselves and their domestic institutions from the consequences, of that company's operations,"[66] a defensive action. Many Democrats and Southerners were concerned about how organized societies would affect political structures. August Hall (IA) spoke for many disconcerted by the new actors in territorial settlement having hoped "that Kansas, like New Mexico, and Oregon, and Washington, would be settled in the natural and ordinary way," but "for the first time in the history of government, emigrants would go out under the instructions of a gigantic monopoly...."[67]

The memorial submitted to Congress with the Topeka Constitution was familiar; many of its arguments were previewed in the Whitfield-Reeder conflict. It stated that free-state supporters had reluctantly come before Congress, but "when further developments of this system of tyranny were made—when the laws enacted by the legislature proved conclusively, to your memorialists, a determination to enslave the people," as freemen they relied upon their constitutional rights and resolved to "throw around themselves that protection which is afforded by a State government." In particular, the Topeka organization drew attention to statutes that zealously protected slavery. For instance, anyone who denied residents' rights to hold slaves was guilty of a felony and subject to two years of hard labor, while those who held antislavery views were ineligible for jury service. These laws denied free-state residents basic political and civil rights. In sum, antislavery activists found local government to be "a perfect failure." With endurance no longer a virtue, "they are compelled to resort to the only remedy left, that of forming a government for themselves...." The memorial asserted that bona fide territorial residents had ratified their path. Because free-state partisans believed most proslavery residents were Missouri residents, the fewer than 1,800 votes cast for the constitution were unimportant given the destruction of ballot boxes and absences prompted by military necessity. The turmoil of the summer lent credence to the argument that their territorial government would not or could not protect them.[68]

In defending the Topeka faction, Grow argued that the lack of an enabling act was irrelevant—Tennessee, Michigan, Arkansas, Florida, and Iowa had all called constitutional conventions without congressional action. Furthermore, he believed Kansas was close to meeting population requirements although other states had been admitted with small populations. For instance, Tennessee joined the Union with only 32,014 residents while Arkansas gained admission with even fewer at 25,671. Procedural questions were unimportant given the grievous wrongs suffered by free-state residents. Grow defended admission by noting that Kansas deserved special dispensation because of its residents' precarious position vis-à-vis the local government, a dire situation unprecedented in territorial history.[69]

The lack of strict standards governing admission meant that members could cite one aspect of a state's admission while conveniently neglecting other salient facts concerning the same state in any given debate. The Committee on Territories' majority and minority reports, which accompanied the Topeka Constitution, well illustrate the malleability of these data. For instance, Felix Zollicoffer (TN) disputed Grow's numbers in the minority report: both Tennessee and Arkansas, admitted in 1796 and 1836 respectively, became states when population requirements were far below the 93,420 required in 1856. Moreover, according to a 1795 territorial census (Grow referred to a 1790 census), Tennessee was admitted with a population of over 77,000 when representation required only 33,000; furthermore, when 47,000 was required, Arkansas had a population of 52,240 according to House documents. Thus, as examples of exceptions, Grow's numbers did not make the case for Kansas.[70]

The minority report also noted that, on average, most territories held that status for 12 to 13 years before becoming a state. Mississippi had been a territory for 19 years, Florida for 26, and Michigan for 32; yet Kansas came before Congress after only 2 years. "Besides, the population of Kansas is entirely too small, too sparsely scattered over the Territory, subject to too much fluctuation and instability, and in almost every way too little prepared to ... assume all the responsibilities of a State government."[71] Moreover, Zollicoffer took exception to the assertion that the Topeka Constitution demonstrated the free-state men were "men of ability, patriotism, and character, [shown] to be devoted to their country, and unmoved by sectionalism or fanaticism."[72] Instead he argued the constitution had been created by a disgruntled, antagonistic group armed "with a questionable list of grievances, and with a temper too impatient, or too prone to disorder, to await the redress of grievances which the due process of law and order are sure to accord to every portion of the American people."[73] On June 30, the House rejected the Topeka Constitution 106–107. However, on July 3, it reconsidered and narrowly accepted it 99 to 97.[74]

Lewis Cass (MI) had presented the constitution to the Senate in the spring, arguing "the worse the story a man has to tell, the more it is your duty to hear him."[75] It had a few ardent supporters such as Benjamin Wade (OH), who believed peace would be established in one hour if only the Senate would accept the constitution.[76] Similarly, William Seward advocated admission "simply because Kansas was held bound, hand and foot, under a foreign usurpation, at the feet of the President of the United States; and that her admission now was not only a necessary measure of relief and redress, but was the only practicable and adequate one." Admission would bring peace; protect property, life, and liberty; and bring Kansas into the Union as a free state. Seward defended the House bill against two main criticisms: against charges it reflected only one party, he contended that all had been invited to participate in the constitutional convention; against complaints that it did not allow changes for nine years, Seward weakly argued that he had not written it and thus could not be held responsible for that aspect.[77] John Crittenden (KY) rejected Seward's rationale. "Can we," he asked, "standing as arbiters of right and wrong between the contending parties in Kansas— all of them being our fellow-citizens—right the one by wronging the other, without a violation of the rights of one party?"[78] But Seward believed these problems were insignificant because Pierce "has perpetrated a *coup d'état*, by which the territorial constitution ... has been absolutely subverted. ..." Moreover, the president controlled all appointments, giving the people no relief to this tyranny.[79] However, there were insufficient like-minded Senators for the constitution to pass the upper house.

Yet the Senate was equally concerned with Kansas. In May and June, three resolutions amending the organizing act were offered, each a tacit acknowledgment of Congress's grave miscalculation in organizing Kansas and

Nebraska. The most important resolution was put forward by Lyman Trumbull (IL), who notified his colleagues in late May that he would introduce a bill to prevent civil war and restore peace in Kansas. On June 9, he announced a two-part plan: first, Nebraska would annex Kansas and extend its statutes over Kansans; second, all Kansas offices and laws would be abolished. Douglas directed debate over the Trumbull resolution, motivated by its attack on popular sovereignty and perhaps by a state rivalry. He was most troubled by Trumbull's negation of self-government, because passage would place Kansas residents under another territory's laws. While such an act would replace Missouri's influence for Nebraska's (seen as more neutral), the end result remained—outsiders would make decisions for Kansans. Trumbull defended his resolution as temporary and preferable to civil war. Moreover, self-government was illusory and imperfect anyway, as territorial residents did not elect their governor or other territorial officers. Douglas reminded Trumbull that such appointments were made by the Democratic Party, to which he belonged.[80] Trumbull countered that the party was divided: "I do not wish to call any harsh names, though I think there is very little Democracy in their ranks, and there are quite as many Democrats out of that organization as in it...."[81] By the summer of 1856, Kansas was taking its toll on party unity—certainly Douglas did not seem to recognize that his state's fellow senator had already defected to the Republican Party.

On June 30, a compromise, the Toombs Bill (S. No. 356), was presented, which followed Pierce's lead by focusing on a future constitutional convention. It provided for a new census to dissuade directed immigration and protect the ballot box; it recommended the president appoint five commissioners to oversee elections and process complaints; and it authorized a constitutional convention on November 1, after which statehood would be granted despite Kansas's insufficient population. Toombs acknowledged that his solution was expedient but believed haste was warranted.[82] When it was reported out of committee on June 30, Douglas lamented the extensive attention Congress had given this issue, complaining that of the 91 days the Senate had been in session, 37 had already been devoted to it.[83]

The beauty of the Toombs Bill was that it addressed territorial problems without forcing an ethical problem upon the senators—that of admitting a state under a constitution sponsored by an extralegal organization and unauthorized by the general populace. While William Bigler (PA) believed accepting the constitution would be wrong, he supported the Toombs Bill because it "strikes at the root of the evil, the source of, danger . . . ," the outside interference that had made Kansas "a kind of battle-ground between the slavery and anti-slavery feelings of the States. A vital object of the bill is to terminate that struggle. . . ."[84] Provided the president would select commissioners of sufficient standing and reputation to convince skeptical residents that their voting rights would be respected, the Toombs Bill was a reasonable solution.

Reluctant to embrace the compromise, other senators focused on the details. John Hale (NH) believed the bill was fair but lacked confidence in Pierce to appropriately implement its provisions. Henry Wilson expressed the same concern, emphasizing his distrust of the president. "I vote for no bill that puts power in his hands red with the blood of murdered people of Kansas." Wade agreed, arguing that Pierce would just appoint former senator David Atchison and Dr. Benjamin Stringfellow, Missouri's two most prominent proslavery activists, thus defeating the Toombs Bill's efforts to ensure a fair test of popular sovereignty.

In trying to move the Toombs Bill to a vote, Douglas summarized two main objections to it: (1) concerns over the appointment of commissioners; and (2) objections that voters previously driven from the territory would be unable to participate. Douglas offered an amendment allowing any individual allegedly driven away to return before October 1 and, after presenting appropriate evidence, to vote. Douglas's amendment was accepted. Wilson then offered one to nullify all of Kansas's legislation, thus ameliorating the failure of the Topeka Constitution by addressing its most critical element. However, the lack of support for the Topeka organization was reaffirmed by the Senate's overwhelming defeat of Wilson's amendment, 8 to 35.[85] But the Senate did approve the Toombs Bill 33 to 12 on July 2, the same day as the Howard Committee presented its report in the House.[86]

Democrats perceived the House defeat of the Toombs Bill as a direct indication that the Republicans were uninterested in peace. Given that it addressed the concerns raised by the Topeka government without embracing its illegal constitution, this was a fair charge. With an important election on the horizon, eliminating the Kansas problem and lessening the impact of Republican campaign propaganda was a high priority for the administration. As one Democrat argued, the House refused the bill "for the same reason that Horace Greeley hopes the 30,000 free state men, who are said to be in Kansas, will let the 5,000 pro-slavery men vote them down—to make a necessity for the election of [Republican candidate John C.] Frémont, to stanch the wounds of bleeding Kansas."[87] Democrats believed Republicans would not settle for anything other than direct capitulation to their demands. The Toombs Bill did not admit Kansas but was a significant compromise. It recognized that Congress needed to protect territorial residents in exercising their voting rights and admit Kansas as a state despite its inadequate population. However, if the opposition was too rigid to be appeased by thoughtful compromises like those represented by the Toombs Bill, how could an accommodation on Kansas be forged?

In the debate on the Topeka Constitution, compromise was undermined by the lack of standards governing the admission of states. Nine states (Ohio, Louisiana, Indiana, Illinois, Alabama, Minnesota, Michigan, Missouri, and Wisconsin) had submitted constitutions after congressional authorization. Four states (Tennessee, Arkansas, Florida, and Iowa) had been accepted despite bypassing congressional permission for a constitutional convention. Moreover, five states had never been territories and thus had unorthodox admissions to the Union. Vermont, Kentucky, and Maine were created from preexisting states, while California and Texas had had independent governments prior to statehood.[88] This autonomy allowed considerable flexibility without which, for instance, the Compromise of 1850 might not have been possible. On the other hand, it also meant Congress could not fall back on preexisting regulations when confronted with a politically sensitive situation.

The Crittenden Resolution and the Army Bill

Prior to Kansas's organization, Western troops had served as agents for immigrants, offering protection during encroachment of American Indian land. As settlement of Kansas turned violent, the military's role became more controversial. This new situation was confusing for both soldiers and settlers, as the military had not been trained to referee disputes between competing territorial residents. The troops were placed between the two factions, and approbation or condemnation of their actions depended entirely on political affiliation.

Pierce and his cabinet were equally conflicted over how to use the military in Kansas. Throughout his tenure as secretary of war, Jefferson Davis had been reluctant to deploy troops along the frontier, an unpopular attitude in the Indian Office, as Davis rarely filled Commissioner for Indian Affairs George Manypenny's requests for military support.[89] After the Wakarusa War of late 1855, military conflicts had escalated and the administration had been discomfited with how each faction tried to persuade federal troops to intervene on their behalf. More importantly, Governor Shannon had indicated that he could not hold Kansas together without troops but was uncomfortable acting as commander-in-chief. Davis supported the troops' removal not because he was sensitive to free-state criticism or uncomfortable with their use, but because he considered General William S. Harney's needs in defending the frontier more critical.[90]

In early June, Crittenden introduced a resolution that signaled the Senate's increased concern over territorial violence. Although the executive branch set military policy, the legislature had a special charge. "The subject is one full of responsibility for us. We are the unquestioned rulers of Kansas. We can throw off the great blame on no State government. We can throw off the blame nowhere," he argued. "It is upon us." Military forces should be "conducted with the greatest discretion and judgment," but the current predicament demanded an officer of "firmness and prudence, energy and conciliation," specifically General Winfield Scott, the commander of the Army, whom Crittenden requested be sent to Kansas to supervise military forces. He characterized Scott as a conciliator, a "man whose great name will speak trumpet-tongued for peace, and will do more than a thousand bayonets to put an end to these troubles. His words of reproof will be sharper than a sword to the refractory and the rebellious." Although this resolution might be perceived as encroaching on presidential prerogative, Crittenden suggested that the president needed prompting. While Pierce recognized how effective Scott could be in Kansas, he might hesitate to trouble such a great man with this minor endeavor.[91]

But Crittenden's timing was flawed, as party conventions had thinned Senate ranks by the time debate commenced on June 11. Few members wished to act under these circumstances, but opponents nonetheless waged a strong effort to bury the resolution. Isaac Toucey (CT), a strong administration man, headed the campaign, arguing the territorial "courts of justice" should address any problems since officials had been nominated by Pierce and confirmed by the Senate, which was "where all wrongs may be redressed."[92] However, as the Howard Committee's investigation demonstrated, an understanding of "justice" depended largely on political affiliation. The validity of Kansas laws, Seward argued, "divides this nation just as it divides Congress." The Senate sees them as "valid, obligatory, supreme, the law of the land." But the House sees territorial laws as "a tyranny, a fraud, a despotism, founded in usurpation." Similarly the South depicts them as "just, humane, merciful, constitutional, and it is treason to disobey them," while in the North "those laws are held and will be held to be unjust, tyrannical, unworthy of obedience, and the people who submit to them unworthy to be the brethren of the free people of the States of the American Union."[93] Given this wide breach, it might be best not to act. "The difficulties in Kansas have grown out of the discussions here to a very great extent," argued Stephen Adams (MS). "I do not believe that anything we can do will remedy the evil, and therefore I am unwilling to make any effort. In my opinion every effort that we make will only make the matter worse."[94] The Senate adjourned without disposing of the motion and did not return to it after the conventions. Although the Crittenden resolution came to naught, it indicated that some senators recognized that after the laissez-faire attitude of 1854 and 1855, legislative action might be necessary.

The debate over General Scott did affect Pierce indirectly. Rebuffed by his party at the Cincinnati Convention, the Crittenden resolution ensured that even though he would not be a candidate, questions over the president's performance as commander-in-chief entered the presidential contest. Where Pierce hesitated to deploy Scott, perhaps another president would be bolder. "The election of Millard Fillmore," one ardent supporter argued, "would put an end to Kansas fighting in a single day. If needful, he would march the entire army of the United States to that scene of blood, with the gallant Scott at its head. He would allow the actual settlers of that territory to settle its government for themselves; and, by exerting the influence of the government for the safety of that people, all strife would cease, and a full sweep be given to the energy and enterprise of settlers in all their free pursuits."[95] Pierce was unlikely to take this suggestion anyhow—the awkwardness of his 1852 victory over Scott (the Whig presidential candidate) aside, Davis and Scott had bickered throughout his administration. Thus, on June 27, Pierce tried to circumvent such suggestions by assigning Persifor F. Smith, commander of the Department of the West and a friend from the Mexican War, to Kansas. In doing so, Pierce emphasized that ending the violence and neutralizing it as an issue were imperative.[96]

On July 10, news arrived in the capital that Colonel Edwin V. Sumner had used federal troops to disperse the free-state legislature at Topeka. Rumors had circulated throughout the territory that proslavery forces planned an attack. As historian Samuel Johnson asserted, Sumner's actions were eminently logical given the situation: "To permit the legislature to be broken up by mob violence, or to permit a majority battle to be fought in its defense, would materially injure the Democratic prospects in the North. On the other hand, to permit it to meet under the protection of federal troops ... would appear in the South to be countenancing abolitionist revolution, and that was unthinkable."[97] On July 21, Davis concluded that given the circumstances, Sumner had acted within his orders even though Governor Shannon had not explicitly asked him to intervene.[98] On July 30, Davis reported to Pierce that no orders had been issued to prevent the meeting.[99] Yet having demonstrated a reluctance to intervene in civil affairs without explicit instructions during the Wakarusa War, Sumner was unlikely to have acted on his own initiative. Moreover, given Shannon's missteps over the previous nine months, it is doubtful that he would have had the confidence to order the move. While the administration disavowed Sumner's actions, the Senate requested relevant papers in late July. The papers exonerated Davis and Pierce and enabled the administration to elucidate their military policy, yet criticism continued unabated.

Meanwhile in the lower chamber, congressmen concerned with military affairs in the territory took a different tack. Administration opponents threatened to constrain Pierce's Kansas policy by withholding necessary funds through serious changes to the Army appropriation bill. This was risky, for insufficient appropriations could cripple the administration's domestic and foreign policies. By strangling the administration's ability to direct and arm troops, delicate campaigns extending beyond Kansas were imperiled: Harney's troops were deployed against the Cheyenne Indians, and civil law had been weakened in the West as martial law was in force in Washington and California, while Utah's renegade governor Brigham Young presented yet another challenge.[100] Despite disproportionate attention, Kansas was not the administration's only trouble spot.

However, the House opposition focused solely on Kansas. The Howard Committee's majority report was frequently cited in debates on the Army appropriation bill. On June 21, Schulyer Colfax (IN) announced he would amend the Army bill such that "no part of the military force of the United States shall be employed in aid of their enforcement; nor shall any citizen of Kansas be required, under their provisions, to act as a part of the *posse comitatus* of any officer acting as marshal or sheriff in said Territory."[101] Some critics argued the removal of the military would result in mob law, but Cumback disagreed because federal laws were automatically in force. Instead, the amendment balanced an activist, proslavery Pierce by preventing him "from continuing his crusade against the free-State men, by enforcing, with the Army of the United States, an abominable code of laws which they had no part in making—laws forced upon them by a Missouri mob."[102]

At the heart of this amendment was the question of whether the territorial legislature's legitimacy was a congressional concern. Stephens did not believe Congress had the right to determine any laws' validity, even those created by "a mere creature of Congress." Sherman disagreed, arguing that Congress had the right to intervene in territorial affairs by denying the president the funds to underwrite his policies. However, Sherman's support revealed an inherent conflict, for while he was unwilling to allow federal troops to enforce proslavery laws, he asked Pierce to deploy troops to protect travelers, disarm the militia, and prohibit "border ruffian" crossings.[103]

The amendment's supporters wanted to remove military influence from the settlement of political questions. "The purpose of the resolution is not to prevent the President of the United States from using the Army in Kansas, or elsewhere, for the preservation of peace," argued Lucian Barbour (IN), "but to prevent its use for the enforcement of the obnoxious laws of the self-styled Legislature of that Territory."[104] It is not clear how Barbour would separate troops' peacekeeping functions in Kansas from enforcement of the legislature's laws, especially given that some of the discord stemmed from the free-state faction's unwillingness to recognize its authority. However, antislavery activists persisted in viewing enforcement of those laws as a political act, whereas proslavery activists maintained the military was merely upholding federal laws in Kansas.

As chair of the Ways and Means Committee, Campbell protested that it was inappropriate to affect military policy by amending the appropriation bill since Congress had "no power to direct the movements of troops. That power belongs to the Secretary of War, under the law. If you would restrict his powers in this regard, the bill for that purpose should originate with the Committee on Military Affairs. . . ."[105] Others like John Quitman (MS) and Abram Wakeman (NY) believed the amendments raised constitutional questions about the government's divisions of power, and they were concerned that violence would increase if territorial laws were not enforced; even Seward believed withdrawing the military might encourage civil war.[106] The main argument, however, was over divining the true purpose of amending this bill. As one congressman argued, the opposition wanted to "stop the wheels of government. . . . The effect is revolution; and I will add, sir, moral treason to the country."[107] Because infringing upon Pierce's powers was of dubious constitutionality, opponents argued that Republicans were once again taking advantage of the Kansas chaos to push their agenda regardless of the likelihood of success or the constitutionality of their efforts.

On August 11, the Senate returned the Army appropriation bill to the House after eliminating all sections extraneous to military funding. It struck out that portion preventing the president from using the military to enact territorial laws and ordering Pierce to disarm the territory. Because the Senate would not support House amendments and the House refused to drop its provisions, Congress adjourned on August 18 without providing military funding.

That same day, Shannon resigned, leaving Pierce without a governor or necessary appropriations to stem the violence in Kansas. Throughout August, territorial violence was on the rise, and it was complicated by Acting Governor Woodson's August 25 declaration that Kansas was in open rebellion. Under these conditions, a fully supported army was imperative. Reflecting on the timing of the appropriations bill's failure, General Persifor Smith wrote Adjutant General Samuel Cooper, "There is a fact that has struck me as a coincidence, if nothing else, that the moment it was ascertained in Washington that the army appropriation bill would fail, the outrages and devastations of the party opposed to the laws here began as though they thought they could no longer have the army to interrupt them."[108] Thus on August 18, Pierce cited Indian troubles and the threat to public peace elsewhere in declaring that Congress's failure imperiled his ability to "perform his duty in relation to the common defense and security."[109] Thus, he called a special session, and on August 21 Congress convened to reconsider the Army appropriation bill.

That day, Pierce told Congress that without appropriations, the military could not provide transportation, equipment, munitions, or pay to soldiers in the field. Moreover, discharged soldiers would be unable to return home. To abandon American soldiers in this manner "would be to subject them to suffering and temptation, with disregard to the justice and right most derogatory to the Government." The president detailed current military challenges in Washington, Oregon, Texas, New Mexico, and Florida. "To refuse supplies to the Army," Pierce wrote Congress, "is to compel the complete cessation of all its operations, and its practical disbandment, and thus to invite hordes of predatory savages . . . to spread devastation . . . and to deliver up the sparse population of a vast tract of country to rapine and murder." Pierce concluded by suggesting that upon reflection, "every patriotic mind" would support an appropriation bill.[110]

The House remained steadfast. On August 22, they returned the same bill (H.R. No. 578) to the Senate, which once again granted the appropriations but struck out their limitations. The vote to accept the amendment was closer than earlier, but it still failed in the House 94 to 96. On the 27th, the House finally agreed to a conference where the same arguments about either the lawlessness of territorial residents or the terrors inflicted by the legislature were rehashed. Douglas accused opponents of inappropriate glee over forcing the president into a corner. "That mischief must result from the defeat of the general appropriation bill for the Army is a fact. That it must have a deranging and disorganizing effect on all the operations of that department of the Government, if it does not entirely paralyze them, is certainly true. That it must bring suffering and distress to a very large portion of the United States, is admitted by all. That it must bring discredit upon this country abroad, in the eyes of the whole civilized world, no one can question. Why, then, should this be a subject of rejoicing?"[111] Douglas complained that the Republicans wanted only to produce civil war in Kansas.

On August 28, the conference committee failed to agree and the House again voted (101 to 97) to reject the Senate's version. The Senate voted to keep its version 32 to 6 and proposed another conference.[112] Under administration pressure and Douglas's arguments that James Lane was merely awaiting the Army bill's defeat to invade the territory with his "Army of the North," the House buckled.[113] On August 30, it concurred to the Senate's removal of its proviso that Army appropriations could not be used to enforce territorial laws, 101 to 98.[114]

Although Pierce ultimately forced Congress to adopt an Army appropriations bill without limitations, the contretemps was costly. Not only was Pierce's ability to fund the military affected, but the administration was deeply embarrassed and angered by the legislature's effort to coerce executive policy. As Smith had argued during the debates, the opposition had risked national security by refusing to fund the military. The Republican Party's desire to seek redress for perceived persecution of antislavery proponents in Kansas seemed unbounded by larger concerns. Here, finally, was an issue for the Democratic presidential campaign, which had been on the defensive all year, to seize. Campaign documents carefully drew parallels between the House opposition and the disunionists of 1812.

> Both attempted to embarrass the Government into compliance with their purposes, by stopping the supplies necessary to national defence. The Disunionists of 1812, by defeating the War loan. The Disunionists of 1856, by withholding the pay of the officers, soldiers and artificers, and thus disbanding the army.
>
> The object of the one was the repeal of the act declaring war against Great Britain.
>
> The object of the other was the repeal of the act authorizing the admission of Kansas with a free or slave constitution.
>
> Are not their purposes identical, and should you not fellow citizens sacrifice your party differences now, as your fathers did then, to the peace of the country and the duration of the Union?[115]

The Army bill proved important in the 1856 election and emphasized the deep gulf between the parties. Moreover, it demonstrated that even a divided Congress could set the agenda on issues entirely within the president's purview.

Conclusion

By December 1855, it was evident that popular sovereignty had not settled the slavery question for the nation. Instead, passions were aroused to an even greater extent in the rush to secure the territory for freedom or for slavery.

Kansas was overcome by chaos and either the executive branch or the legislative branch had to act to prevent civil war. Although Pierce had made the Kansas-Nebraska Bill a party measure, responsibility for its passage rested squarely on Congress. Similarly, Pierce had made mistakes in directing the territorial government and was responsible for part of the resultant trouble, but he had urged Congress to calm tensions by passing an enabling act allowing residents to proceed toward statehood legally. However, Congress proved too divided to enact genuine reform for Kansas, both in party and in temperament across the upper and lower houses.

The Democratic Party approached the legislative session hoping to restore the luster lost during the electoral campaign and territorial difficulties of 1855. As Congressman John Wright argued in March 1856, "The Democratic party have been charged, here and elsewhere, as being factious and disorderly and disposed to break over and trample down law...."[116] Wright hoped the party would disprove these charges during the congressional session, but as the summer progressed, the reputation of the Democratic Party continued to decline. In May, Brooks attacked Sumner in an act so reprehensible it garnered notice throughout the Union and abroad.

> That a Senator should be assailed not in the heat of debate, by one of his fellows, but deliberately and of malice purpose, brutally beaten to the earth by a member of the lower house, for language uttered in his senatorial capacity, and stamped as Parliamentary by the acquiescence of all who listened to it,— this is a feature so new and strange in the aspect of political affairs beyond the Atlantic, that too great importance can scarcely be attached to it as significant of a state of feeling in America, upon which no Englishman can look with indifference. Not less significant is the dread reality of armed strife now raging between citizens of the Northern and Southern sections of the Union upon the plains of the Territory of Kansas.[117]

Sumner's caning was hardly a party measure, but it reflected negatively on Democrats and underscored popular myths about Southerners and their culture of violence. On the heels of Sumner's caning in the Senate—violence which mirrored all too clearly the violence in Kansas Territory—came news of other excesses. "William Smith, an ex-Governor of VA and member of the House, assailed and beat the Editor of the *Evening Star* in the street outside the House; Albert Rust, a House member from AK, did the same to the editor of the NY *Tribune* in the grounds of the Capitol after leaving the House; Philemon T. Herbert, of Alabama, and a member from CA, shot and killed an Irish waiter at Willards and is awaiting trial; In 5 months: 'four flagrant breaches of the peace on the part of members of Congress who were born and bred in slave States, and who are necessarily, demoralized by that institution...."[118] If the party could not control their own members in the capitol, how could they control inchoate Democrats in Kansas? To blunt such criticism, Democrats were reduced to describing Republican presidential candidate John Frémont as a "cool calculating, revenge-seeking duellist."[119] Although there were sufficient atrocities in Kansas to tar both factions, the Democrats were less able to distance themselves from the violence or from the charges of indifference.

The Republican Party tried to press the administration on the Kansas issue in Congress, but its members were disproportionately concentrated in the House. Without the cooperation of other parties, Republicans could not push genuine change. Although they were unable to parlay their victories in the House (the repudiation of Whitfield, passage of the Topeka Constitution, and embarrassment of the president by withholding military funds) into the White House in 1856, they demonstrated augmenting strength and spread their message throughout the North without much difficulty or expense. Moreover, the party's ability to keep the Kansas issue front and center of the national debate contributed to their considerable growth over this election year. Ultimately, however, House Republicans were uninterested in any solutions for Kansas short of immediate admission under the Topeka Constitution.

Perhaps the greatest obstacle to congressional compromise was that the debate over slavery had degenerated too much to be withstood by a fractured Congress. This was especially so given that 1856 was an election year and the legislative debates were a forum to establish the issues for the forthcoming presidential contest. In the days of the greatest national compromises in the 1830s, the two-party system was at its strongest. Even the Compromise of 1850 was forged by two clearly defined parties. By mid-decade, however, party politics had fragmented. With the decline of the Whigs and the confusion of the Know-Nothings, the continuing ascendancy of the Republican Party spurred a political realignment. However, compromise requires parity to succeed and although the Republican Party was on the rise, it had not yet solidified sufficiently to add weight to a congressional compromise. Moreover, it was unclear whether either side would agree to the concessions compromise requires.

In October 1855, William Seward predicted that if Southerners, "in a season of madness," seceded from the Union, threats of a "servile war" would quickly bring them back.[120] Such a season did not arise in 1856; however, the tumultuous 34th Congress presented its own version of madness to the nation. Charged by the president with ameliorating conditions in the territory,

Congress did not respond constructively. The Senate was unable to persuade the House to agree to the one true compromise of the session—the Toombs Bill, which would have settled existent constitutional questions. However, by rejecting the Topeka Constitution without arranging for a substitute, Congress fomented the agitation. The extensive debate prompted by the Whitfield-Reeder conflict and the Howard Committee inflamed public opinion. Even the more innocuous and ineffective resolutions, like the Crittenden Resolution regarding General Scott, contributed to the factious discourse of the electoral season. Ultimately, Congress helped neither the president nor territorial residents. And with solutions in short supply in both the executive and legislative branches, attention turned to the election of 1856.

5

The 1856 Presidential Campaign and Kansas as a Party Issue

On the national stage, the fall of 1855 had seen a mad scramble to unite, disband, or consolidate parties in preparation for upcoming state elections and the 1856 presidential election. Many politicians were confounded by the fluidity of the parties; others were stranded by platform changes but were hesitant to abandon weakened parties and appear disloyal. "Fickleness in political associations is a weakness, and precipitancy in public action is a crime," Senator William Seward (NY) noted in October 1855. "Considered by itself, it is unfortunate to be obliged to separate from an old party, and to institute a new one."[1] In this atmosphere, he urged Whig compatriots to join the Republican Party, for now was the time for "a bold, out-spoken, free-spoken organization."[2] For those concerned with freedom and "the dereliction of Congress and the Treachery of the President of the United States," only the Republican Party could rectify the administration's failures in Kansas Territory.[3] Indeed, it superbly negotiated this transition, transforming itself from a fringe party into a formidable organization.

The Republican Party's success derived in great part from the government's difficulties in controlling the chaos in Kansas. President Franklin Pierce was damaged by his laissez-faire attitude. In fact, he came to rue his decision to ask the first governor, Andrew Reeder, to postpone his departure to Kansas for six months. Moreover, Pierce's delay in removing his incompetent governor allowed Reeder to transform himself into a sympathetic free-state figure, embraced as a martyr sacrificed to encroaching proslavery forces. Although Pierce dismissed Reeder for malfeasance, free-state partisans insisted such charges merely masked the president's true rationale, a need to kowtow to the slave South.[4] Although necessary and justifiable, Reeder's removal came too late to pacify residents angered by electoral fraud. Further, the Democratic Party was tarred as so committed to making Kansas a slave state that it would ignore electoral violence and accept a territorial legislature chosen by "border ruffians" from nearby Missouri who were stripping their opponents' rights such that "mob-law is in the ascendant."[5] Once Reeder joined the free-state movement, his previous actions such as allowing the dismissal of free-state men elected in a May 1855 special election without comment were ignored. Although Reeder's greed directly led to his dismissal, it infuriated those who questioned why he was fired when other equally suspect territorial officials were retained.

Reeder was not an exemplary free-state spokesman, but he became a pivot during the 1855 elections. Senator Charles Sumner (MA), for instance, contrasted Pierce's refusal to support Reeder with his willingness to enforce the fugitive slave law. "Though prompt to lavish the Treasury, the Army and the Navy of the Republic, in hunting a single slave through the streets of Boston," Sumner charged in November, "he could see the Constitution and laws which he was sworn to protect, and those popular rights which he had affected to promote, all struck down in Kansas, and then give new scope of these invaders by the removal of the faithful Governor—who had become obnoxious to the Slave Oligarchy because he would not become their tool. . . ."[6] Throughout the fall campaign, Pierce's Kansas decisions became a crucial electoral issue that would be honed during the 1856 presidential campaign into a central strategy for the Republican Party around which other presidential contenders had to maneuver.

Within the territory, the proslavery faction recognized they were losing the propaganda war, and some chose to pursue a less offensive strategy. Considered extremely partisan, Surveyor-General John Calhoun nonetheless attempted to forge a "state's rights" party to gather proslavery partisans, free-state Democrats, and Whigs. By doing so, he hoped to strengthen the national party, and as he wrote in late November 1855, to repudiate "the extravagant follies of Atchison and Co."[7] But initial efforts at moderation suffered a setback in Wakarusa in December when it became clear that conflict was imminent. Even the most vehement proponent of a slave Kansas recognized the dangers. "If you attack Lawrence now," former Senator David Atchison (MO) warned, "you attack it as a mob, and what would be the result? I tell you it would cause the election of an abolition President, and the ruin of the Democratic party."[8] Although Governor Wilson Shannon's dubious diplomacy averted the feared skirmish, as 1855 came to a close the Kansas issue continued to ferment.

Party Politics

Kansas entered the national consciousness mired in controversy, and two years later it continued unabated. Had Kansas's settlement been as quiet as

Nebraska's, Pierce might have mitigated the hullabaloo that had erupted over the Kansas-Nebraska Act. However, the 1854–1855 territorial disarray ensured the nation's focus remained on Kansas precisely when political parties jockeyed for position for the next presidential election. After devastating Kansas-tinged losses in the 1854 midterm elections, the Democratic Party rebounded after Pierce initiated a campaign against the Know-Nothings, stripping them of federal patronage. As a result, the party had reacquired Pennsylvania, Indiana, Illinois, Wisconsin, and New Jersey.[9] However, success was short-lived, as a new and more formidable foe presented itself.

By the end of 1855, a mere 18 months into Kansas's existence, territorial divisions were clear, and the coming year only made the national ramifications of these issues more stark in the minds of voters. A preview of the presidential campaign was seen in Congress as a deeply divided House of Representatives was unable to organize. Already demonstrating national strength, Republicans forced round after round of voting for speaker. After weeks of wrangling, "in truth," the *Charleston Mercury* noted, "the House is at sea. No one can predict the time of organization, or the Speaker. This, however, is certain; that Abolitionism is at the bottom of the strife, and that a Freesoiler will be chosen."[10] Indeed, the paper reported that Republican Nathaniel Banks showed surprising strength, and as Sumner summarized when the new year began with the position still vacant, the "Slave Oligarchy now says, 'anybody but Banks.'"[11] However, after eight weeks of gridlock, Banks triumphed when the House agreed to a plurality vote, which he won. He had been regularly polling 105 votes before the membership agreed to change the rules; this crucial demonstration of "unity & organization," Sumner wrote, would "affect the country more than any speech. It is an *act*, which you know is better than *words*."[12] Although he correctly stated that Banks's election was better than words, the speakership allowed Republicans to flood Congress with a plethora of words during the presidential campaign. This crucial victory allowed Republican agitation on the Kansas issue before Congress and the public throughout 1856. Without Banks's ability to make committee assignments, the Republican Party would have not have had the power to place the administration and its party on the defensive.

The Democrats

As the territorial troubles of the winter settled into an uneasy truce, the Democratic Party was forced to deal with Kansas. Pierce defined the party line in January 24 and February 11 messages that blamed Reeder and the free-state faction for the turmoil. He asserted that the conflict within Kansas was "between lawless violence on the one side and conservative force on the other, wielded by legal authority of the general government."[13] Pierce's indictment of Reeder, now the standard-bearer for the Topeka faction as its territorial delegate to the House of Representatives, clearly indicated his administration would remain deaf to free-state pleas to overturn the electoral results and rebuff the territorial legislature. Reeder was understandably outraged by being singled out for censure, but his reply indicated the Topeka faction expected such behavior from an executive "unmoved by a single sympathy in favor of an unoffending people innocent of all wrong."[14] Although Pierce defended his Kansas decisions, his messages reveal a sensitivity to the criticism and heralded a national campaign in which the party in power had to justify its territorial actions rather than run on its accomplishments.

Even without the opposition's ability to keep the territory before the nation in House debates over the contested delegate seat, the Topeka Constitution, and Army appropriations, the issue of Kansas was amply disseminated by Republican newspapers. The turmoil of 1856 provided journalists with plenty of grist to publicize, and broadsheets like the *New York Tribune* ensured constant coverage and criticism. "All the gas for Republican balloons is manufactured in Kansas," one Democrat complained. "They kill men and bring them to life two or three times over just to suit the market."[15] Such charges were difficult to refute, and even the few retractions or corrections that appeared were inevitably buried beneath yet more sensationalized news. Moreover, the 1854 uproar over the Kansas-Nebraska Act had had a tinge of religious fervor, and by 1856 Kansas became a modern crusade. "That [the Crusades] was a Holy war; so is this," Joseph C. Lovejoy asserted. "That was preached up by a flaming St. Peter,—St. Bernard and their associates. This crusade is fanned into flame, by St.-Henry-Ward-Rifle-Killam-Beecher, and his associates. 'They mistook' then, says the historian, 'the enthusiastic shouts of madness and folly for the approbation of God.' So they do now."[16] Senator James A. Pearce (MD) similarly described Republican presidential candidate John Frémont as motivated by the same feeling "which animated the preacher who proposed to supply the brethren in Kansas with bread and *powder* too, and which has stimulated other preachers and their congregations to subscribe Sharpe's rifles as the most efficacious instrument in the adjustment of the controversies in that Territory, which all good men deplore, however they may differ as to the causes of the unhappy anarchy which prevails there."[17] The infusion of morality into the conflict made such propaganda difficult to counter and placed the Democratic Party in an unenviable position—emphasizing policy of dubious efficacy while their opposition emphasized principle.

Throughout the year, they remained on the defensive. The Democratic National Committee issued a *Democratic Hand-Book* to regain the initiative by tarring House Republicans with disloyalty, comparing their actions with those of the 1812 disunionists.[18] On the campaign trail, partisans disassociated the party from the Kansas debacle: "The Democratic party is no more responsible for the evil passions exhibited in Kansas than they are for the excessive rains that spoiled so many hundred tons of hay in Maine."[19] The party defended its record, deflecting criticism by emphasizing the free-state party's tendency to exaggerate. The Republican method, one Democratic booster remarked, was to make their party "the scapegoat of all that was wrong, or imagined to be wrong anywhere, or with any body; every Kansas row, real or of newspaper fabrication, was attributed to unwise legislation of the *Democratic* party, or the maladministration of the Democratic executive."[20]

In Congress, members emphasized they were answering Pierce's call to find a solution. Congressional Democrats were not indifferent to the plight of Kansans; for instance, the Toombs Bill might have settled the question of admission, but Republicans more concerned with politics than solutions had blocked it by continuing to push the Topeka Constitution. "There what could the Senate do more?" Joseph C. Lovejoy inquired. "Why did not the House accept and pass it? . . . The Republicans are orphans. The fountain of their tears is dry. That must be a sad cause which rejoices in domestic strife and flourishes when fed on fraternal blood."[21] Indeed, press coverage was so extensive that it even caused some to question their assumptions. "The wild and irrational ravings of the abolition press proper was supposed to be confined to a few fanatics," the *New Orleans Bulletin* wrote, "small in number and despicable in character, and by no means representing the opinions of the Northern people in the aggregate. Most unfortunately, different impressions begin to prevail. We cannot beguile ourselves any longer with such delusive hopes . . . this feeling of hostility to the institution of slavery, and to the section of country where it exists, is getting to be wide-spread, bitter and insatiable."[22]

In order to shift the focus from Kansas, Democrats highlighted opponents' weaknesses. New York Democrats, for instance, emphasized their problematic approach to the slavery issue. "They [Abolitionists] ask for congressional intervention on the assumed ground that slave-holding, under all circumstances, is absolutely incompatible with religion, as well as republican principles; so much so indeed that government cannot innocently *let it alone*! And when told that the constitution was fashioned upon a different theory," Albany's Nicholas Hill argued, "they admit and lament the fact, exalt themselves above the constitution, above the government, and appeal to a 'higher law!' The light by which our fathers walked and toiled will not do for them."[23] The administration operated lawfully in Kansas; other parties pushed beyond American laws and institutions in service to their beliefs. Nonetheless, the Kansas-Nebraska Act, which the Pennsylvania Democrats called a "work of patriotic sacrifice," would be pivotal in 1856, for, as Senator William Bigler (PA) argued at his state's convention, "on this broad ground [the rights of the people in a territory], they [Abolitionists] intend to contest the next Presidential election."[24]

The first question Democrats had to address was who would be their candidate. An obvious choice was the incumbent and Pierce still had his supporters, especially in the South. Thomas W. Thomas (GA), for instance, claimed he would best serve Southern interests because Kansas was clearly "the very turning point of the battle between the North and the South which has raged for 35 years." Pierce was the most committed to a slave Kansas, having "cast in his lot with the South and he must sink or swim with us."[25] But others recognized that however well he served the region, his candidacy simply was not viable. Indeed, reelection would require enormous effort, especially in a North still seething from the Kansas-Nebraska Act. Hannibal Hamlin (ME) dismissed Pierce's chances in early January. "He has been used, and is now to be thrown away, as we do a lemon after we have squeezed it. . . ."[26] Indeed, as Alexander Stephens (GA) explained, Pierce's appointment of former Free Soilers to federal office had alienated many members; further, having "'shot down' all the true friends of the Kansas Bill in the Northern States two years ago—not with gunpowder it is true but with executive patronage by putting their enemies in power over their necks and heads," he would not be renominated.[27]

Pierce had so few friends that a second term seemed impossible. Indeed, an opposition song entitled "Franklin Pierce's Farewell" well captured the dilemma his policies created:

> Farewell to the chair which has lent me its glory!
> Farewell to the party which leaves me in shame!
> It abandons me now; but the page of its story
> The feeblest and blackest is linked with my name.
> I have warred with the North, which vanquished me only
> When the light of the slave-owner allured me too far;
> I have battled with freedom, yet, wretched and lonely,
> I'm left without even one feeble hurrah.

> Farewell to thee, South!—with thy chivalry round me,
> I promised thy slave-flag should cover the land;
> But thy weakness decrees I should leave as I found thee,
> —Decayed in thy glory—thy wealth on the sand
> O for the fast-fleeting hours that were wasted
> In idle endeavor to frighten the North!
> O, would that the cane of your Brooks had been blasted
> Before it had scattered my party like froth![28]

With Pierce so weak, the time seemed propitious for Senator Stephen Douglas (IL), the force behind the Kansas-Nebraska Act. However, critics faulted the party's tendency to conciliate the South and nominate doughfaces. "Of late years the South have adopted the policy of nominating Northern men with Southern principles," John Read asserted, "and to them has virtually been given the privilege of selecting the candidate, and announcing the principles upon which his administration is to be conducted. Thus, though in a decided minority, by always acting as a united force, they have secured to themselves the whole power of shaping the policy of the government."[29] However, as another observer noted, the utility of doughfaces may have passed. "The illustration presented in the case of Pierce, with his throat cut and his back broken, may be worth something."[30] However, Democrats again bypassed Douglas and selected another Northerner, but one with greater Southern ties and without his liabilities.

The groundwork for James Buchanan's elevation began with his home state's convention. In an amusing hodgepodge of mythmaking, Pennsylvania Democrats presented Buchanan as "the log cabin boy, with the laughing cheek and open brow" who rebuked the British monarchy with his "plain and simple dress of an American gentleman."[31] They emphasized his early support for Andrew Jackson, the party's most famous president, while Buchanan's 1836 statement that "the older I grow, the more inclined I am to be what is called a states rights man,"[32] was recalled to make him even more palatable to Southerners. As the *Cincinnati Commercial*'s Murat Halstead wrote, Buchanan could "combine the radical and conservative sections of the party North and South, while his great caution, extreme respectability, and Federal antecedents will secure to him a large body of the Whigs, the debris and rubbish of defunct organizations, and other fossil remains—the deposits of previous political revolutions. . . ."[33]

Buchanan had long wanted to be president and after his 1852 disappointment, he found himself in a great position across the Atlantic when prominent Democrats took stock of potential candidates. After dismissing Pierce and his cabinet as candidates, Howell Cobb assured Buchanan his chances were excellent since he was "not the strongest but perhaps the only man that can succeed in 1856.... First, you have been absent from the country during this bitter Nebraska contest and are not therefore complicated with it personally."[34] Unlike Pierce, Buchanan's lengthy record of public service was distinguished. In addition to serving in both houses of Congress, he had been secretary of state and minister to both Russia and Great Britain.

Yet this very record opened him to charges of ambition and excessive proslavery sentiment, and Republicans relentlessly portrayed Buchanan as devious and ruthless. The sardonic pamphlet *Justice to "Buck,"* for instance, depicted him as utterly lacking in principle: "if it was dangerous to stand at the front of a great issue, why, he prudently got behind it; and if that would not do, he was not too indolent to travel around it again and again, knowing well that time never fails to point out the true policy and road to popular favor, or that death was a common leveler, and that great issues, like great men, had some day to die of themselves, then they could be spoken of with more safety and without giving offense!"[35] But Buchanan's diplomatic ability was what most recommended him, as many Democrats believed Pierce's relative inexperience had contributed to his difficulties. Thus, they eagerly embraced his record.

In accepting the nomination in June, Buchanan pledged to use presidential "power and influence" in a "firm but conciliatory spirit, during the single term I shall remain in office, to restore the same harmony among the sister States which prevailed before this apple of discord, in the form of slavery agitation, had been cast into their midst."[36] The Democratic platform on which Buchanan would run was familiar, especially its insistence that the slavery issue be removed from Congress, and its support for the 1850 compromise measures. Yet in a reflection of the challenge posed by the newest party, the platform pledged to "more distinctly meet the issue on which a sectional party, subsisting exclusively on slavery agitation, now relies to test the fidelity of the people...." Thus, the platform defined the "paramount issue" as "preservation of the Union." To that end, Democrats deplored those who "seek to embroil the States and incite to treason and armed resistance to law in the Territories" and recognized the right of territorial residents to form a state regardless of the nature of its constitution. Although Pierce had been jettisoned in favor of Buchanan, the platform defended his policy with "unqualified approbation."[37]

The selection of John C. Breckinridge as the vice presidential candidate was a key concession to those who had preferred Douglas. Kentucky had not voted Democratic since 1828, and selecting a native son helped ensure the state's support in a contest where every electoral vote would be crucial. After Maine was carried by the Republicans in September, Breckinridge urged Pennsylvania managers to unite and work together, for without that state "I fear that violence will not be confined to the plains of Kansas." He also undertook an important and unprecedented campaign though Indiana, Ohio, Michigan, and Pennsylvania to help his party. In speeches such as one at Tippecanoe, Indiana, Breckinridge emphasized moderation, arguing that the South did not want to spread slavery throughout the territories.[38] Although Republicans had made slavery a national question, Democrats hoped to refocus on what they considered the central issue: the growth of slavery in the territories.

Democrats emphasized that the differences between Nebraska, "which is equally subject to all these historical influences, as tranquil as a summer lake," and Kansas was due to the fact that the former had not "been taken into the keeping of the emigrant aid societies and Sharp's-rifle Christians."[39] Their central strategy was to emphasize the Republican Party's radicalism. Democrats collected Republicans' inflammatory statements in one pamphlet to emphasize the lengths to which they were willing to go to abolish slavery. For instance, one Republican cherished hopes that "a *civil war* may soon burst upon the country. I want to see American slavery abolished in my day—it is a legacy I have no wish to leave to my children . . . and when the time arrives for the streets of this 'land of the free and home of the brave' *to run with blood to the horses' bridles*, if the writer of this be living, there will be one heart to rejoice at the retributive justice of Heaven. This, of course, will be treason in the eyes of the doughfaces in this land."[40] Rash statements from Republican congressmen—like Banks who said he was willing to let the Union "slide"; Joshua Giddings (OH), who looked forward to a servile insurrection to "hail it as the dawn of a political millennium"; or Gerrit Smith (NY), who yearned to learn of a "collision at Topeka" that should lead to "the gratifying intelligence that the northern States have arrayed themselves against the Federal Government in Kansas"[41]—worried Democrats already inclined to believe that Republicans threatened the Union's stability. Such speeches demonstrate a remarkable disregard for the demands of civil war, for the difficulty of conflict, and for the ramifications of creating the blood-drenched scenarios many abolitionist speeches advocated. Yet despite efforts to publicize these aims and the threat of civil war should a Republican win, Democrats were in danger of losing the presidential election.

The Republicans

Banks's elevation to the speakership eased the path for Republicans in determining the issues for the election. According to Sumner, the Kansas debate began in earnest when Senator Henry Wilson (MA) denounced Shannon in chambers and advocated his removal in February. Yet, despite harsh criticism and a damning review of his record and qualifications, Shannon was confirmed. Afterwards, Sumner stated, "you will hear nothing but Kansas from this time forever. . . ."[42] The Republican campaign gained momentum, as territorial developments that spring suited antislavery advocates who had been waiting to press their agenda. "For a time," Sumner wrote, "my desire has been to make an issue with the Slave oligarchy; & provided this can be had, I am indifferent to the special point selected. Of course, at this moment Kansas is the inevitable point. In protecting this territory against tyranny we are driven to battle with the tyrants, who are the Oligarchs of Slavery."[43] The Republican Party quickly comprehended that the territorial disarray and Pierce's missteps offered a golden opportunity, especially since their control of the House allowed for constant criticism of the president.

In late February, the Republican National Mass Meeting issued a 50-page report devoted to Kansas wherein delegates unanimously agreed "(1) to repeal all laws for the introduction of slavery into the territories, (2) to admit Kansas as a free state, and (3) to overthrow the Administration for its reprehensible conduct of the Kansas question."[44] Not surprisingly, they followed this initial salvo with a platform indicting Pierce for his conduct and pledging the rescue of Kansans whose "dearest Constitutional rights . . . have been fraudulently and violently taken from them." The platform issued at the Republican national convention in June reiterated charges party members had repeatedly levied against the administration throughout congressional debates. They charged that Kansas events happened "with the knowledge, sanction, and procurement" of Pierce's administration and so constituted a "high crime against the Constitution, the Union, and humanity . . ." for which they would seek appropriate punishment. Thus, the party advocated Kansas's immediate admission under the Topeka Constitution.[45] Congressional Republicans had been pursuing this course for months; in March Sumner had embraced it as "something practical; and on this we must fight the Presidential election."[46] Ultimately, they could not score any significant legislative victories, but then they had not anticipated success. Rather, as the *New York Tribune* indicated, "it does not follow that their efforts in behalf of those provisos were in vain. . . . The Issues are fairly made up. Their decision rests with the people."[47] Indeed, keeping the issues before the public was the significant victory.

The connection between Kansas and the Republican Party was underscored by the political ties between John Frémont, a leading contender for the nomination, and Charles Robinson, with whom he shared a background in California politics. Although then a Whig while Frémont was loosely tied to the Democratic Party, Robinson had been one of his "most determined supporters in the California Legislature."[48] Throughout the campaign, Frémont exchanged letters with Robinson expressing his intense devotion to an antislavery Kansas. One such letter was reprinted in the *New York Tribune*. Frémont wrote that he expected Congress to highlight the truth about Kansas and "neither you nor I can have any doubt what verdict the People will pronounce" once they understand. "It is to be feared, from the proclamation of the President, that he intends to recognize the usurpation in Kansas as the legitimate government, and that its sedition law, the test oath, and the means to be taken to expel its people as aliens, will all directly or indirectly be supported by the army of the United States."[49] Written by Frémont's advisers, these letters were carefully orchestrated to publicize his alliance with Robinson. "Frémont is for *doing something*, which alone can save Kansas," the *New York Tribune* editorialized, "the others are for *keeping quiet*, which is to give her up to eternal Slavery and oppression. Between active correction and passive acquiescence the real issue lies."[50] In addition, this correspondence further disseminated a major Republican contention—that Pierce's Kansas policies constituted a failure of democracy enforceable only with military force. The events of the spring and summer aided the party in publicizing this message. After the sack of Lawrence, the summer was marked by intermittent warfare in the midst of which Colonel Edwin V. Sumner disbanded the Topeka legislature. This ensured that Frémont was seen as a last hope for besieged free-state settlers, and his supporters adamantly insisted that his defeat would be disastrous for the country.

As the *New York Evening Post* stated, the struggle thus far "will be but pastime and holiday sport in comparison to what will follow. . . . We have often seen the public mind agitated by political controversies, but we have never seen the moral nature of the people moved as it is moved now."[51] Summer events were a political boon for Republicans, and the territory's famous free-state prisoners understood their contributions. Henry H. Williams, for instance, urged his correspondents to publish news of his arrest for treason after the Pottawatomie massacre in the local paper for "political effect" and to "come to my assistance by voting for Fremont and Freedom" as "our oppressors are working scheming & fighting for its continuance in power with Buchanan for a leader & slavery for a motto they are trying to ride rough shod over the free men of Kansas."[52] George W. Brown, the editor of the *Herald of Freedom*, also sat in an Army camp that summer on charges of treason but was buoyed by the positive aspects of his arrest and the destruction of his press at Lawrence. "The prospects of Kansas were never brighter to me than at present. With our presses destroyed, our principal citizens fugitives and outlaws, else deprived of their freedom. This, at the first appearance, to the superficial observer, a gloomy aspect; but look again; the presses now apparently silent are speaking in thunder tones and arousing a notion to action. Cast your eyes over the Northern States and there never was a time when the people were so determined in defending the rights as now. There is but one voice in the North, and that is for freedom."[53] Those jailed for treason were not at serious risk—one prisoner reassured his correspondent that federal soldiers would "aime too high to inflict injuries" if forced to fire upon them—but they were nonetheless a powerful symbol of Democratic oppression.[54]

Campaign documents further underscored the complicity of Pierce and the Democrats. One such publication, *The Reign of Terror in Kanzas: By Which Men Have been Murdered and Scalped; Ministers of the Gospel Tarred and Feathered; Women Dragged from their Homes and Violated; Printing Offices and Private Houses Burned; Citizens Robbed, &c., by Border Ruffians*, declared these events were "encouraged by President Pierce, and Carried out By the Southern Slave Power." This pamphlet was filled with purple prose lifted from Kansas proslavery papers. A quote from the *Squatter Sovereign*, known as David Atchison's paper, underscored the venality of the actors against freedom in Kansas and their extremist positions, all of which explicitly tied them directly to the Democratic Party. "We are determined to repel this Northern invasion, and make Kansas a *Slave State*; though our rivers should be colored with the *blood of the victims*, and the carcasses of *dead abolitionists* should be so numerous in the Territory, as to bread disease and sickness, we will not be deterred in our purpose. Let those who desire GRAVES in Kanzas, engage in this unholy and unjust war against the *extension* of our BELOVED INSTITUTION, that is now being waged against the South by the fanatics of the North."[55] Although Pierce had not acted personally in Kansas, prominent Democrats such as Atchison and Kansas Territorial Delegate John Whitfield had, and the accusation that Whitfield, for instance, actively led "border ruffian" posses following the sack of Lawrence hurt Democrats. Indeed, the party was ill-served by these men and others such as Congressman Preston Brooks (SC), who retaliated for perceived slights against his state and relative, Senator Andrew Butler (SC), by attacking Sumner in chambers in a bloody spectacle that riveted the nation.

Republican campaign documents selectively excerpted from the most reactionary Democratic papers to imply that Democrats were frightened of change and progress. For instance, a selection from the *South Side Democrat* was most likely chosen to portray the party as a relic reduced to clinging to old ideas. "We have got to hating everything with the prefix *free*," one editorial opined, "from free negroes down and through the whole catalogue, free farms, free labor, free society, free will, free thinking, free children and free schools, all belonging to the same brood of *damnable isms*."[56] One frequent tactic of Republican propagandists was contrasting the youth and vigor of Frémont with the maturity of Buchanan. "Poor Old Buck" presented the Democrat as too exhausted to be of use: "There is an old donkey, a worn-out Jack / Too old to live very long / He has no bone in the middle of his back / Where the bones *ought* to grow very strong. . . . . What's the *use* of a nag with so many bad ways / So stubborn, so old, and so slow? / The best we can do is turn him out to graze / In the fields where the short grasses grow."[57] On the other hand, another song, "The Four Years' Race," left voters in no doubt a better option existed. For while "slavery's load had strained his [Buchanan's] back," there was no need to fear. "For freedom's colt is training / For a few days, a few days / He'll run without spur or reigning: O, take 'Buck' home!"[58]

Just as Buchanan was decrepit and faltering, so too was his party. One campaign song lamented that although only 80 years had passed since George Washington, the country was now represented by enemies of freedom. Frémont was "young, but he is very keen," unlike the opposition: "It's Only eighty years ago! / But *times* have changed since then! / For Franklin Pierce and Preston Brooks / Are a different sort of men!"[59] Not only was Brooks a central figure in anti-Democrat propaganda, but considerable ink was devoted to his "cowardly brutality." As William Cullen Bryant editorialized, "The friends of slavery at Washington are attempting to silence the members of Congress from the free States by the same modes of discipline which make the slaves unite on their plantations." In the *New York Evening Post*, he explicitly compared Southern attitudes toward their slaves with their conduct in Congress, stating that violence was "the proper instrument of its [proslavery] designs."[60]

Brooks's brutality was undeniable and although some defended him by noting the inflammatory nature of Sumner's speech, the latter's caning forever linked Southern brutality to Kansas's oppression.[61] Even Sumner's greatest defenders acknowledged that his speech might have skirted parliamentary rules although such retaliation was inexcusable.[62] The subsequent tension in congressional chambers was extraordinary, as many came to work armed. As Hamlin wrote William Fessenden (ME), "We are having rare times here, such as I have never seen. It is my candid opinion that some will be shot down before the session closes. All I have to say is, *let it come*. If we do not stand manfully and fearlessly to the work before us, *we ought to be slaves*."[63] Amidst rumors of duels and other challenges, Brooks defended himself by noting that despite an "unalterable determination to punish" the senator, he had not intended to kill him. After all, despite Sumner being his "superior in strength," he had selected an ordinary cane.[64] Brooks resigned to allow his constituents to vote on his conduct, and his reelection further tarnished the party, especially since Congress had not rebuked him.

Throughout the summer the Republican Party successfully depicted an avaricious Pierce willing to sacrifice Kansas to his ambition. Party leaders like J. Watson Webb, the editor of the *New York Courier and Enquirer*, frequently charged that the president acted due to his desperate need to conciliate the South and earn a second term. In doing so, Pierce had "winked at and encouraged the Border Ruffians of Missouri in violating the free soil of Kansas, and, with bowie-knives and rifles, driving her freemen from the polls and then electing creatures of their own, to accomplish the infamous purpose of making her a Slave State." Like many others, Webb believed that "resistance to the administration of the so-called Democratic party and its murderous and blood-stained acts of oppression toward our brethren of Kansas, is more imperatively demanded at our hands now, than was resistance to George III and his minions by our patriot sires in 1775."[65] As Webb's paper further stated, the United States was in the "midst of a revolution" against the slavocracy and should they fail at the polls, they would "do as our fathers did before us—stand by our inalienable rights and drive back with arms those who dare to trample upon our inheritance."[66] This view was echoed by Kansas residents such as Sarah Everett, who believed that only Frémont's election could save them; without it, "we can no longer speak of our glorious Republic! Liberty and Democracy will be utterly overthrown to be raised again only by strife and bloodshed! It is a shame that a government commenced as was ours, should now be overthrown by a spirit darker and more malignant than that which provoked its origin."[67]

For many Republicans, their greatest problem with Buchanan was that he was too much like Pierce. As reformer Theodore Parker wrote, "The principles of the Administration will be the same as now; the measures the same; the mode of applying the principles and executing the measures will be slightly altered—no more."[68] Others warned that dire consequences would arise for Kansas if the Democratic ticket won; as one broadside insisted, Buchanan had to be repudiated because he supported Pierce. "But let John

C. Fremont be elected and justice will be done to Kansas.... The man who votes for Buchanan, votes to have me and all the settlers of Kansas murdered, and he should be denounced as a doughface. Tell every voter to go to the polls and vote for John C. Fremont, or be denounced as a man who upholds murder."[69] By linking Buchanan to Pierce, Republicans hoped to reinforce the idea that salvation for Kansas residents was impossible under any Democratic administration. As a result, Kansas residents closely watched the election, especially since they could not vote. "We are still in a painfull suspense,..." Jonas Colburn wrote, "I will not believe that it can be true that Buchanan is elected. But should it be so, we are in no worse condition than we have been. I do not think our position will be changed much of any. It may bring war upon us soon, but it was sure to come whatever the result might have been...."[70]

Conclusion

One major aspect of the 1856 campaign was the strange amalgamation of the Whig and American parties. In late February, the Know-Nothings held a convention during which one Connecticut delegate indicated that Kansas would be a party issue necessitating any candidate to clarify his stance on the organizing act. "The South admits that the Kansas-Nebraska Act was a fraud; they cannot and dare not deny it. This question cannot be ignored; it must be met; no candidate can be nominated whose position on that question is doubtful."[71] The American Party nominated Millard Fillmore even though he was not "an avowed advocate of Know Nothing principles."[72] Their platform straightforwardly professed its central tenet: "*Americans must rule America.*" Otherwise, it advised party members to unite behind national questions, urging non-intervention on the slavery question. Like the Republican Party, the Americans criticized the administration's conduct. The thirteenth plank of their platform termed Pierce's Kansas course "reckless and unwise" and angrily protested the president's removal of Americans from office; the repeal of the Missouri Compromise; and the extension of suffrage to unnaturalized foreigners in Kansas and Nebraska.[73]

Although this criticism was fairly mild and centered on small aspects of the Kansas question, during the campaign Fillmore's boosters proved a distraction for the Democratic Party. One supporter relentlessly publicized Pierce's perceived failings as "it was his imperious duty to have provided a new legislature, which would have expressed the free will of the real settlers of Kansas, which would have satisfied the North and the South, and prevented the subsequent effusion of blood."⁷⁴ Although Fillmore did not take a public stance on Kansas, he assured prominent advocate Amos Lawrence that he would "act promptly."⁷⁵ The Fillmore candidacy was not a serious threat, but Democrats feared the Americans would cull their support and force the election to the House, where Frémont would be elected. On the other hand, some Republicans worried that the Democrats and Know-Nothings were acting together to deprive Frémont of a victory should it be thrown to the House.⁷⁶ But the choices members of the American Party were making in 1856 simply were not clear because Senator Jesse Bright (IN) reported that "[t]he Fillmore party in Ind[iana] is rapidly being absorbed by the Fremont & Abolition party, we have to beat the anti Democratic party. . . ."⁷⁷

The strange collection of candidates confounded Kansas partisans. In a public letter to the editor of the *New York Evening Post* on September 18, Reeder emphasized that if the Democrats won, all hope would be lost because their congressmen were "laboring in earnest zeal, by speech and vote, to cover up the iniquities of this administration and the border ruffians of Missouri, and to suppress a fair investigation of outrages which shock both humanity and republicanism and defy the constitution and laws." Although he refrained from directly criticizing his fellow Pennsylvanian by stating that the party would force Buchanan to act in a certain direction "whatever may be his own private feelings," he faulted the party for being "fully committed to Southern sectionalism." Although Reeder was obviously no longer a Democrat, he timed his formal break from the party during the election for propaganda purposes, stating that he did so because duty demanded the "sacrifice of personal feeling."⁷⁸

That summer, poet Walt Whitman wrote that Fillmore and Buchanan were dregs of the past. "Stript of padding and paint, who are Buchanan and Fillmore? What has this age to do with them?" Whitman asked. They were

> two galvanized old men, close on the summons to depart this life, their early contemporaries long since gone, only they two left, relics and proofs of the little political bargains, chances, combinations, resentments of a past age, having nothing in common with this age. . . . It is clear from all these two men say and do, that their hearts have not been touched in the least by the flowing fire of the humanitarianism of the new world, its best glory yet, and a moral control stronger than all its governments. It is clear that neither of these nominees of the politicians has thus far reached an inkling of the real scope and character of the contest of the day. . . .⁷⁹

Both men were safe choices whose nominations reflected the "climax of political cynicism."[80]

Ultimately, Buchanan won the election with 174 electoral votes to Frémont's 114 and Fillmore's 8. However, Buchanan's 1,836,072 votes were fewer than the combined votes of his opponents. Although it is impossible to know how the 873,053 voters who selected Fillmore might have voted without his candidacy, especially given the conservatism of the Whig element of those votes, the 1,342,345 votes Frémont garnered were impressive.[81] Indeed, both sides had reasons to cheer and fear the results. For Republicans, their competitiveness boded well for continued growth and influence. As Bryant explained, the popular mind had shifted in the eight years since the extension of slavery had been made a question in a presidential election. "We were then comparatively weak, we are now strong; we then counted our thousands, we now count our millions; we could then point to our respectable minorities in a few states, we now point to state after state. . . . The cause is not going back—it is rapidly going forward. . . ."[82] Even within the territory, residents accepted the outcome with equanimity. As John Everett wrote, "It has not depressed the feelings of free State men here as I thought it would." Indeed, not only did they have justice and principle on their side, but "a great majority of the intelligent, upright, thinking Northern public is strongly and actively with us." On the other hand, "a bare plurality of votes of the ignorant and prejudiced, obtained by the grossest misrepresentation and fraud is all that our enemies can boast of against us."[83] Free-state advocates recognized that while a Frémont victory might have hastened the territory's admission, the fight would continue in Congress as that body again debated a Kansas constitution.

Though bound to be disappointed that Buchanan was a minority victor who owed a debt to Fillmore's third-party candidacy, Democrats nonetheless had four years in which to capitalize on their victory. An important arena was bound to be in Kansas—after all, a quick settlement of the issue would allow the next presidential campaign to be decided on more typical issues. The Republicans, of course, hoped that Buchanan would break with Pierce's policy by recalling his territorial appointments, but although he accepted Kansas governor John Geary's resignation, he was unlikely to distance himself entirely from his predecessor.[84] Yet the election had not settled the question of slavery or freedom for the territory. As Congressman William Cumback (IN) explained, "The Presidential canvass has settled no great principles—that on the great living question of the times, we are as much at sea as before." Indeed, one's expectations of Buchanan depended on one's point of view. "The election of the successful candidates has been advocated in one section of the Union by claiming for them that Slavery would be extended into Kansas; while in the other section," Cumback noted, "on the banners of the same party, were emblazoned 'Buchanan and Breckinridge, and Free Kansas. . . . '"[85]

Perhaps the most significant result was not about parties, but about a sense that this election marked a transition from which the country could not recover. The *Charleston Mercury* admitted that a victorious Buchanan would undoubtedly do his best to eradicate the sectional strife sweeping the country but was not optimistic. Buchanan "cannot extinguish this fire through which he has waded," the paper editorialized in November. "It still burns undiminished; and the mere fact that it has almost succeeded in casting its lurid flames upon the temple of our common Confederacy, is sufficient to show us that we have no safety in this Union. We may linger in it a few years longer, but always at our peril. The hope of peace, of good understanding, has all passed away. Henceforth we are, necessarily, two peoples—the North and the South."[86] Indeed, while the Kansas issue for Republicans was about the spread of slavery, even in defeat they were able to celebrate a cause that was not going backward, but forward with ever augmenting strength.[87] Southern Democrats in particular understood Kansas to be a test of the nation's willingness to recognize their institutions.

6

Pledges and Principles
Buchanan, Walker, and Kansas in 1857

In accepting the presidential nomination in June 1856, Democrat James Buchanan had written, "[L]et the members of the family abstain from intermeddling with the exclusive domestic concerns of each other, and cordially unite, on the basis of perfect equality among themselves, in promoting the great national objects of common interest to all, and the good work will be instantly accomplished."[1] Despite this pledge, harmony proved elusive. Democrats did not perceive the transition from Franklin Pierce as being a sea change so much as a substitution for an experienced statesman better equipped to meet the challenges that had shaken his administration. The presidential election, however, had been contentious and hard fought. In his 1857 inaugural address, Buchanan reminded Americans that the election had heightened passions but then "the tempest at once subsided, and all was calm." He hoped that the passions in Kansas could be calmed just as expeditiously. The government had an obligation to ensure residents were protected in exercising their rights but beyond this, he asserted, "nothing can be fairer than to leave the people of a Territory . . . to decide their own destiny for themselves, subject only to the Constitution of the United States."[2]

Buchanan began his administration convinced that the Kansas question had assumed greater importance in the public mind than it deserved. "Indeed, viewed in the eye of sober reason, this Kansas question is one of the most absurd of all the Proteus-like forms which abolition fanaticism has ever assumed to divide and distract the country," Buchanan asserted. "And why do I say this? Kansas might enter the Union with a free constitution to-day, and once admitted, no human power known to the Constitution could prevent her from establishing slavery to-morrow. "[3] This belief in the mutability of constitutions contributed to Buchanan's support for the measure, which would define his Kansas policy. In his writings, the president indicated that the Lecompton convention would submit the constitution they created to a general vote, as Minnesota recently had done. As such, Buchanan's main concern was protecting the franchise from fraud or violence.[4]

In his memoir, Buchanan posited that his options in Kansas were severely limited because the territorial government was already in place when he took office. Although the initial elections were imperfect, Congress's rejection of the Topeka Constitution had settled any remaining questions of legitimacy. As such, he could not "adjudge it to be null and void. In fact, he had no alternative but to sustain the Territorial Government."[5] If he had any lingering doubts about how to approach Kansas, the Dred Scott decision, issued by the Supreme Court soon after his inauguration but referenced in his address, settled them. This decision, "so full and explicit," established the rights of slave owners to convey their property into any territory, even if the territorial legislature outlawed slavery, until it entered the Union and finalized the question in its constitution.[6] Buchanan lauded the Court's decision, which granted slave property equal protection under law, placing them "on the same ground by the fifth amendment to the Constitution, which provides that no person shall be deprived of life, liberty, and property without due process of law."[7] Buchanan clearly believed the key to interpreting the disturbances in Kansas lay in these legislative and judicial decisions. Given that antislavery proponents had been dealt setbacks by both Congress (the 1856 rejection of the Topeka Constitution) and the judiciary (the 1857 Dred Scott decision), the free-state party should reject their extralegal organization and effect change through the constitutional convention set for September 1857 in Lecompton.[8]

Although Congress rejected the Topeka Constitution, Kansas's eligibility for admission remained ambiguous, for the legal and ethical questions surrounding it had detracted from the more significant issues of population and self-sufficiency. The first territorial census of February 1855 established the population at 8,601 residents, and while many suspected rapid growth, the population was in flux and difficult to estimate.[9] Perhaps a more relevant question, then, was whether the territory could meet self-sufficiency standards with any population.

Because of the continuing conflict and the decision to delay land sales, only a small portion of the property tax due was collected; most of Kansas's revenue between 1855 and 1859 derived from the dollar poll tax levied on voters. The territory had proven physically challenging—winters had been severe, drought prevalent, and immigrants arrived unprepared for differences in climate and situation. As a result, most settlers suffered financial reverses. By 1860, two-thirds of personal income was derived from the agricultural sector, but per capita income remained low at $84, slightly more than half that of free residents throughout the United States. Moreover, the territory was already in debt for more than $61,000. Its disorder decimated the budget established by Congress, with the most significant outlays allocated to electoral fraud investigations; constitutional conventions; construction of territorial roads; and legislative expenses.[10] Without federal support, Kansas was unlikely to meet its financial obligations. Nonetheless, its legislature pursued statehood in 1857, setting delegate elections for three months before the constitutional convention.

The New Executive Team

Although Buchanan's analysis was provided in retrospect and through the lens of civil war, he signaled that he would forge his own path in Kansas by accepting Governor John Geary's resignation. Buchanan's nomination of Robert John Walker to replace him was a surprise. Although a well-known, well-regarded Democrat, Walker had opined during the presidential campaign that Kansas was "a graveyard for governors" and would never be a slave state.[11] But he also had expressed concern that the South's inability to contend for Kansas was unconstitutional. Rather than a "division of the common territory," the North would have all of it while the South "shall have no voice or vote in the matter. . . ."[12] Walker's national reputation was so well established that, having previously served as secretary of the treasury, he was expected to join the administration as secretary of state if at all. But Buchanan insisted the Kansas post was "the most important position in the country" and pressured Walker to serve on the frontier. "It was said," Walker recalled, "that I was a northern man by birth and a southern man by long residence and adoption, and perhaps enjoyed the confidence of the whole nation as to my impartiality upon this question, and that possibly I could do more, from these peculiar circumstances, to reconcile conflicting elements in Kansas than any other person."[13] Originally from Pennsylvania, Walker manumitted his slaves in 1832 and denounced nullification and secession as treason; yet he represented Mississippi in the Senate from 1836 to 1845.[14] Despite the perception that he considered the position "beneath the dignity of one of his national reputation" and feared that "failure in Kansas would be his political ruin," Walker's concerns for the Union prompted his acceptance.[15] His unexpected acquiescence was combined with his standing and reputation to foment rumors that he was clothed with an "almost unlimited" authority.[16] Indeed, he accepted only after Buchanan pledged his unqualified support. As Walker wrote in his letter of acceptance, he understood that the president and his cabinet agreed that Kansas residents, "by a fair and regular vote, unaffected by fraud or violence, must be permitted, in adopting their state constitution, to decide for themselves what shall be their social institutions."[17]

A question central to understanding Kansas evolved around the antislavery faction's decision to forgo voting. As Walker reassured his sister after his appointment, "[T]he slavery question in Kansas, is not so *unsolvable* as you suppose. It is reduced to the simple issue, if slave or free state, and must be decided by a *full* and *fair* vote. . . ."[18] Thus Walker spoke extensively on the importance of complete participation in territorial elections, especially since Secretary of State Lewis Cass's instructions that "freedom and safety for the legal voter, and exclusion and punishment for the illegal one—these should be great principles of your administration" mirrored his own sentiments.[19] But antislavery newspapers dismissed Walker's concerns. "If they really mean this," the *New York Daily Tribune* asked, "what has kept their mouths padlocked during the two years' earnest struggle for and against the usurpations and tyrannies of the bogus Legislature imposed on Kansas by the Border-Ruffian invasion of March 30, 1855?"[20]

Congressman Schulyer Colfax (IN) wrote free-state leader Charles Robinson with suggestions on how they might use Walker's speeches advantageously. The new governor, Colfax explained, "expects you to decline participating in the election in spite of his appeals, and he will return with the Border Ruffian Constitution declaring that he was there expecting that Kansas would be free, but that her Free State people would not vote, and consequently a Slave State Constitution was inevitable."[21] Despite this warning, the free-state faction continued to repudiate participation. "[We will] wait for those who are coming," one partisan wrote. "The advocates of voting want to go to the polls and expect they would have to vindicate their rights there with blood. But our policy is peace. We wish to do nothing to provoke collision, at least till we are strong enough to awe and look down all opposition."[22]

The antislavery party's ascendancy continued, but the Republicans' failure to win the presidency and the 1856 membership shift in the House of Representatives meant that the Topeka government had to reassess its strategy. Colfax warned Robinson that the local organization must take the initiative because Republican presidential candidate John C. Frémont's defeat meant that "a grave responsibility is devolved on its friends in Kansas. . . ."[23] Moreover, since their constitution was no longer viable, especially with the Lecompton process already in motion, "you ought to at least try voting once; and I fear if you do not meet Gov. Walker's plausible proposition with some proffer to vote . . . your case will be materially and perhaps fatally weakened."[24] Indeed, criticism was burgeoning that any organization staking a moral claim to greater democratic form had to work through the political system, however flawed the territorial mechanisms.

As Walker continued to stump for full participation in the capital, Frederick Perry Stanton, the new territorial secretary, left for Kansas. Although the previous secretary, Daniel Woodson, had proven divisive, Cass informed Stanton that he had not been recalled because Buchanan disapproved of him. Instead, Walker requested "a gentleman known to him, and in whom he has confidence" to go in his place since he could not leave Washington before May 11. Stanton initially rejected the offer, but the administration persuaded him to accept.[25] Like Walker, Stanton had represented a Southern state (Tennessee) in Congress from 1845 to 1855. Yet Stanton's prominence both reflected Kansas's importance and rendered his acceptance suspicious. The *New York Tribune* reported that Stanton's acquiescence had been purchased with the promise that they would help him become a senator after Kansas's admission. "This is a new illustration of the doctrine of popular sovereignty. The people of Kansas have a Constitution cut and dried out for them by Missouri Border Ruffians, and the Senators picked out at Washington, even before the Constitution is formed."[26] Furthermore, local activists worried that Buchanan's appointment of two Southerners was inauspicious.

Stanton arrived in Kansas on April 13. Four days later, as acting governor, he issued an address supporting the upcoming convention because it would submit "the great distracting question regarding their social institution" to residents. Moreover, he revealed his preference for a general amnesty, a suggestion he floated to the administration that same day. It would "promote peace and harmony" and "calm the excited passions of the people and to prevent similar occurrences in the future.[27] The next day in Lawrence he revealed a harder stance and dissipated any positive feelings this initial conciliation might have inspired. "If any man here is prepared to say that he will resist those [territorial] laws," Stanton warned, "with that man I declare war!—war to knife and the knife to the hilt."[28] But Walker cautioned him from Washington that "the force of *argument* should be exhausted, before *force* should be called in."[29]

Stanton told Robinson that free-state men must accept responsibility for their situation, emphasizing the availability of other remedies and expressing the increasingly popular view that they had to vote. "The trouble is," Stanton complained, "you Free-State men are not willing to take any steps looking to the correction of the evils you complain of." He assured him that the governor was in Kansas to administer "impartial justice" and only after it had been denied would Walker admit "there is something radically wrong in the government of Kansas." But Robinson responded that free-state men could not "go hunting a sheriff or a census-taker, especially if he [the census worker] spends most of his time in another state."[30]

With Walker in Washington for another six weeks, Stanton arranged for the census and delegate election. The free-state faction placed conditions on their participation: appointment of one proslavery and one free-state man to correct the registry list in each district and four judges of election per precinct, two of each party, with a majority vote settling any disputes.[31] Although Stanton favored one Republican, one free-state Democrat, and one proslavery Democrat judge in each precinct, he rejected this request because only Congress could overturn territorial laws. Moreover, he chastised the group for their "unreasonableness" in asking to "set aside the law in order to accomplish what you have refused to do in obedience to its provisions...."[32]

On May 20, Stanton announced the apportionment for the June 3 delegate election. With only nine thousand out of an estimated twenty thousand eligible voters registering, almost two-thirds of the sixty delegates would come from Missouri border counties.[33] Charges were quickly levied that districts had been "gerrymandered" to ensure maximum Missouri votes, which would render free-state participation irrelevant. However, they likely would not have participated anyhow. In fact, in several counties where there was no registration, few if any eligible voters lived. This resulted in countercharges that Republicans wished only to create the appearance of foul play. Five days after Stanton announced the results, the free-state faction requested a new census and apportionment, insisting that half the election judges come from their faction. Again he rejected these requests. As the *New York Tribune* complained, "[T]he moment they are asked to do anything in justification of their pledges, they plead want of power."[34] Stanton would later regretfully recall that he "was ignorant of the circumstances, and greatly perplexed," but had no other option.[35] At the time, however, the acting governor believed his actions were appropriate.

After this announcement, free-state partisans became even more convinced that their situation was untenable. "Kansas is now governed partly by a military despotism, partly by an outside oligarchy, under the form of the most unlimited democracy," one activist wrote. "This government is carried on by a party whose national strength consists in their professions of devotion to the broad principle of the sovereignty of the actual settler. This unnatural state of things cannot exist long."[36] Partisans actively wrote Northern newspapers, disputing the value of voting. As one free-state man wrote to the *New York Times*, "[T]he argument for participation would be ten-fold stronger" if a fair vote were possible, but given the flawed registry and census, "what madness would it be for the people of Kansas to abandon their now impregnable position, and mingle in this election, *thus indorsing the frauds on which it is based*, without even a remote hope of either success or justice."[37]

Walker arrived in Kansas determined to mold it to his submission policy. He had emphasized after his appointment that he represented a fresh start and would guarantee equal protection to voters. Although the new governor arrived after protests had arisen about the delegate apportionment, he neither acknowledged the dispute not adjusted his strategy. Walker's inaugural address on May 27 powerfully stated his goals and elucidated the rumored understanding between him and the president. Buchanan and his cabinet believed the territory's condition was "fraught with imminent peril to the Union," and Walker thus had been asked to settle the question "which has introduced discord and civil war throughout your borders, and threatens to involve you and our country in the same common ruin." Although the Lecompton process was already underway, he assured residents that Buchanan and Congress would not force a constitution on them. "I repeat then, as my clear conviction, that unless the Convention submit the Constitution to the vote of all the actual resident settlers of Kansas, and the election be fairly and justly conducted, the Constitution will be, and ought to be, rejected by Congress." Walker reminded residents that Congress could not compel statehood; rather, through the convention process, they controlled their own fate.[38]

While thus reassuring free-state men that they had a right to contribute to a state constitution, Walker reminded them that rights were tied to responsibilities. He emphasized the legislature's validity; without it, Kansas would have no law. Moreover, residents were subject to all laws and could not selectively choose among them. Walker invited all Kansans to vote, for to do otherwise would remove them from the process of state-building. With or without the free-state party, the territory was moving toward statehood. "The law has performed its entire appropriate function, when it extends to the people the right of suffrage; but it cannot compel the performance of that duty," Walker wrote. But when voters absented themselves from the polls, they "authorize those who do vote to act for them in that contingency, and the absentees are as much bound under the law and Constitution, where there is no fraud or violence, by the act of the majority of those who do vote, as though all had participated in the election."[39] Residents opting out of the electoral process were equally bound by the certified will of the people.

Finally, Walker asked residents to place their territorial experiences into the greater context of democracy. "What is Kansas with or without slavery," he speculated, "if she should destroy the rights and Union of the States?" The issue was moot, the new governor argued, for climate necessarily closed the territory to the institution. Moreover, antislavery partisans foolishly imperiled the Union for slaves for whom they had little genuine empathy and whose labor would not thrive in this climate. Is it, Walker asked, "for the handful of that race now in Kansas, or that may be hereafter introduced, that we should subvert the Union . . . ?" Citing the black laws of the Topeka Constitution which revealed an antipathy toward free blacks, Walker wondered why free-state advocates placed the interests of the African race above those of the "Great American and European race."[40]

Despite this criticism, free-state reaction was largely positive. The *Herald of Freedom* stated that the people of Kansas had "reason to hail with delight" Walker's course because it would "release them from political thraldom, it will give them possession of all their God-given rights."[41] If Walker's inaugural satisfied the free-state faction, the proslavery faction was unimpressed. At a dinner for the new governor, L.A. McLean, Surveyor-General John Calhoun's clerk, gave a worrisome toast: "And do you come here to rule over us?—you, a miserable pigmy like you? You come here with ears erect, but you will leave with your tail between your legs. Walker, we have unmade governors before; and by God, I tell you, sir, we can unmake them again!"[42] Although Walker did not respond, such a reception could not but shake his faith in the men of his party.

In Washington, the cabinet and the president were purportedly surprised by Walker's explicit promises. In private correspondence, Secretary of the Treasury Howell Cobb claimed not to have seen or heard of these pledges until he read news reports and assumed Walker made them to satisfy the free-state faction. Cobb reported that Buchanan had not wanted any administration official to "use his position to affect the decision of the slavery question, one way or the other. He was indifferent to that question, so it was fairly and honestly made by the people of Kansas, and this was the position of the cabinet."[43] Although Walker asserted that the administration supported a fair vote, his emphasis on the unlikelihood that Kansas could support slavery seemed to indicate the administration favored a free state. Buchanan most likely favored a slave state not because of any personal preferences, but because he believed a sectional balance was imperative to preserve the Union. Moreover, he genuinely thought the proslavery party was in ascendance in the territory but was being outmaneuvered by a small, abolitionist minority whose stridency masked their true numbers. Buchanan's inability to recognize the rise of antislavery sentiment in the North was exacerbated by his absence from the country in 1854 and 1855, two years of considerable growth for the movement.

Walker's inaugural address also caused an uproar among Southerners, many of whom attributed its contents to ambition. "Everything was quiet, going on smoothly, to some decision and determination, ... when he [Walker] puts in, and merely to give himself consequence to seem the settler [of] what was rapidly settling itself, raises the devil all over the South," Senator Robert Toombs (GA) complained. "And this is not the worst of it. B[uchanan] intends to sustain him, and thereby ruin himself and his administration."[44] Moreover, soon after Walker's appointment, he met and disappointed a local proslavery contingent by his intention to deal with both factions impartially leading prominent activists to declare that "Walker would not do."[45] Some proslavery residents recognized the tide was turning against them. "I fear ... that this will be made a Free State at last," Axalla Hoole wrote in July. "'Tis true we have elected Proslavery men to draft a state constitution, but I feel pretty certain, if it is put to a vote of the people, it will be rejected, as I feel pretty confident that they have a majority here at this time. The South has ceased all efforts, while the North is redoubling her exertions."[46]

Walker's immediate concern was how to move beyond his inaugural's reassurances to persuade the free-state party to fully participate. He urged those who wrote to complain about not being counted in the census to send delegates to the convention anyhow (although it would be up to the convention to seat them).[47] He told a mass meeting in Topeka on June 6 that Buchanan supported submitting the constitution to a vote. Walker's speech further tied the administration to his policy when he argued that if the convention "do not thus submit it, I will join you, fellow citizens, in lawful opposition to their course [Cries of 'good,' and cheers.] And I cannot doubt, gentlemen, that one much higher than I, the chief magistrate of the union, will join you in opposition."[48]

Despite Walker's encouragement, free-state activists continued their "masterly inactivity" while awaiting final victory through immigration. When the delegate election results were announced, merely 2,071 of the 9,251 registered voters participated. As a result, only one-tenth of the eligible population selected the delegates who would write the territory's constitution. This result convinced the free-state faction that their strategy had been vindicated.[49] Because this outcome emphasized the convention's nonrepresentative nature, they turned their attention toward the constitution. As friends in Washington had warned, the new Congress was not disposed to view the Topeka movement favorably. In an editorial entitled "The Past—

A Plan for the Future," the *Herald of Freedom* presented new tactics knowing that they would have to let the Topeka Constitution go. First, if the Lecompton Constitution were submitted, "we must vote, and vote it down." Second, if not submitted, then they "must take possession of it, and elect every officer, executive, legislative, and judicial, under it; and although we cannot produce an abortion, we can *strangle* it at its birth, by getting possession of the *monster* when it begins to give evidence of life." Their statement that "the character of that Constitution" was irrelevant to their strategy reveals their rigidity—even should the delegates construct a neutral document, free-state activists were determined to oppose it.[50]

Throughout July, Walker was in constant communication with Washington over whether free staters would participate in the October elections. On July 11, the free-state legislature convened at Topeka to discuss their options. Walker urged them to abandon their illegal path and vote on the constitution. The governor was confident that delegates would write a constitution allowing slavery but prohibiting further importation, an outcome that could unite free-state Democrats and proslavery advocates. On July 15, Walker wrote Cass that they would participate. Indeed, resolutions issued at Topeka quoted his assurances in recommending a mass meeting at Grasshopper Falls to decide their participation.[51]

That same day, however, the Lawrence group outraged Walker and further diminished his opinion of them. Although the legislature had granted Lawrence a charter to organize, they would create an "independent municipal organization" instead. In a printed address, they justified their course by declaring, "[I]n the absence of constituted authorities and organized governments, the people are left to act in their primary and independent capacity, and form a government for themselves." Furthermore, "political and social rights are not dependent upon the gift of organizations, but are inherent in the people."[52] Walker decried this endeavor as an effort to implement the Topeka Constitution on a smaller scale, to "do in detail what they dare not attempt as a whole; then with the machinery of government in operation in the principal localities of the Territory; they could set in motion their State machinery and run out the Territorial government."[53] Walker issued a proclamation on July 15 stating that by disseminating these resolutions they intended to "renew the scenes of bloodshed and civil war." He warned against "conspiring to overthrow the government of the United States in this territory.... Let me implore you not to compel me to appeal to that military power which is required in the last resort to protect the government of your country."[54]

The likelihood that the administration and the Topeka faction would come to blows was so high that summer that Supreme Court judge John

McLean advised Cass against a military response. "Let them go on in their folly, as they can do no harm, only to themselves, and their instigators," he urged; the "few unprincipled demagogues" who directed events thrived on agitation for "they must have war, to save themselves."[55] Nonetheless when Lawrence officials dismissed the governor's warnings that electing local officials would violate federal laws, he dispatched federal forces to arrest them. But the conflict ended peacefully after dragoons moved into position.[56]

Walker would later distinguish between the Topeka statehood movement and this Lawrence effort by arguing that the former, however ill-advised, awaited congressional recognition while the latter "not only passed laws, but required, by seizure and sale of property, their compulsory execution, under the requisition of an oath. . . ."[57] Based on this quarrel, Walker asked Cass for additional troops. Denying that he was an "alarmist," he demanded more dragoons (only 262 were present), valuing their rapid response and ability to traverse the vast territory. Given that "to order out the militia is simply to renew the civil war in Kansas," Walker requested two thousand troops and asked that General William S. Harney be placed in command.[58] Military forces in Kansas had been reallocated because they were needed elsewhere, but on September 1 Cass promised to deploy thirty-six companies (approximately the two thousand men requested).[59]

As the summer progressed, Southern discontent with Walker simmered. The *Charleston Mercury* condemned his plans to send a constitution to the people as "a violation of the promised neutrality—an insidious and high-minded breach of faith towards the south and southern men in Kansas. . . ." Similarly, the *Richmond South* insisted that a popular vote would have "disastrous consequences. In the first place, it would inflame and prolong the controversy, and would ultimately throw Kansas into the arms of the abolitionists."[60] Of course, neither paper considered that Kansas might very well be in the hands of antislavery men already.

Even as Southern criticism became more strident, Southern critics were diversifying beyond the usual malcontents. The Democratic State Convention in Georgia, for instance, believed Walker had gone too far in enticing free-state participation, that it represented "a presumptuous interference in matters over which he has no legitimate control. . . ." Even more, his "gross departure from the principles of non-intervention and of neutrality which were established by the Kansas bill" was such that they had "full confidence that Mr. Buchanan will manifest fidelity to the principles which carried him into office, by recalling Governor Walker." Mississippi Democrats adopted a similar resolution and the governor of Florida criticized Walker in his inaugural address.[61] Even Cobb conceded that although he still believed the governor's "isothermal and climate arguments were ill-timed and out of place and his threat to oppose the admission of Kansas . . . wrong and unjustifiable," nonetheless Walker "had been too harshly judged" in Georgia and Mississippi.[62]

In the territory, Walker blamed Southern extremists for causing free-state Democrats to abandon their conservative position. The governor believed he had gained this faction's support, but increased Southern agitation had forced a realignment. "This policy was making great and successful progress when the violent attacks made upon it and upon me by southern extremists reached the territory," Walker wrote Cass. However, afterwards it seemed likely that some free-state Democrats might join the Republicans on the necessity of a free-state constitution. If this happened, they "would constitute an admitted and overwhelming majority of the people of the territory, and, if effected, would produce the most deplorable results. . . ."[63] However, local politics did not lend itself to moderation. As Surveyor-General John Calhoun stated, "A man must be Pro-Slavery or Free-State; there is no half-way ground."[64]

Writing to Walker in mid-1857, Senator Stephen Douglas (IL) also reassured him that it was just politics. The South was "dissatisfied with the nation's administration, and seized upon the Kansas question as a pretext, and made you the scape goat. But the present state of the question will compel them to rally under your banner. . . ." But Douglas regarded the Lecompton Constitution optimistically, believing that free-state participation was irrelevant to Democrats' success. Even "if they do vote, I still have faith that the law and order party will be able to out vote them [the abolitionists] and adopt the constitution."[65] This analysis, common among Democrats who believed that all free-state men were abolitionists, seriously underestimated free-state strength. Moreover, Douglas did not seem to realize that the Law and Order Party was unlikely to place terminating the controversy above making Kansas a slave state.

In late July, Walker warned Cass that despite proslavery support and the likelihood of full participation in the election, free-state men might be driven from the Democratic Party. To mitigate this, Walker believed he had to respond to "unmerited attacks upon me and my policy" by Southern extremists and would do so without embroiling the administration. However, Walker's submission policy was controversial because both sides viewed his rationale suspiciously—the South believed he intended to allow "abolition vagrants and interlopers to control the result" while local Republicans believed his policy would allow Missourians to do so.[66]

Walker continued his analysis of local politics in a letter to Buchanan. He believed free-state Democrats were prevalent among Kansans, followed by Republicans, proslavery Democrats, and a small number of proslavery

Know-Nothings. His inaugural's "climate doctrine" had restrained the free-state party and once again he insisted that, without submission, Kansas would be consumed by civil war.[67] Buchanan reassured Walker that he would support submitting the constitution to a vote. More importantly, "on the question of submitting the constitution to the *bona fide* resident settlers of Kansas," Buchanan wrote, "I am willing to stand or fall. In sustaining such a principle we cannot fall.... Should the convention of Kansas adopt this principle, all will be settled harmoniously; and, with the blessing of Providence, you will return triumphantly from your arduous, important and responsible mission."[68] Buchanan was as optimistic as Douglas about the constitution's chances for success. However, when he was proven wrong, Buchanan emphasized the qualifier in his statement, not the pledge. He began to stress that his promise to stand or fall on the issue was only relevant if the convention itself chose to submit it; the constitution retained its validity whether or not it was submitted to the people. Moreover, the same Southern critics who irritated Walker worried Buchanan and confounded his cabinet. Secretary of the Interior Jacob Thompson, for instance, complained to Attorney General Jeremiah Black that "I get lost in following the path with the Administration and its true position on one side and Gov. Walker and his many givings on the other. Walker evidently has one purpose and the Administration another; and it requires a tactician to do justice to the President and not wound the sensibilities of Walker."[69] Given Walker's prominence, reining him in to better reflect administration policy was a delicate operation.

Over the summer, Northern activists increased their pressure. Forty-three prominent citizens of Connecticut, for instance, sent the president a memorial about how his policy was misguided. It discussed the bogus laws of the bogus legislature, considered the use of the Army to enforce them, argued that Buchanan was waging war against a portion of the United States, and closed by praying that "Almighty God will make your administration an example of justice and beneficence, and with his terrible majesty protect our people and our Constitution."[70] Although Buchanan addressed the Kansas situation throughout his administration, he later isolated his August 16 response to this antislavery memorial as the clearest statement of his policy. He was unsympathetic to the contention that the federal government forced "the people of Kansas to obey laws not their own, nor of the United States,"[71] for the territorial government was as established as that of any other territory. "Under these circumstances," Buchanan asked, "what was my duty? Was it not to sustain the government? to protect it from the violence of lawless men, who were determined either to rule or ruin? to prevent it from being overturned by force?... Would you have desired that I should abandon the Territorial government, sanctioned as it had been by Congress, to illegal violence, and thus review the scenes of civil war and bloodshed which every patriot in the country had deplored? This would, indeed have been to violate my oath of office and to fix a damning blot on the character of my administration."[72] Congress had supported the official government by refusing to repudiate the territorial legislature. His sole duty, then, was protecting local institutions, even if it required military force. The memorialists continued to debate Buchanan, arguing that Congress could not have sanctioned the territorial government because it was not legitimate, and asked why he had not considered the testimony recorded by the Howard Committee. Finally, they condemned Buchanan for accepting the presidential nomination if he was unwilling to take responsibility for Kansas.[73] Buchanan did not respond to this rebuttal.

On August 26, the free-state party decided at Grasshopper Falls to participate in fall elections. "The Territorial legislature belongs to us," James Lane asserted, "and we are going to have it—by the ballot if we can, by the rifle if we must. If we elect only one member we intend to make him a good working majority."[74] The convention as a whole, however, passed a more temperate resolution: "*Resolved*, That in thus voting we rely upon the faithful fulfillment of the pledge of governor Walker."[75]

The Lecompton Convention and the October Election

The Lecompton constitutional convention began on September 7. Despite strong border representation, the delegates were not stereotypical ruffians as critics charged, but professional men active in politics. Even though only 12 had been born in free states, a majority had emigrated from the Ohio and Mississippi valleys, a region known for its conservatism.[76] After making committee assignments, the convention recessed to await the upcoming election results, which included both factions for the first time since 1855. Although no reason was given for the break, it was widely believed that these results would determine the question of submission.[77] Nonetheless, recessing was odd. Unless the delegates were sensitive to charges of illegitimacy, there was no persuasive reason to delay deliberations. Given that the worst that could be said about the convention was that they were unrepresentative but not illegitimate, this recess would prove ineffectual.

In the run-up to the October 5 and 6 election, Walker defined his role. In July, he had asked Cass to advise on voter qualifications and whether payment of a territorial tax was necessary to vote.[78] In September, Cass finally responded that the president and the cabinet concurred in Walker's opinion that payment of the poll tax was not required. But "the President had no idea, as I have already stated, that it can have any legal effect in determining the qualifications" of voters. In addition, Walker had no authority to rule on disputed elections because the legislature had jurisdiction over its membership. As such, the governor's role was simply to "see that the laws of the territory are faithfully executed, to take care that the elections shall be free and fair." However, Walker was buoyed by Cass's admission that the territory was "in a peculiar condition" and that as governor, his views were "entitled to great weight."[79]

Based on this letter, Walker issued an address about the upcoming elections. While he regretted that the census and registry had been incomplete, he could not rectify this error. He blamed local officials' negligence for the missing 15 counties' registrations but asserted that it had no bearing on the election. He reminded residents that the Kansas-Nebraska Act established voter qualifications for the first election only, deferring to the legislature to define subsequent qualifications. The 1855 election law assigned questions on voter qualifications to judges of election, not the governor or other officials, while the 1857 convention law only required three months' residence and registration. Walker concluded by stating that he would not support anything that would deprive men of their rights.[80]

On September 26, Walker reported to Cass that his speeches had been effective, but Washington's support was what swayed the populace toward complete political participation and would secure a fair election.[81] He was so convinced of his path's correctness that he allegedly dictated an editorial to the *Herald of Freedom*'s editor, George Brown, which clarified what the free-state faction should do if Walker failed to fulfill his pledges. "If the last resort of freemen shall become necessary, let us first know whether Governor Walker will not do his whole duty, and render the last alternative unnecessary. Let us have our rights, '*peaceably* if we can, *forcibly* if we must.'"[82]

On election day, early returns promised the proslavery party would retain some strength, but there was an anomaly: while the free state congressional delegate won his seat by over four thousand votes, the proslavery party retained control of the legislature.[83] Rumors of fraud concerning two Southern counties quickly circulated, and Walker and Stanton headed to Johnson and McGee counties to investigate. Although free staters were skeptical of Walker's support—one diarist reported that he was "afraid of his head I suppose or he would wink at it and let it go. Freestate men are bound to have their rights at all hazards and he knows it"—he exceeded such low expectations.[84] Stanton recalled that they were determined to reject fraudulent returns, and he "would have resigned my office in order to testify my sense of the enormity of the wrong" had he been required to certify them. However, both men were "gratified" to find the papers "so imperfect" as to give them legitimate grounds for rejection.[85]

Walker acquitted Missourians of any complicity, finding that the pollbooks had been modified and the Oxford perpetrators none too wisely had derived their poll list from an old Cincinnati directory that included Salmon P. Chase.[86] A village of six houses, Oxford could not have produced its 1,828 votes even if it included the adjacent village of New Santa Fe, Missouri, with its 20 houses located across the street. "Under these circumstances we do not feel embarrassed by any technical difficulty as to our right to go behind the returns. We hold the returns themselves to be defective in form and substance, and therefore inadmissible." In McGee County, which reported 1,226 votes, Walker found the same residential scarcity in this southeastern county formed from Cherokee lands closed to settlement, but again exonerated Missourians of fraud. Walker rejected the McGee returns and reiterated that he and Stanton were not judging voter qualifications or excluding illegal votes; as such, they were "not going behind the returns, as we have been unjustly charged with doing."[87]

In his testimony before the Covode Committee investigating corruption in 1860, Walker stated that this election represented the first attempt to make Kansas a slave state. However, given the "terrible forgeries in the pretended returns—they were not legal returns," he rejected them, which "gave a majority of the territorial legislature to my political opponents, the Republicans, at which, I am free to say, I was deeply grieved."[88] Nonetheless, although acting against strict orders not to intervene, he was determined to ensure a fair election and likely believed Cass had provided a loophole: this time, the fraud derived from illegal returns, not illegal voters. "We have never proposed to go behind genuine, legal and valid returns, to purge the polls, or judge of the qualifications of voters, but that we have rejected the papers therein referred to," Walker argued, "because they are not 'returns' in the language of the law, and because they are spurious and fictitious." To do otherwise would have involved them in fraud.[89] While the administration was displeased, they were not rebuked.[90] Indeed, Stanton later recalled feeling "aggrieved when I received no word of approval from Washington, but was greeted, instead, with volleys of unmeasured abuse from Democrats in all quarters of the country."[91]

After Walker disqualified the Oxford and McGee county votes, the free-state party won majorities in both houses. The outcome was controversial, as the legislature hinged on those votes: if included, it would remain proslavery; if disqualified, it would become antislavery. Including the Oxford vote would have given the Democrats 7 seats in the council to 6 for the free-state party and 23 to 16 in the House. Without these illegal votes, the free-state party won 9 seats in the council to the Democrats' 4, and 24 seats to the 15 Democratic seats in the House. The free-state majorities came only after Walker eliminated these fraudulent returns.[92]

Walker's decision enraged the proslavery men, and they passed 17 resolutions condemning the executive team at a Democratic meeting in Lecompton. Many thwarted candidates were violently unhappy; Samuel Jones, for instance, drew a knife on Walker when refused his certificate of election.[93] They attempted to enjoin the governor to grant election certificates, but Walker and Stanton ignored Judge Sterling Cato's writ, citing a lack of jurisdiction; requiring them to issue certificates would be "an usurpation of power, and therefore a nullity, which, under their oath of office, it would be their duty to disregard."[94] The protests and legal maneuvers failed. Despite this severe setback, the proslavery party nonetheless had another chance to ensure Kansas's admission as a slave state.

Even though the free-state faction had not voted for delegates, the convention was legal and authorized to write a constitution. Though now clearly at odds with the general population, they proceeded in their work. Many delegates undoubtedly wanted to establish slavery, but more farsighted Democrats recognized the threat presented by the burgeoning free-state population: if put to a general vote, the constitution would be rejected. Moreover, even if Kansas became a slave state, the institution would be at risk. As one antislavery proponent stated, "even if our state is slave in form and name, it will be a slave state with a great majority actively hostile to slavery.... If a slave state at all, it will be a slave state without slaves."[95] In addition, once it became a state, Kansas's elected officials would be Republicans, with James Lane and Charles Robinson likely congressmen, an unpalatable proposition.[96]

Surveyor-General John Calhoun presided over the Lecompton convention and claimed to speak for the Buchanan administration. According to Walker, Calhoun had approached him to discuss the proposal to split the slavery clause from the constitution, which he characterized as the administration's preference. Walker cited Buchanan's various letters in informing Calhoun he was wrong, but Calhoun countered that the administration's policy had changed. Walker warned Calhoun that having staked his reputation on a free vote, he "would never change or modify my views on that question in the slightest respect; that I would fight it out to the end, be the consequences to me personally or politically what they might." When Calhoun suggested he broach this topic with the president, Walker said he would never assent to such a change no matter how reliable Calhoun believed his information, that regardless of his position in the convention, he was merely a surveyor without civil authority. Even in 1860, Walker refused to believe that this "programme" emanated from Buchanan, especially given the "infamous manner in which Calhoun behaved, forfeiting all his pledges, and from the fact that he must have been privy to the forgeries of the returns from Oxford, and also many other forgeries, I have long since ceased to have the slightest confidence in his veracity."[97]

However, if Buchanan had not sent orders directly to Calhoun, his cabinet actively directed events. A clerk in the Department of the Interior, Henry L. Martin unofficially participated in the convention. He left for Kansas after a conversation with Thompson in which his boss emphasized that legislative resolutions from Georgia and Mississippi indicated their close interest in the convention. Martin quoted Thompson as stating that the cabinet favored full submission but he was "not prepared to take ground against the admission of Kansas if a pro-slavery constitution should be made and sent directly to Congress by the convention." According to Martin, Thompson believed that if Congress rejected the constitution because it had not been submitted for a vote, the South would claim it was because it was proslavery and disunion would result. Martin was friendly with Cobb as well, and these Southern resolutions arose in conversation once again. Cobb entrusted Martin with a letter for delegate Hugh H. Moore, although he denied carrying any such document.[98]

"Public business required an agent to be sent from the office about that time," Thompson explained to the Covode Committee, "and I was very willing to avail myself of the occasion to select an agent [Martin]—who would necessarily be thrown in contact with the members of the convention— whose views would harmonize with my own." He believed the convention could submit a constitution straight to Congress, although doing so without a popular vote would be "unwise and impolitic." Thompson testified that he wished "to secure the question of slavery, and yet secure the cooperation of the free State and pro-slavery democrats." Furthermore, he did not want to separate out the slavery clause because it was "the weakest form in which the question could be presented." He again expressed how Southern pressure affected their view of the Lecompton process. Thus, the administration was very aware of non-territorial pressures in considering the Kansas problem.[99]

Martin reported that the decision to submit only the question regarding slavery to a referendum came after an intense battle. One faction led by Calhoun favored full submission; the other led by Blake Little wanted to bypass a referendum. Martin attributed the shift against full submission to the dispute with Walker over the certificates of election, which was still raging when the convention reconvened on October 19. After Walker rejected Cato's writ and it became clear that the free-state party would be victorious, "some of the extreme anti-submission members of the convention, with friends of the thus defeated democratic candidates for the legislature, called a meeting to denounce" the executive team's course, arguing that they "were not judges of election, and had no authority of law for going behind the returns. . . . That made a breach between the governor and a large portion of the convention, which I labored in vain to prevent and afterward to heal." Afterward several delegates who had supported full submission in caucus changed their vote. Full submission was defeated by one vote whereby a reconsideration of the partial plan passed by three votes. Martin believed it was a compromise for those who believed full submission would lead to a defeat at the polls.[100]

Presented to the people on November 7, the constitution was similar to other frontier constitutions. Although it did not allow amendment until 1864, neither had the Topeka Constitution.[101] Moreover, it addressed many of the statutes that had garnered so much criticism during the 1856 legislative session. For instance, the bill of rights stated that all elections "shall be free and equal" and "every citizen may freely speak, write and publish his sentiments on all subjects."[102] Article VII provided for slavery, but a December 21 referendum would determine whether the constitution would be endorsed with slavery or without it. If a majority wanted slavery, then they would simply send Congress the constitution. If a majority rejected it, "then the article providing for slavery shall be stricken from the constitution by the president of this convention . . . and no slavery shall exist in the State of Kansas, except that the right of property in slaves now in the Territory shall in no manner be interfered with. . . ."[103] This too was typical, as states outlawing slavery generally allowed a period of adjustment for slaveholders.

Although on the surface this clause seemed to give Kansans an antislavery option, it was widely perceived as a trick. "Everybody knows that . . . no matter which vote should have prevailed," Stanton recalled, "the State would still have been left as completely slaveholding as many of the Southern States which prohibited the introduction of more slaves within their borders."[104] Without an emancipation policy, the constitution did not allow residents to outlaw slavery entirely; however, slavery was not deeply entrenched in Kansas. And while the South had long thrived without additional importation, it was difficult to see how a slave empire could be constructed with so few slaves. By 1857, there were approximately 450 slaves in Kansas, few of whom were engaged in plantation labor. Instead, they "plied the ferry, operated printing presses, cooked and baked in homes and hotels and on river boats. . . ." Few slaveholders had relocated and it is difficult to envision many coming to the territory after the October election and the loud outcry against the constitution.[105]

On November 18, the attorney general wrote an editorial for the *Washington Union* confirming administration support for the constitution. Although Buchanan had approved a draft affirming Walker's course, Black deleted that reference, leading Buchanan to complain afterward. "What is the reason for this?" the president asked. "It will give just cause of offense to Governor Walker's friends; and I confess I am much worried myself at the omission." Given that Black had previously dismissed Buchanan's autonomy—writing in 1856 that "Mr. Buchanan has very little to do with a cabinet appointment and of course will not presume to have a will of his own"—it is not surprising that he would revise this editorial after Buchanan approved it. Moreover, as one historian posited, perhaps "the conjunction [was] too incongruous or [Black] thought that a pat on the back after a stab in the back was too much."[106]

By the end of November, Walker had left Kansas on a preapproved leave of absence, so Stanton would oversee the referendum. Before his departure, Stanton asked Walker to call a special session of the legislature, but he left without doing so and offered neither opinion nor advice about Stanton's plan to do so.[107] Cass instructed Stanton to ensure a fair, peaceful election, writing that the president was pleased that "the great question which has so long agitated Kansas" would be put before the people. He sent him that portion of Buchanan's annual address relating to Kansas beforehand with instructions to publish it prior to the election so voters would be aware of his views. However, Stanton became increasingly concerned that the referendum could not be held without "collision and bloodshed" and that only a large military force could maintain order.[108]

On November 28, a group of incoming legislators petitioned Stanton to call an extra session to allow them to "counteract the proceedings for the pretended submission of the so-called Lecompton constitution to a vote of the people, or to give the *bona fide* citizens of the territory a fair and impartial opportunity, through the ballot box, to express themselves in favor of or against that instrument."[109] Although some might argue that the antislavery party's refusal to participate in the census and delegate election was at the heart of the Lecompton problem, many were sympathetic to the view that the convention was illegitimate in spirit if not in form. On December 1, Stanton called a special session to begin five days, later fully aware that a separate, free-state referendum would result. By convening the legislature "to consider matters of great moment pertaining to the public welfare," he hoped to show Congress the depth of territorial disapproval before it began debating admission. However, given that the free-state legislature was not due to convene until January, Buchanan had hoped they would not interfere with the referendum and so fired Stanton when he facilitated their action.[110]

On December 2, the free-state group repudiated the referendum, resolving that "everything connected with the Lecompton constitution was a swindle."[111] Aside from formalizing their non-participation, they revealed the depth of their hostility by forming a "league and covenant with each other that we will never, under any circumstances, permit the said constitution so framed and not submitted to be the organic law for the state of Kansas, but do pledge our lives, our fortunes and sacred honors in ceaseless hostility to the same."[112] One participant described the general atmosphere as full of joy at their resolve, that none of the territory's many conventions had so "much heart in them. . . ."[113]

On December 8, Buchanan issued his first annual message. He insisted that neither party nor ideology divided the two factions in Kansas; instead adherence to national laws was the significant division "between those who sustain and those who have done all in their power to overthrow the territorial government established by Congress."[114] The president acknowledged the uproar over the Lecompton Constitution but defended the convention. Given that many Kansans had not participated when given the opportunity, "their refusal . . . could in no manner affect the legality of the convention."[115]

As for the right of the people to vote on the constitution, while Buchanan had hoped that Kansas would follow Minnesota's example, neither Congress in its organizing act nor the territorial legislature in authorizing the convention had required it. Moreover, he believed that the option of accepting the constitution "with slavery" or "without slavery" adequately allowed the people to express their will. The president then echoed his 1856 Wheatland speech emphasizing the basic right to amend any state constitution as "no human power can prevent them from changing it within a brief period. Under these circumstances it may well be questioned whether the peace and quiet of the whole country are not of greater importance than the mere temporary triumph of either of the political parties in Kansas." Buchanan emphasized that this constitution presented an opportunity to decide Kansas's fate; if Congress let it pass, the territory might descend into "domestic discord" and civil war before another such opportunity arose.[116]

Despite having been fired, Stanton convened the special session the same day Buchanan's speech was released to the nation. He told legislators that the convention ought to have considered the electoral results when it wrote the constitution but also blamed free-state men's noncompliance in the spring for "all the evils and dangers of the present critical hour." Without legitimately representing the people, they had organized a government that caused residents to fear that Congress would admit Kansas under its own unrepresentative constitution.[117] Because of the "sense of wrong and injustice, whether well- or ill-founded, and an apprehension of greater evils to arise therefrom," he was calling the legislature into session, but while some advocated repealing the law authorizing the convention as a way to subvert the Lecompton Constitution, Stanton warned against this option. Instead, he suggested they authorize a referendum for residents to vote for it "in either of the forms presented by the convention, and also against that constitution in both forms."[118] Stanton hoped for the best, although he feared these men had "nothing good or sensible in them."[119]

Acting as the legal representative of the territory, the legislature asked Congress to admit Kansas under the Topeka Constitution. Additionally, although a referendum was set for December 21, the newly convened free-state legislature arranged for a second referendum on January 4, the same day voters would select state officers under the Lecompton Constitution.[120] Moreover, on December 16, the legislature placed James Lane at the head of the militia over Stanton's veto; as the governor headed the militia and the president had denounced Lane as a "turbulent and dangerous character," this was a direct affront to the Buchanan administration.[121] This final act demonstrated the free-state faction's determination to ignore territorial law even when it controlled the legislature.

Local Democrats were as committed to their constitution as free-state men were opposed. On December 9, a proslavery convention at Lecompton nominated state officers, passed resolutions praising Buchanan, and emphasized "the duty of every true Democrat to support the Lecompton Constitution." They expressed disappointment with their executive team, accused Stanton of being in a "corrupt contract with the Black Republicans," and mourned the path taken by other national Democrats. The convention resolved "that though a Reeder, a Geary and a Walker have sought to reduce and prostitute the Democracy to the unholy ends of the Abolitionists, yet we rejoice that their careers have closed in Kansas in contempt and infamy to themselves and without injury to the Democratic party." The proslavery faction called the Lecompton Constitution a test of devotion to Democratic principles.[122]

Two weeks after Buchanan's annual message, on December 21, in the referendum set by the previous legislature and boycotted by free-state men, the Lecompton Constitution with slavery was overwhelmingly approved: 6,226 voters in favor and 569 against it without slavery. Typically, fraud was reported, especially in proslavery counties. For instance, in Kickapoo County, James

Buchanan, William Seward, John Frémont, and Horace Greeley all voted for the proslavery constitution.[123] This resort once again to fraud where it was not needed demonstrates the proslavery faction's increasing desperation. Convinced they had won the October elections, they now witnessed a free-state legislature called into special session, a month before previous legislators' terms expired, undo their actions.

On January 4, 1858, 10,226 residents voted against the Lecompton Constitution as a whole (instead of on its provisions) in the free state legislature's referendum, while 138 accepted it with slavery and 23 accepted it without slavery. At the same time, voters selected potential office holders electing the free-state ticket narrowly over the proslavery ticket. For instance, George W. Smith was elected governor over F. Marshall by only 330 votes; the other offices were also within this range, with the narrowest victory margin being 301 votes for secretary of state and the widest being the 696 votes that would have sent Marcus Parrott to Congress over Joseph Carr. Buchanan interpreted the free-state men's willingness to cast votes for state officers as acceptance of the Lecompton process. In actuality, however, their strategy was to elect "tried and true Free State men" to prepare for the possibility of admission; if Congress accepted the constitution, these candidates pledged to "favor an immediate call of a convention, to wipe out every vestige of that odious constitution, and to frame and adopt a new one...."[124]

Yet despite the triumph of the free-state ticket, the narrowness of victory reveals residents' disinclination to participate in elections relevant to actual governance as opposed to the form of government. Indeed, the willingness of both sides to argue principle when thwarted but to ignore it while in power demonstrates that at both extremes, these opposing factions were concerned with outcome, not process. While the election of a free-state ticket for state government positions did not reveal overwhelming strength, it represented a shift of momentum in favor of a free state and a Republican one at that. At the beginning of the year, the proslavery *Squatter Sovereign* had recognized that a shift in strategy might be needed. "Let us make Kansas a slave State and Democratic if possible," the journal opined in February 1857. "If not, then next best we can, which is to make it a National Democratic State should slavery be abolished."[125] However, 11 months later, even this lesser goal seemed out of reach.

Conclusion

Over the fall, Walker had come to oppose the Lecompton Constitution, a process prompted no doubt by the fraud that marred the October elections. Thus when he left Kansas on his leave, Walker went to Washington to personally impress upon Buchanan the necessity of defeating the now tarnished constitution. Democratic Party loyalists were wary of his anti-Lecompton stance, and the *New York Herald* decried that the party was divided by "technicalities and secondary issues," referring to the governor's insistence that the constitution be submitted to the people as "this Walker movement for the annihilation of the Democratic Party, and the reduction of all parties to hostile sectional and disunion organizations."[126] Although the November 18 editorial in the *Washington Union* ought to have forewarned him, a cabinet meeting provided Walker's final shock. After what was described as a "cordial" meeting with the president, he updated the cabinet on Kansas affairs and informed them of his implacable opposition to the constitution. He found the cabinet, particularly Black, Cobb, and Thompson, equally implacable in expressing their full support for both the convention and its constitution. Walker then "wrapped about him the garb of the martyr, stalked from the meeting," and began his break with the administration.[127]

On December 15, Walker resigned. Writing Cass that he would no longer be able "to preserve the peace or promote the public welfare" after Buchanan's message, he maintained that the administration had placed him in an untenable position. Walker reiterated that his acceptance of the governorship had been predicated on submitting the constitution to the people, which the president and the cabinet fully understood. "These pledges I cannot recall or violate without personal dishonor and the abandonment of fundamental principles."[128] Unlike Reeder, who embarrassed Pierce by returning to Kansas after discovering their differences of opinion, Walker chose to resign rather than force Buchanan to remove him for disobeying his instructions; doing otherwise would transform him into a "public martyr in the defence of the great principle of self government."[129] Thus, despite a strong start brimming with confidence, he resigned his post a mere six months after his inauguration.[130]

By the time Walker resigned, he felt bitter, betrayed, and abandoned. Unlike his predecessors, he had not had any great disasters; yet he had shown a tendency toward creative interpretation of his instructions. Buchanan's insistence that the Democratic Party support the Lecompton Constitution, regardless of whether it commanded territorial support, forced his resignation. The president held firm, however, because he did not share Walker's understanding of their agreement. In responding to Walker's letter of resignation, Cass bluntly conveyed his disapproval. He wrote that it was odd for an officer of the government to pursue this "unusual course" of placing in the State Department's files "criticism" of administration policy, especially given his lack of obedience to his orders. Cass disputed Walker's allegations, stating that the convention had exercised their right to decide what, if any, part of the constitution to submit to a referendum. Buchanan believed that the convention had submitted "the all-important and dangerous question of slavery" to the people. Moreover, Cass postulated that Walker charged Buchanan with changing his Kansas policy merely because "he had not treated the submission of this momentous question as a mere nullity." According to Cass, the president "never entertained or expressed the opinion that the convention were bound to submit any portion of the constitution to the people, except the question of slavery, much less that the other portions of the constitution would be invalid without such a submission." Finally, he reminded Walker that "with the question, whether Kansas was to be a free or slave state, you were not to interfere. You were to secure to the people of Kansas a free and fair election, to decide this question for themselves."[131]

Walker deserves approbation for convincing free-state men to participate in the election, which was imperative to normalize local government, but he also was excessively independent. As Walker's biographer states, "[T]hat Buchanan and his cabinet had committed themselves to support Walker without qualification cannot be doubted."[132] However, even accepting that Buchanan issued such a broad pledge to Walker, it is unlikely the president expected him to aggrandize it as he did. The explicitness with which Walker issued pledges and tied Buchanan to them was bound to make the president uncomfortable, regardless of how much he might have agreed with him. Even the *Boston Journal* criticized Walker's "restless officiousness": "He has no idea of the negative virtues of a judicious abstinence from acts and words. He overdoes his part, and gets himself into trouble by talking, writing, and acting where there is not the slightest need for it."[133] Walker's speech at Topeka the week after his inaugural exemplifies this tendency. He assured the audience that "the chief magistrate of the union, will join you in opposition." In his many speeches, he was remarkably free with Buchanan's name and frequently made promises on his behalf. After such explicit statements, the president's repudiation of Walker humiliated him, which alone could account for his subsequent hostility.

It is also possible that Walker continued to think of himself as Buchanan's equal based on their service in President James Polk's cabinet and had difficulty understanding, as Cass pointed out, that in accepting the Kansas post he was obligated to follow Buchanan's directives. However, after a few weeks in the territory, both Stanton and Walker had gained a different perspective and began to see themselves as apart from the national administration. Stanton would later assert that he and Walker had a greater duty than that which they owed Buchanan. "It is true the organic act, alike binding on the President and myself, gave certain powers and imposed certain responsibilities on the Governor, which were independent of the President and rested solely on the conscience of the Governor so long as he held that position." Stanton seemed surprised to discover that the executive team was "in a certain sense only the agents of the Washington government, inasmuch, as you well know, they were wholly at the mercy of the President, to be dismissed at any moment at his own whim and caprice, or at the suggestion of such heated partisans as might at any moment reach his ear and command his confidence. . . ."[134] Walker's and Stanton's conduct led the *New York Tribune* to describe them as assuming a new function: "Instead of confining themselves to enforcing the bogus laws, they become political missionaries."[135]

Both Buchanan and Walker made promises, but as the months passed each began to emphasize separate aspects of their statements. In his inaugural, Walker had spoken of the convention as an inviolable entity and warned that "the absentees are as much bound under the law and Constitution, where there is no fraud or violence, by the act of the majority of those who do vote, as though all had participated in the election. Otherwise, as voting must be voluntary, self-government would be impracticable, and monarchy or despotism would remain as the only alternative."[136] The delegate election had been conducted without significant fraud, and while some districts were inadequately registered, free-state men had opted out of the process beforehand as a matter of principle. The pertinent fraud under Walker's watch affected only the October elections, not the convention. Over time, however, he began to conflate the two and to perceive the convention itself as fraudulent. Thus, Walker began to focus on the "no fraud or violence" aspect of his inaugural in deciding to repudiate the Lecompton Constitution.

On the other hand, Buchanan had written Walker that he was "willing to stand or fall" on the question of submission. However, this letter contained a restriction. In the same paragraph, he had stated that "should the convention of Kansas adopt this principle, all will be settled harmoniously. . . ."[137] As the months passed, the president began to favor this qualifier in recalling his instructions to Walker. He maintained that the question of submission belonged solely to the legitimately constituted convention and that to obstruct the convention's judgment would be to violate the will of the people. Yet even as it became clear that Walker and Buchanan understood their obligations differently, the president was in a delicate position. Buchanan had had to make an extraordinary effort to persuade such a national man to go to Kansas when Walker expected a cabinet post. Thus reining in Walker as he embraced his position with admirable enthusiasm was awkward. Was Buchanan sincere when he pledged his support? Yes, but Buchanan and Walker most likely agreed on the vital issues when the president tendered the offer and Walker allowed himself to be persuaded. Both were Union men whose formative political experiences had been forged in the same national cauldron. But Walker's experiences in the territory altered his understanding of what threatened the Union, and he came to see the illegal graspings of the proslavery party as the greater hazard. In Washington, Buchanan remained convinced that the greater threat to the Union would be allowing abolitionists to thwart the will of the people as expressed in their convention. Despite overwhelming evidence to the contrary, Democrats like Buchanan persistently regarded the free-state men as an abolitionist fringe group. This inability to read the actual political layout accurately in the distant territory negatively affected the administration's ability to forge an effective policy for Kansas.

7

"The Noise of Democracy"

The Struggle over the Lecompton Constitution in Congress and Kansas

At the end of 1857, President James Buchanan stood at a crossroads. Although he had clearly supported the Lecompton Constitution in his annual address, it was written before territorial residents had voted in what turned out to be two referenda on the question. Buchanan had concluded his section on Kansas by stating that the territory had "for some years occupied too much of the public attention," which could best be devoted to far more significant issues. "When once admitted into the Union, whether with or without slavery, the excitement beyond her own limits will speedily pass away, and she will then, for the first time, be left, as she ought to have been long since, to manage her own affairs in her own way."[1] The president's initial Kansas policy, then, was to normalize Kansas by having his governor ensure full participation in the political process, focused on the production of a state constitution. However, presented with such a negative vote, it was unclear if Buchanan would drop his support or how Congress would respond to its submission.

Two successive governors advised him that the constitution was flawed, but would the president consider whether these men discerned a reality imperceptible from distant Washington? Would he listen to a growing outcry against the constitution evident in both Kansas and Congress? Ultimately, Buchanan would not reassess his plans for the territory. Driven by party concerns in advance of the 1860 presidential election and a genuine belief that the ongoing Kansas conflict endangered the Union, Buchanan insisted that apprehensions about the constitution's legitimacy and whether the people's will was being respected simply were not as important as seizing the opportunity the Lecompton Constitution presented to settle the Kansas controversy through admission. Ultimately, the combination of an overly invested president and a dutiful but reluctant governor shaped the constitution's fate.

Buchanan's Second Selection: The Reluctant James Denver

With Kansas governor Robert Walker and Secretary Frederick Stanton absent from their posts (the former had resigned and the latter had been removed) and the Lecompton dilemma still unresolved in December 1857, the administration needed a loyal emissary, and Buchanan tapped former California congressman James Denver. As one antislavery advocate recounted, his appointment came as proslavery forces were losing, when "politically dead Kansas Governors were strewn all over the country, and the Administration was advertising for some Goliath of Gath to overcome the armies of Kansas. . . . Seven Governors—all, all sent as messengers to plant slavery on Kansas soil—had been thwarted, and failed. . . ."[2] Denver's selection to be this Goliath came as a surprise, most of all to Denver himself.

On December 10, during a tour of Kansas as commissioner of Indian affairs, Denver was unexpectedly appointed secretary of the territory he toured. His frontier experience had come in California: in 1850, he served on a relief committee to protect immigrants; became a state senator in 1852; was appointed secretary of state in 1853; and then served in Congress from 1855 to 1857, when he was appointed to the Indian Bureau.[3] However, Denver was loath to leave his position, a reluctance likely fed by his predecessors' fates. As one Missouri friend worried, "Four politically dead governors attest the graveyard tendency of Kansas statesmen, but your good judgment & prudence with the beacon light of the past may save you—but *we fear* the end will be unfavorable—nevertheless you have our best wishes—for we are Democrats. . . ."[4] Only after Stanton emphasized that the federal government would be unrepresented unless Denver accepted did he relent, but he insisted on being replaced after the session.[5] Eleven days later, however, he was promoted to acting governor; in February, he was appointed governor. In his instructions to Denver, Buchanan emphasized the Lecompton Constitution's legitimacy, insisting that the people had the duty to vote upon its provisions and the right to do so unimpeded. He informed Denver that his chief duty was to preserve the peace, authorizing him to call upon federal troops if necessary and suggesting their dispersal to polls beforehand. Moreover, Buchanan recognized the special session of the legislature that Stanton had called a month before legislators' terms were to have commenced, stating that its "rightful action must also be respected" but insisted they not interfere with the elections set by the convention.[6]

Denver's appointment as acting governor came on December 21, the same day residents would vote on the constitution. His inaugural address conveyed a disbelief that Kansas was devoid of anyone willing to listen to "the voice of reason," for there had to be "enough of the conservative element remaining to uphold and enforce the laws. . . ." Denver reminded free-state men that "abandoning the elective franchise . . ." was not appropriate and could be perceived as indifference. He dismissed concerns about potential fraud, arguing that even if they were true, choosing not to vote was not how Americans should protect their right to vote. Finally, Denver warned residents against making personal disputes political and being drawn into conflicts over land claims.[7]

Although this election passed without incident, rumors persisted that the January 4 elections (for state officers under the Lecompton Constitution and the free-state referendum on the constitution itself) would be disrupted, leading Denver to announce plans to use troops to protect the polls. He also addressed a long-standing electoral issue: who was a bona fide Kansas settler. Congress had declared that resident white men over the age of 21 could vote, but the territory had been plagued by differing interpretations of a "resident." He cited Webster in clarifying that presence in the territory alone did not convey residency and warned that anyone violating these provisions would be arrested and, if necessary, extradited.[8] Finally, he instructed U.S. Marshal E.S. Dennis on his duties in protecting all voters, not just those in Oxford and Shawnee in Johnson County, the scene of fraud the previous October, as Dennis had planned. Moreover, although the marshal believed his deputies could judge the legality of votes, Denver emphasized that only judges of election could do so, since "to place the troops under the control of violent partisans and giving them unlimited powers may involve you in very serious troubles, and defeat the end we have in view—a fair election."[9]

As these dispatches reveal, the marshals assigned to preserve the peace continued to plague this governor as they had the others. On January 9, federal troops had to intervene when a mob searched private homes in Leavenworth for arms. Denver was forced to reprimand Dennis, emphasizing that local law enforcement had to instill confidence among the populace, but "when the officers of the law choose to look on carelessly, and to allow a mob to run wild without attempting to interpose their authority to preserve the peace, it is no wonder if the people should be dissatisfied with them."[10]

While Denver had the requisite skills and conscientiously fulfilled his responsibilities, his greatest challenge was his utter disinterest in the position. "I am greatly in hopes that the whole thing will be closed up in this month, and let me off," Denver complained barely two weeks after his appointment. "Confound the place, it seems to have been cursed of God and man. Providence gave them no crops last year, scarcely, and now it requires all the powers conferred on me by the President to prevent them from cutting each other's throats." Moreover, unlike John Geary who embraced even the smallest task, Denver was taken aback by residents' expectations. "Many people here seem to think that the Governor is all powerful, and if one man makes mouths at another, he must run with a complaint to the Governor about it. If a desperado is to be taken, it is expected that the Governor will do it." Not surprisingly, Denver's immediate focus was extricating himself from the "cursed" territory.[11]

On January 11, Denver wrote Buchanan that not all the administration's goals were within reach. Even though a majority of residents wanted a free state, the party could still have a strong presence because the slavery question forced otherwise moderate men toward extremes. Although most Democrats wanted slavery, many would be satisfied with a free state so long as the subsequent congressional delegation was not full of Republicans. Denver believed the party would rebound after admission, but Lecompton was not the answer. If Kansas was so admitted, it would further inflame tensions because "an organization exists here whose purpose is to assassinate every man who takes an oath of office under the Lecompton Constitution."[12]

Instead, Denver believed he had "a remedy which will localize the Kansas question, heal all breaches in the Democratic party on that subject, and effectually stop abolition clamor." If the government would put aside the Lecompton process, Congress could enable a new convention. He then envisioned Congress directing Kansas to send a new constitution straight to the president, who would simply proclaim the state admitted. Alas, this plan was unfeasible—the legislative branch has power over the territories and bypassing it would be unconstitutional.[13] And given that the South was unlikely to want to set aside a legal, proslavery constitution, it was politically unviable as well.

Although Buchanan did not reply until late March after the constitution had begun its legislative journey, in late January Secretary of the Interior Jacob Thompson expressed his disappointment with Denver's views. He believed the administration risked criticism from both sections unless it stayed the course. Until Congress accepted it, Denver had to control the legislature and ensure Republicans did not benefit from the Kansas issue as they had in 1856. "We are like the man who held the wolf," Thompson warned, "to hold on is bad enough; to let go is inevitable death."[14] As Thompson demonstrated, the administration was irrevocably committed to Lecompton. Two successive governors advised that the constitution was flawed, but White House officials did not consider whether territorial appointees might discern a reality imperceptible from distant Washington.

Denver tried to follow Thompson's advice, but the free-state legislature proved as aggressive and intransigent as its proslavery predecessors. Further, James Lane continued to torment the local government despite the ascendancy of his party. During the special session of the free-state legislature in December, he had been given command of the militia over Stanton's veto; the next month, the regular session passed a similar bill. Denver condemned this effort because it encroached on his powers,[15] but the bill passed over his veto, leading Lane to blast him as "a calumniator, perjurer and tyrant."[16] The legislature also repealed the more repugnant territorial laws such as the harsh punishments for interfering with slaves. However, Denver found the bill too stringent since slave owners had a right to protect their property, and he vetoed it.[17] This too was overridden. The free-state legislature also tried to relocate to Minneola over Denver's veto, but he refused to move, would not transfer records, and was vindicated when Attorney General Jeremiah Black declared the move unconstitutional.[18]

Finally, to Denver's displeasure, the legislature passed an act for another constitutional convention. "I concluded that we had constitutions enough," he recalled. "We had then pending before Congress the Lecompton Constitution, which was a pretty ugly-looking affair all around. We had the Topeka Constitution, which was objected to on the other side just as much; and then we had the Territorial Government established by act of Congress, and I thought we had about as much government as one little Territory could very well live under." He pocket-vetoed the bill to prevent an override. Although a bill became law if not returned within three days, this was only when the legislature was in session, which it was not. Undeterred, they endorsed it as if it had been returned and re-sent it to Denver, who promptly burned it. Undaunted, the legislators merely took the burnt bill, declared it legal, and moved forward with convention plans.[19] This latter episode demonstrates that neither the proslavery nor the free-state legislature held fast with legality in advocating their views.

Introduction of the Lecompton Constitution

In Washington, Buchanan was undeterred by the January 4 election, in which free-state men repudiated the constitution by more than ten thousand votes. "The Kansas question, from present appearances, will not be one of much difficulty; *& all is not yet told*," Buchanan wrote a friend in January. He believed Congress would accept the constitution or be punished by voters in the fall for "their safety consists in their firmness & fidelity."[20] The president believed so strongly in this measure, he declared passage "vital to his administration."[21] He was not alone in discounting the recent referendum, because as one Washington newspaper observed, it was unauthorized and "can in no way affect" the constitution's legality.[22] Although Buchanan was disappointed the convention had not submitted the entire constitution to a vote, it was valid.[23]

On February 2, he sent Congress his copy of the constitution. Because it realized the Democratic principle of non-intervention while removing the slavery question from the halls of Congress, he urged their endorsement.[24] The president reminded legislators that "a great delusion seems to pervade the public mind" due to propaganda that gave the impression that the territory had two parties divided on the slavery question. Instead, Kansans were divided by adherence to the law. There were those who "are loyal to this government and those who have endeavored to destroy its existence by force and by usurpation. . . ." But the Topeka faction continued to cling "with such treasonable tenacity" to their revolutionary course, and it would "prove fatal to us as a nation" if the nation put aside its adherence to the law.[25] Buchanan emphasized the convention's legality, dismissing free-state protesters because they had willingly opted out of the process. He would have preferred a popular vote but deferred to the convention. Moreover, repudiation in favor of "the disaffected" would likely increase agitation. On the other hand, accepting the constitution would allow local questions to be decided at the ballot box and federal troops to be withdrawn. Finally, if Kansas were admitted, the "dark and ominous clouds" hovering over the nation would "be dissipated with honor." To do otherwise would leave Kansas under even greater threat.[26]

The winter proved vexing for the Buchanan administration as anti-Lecompton forces gathered steam. The plan, former Illinois congressman John McClernand wrote, was to "Agitate! Rouse the people!"[27] And this strategy succeeded as an outcry arose. Even if Congress accepted the constitution, it "will *never* be submitted to by the people of Kansas, *civil war first*," wrote one antislavery advocate. "[T]he plans of the slave power for our subjugation will be thwarted, *peaceably* if they can be, *forceably* if they must—*at all events Kansas must be free*."[28] But proslavery proponents were equally angered by the possibility that a legal constitution would be set aside. "We look upon all these suggestions as pleasing deceits—baits manufactured for party purposes—to quiet the South in the progress of the North to mastery in the Union . . . ," the *Charleston Mercury* wrote in dismissing lures like Cuba. "Now the fight is for a tardy and one-sided justice in Kansas. . . . No distraction now—no squintings toward the ever green isle. The South must be earnest and united, and Kansas is the battle-field."[29]

Senator Stephen Douglas (IL) was the most prominent critic of the constitution, and he began his assault the day after Buchanan's annual address. But there had been earlier indications that he might break with the administration. The *Washington Union*'s editor warned Buchanan in August that if Douglas went "with the extreme South, he will be strangled in Illinois, and he is no more in all the North, if he supports your Kansas policy he will strike from his support all the . . . forces which have made him what he is. . . ."[30] Indeed 55 of 56 Illinois newspapers condemned the constitution. In this atmosphere, backing the administration was too risky for an aspirant to the presidency.[31] In December, Buchanan threatened to oust Douglas from the party and remove his state's patronage appointments. Douglas persisted and although the president failed to oust him, by the end of February, he was complaining that his friends had been removed from office; that promises of hostility toward him were demanded of new appointees; and that the administration was directing a campaign to defeat him.[32]

On February 6, Douglas wrote John W. Forney, the organizer of an anti-Lecompton rally in Philadelphia, that the convention lacked the authority to create a constitution. Instead, it should only have determined the people's views on admission and sent Congress a memorial to that effect. Therefore, anyone who "cherishes the time-honored principle of his party, and is determined, in good faith, to carry out the doctrine of self-government and popular sovereignty," should repudiate the constitution.[33] Although Douglas had claimed the convention did not have to submit the constitution to a popular vote the previous June, he now attempted to lure Democrats away from the administration by tying its repudiation to older party principles.

Kansas's most recent executive team joined Douglas in dissent. Despite Walker's December pledge not to embarrass the president, by the spring he and Stanton openly denounced the constitution before a variety of large, anti-Lecompton demonstrations. Stanton alone spoke in Columbus, Albany, Philadelphia, and New York, intent on using his influence to defeat it.[34] Removed for calling a special legislative session, Stanton expressed little regret because the "people had a fair claim to be heard . . . ," and despite the cost, he was pleased his actions allowed that. Now that the people had spoken, the Democratic Party had an "opportunity to defend the true principles of constitutional liberty, and to save itself from disastrous division and utter overthrow." If Congress would just listen, Kansas would be at peace.[35]

Walker's speeches emphasized that he had accepted the Kansas post due to a shared understanding that the constitution would be submitted to a popular vote. Although he denied charging Buchanan with "willful deception," Walker's speeches did just that. He decried the president's annual message in which

Buchanan focused solely on the constitution's slavery clause as evidence of duplicity. Had he known the president harbored such opinions, Walker would have refused the assignment. Instead, to his "surprise and astonishment," Buchanan had developed a new theory of submission.[36] Combined with the wide dissemination of Walker's resignation letter, these speeches helped rally anti-Lecompton forces. To parry this damage, Buchanan carefully noted Walker's letters to Secretary of State Lewis Cass, then before the Senate, to demonstrate the illegality of the Topeka government and how it threatened the territory's peace.[37] Moreover, given the danger the renewal of antislavery agitation posed, there simply was not time to elect delegates, hold a convention, and frame a new constitution.[38]

Over several months Congressman William Maclay (NY) defended the convention's right not to submit the full constitution to a vote. Like Douglas, he based his position on the party's popular sovereignty and non-intervention doctrines but believed these doctrines were best expressed by insulating the convention from national pressure. While the constitution could not be amended for a few years, the Topeka Constitution had the same provision. Moreover, Congress could not "force" a constitution on the territory, since it had been written by a legally convened body of Kansans. Maclay argued that "patriotic regard" demanded admission. "The prolonged, perpetual agitation of this subject may promote the ends of some political party or faction, but cannot fail to aggravate the sectional animosities which already exist. . . ."[39] However, Northern Democrats like Maclay were no match for the Douglas-Walker-Stanton trifecta.

The United States Democratic Review, a prominent Democratic journal, put a Pollyannish spin on the struggle and resultant bloodshed in the territory. The journal argued that daily violence in California in 1852 far outstripped Kansas's violence, and while there existed a "revolution in progress," this agitation defined the nation. Viewing the state as an evolving entity existing solely for convenience, the *USDR* held that as a constitutional issue slavery was irrelevant since any constitution could be amended to more accurately reflect the people's views whenever they saw fit. As long as the constitution established republican government, Congress could not reject it. The journal did not address the difficulties of amendment (requiring a two-thirds vote) versus passage (a one-half vote) or the ethics of accepting a constitution rejected by the majority of residents.[40]

Canvassing Congress, Buchanan was cautiously optimistic, believing 36 of 39 Democratic senators would support the bill. As usual, the House would be a greater challenge, as there were 92 Republicans, 14 Americans, 100 Administration Democrats, and 21 anti-Lecompton Democrats. Of these,

Buchanan believed 110 would vote for passage.[41] Although Senate opposition was too weak to represent a genuine threat, the real surprise came from Douglas—although his opposition was anticipated, its depth and tenor came as a shock.[42]

The Lecompton Bill in the Senate

Douglas had hoped to sway the Committee on Territories to his side, but ultimately decided there was "no hope of an amicable adjustment of the Kansas question" within the committee. Rather, "it has become apparent," he wrote a friend, "that the administration is more anxious for my destruction than they are for the harmony & unity of the Democratic Party."[43] Indeed, on February 18 the committee issued three reports instead of the typical two. James Green's (MO) majority report supported Buchanan, and he offered the bill on the floor. Jacob Collamer (VT) and Benjamin Wade (OH) issued a Republican minority report that reviewed the territory's history through the lens of the Howard Committee, indicted the Lecompton convention, and supported Walker's and Stanton's actions, concluding that admitting Kansas under this bill would "give success to fraud and encouragement to iniquity. . . ."[44] Finally, Douglas issued a report representing the Democratic minority and echoing by now familiar arguments that the constitution did not reflect the will of the people. He asserted that Buchanan was wrong—rather than bringing peace, admission risked establishing two competing state governments, one supporting the Lecompton Constitution, one opposed.[45]

James Hammond (SC) refuted Douglas's understanding of the "will of the people," for a convention could not be dismissed as a mere "creature of the Territory Legislature." Compared to a convention, it was a "petty corporation, appointed and paid by the Congress of the United States, without a particle of sovereign power." Because of rapid immigration, conventions represent the people when called; allowing legislatures to subsequently annul their decisions would engender an endless cycle. Like many Southerners, Hammond believed opposition masked a sectional bias. In an early speech, William Seward (NY) had noted the North could not know whether the South would interfere if Kansas abolished slavery, but neither side had guarantees. How could the South know the North would not "plunder us with tariffs," Hammond asked, "that you will not bankrupt us with internal improvements and bounties on *your* exports; that you will not cramp us with navigation laws, and other laws impeding the facilities of transportation to southern produce?"[46] Kansas's admission had ramifications beyond its borders.

Lafayette Foster (CT) disputed Buchanan's rationale for submission, arguing that he had not provided a "statesmanlike reason" to accept the constitution—the president was merely a party man wanting to institute slavery—and urged fellow Senators to "be just and fear not."[47] However, despite such views and Douglas's active dissent, with 39 Senate Democrats, the bill was safe. However, a number of senators offered amendments. Robert Toombs (GA) wanted to clarify that residents could alter the constitution after admission, but his proposal to make explicit what was widely understood failed, most likely due to opponents' reluctance to help in any way.[48] Samuel Houston (TX), an independent, atypical Southerner who had opposed the 1854 Kansas-Nebraska Act, proposed submitting both the Topeka and Lecompton constitutions to a popular vote and enabling a new convention if neither passed.[49] Green wanted to tie Kansas's and Minnesota's admissions together but was also rebuffed.[50] Garnering more support was John Crittenden's (KY) proposal to return the constitution for a popular vote: if accepted, Kansas would become a state without further debate or action, but it was defeated 24 to 34. On March 23, the Senate accepted the constitution 33 to 25; Douglas was joined by three other Democrats: Charles Stuart (MI), David Broderick (CA), and George Pugh (OH).[51]

Buchanan Increases the Pressure

Warily watching these proceedings, Buchanan was convinced that the Crittenden resolution would be disastrous, but his relief at the Senate's rejection of it was short-lived, since the House resurrected it. Thus the president intensified his offensive. First, he reached out to Denver in March, flattering the governor by commenting that had he been sent to Kansas "instead of Walker, the territory would have been in a much more quiet condition than it is at present." Buchanan believed the bill had to pass because a defeat would cause Americans to worry about the integrity of the Union and would lead to a decline in property values and foreign trade. Passage would greatly diminish sectional tensions while a rejection would damage the party. In addition, another constitution could not be framed and Kansas admitted in time, leaving the territory to be "the sport and the capital of the Black Republicans in the Presidential election of 1860." As such, Buchanan was sufficiently confident of passage that he told Denver he would rely upon him to distribute the new state's patronage.[52]

Maneuvering for the presidential contest of 1860 complicated this struggle. Lecompton's opponents included typical Democratic standard-bearers like Douglas and Walker whom Buchanan suspected of harboring presidential aspirations. There is no doubt that Walker had national ambitions and success in Kansas would strengthen his position. While it is difficult to understand a strategy that alienated the South, given his violation of Cass's instructions and insistence on a fair vote, Walker could not deviate from this course without damaging his reputation. Moreover, the president had to contend with his cabinet's ambitions; for instance, Secretary of the Treasury Howell Cobb's advice to support Lecompton might have been tinged by his own presidential plans.

Determined to prevent further bolting, Buchanan pressured party members. "The President is perfectly wrapped up in the sole idea of 'putting the thing through,' and all in office who oppose him, are compelled to walk the plank," R.S. Stevens, a former colleague from the Indian Office, wrote Denver, "while those who want office, must first be weighed in the Lecompton balance."[53] As the constitution moved through the House, former senator Henry S. Foote (MS) reported that "the anxious President had urged them, in language almost of imprecation, for God's sake, not to forsake him and the Democratic cause at this crisis."[54]

The House and the Lecompton Constitution

While the administration pushed the bill through the Senate comfortably, it immediately faltered in the House when it was referred to a special committee chaired by Thomas Harris (IL), a friend of Stephen Douglas, instead of being sent to the Committee on Territories. In a close vote, the absences of 2 Southern Democrats and 2 administration Democrats hurt; nonetheless, the negative votes of 22 Northern Democrats revealed the administration's weakness.[55] Harris's chairmanship was worrisome because his feelings on Lecompton were well known. In early February, he had written an anti-Lecompton meeting in Philadelphia that "sound Democratic doctrine" held that the people could not yield their rights to a convention, and despite being "stigmatized and abused by its [the administration's] hireling and plunder-gorged presses as renegades and demagogues," he would not be deterred. While Harris appreciated a strong executive, Buchanan was unlike former President Andrew Jackson, who always "went with the masses of the people, never against them. . . ."[56]

Similarly Samuel Cox (OH) warned that "expediency is a dangerous doctrine, when in collision with principles."[57] The House opposition held fast to principle, rejecting the president's pleas and attacking the constitution's legitimacy. Kansas delegate Marcus J. Parrott asserted that the Topeka and Lecompton constitutions differed significantly. Topeka "sprang spontaneously from the people, asking the restitution of their rights," while Lecompton was "the evil spawn of usurpation." Without popular support, it slinked along "like a convicted felon. . . ." Parrott acknowledged the free-state men had not participated in the Lecompton process but blamed Buchanan and Walker for promising they would later be able to vote on the constitution. Instead, the free-state faction had been betrayed, "lulled into indifference or deluded into inaction by this pledge. . . ." As such, Parrott insisted that the constitution violated the rights of Kansans and must be repudiated.[58]

However, Buchanan firmly believed he combined principle with peace and expediency and so the administration's friends stressed the legality of the process. Additionally, the need for Southern guarantees that Hammond had touched upon in the Senate were echoed in the remarks of James Dowdell (AL), who pointed out that many state constitutions used the phrase "we, the people" but had not been subject to popular suffrage. Moreover, conventions were "*the people* in an *organized* capacity." To then poll the people after the fact to see if the convention accurately expressed their will would be the actual violation, an exercise of "arbitrary power." Dowdell mentioned that his state legislature, like that of Georgia, was ready to "resist aggression" should Lecompton be abandoned. But he also condemned Northern Democrats who abandoned their party to ally with Republicans.[59]

Many hoped these desertions could be offset by Know-Nothings or those with "Southern affinities," but it became clear that "they can't be relied on and Lecompton is bound to be beaten."[60] Indeed, Douglas Democrats and House Republicans forged a formidable alliance. Their union was difficult to fathom; aside from this one issue, they had little in common, but these strange bedfellows emphasized January's free-state vote and ensured the Lecompton Bill would fail in the House.

Congress had not required previous territories to submit their constitutions to a popular vote, but Cox argued Kansas was so divided that doing so seemed prudent. "When the voice of the people is ambiguous, or in doubt, or against the constitution, it is clear Congress should require a popular verdict before it should pass judgment."[61] Because of such views, the House began to favor the Senate's rejected Crittenden resolution. Thus William Montgomery (PA) proposed returning the constitution to Kansas, where a new constitutional convention could amend it before submitting it to a popular vote.[62]

But accepting the Lecompton Constitution by relying on future amendments was risky. As Daniel Gooch (MA) stated, "If we wish to see civil war in Kansas, I know of no way in which we can so surely bring it about, as by admitting her into the Union under this constitution, and then telling her to alter or amend it. If ever there was a people of the globe, that needed a constitution, which should not be touched or altered for years to come, that people are to be found in Kansas."[63] Nonetheless, on March 31 the Crittenden-Montgomery Bill passed the House 120 to 112.[64] The House's refusal to accept the constitution outright prompted a large celebration in Leavenworth, where three to five thousand people gathered to "celebrate the downfall of the Lecompton swindle..." and offer cheers to the "120 who defended our cause in the House of Representatives."[65]

Into Committee

The Senate refused the substitution and requested a conference. The conference committee included Senators Green, Robert Hunter (VA), and Seward and Congressmen William English (IN), Alexander Stephens (GA), and William Howard (MI). They embraced English's compromise, which was based on resubmission. Congress would return the constitution to voters stipulating that, if rejected, Kansas could not become a state until it had 93,420 residents, sufficient for one representative. If accepted, the new state would receive a generous land grant, although the bill trimmed the convention's request by 20 million acres.[66]

This compromise convinced congressmen like Cox who did not want "to see or talk with any member of the administration," to support the constitution so they could deny being unduly influenced.[67] As Cobb's brother-in-law, Cox was in a difficult position. But he was one of the pivotal Northern Democrats who saw resubmission as granting the people an opportunity "to kill it if they did not like it" while ensuring they could continue to insist that they had never supported the Lecompton Constitution.[68] In the House, those who opposed the constitution but agreed to the English Bill included John Gilmer, an American from North Carolina, and the following Democrats: English and James Foley of Indiana; Joseph Cockerill, Cox, William Groesbeck, Laurence Hall, William Lawrence, and George Pendleton of Ohio; and Owen Jones of Pennsylvania.[69] This compromise was especially attractive for Democrats fearful of constituents' reactions.

The conference committee issued its report on April 23, and it passed both houses seven days later: the Senate accepted it 30 to 22, the House 112 to 103.[70] Buchanan greatly preferred the Senate bill, but was pleased with the compromise because "the Kansas question as a national question is at an end."⁷¹ But Buchanan was overly optimistic in believing the agitation had ended. On the night after passage, a victory celebration was held in front of the White House, and applause rang out when Senator William Gwin (CA) described the possible consequences of a no vote. "If she rejects it," he warned, "... then let Kansas shriek and let her bleed, for she shall never come in until she has sufficient population."⁷² Ultimately, Gwin was stating that there was one standard for a slave state, another for a free state.

Back in Kansas Territory

The Democratic Party line emphasized that Congress had spoken decisively and left the question of Kansas's future up to its residents. However, as the January vote ought to have indicated, the English Bill's conditions would prove unacceptable to the majority of Kansans. Many critics focused on the land grant—while its size was not at issue, its conditions were unprecedented, and so it was derisively termed the "English Swindle" or "Lecompton, Jr." for resembling a bribe. "The Infamy is Consummated" decried the *Freedom's Champion*. "Thus on the one hand they insult the honest settlers by attempting to *buy* their manhood, and *bribe* them to accept this infamous swindle with a few acres of land, while on the other hand they *threaten* and declare that we shall remain a territory unless we do accept it."⁷³ Most worrisome was the bill's failure to describe the land grant Kansas would receive if it repudiated the bill. Would Kansas get a land grant at all?

The land grant question reanimated a long-standing debate over land sales. In December 1856, after receiving President Franklin Pierce's instructions on land sales, then-governor John Geary had urged a delay arguing that peace was "of greater importance to the country than the entire value of the lands."⁷⁴ In addition to the overriding question of slavery, expansion also involved settlers' rights and federal land policy. Since the Northwest Ordinances had first codified territorial policies, land policy had been evolving ever favorably toward easing the path of settlement and encouraging infrastructure development. By mid-century, historian Paul Gates asserts, "settlers had been granted the right to buy land at low prices, the right to enter upon and select the public land before speculative monopolists could anticipate them, and the right to have at least a year of residence and development before they had to pay for their tracts."⁷⁵ However, under Pierce and Buchanan, land was offered directly to individuals rather than first being converted to public domain, which would subject it to public-land laws; this led to rampant speculation that, when combined with administration efforts to increase revenue from land sales, alienated settlers from the party.[76]

When Buchanan commenced land sales while simultaneously encouraging territorial support for the English Bill, the situation deteriorated. Although he might not have intended to link the two, residents viewed his timing with suspicion. Because few surveys had been completed, many settlers assumed it would be years before they needed to pay for the land.[77] Any income derived from the sales would have swelled the treasury, but it was not desperately needed—in comparison with the government's total income, land sales contributed 12 percent in 1856; 5 percent in 1857; and 4-7 percent in 1858.[78] John Everett was one of many residents infuriated by Buchanan's new policy. "The approaching land sales are being used as a screw to force the poor settlers to vote for the Lecompton Constitution," he wrote. If they voted yes, sales would be postponed; if they voted no, they would continue. Besides, money was scarce, and residents were convinced the "land sales were ordered for the express purpose of being able to exert the power of the creditor which the President possesses to force the poor debtor to vote according to his will." Everett argued this was "a new illustration of popular sovereignty truly!"[79]

Like Geary, Denver had advocated delaying the land sales until the spring of 1859, since allowing his unnamed successor to announce this policy would give him "an excellent start with that class of the people who are most interested in having it done." The land sales were delayed until November 1, but the controversy damaged Buchanan's administration.[80] In such an atmosphere, Denver's duties were "of the most delicate and important character. . . ." In sending him the English Bill, Cass noted that Congress had found the Lecompton provisions lacking and its land grant request excessive. Now Kansas residents were asked to agree to a more appropriate grant such as the one given Minnesota, whose admission was then being debated. Moreover, Cass reassured Denver that the bill ensured a fair election by making key territorial officials into an electoral board of commissioners.[81]

In the southern part of the territory, however, the people were distracted by ongoing disturbances that had started in mid-December 1857. Unable to fulfill his duties, the sheriff of Bourbon County had requested federal troops.[82] His situation was made more difficult when James Lane, the alleged head of the militia, organized two companies and placed James Montgomery in command of one. These companies clashed with local authorities, and a federal soldier was killed. Montgomery and his men then terrorized the countryside and drove many residents from the territory; some were forced out, some fled out of fear. While the free-state men seemed to support these activities, they soon began to worry that "some of those who had been driven away might return and take vengeance for the wrongs they had suffered."[83]

In fact, one such party, commanded by Charles Hamilton and composed of 21 proslavery and 7 free-state men, returned in May. On the 19th, at a trading post 12 miles from West Point, Missouri, on the military road between Forts Scott and Leavenworth on the Marais des Cygnes [Osage] river, they arrested a number of free-state men and fired on 11, killing 5 and wounding 4. As Denver acknowledged, these were revenge killings, but none of the dead had been implicated in earlier events (though such actions were unjustifiable regardless). At most, these men had "sympathized with Montgomery and his band" and had not acted to "protect their neighbors, who differed with them in political opinions, from their depredations. . . ."[84]

Denver sent Lieutenant J.P. Jones to investigate. He reported that Missourians wanted their property returned and Montgomery arrested. If not, they would not hinder Hamilton in his goal "to take Montgomery, dead or alive." Jones also blamed Linn County Sheriff Calvin McDaniel for inefficiency and a likely affiliation with Montgomery. The situation remained volatile, and perhaps hoping to avoid the interference of Missourians in southern Kansas, Jones recommended troops be dispatched to restrain Hamilton and protect Montgomery.[85]

In late May, after hearing rumors of more skirmishes, Denver followed Jones to Fort Leavenworth, intending to dispatch troops if needed. Upon arriving, however, the governor was "greatly astonished" to learn that the Second Cavalry had remained in Texas, leaving him only foot soldiers, the "equivalent to withdrawing the troops entirely from the territory, for infantry is useless as a posse in a country such as this." Without the cavalry, Denver had to rely upon often complicit local citizens, free-state men who might have "preserved the peace had they been so disposed," he complained to Cass, but whose "fanaticism and bitter political feelings induced them to allow the robbers to plunder the pro-slavery people first, and next the free-state democrats and conservative men generally, without restraint."[86] In June, there were renewed depredations after the troops were reassigned to Utah. Denver needed these troops to keep the peace because without them, he was dependent on partisan territorial courts, which amounted "almost to a denial of justice." Finally, he lacked sufficient funds to carry out his duties. "Left powerless by the government and unable to enforce the laws when violated," Denver could only be relieved that the "lawless men" of the territory were unaware of his situation.[87]

Next, after hearing that Montgomery had tried to burn Fort Scott, Denver traveled there. "Had such an act been done by savages," the governor noted, "it would have produced a thrill of horror throughout the whole country...." But many free-state men supported Montgomery despite "this most outrageous attempt at arson and murder." Moreover, when Denver arrived on June 11, "the people seemed to have forgotten that they had a civil governor." But he soon found them more disposed to uphold civil authority. Town residents accepted a series of resolutions and pledged to avoid land quarrels, stop frivolous arrests and prosecutions, restore peace, and enforce the laws, while Denver pledged to withdraw troops once he was convinced the community was at peace.[88]

Although the Fort Scott agreement settled the immediate problem, the military continued to trouble Denver. On June 28, Brevet Major Thomas W. Sherman, in command at Fort Leavenworth, informed him that the Department of the West had ordered the Second Infantry from Fort Leavenworth to Fort Randall in Nebraska Territory. As such, the two companies, which were in detached service at Fort Scott, had to return immediately to Fort Leavenworth for reassignment. However, Denver refused this relocation, citing his authority to use federal troops to keep the peace; additionally, he worried that "any new and unexpected movement of the troops among a people greatly alarmed and very suspicious cannot but be very prejudicial and the results of which I will not be answerable."[89] Denver conveyed his concerns to Sherman by letter and in person and believed Sherman had agreed not to order the troops' removal from Fort Scott until he received direct orders from headquarters or from Washington. On July 6, Sherman again asked permission to recall the troops and again was refused, this time by Acting Governor Hugh Walsh since Denver was in Washington. Despite Denver's orders and his own agreement to not act, Sherman ordered the two companies to return to Fort Leavenworth, 150 miles north, only to have them turn back after 100 miles when the War Department's order to stay put arrived. In doing so, Sherman thus effected precisely what Denver wished to avoid—marching troops back and forth through a still uneasy region in what might be perceived as a show of force rather than a relocation. Denver insisted Sherman be removed; soon after, Secretary of War John Floyd assured Cass that Sherman would explain himself, from Minnesota where he had been transferred.[90]

These troubles in the southern counties were not directly relevant to the English Bill but demonstrate how easily partisan fighting could destabilize the territory. Over the summer, Denver juggled these troubles in Bourbon and Linn counties, a recalcitrant commanding officer at Fort Leavenworth, and ensuring a fair election on the English Bill while attempting to govern the territory. In addition, his predecessor had spent a year's contingent expenses in a quarter—which left him in financial straits—but he found little sympathy in Washington.[91]

Throughout, Denver pursued his favorite project: persuading Washington to relieve him and trying to resign so he could return to the Indian Bureau. But the administration did not want to lose another governor. Instead, they relied on his party loyalty to compel his continued presence and linked his release to the territory's acceptance of the compromise. "Should the people accept, you can be early relieved, and your work is done; if they reject, your influence will be needed to keep peace, and prevent an effort to come here with a new and another constitution," Thompson wrote. "I believe you can hold the ship steady & keep this question from becoming a dangerous and alarming element in the canvass of 1860."[92] But Denver had scant hopes the English Bill would be accepted; without passage, he would be stuck as governor until 1860. He disagreed with the administration's Kansas policy, but proved his loyalty by keeping his feelings private. Although Denver withdrew his resignation after receiving this June letter, he found his backbone at summer's end.

On August 2, Kansans overwhelmingly rejected the English Bill, 11,300 to 1,788. As always, some clung stubbornly to their hopes. "We have gained at least a respite," the *Richmond South* reported in September, "in which, with proper effort, we might yet establish slavery in Kansas."[93] However, this rejection clearly signaled that Kansas was lost both to the Democratic Party and to slavery. As the *New Orleans Daily Picayune* reported, the vote revealed the preponderance of free-state settlers and showed that Kansas was "finally and irrevocably a free State, as it has for a long time been perfectly evident that it could not be permanently anything else."[94] Buchanan's only possible consolation was that Kansas would not send Republicans to Congress that winter.[95]

Even after Kansans rejected the English Bill, fallout continued because of the breach between Douglas and Buchanan. Douglas's course—both his refusal to support an administration measure and the verve with which he threw himself into the battle—continued to reap bitter fruits until the 1860 election. In early August, Attorney General Black wrote that since Douglas Democrats had started the war, they must end it, having "made common cause with the black republicans against us," while supporters would be "conciliated, treated kindly, and supported. . . ."[96] Douglas's defection also annoyed Cobb, who charged him with abusing both himself and the president and "doing more than any other man in the country to arouse and organize opposition to the only feature in the English Bill which made it acceptable to the South. . . ."[97]

On August 26, Denver requested a replacement; on September 1, he simply notified Cass he was resigning effective October 10, noting "peace now reigns where but lately all was confusion."[98] The administration reluctantly accepted Denver's resignation; but even on his last day, Thompson was unprepared to relent, sending Denver a pointed letter emphasizing the larger goals at stake. He thought Denver had sufficient influence to prevent Kansans from putting forward another constitution until they had the requisite population. He closed his letter by wishing Denver would stay, for "you have the wolf by the ears, holding on may be a sacrifice of personal interest, but letting go will surely sacrifice your party and compromise its strength."[99] Despite such heavy pressure, Denver was determined.

In his final address, the governor told residents that although he had quieted the territory, it was up to them to keep the peace. Federal intervention was "a stigma on the American people who boast of their voluntary obedience to the laws and their ability to govern themselves." Although he appreciated the regrets expressed after his resignation, Denver advised Kansans that the executive made "but little difference" so long as "the people are true to themselves and true to American institutions."[100] Now that the latest controversy had ended, it was time to behave in an orderly manner.

Denver's popularity was probably due to a professional attitude uncommon among his predecessors. As he later recalled, "I did not belong to the Territory. I was not here as a citizen of the Territory; I was here as a representative of the Federal Government. I therefore took no part in the local affairs of the Territory, only so far as was necessary to represent the Federal Government. While I had my own views as to the great question that agitated the country . . . I did not propose to mix with it."[101] As Thompson had remarked, Denver was among the more popular territorial governors; indeed, after his resignation both factions attended his farewell banquet.[102]

Although former governor Wilson Shannon dismissed Denver's accomplishments—"If I were a Governor again," he groused, "I would do as Denver does—sit in my chair and do nothing"[103]—Denver did have the smoothest administration, perhaps partly because he was the least invested in the position and its future rewards. Everyone appointed was ambitious, but he was well satisfied as commissioner of Indian affairs and unwilling "to sacrifice myself and the best days of my life, subjecting myself to all manners of privations and dangers, for glory alone."[104] Unlike even those governors who began by declaring neutrality but soon revealed marked preferences, he remained apolitical in his public persona. He remained a loyal national Democrat, and while his letters reveal considerable antipathy for the free-state legislative leaders, Denver approached his duties in a businesslike manner, impatient to calm the territory so he could leave. His letter of resignation reveals satisfaction with the August vote; although Kansas was not admitted, "peace now reigns" and the administration could "count with certainty" there would be "no more 'Kansas troubles.'"[105]

More important, Denver handled the Marais des Cygnes massacre, the 1858 equivalent of the Pottawatomie Massacre, without allowing the territory to descend into the guerrilla warfare of 1856. Despite weak responses to the havoc Lane and Montgomery engaged in, Kansas did not see the type of disorder or organized violence of two years earlier. This might have been due to a widespread sense that because the free-state party was in control of state offices, it was only a matter of time until Kansas would become a free state. Moreover, the *St. Louis Republican* reported that Denver had made "sincere admirers and steadfast friends" of the free-state faction.[106] Whether from a sense that such behavior would no longer be tolerated, as the *St. Louis Republican* speculated, or from sheer exhaustion from the years of turmoil, Denver left the territory in far better shape than he found it. Furthermore, he bequeathed Samuel Medary, his successor, "a different population there from what I expected, a population that was disposed to listen to what was said to them, who were disposed for peace."[107]

Within the territory, the two factions evolved into typical party rivals. On November 25, Democrats called a convention at Leavenworth where they pledged slavery would not be an issue. Among the resolutions passed was one acknowledging that "the causes which have hitherto divided and estranged the people of Kansas no longer exist." However, Democrats remained suspicious of Republicans for their "negro-equality tendencies" and favored excluding free blacks from Kansas.[108] Similarly, the original free-state party, a fragile organization due to its overreliance on personality, was finally replaced by an official Republican Party.

Kansas's subsequent path to statehood was far quieter than may have been expected. Despite Denver's exhortations against more constitutions, the territory submitted a free-state constitution on January 6, 1859, but since Kansas was still underpopulated, Congress ignored it. In a referendum held two months later, residents voted to begin the statehood process anew that summer in Wyandotte.[109] The delegate election on June 7 was closely contested, with Democrats polling 6,155 to Republicans' 7,374 votes, but due to districting, Democrats could only claim 17 of 52 seats.[110] Republicans' strength continued to grow, and in the December 1 legislative elections, they carried the entire ticket with a 64 to 11 edge in the House while Democrats only managed 3 seats in the Senate.[111]

The Wyandotte convention was less controversial than that at Lecompton.

On October 4, Kansas accepted its constitution, 10,421 to 5,530.[112] Free-state activists saw the vote as slavery's final defeat. "'Atchison precinct' is the strongest pro-slavery of any in this part of Kansas," Julia Lovejoy reported, "and it gave a majority of one! We heard the booming of cannon along the river, that told us that free principles were triumphing, and pro-slavery subserviency was breathing its last gasp in Kansas."[113] Congress received the constitution in February 1860, and while the House accepted it on April 11, the Senate postponed consideration until after the presidential election.[114] During the debate on Kansas's admission from December 11 to January 21, 1861, six Southern senators returned home; although it had no real effect on passage, their departure lent it a certain irony.[115]

Conclusion

Despite Buchanan's disappointment when Kansas rejected the English Bill, he believed he had diverted attention "from fighting to voting, a most salutary change."[116] In the spring, the *Freedom's Champion* had warned that the bill it denigrated as "The Settler" would have unintended consequences. Eastern papers "proclaim that the Democracy have *settled* the Kansas question. They are only mistaken a little in the terms. Instead of the Democracy *settling* the Kansas question, the *Kansas question* has most effectually *settled* the *Democracy*."[117] But although the party was hurt in midterm elections, the country was in a recession, which hurts incumbents.[118] In the House, Democrats declined from 128 to 92, but nearly 60 percent of these came from Pennsylvania and New York, states with active oppositions and party divisions throughout the 1850s. Also, Northern losses included 12 Democrats who had voted against Lecompton.[119] In Pennsylvania, Republicans joined with anti-Democratic groups such as the "People's Party" and campaigned on a pro-tariff, anti-Lecompton platform to defeat the party.[120] These successes in Buchanan's home state led many to believe that Lecompton was a pivotal issue, but he was more sanguine about this rebuke. "Poor bleeding Kansas is quiet and behaving herself in an orderly manner; but her wrongs have melted the hearts of sympathetic Pennsylvanians or rather Philadelphians. In the interior of the State the Tariff was the damaging question. . . ." Remaining resolute, the president reassured his niece that the upcoming congressional session would be successful.[121]

Because of his identification with such a widely despised bill, the president was forced to deny he had violated various pledges and principles. In his second annual message on December 6, 1858, Buchanan justified his support of Lecompton. "In the course of my long public life," he wrote, "I have never performed any official act which, in the retrospect, has afforded me more heartfelt satisfaction. Its admission could have inflicted no possible injury on any human being, whilst it would, within a brief period, have restored peace to Kansas and harmony to the Union." Buchanan admitted that he had advocated submission of the constitution to the people but had had to defer to the convention. He was implacable that his position was just, and neither the election results nor the bluster of his prestigious critics could budge him.[122] In truth, the English Bill's defeat had settled the Kansas question—it was not admitted, but unlike in earlier rejections, the terms for admission were clear; without the requisite population, it would remain a territory. However, if by the elusive peace and harmony he mourned in his speech Buchanan meant that in national elections the Kansas issue would continue to haunt the party, then he was correct.

But Buchanan recognized the Kansas conflict meant that the government had to reassess its relationship to its territories. "The federal government has ever been a liberal parent to the Territories, and a generous contributor to the useful enterprises of the early settlers," especially given the financial arrangements territories enjoyed, but this generosity distracted residents "by prematurely exciting angry political contests among themselves, for the benefit of aspiring leaders." He partly blamed ambition and urged Congress to ensure this experience would not be repeated. "It is surely no hardship for embryo governors, senators, and members of Congress, to wait until the number of inhabitants shall equal those of a single congressional district. They surely ought not to be permitted to rush into the Union with a population less than one-half of several of the large counties in the interior of some of the states."[123] This was reasonable but myopic nonetheless, as Buchanan had tried to usher Kansas into the Union under precisely these circumstances.

In his memoir, a defensive Buchanan argued that civil war would not have arisen had Kansas residents respected the Dred Scott decision. It was this disappointment—seeing the Supreme Court decision supporting their rights rejected by the Republicans—that swung many Southerners into "the hands of disunion agitators."[124] Not surprisingly, Buchanan found criticism of his conduct unfair, convinced as he was that once he became president, he could not favor a political platform above a Supreme Court decision.[125] However, he wanted and helped produce this decision, so his actions were not as objective and manifest as he preferred to remember. Moreover, he did not adequately address the more important defection from within his own party—"the Douglas Democracy."[126] In responding to Kansas events, Buchanan completely embraced the Southern perspective, as Howell Cobb noted in defending the president's record in 1857. "He is the first President who recognized the right of the southern man to go into the common territory with his slave property—denying both to Congress and the territorial legislature the power to forbid it—thus putting himself upon the southern construction of the doctrine of popular sovereignty. . . . and in all his appointments *every where* refuses to recognize any man as worthy of his patronage and confidence who is not fully committed to these great cardinal principles upon which he has planted his administration."[127] As such, it is not surprising that the carving off of support from both sides left him standing alone on a very narrow plank, propped up by only the most vehement slavery proponents. Finally, the issues the Dred Scott decision were to have settled were not relevant in Kansas, where voter fraud and the inability of the populace to vote on the Lecompton Constitution, not the status of slavery in the territory, were the critical issues.

When Buchanan returned from England on April 23, 1856, a great New York crowd had greeted his steamer. Gratified by his reception, he told the crowd that he had "been for years abroad in a foreign land, and I like the noise of democracy." When Buchanan was selected to head the Democratic ticket for the upcoming presidential election, he was hailed as "the consistent statesman, the pure patriot, and the honest man." He was described as having a "progressive view of public questions" but, at the same time, having "that healthful degree of conservatism which checks excesses, guides events within the bounds of reason, and in fact sustains that healthful progress of society which is equally removed from rashness as from the dead calm of inactivity."[128] Buchanan could not but have been shocked that merely two years into his presidency the enchanting "noise of democracy" had transformed itself into a deafening roar of disapproval and dissent. In the end, his policies contributed to the Democratic Party's loss in the 1864 election; in its first presidential election, with just 1 in 50 votes cast for his vice president John Breckinridge, Kansas gave 79 percent of its vote to Republican Abraham Lincoln, a greater proportion than any other state.[129]

Conclusion
"To the Stars Through Difficulty"

On January 29, 1861, President James Buchanan signed legislation admitting Kansas into the Union. As its motto, the thirty-fourth state adopted "to the stars through difficulty," an apt description of its nearly seven-year journey to statehood. Just as Kansans celebrated the end of their quest, the nation's greatest challenge commenced, as the stars themselves were falling away one by one over disagreements that the Kansas-Nebraska Act had been designed, in part, to subdue. Given the break with national policy this legislation represented, it is tempting to view the bill's passage as the first step in an inexorable march toward separation. Yet the Kansas-Nebraska Act did not make war inevitable. Instead, territorial events augmented sectionalism while impairing the ability of the executive and legislative branches to successfully temper it.

Kansas's topography and proximity to Missouri lured Southern expansionists while vexing free-labor advocates concerned that its transformation into a slave state would herald an erosion of freedom. Given its remoteness and lack of settlement prior to organization, the chaotic nature of Kansas's local politics could have been foretold. Territorial organization has often been affected by the competition among federal officials and local boosters to influence political decisions, as their economic well-being was often affected by territorial decisions.[1] In Kansas, the typical territorial competition was exaggerated by extraterritorial interference, from outside agents directing immigration through aid societies or bounties and, more locally, from those crossing into the territory from nearby Missouri. As Governor John Geary informed President Franklin Pierce, outsiders were responsible for the ravages of 1856. "These damages cannot be considered in their origin as springing from purely local causes and as such the subjects of Territorial redress. Their exciting cause," Geary asserted, "has been *outside* the Territory and the Agents in their perpetration have been *the citizens of nearly every state in the Union*. It has indeed been a species of National warfare waged upon the soil of Kansas, and it should not be forgotten that both parties were composed of men rushing here from various sections of the Union, each impelled by a common object that both committed acts which no law can justify and that the peaceful citizens of Kansas have alternately been the victims of both."[2] The influence of nonnative agencies can be detected in the political careers of key players within Kansas—the state's first governor, Charles Robinson, for example, came to Kansas as an agent for the New England Emigrant Aid Company.

With the nature of popular sovereignty being untested, an executive officer of principle and purpose was vital for orderly settlement. Even before the Kansas-Nebraska Act had passed, intensifying interest in the region was evident, and the rhetoric and bitterness of the national debate indicated the president had to exhibit sensitivity in territorial appointments. As commander-in-chief of the territorial militia and superintendent of Indian affairs within its boundaries,[3] governors oversaw the establishment of political institutions and ensured that residents were protected from foreign threats, but they were ill-prepared to cope with threats from the settlers themselves. Partisans were engaged in "one continual struggle for the ascendancy" in which "all means are resorted to fair or foul, to effect their object."[4] Efforts to control them were hampered by an ill-equipped militia fortified only by an army whose authority to intervene was unclear. From the commission of the first governor on June 29, 1854, to the end of its territorial status six and one-half years later, frequent absences and vacancies led to the installation of 26 different executive terms before statehood was granted.[5] This instability in the territory's most important post contributed to Kansas's upheaval. Additionally, its resources were inadequate to meet administrative challenges. The judiciary could have provided stability absent in the executive, but although the judicial branch was well represented with three judges and a district attorney, in two of Kansas's most violent years only one conviction "for stealing and another for killing a horse; three or four for assuming office; and some eight or ten [convictions] for selling liquor without a license" were achieved. Further, as Geary's personal secretary complained, significant crimes were often overlooked because the district attorney refused to prosecute or defendants were found innocent by "a packed jury of criminals like themselves."[6]

Although Kansas's journey to statehood was fraught with typical frontier violence, its ideological overtones were atypical. Bolstered by numerous national newspaper correspondents, many of whom actively participated in events, the thriving newspaper industry provided a framework for understanding the struggle but imposed an ideological cast upon it. The resultant propaganda transformed Kansas into a conflict of "absolute rights and wrongs."[7] The ability of free-state partisans to focus the public gaze on the territory was greatly aided by the Republican control of the House of Representatives in 1856, but journalists played the pivotal role. The caliber of reporting was dramatically affected by the eager presence of national correspondents focused on swaying public opinion back home. The Kansas conflict occurred during a time of rapid expansion of the news industry. From 1840 to 1850, the number of dailies in the United States nearly doubled from 138 to 254; this growth was supported by the increasing reliance on national correspondents and lent itself well to keeping the Kansas issue alive.[8] During the territorial period, more than one hundred newspapers were established in Kansas. Of course, many were short-lived, some designed solely to advocate a single issue or candidate or founded to promote a newly erected town, but to significant effect.[9]

In his investigation of the territory as a frontier institution, historian Earl Pomeroy described immigrants' politicized experiences, noting that "visitors to the territories often remarked [on] the absence of subordinate attitudes; residents took so keen an interest in national affairs that in later years, they sometimes thought that they remembered voting in national elections."[10] This interest was even more marked in Kansas, as residents would be profoundly affected by the constitution under which they entered the Union. Underscored by increasingly strident disagreements over the slavery issue and the ramifications of popular sovereignty, partisans escalated the usual rhetoric that politics inspired until Kansas ceased to be just another territory and became a symbol of the struggle between freedom and slavery. Mythologizing within and without Kansas heightened the feeling that its importance transcended mere questions of party affiliation or the character of its constitution. This mythmaking was at its peak during the presidential campaign in 1856. Poems written during the conflict, the presence of genuine ideologues within the territory, affiliation to and creation of secret societies, the elevation of heroic status to bit players, and martyr-making—with the imprisonment of editors, former governors, and others for treason—all contributed to the construction of the "bleeding Kansas" myth.

By 1856, Kansas had transcended its territorial status and served as a unifying myth for both sections in a growing national schism. Although perceived differently across party and section, "Kansas" was used by individuals like Senator Charles Sumner, editor Horace Greeley, and Colonel Jefferson Buford to motivate partisans; by political parties such as the Democrats, Republicans, and Know-Nothings to lure voters; by organizations like the New

England Emigrant Aid Company and the Platte County Missouri Self-Defensive Association to spur migration; or by writers like Ralph Waldo Emerson and Henry Thoreau to construct martyrs to the cause. Once it opened for settlement, the territory became larger than itself. Although inhabitants of American territories typically rejected suggestions that emigration from established states to a nascent one reduced their capacity for citizenship, residents felt their lack of agency keenly in Kansas. Since they were unable to select their governor, the position was ever more important because of electoral disputes and the autonomy that popular sovereignty promised. With former governors Andrew Reeder and Wilson Shannon unwilling to overturn tainted elections, the perception intensified that the national administration had such a vested interest in the territory's institutions that it was willing to embrace unethical behavior to acquire Kansas for slavery.

Because they were more divided than usual, political parties could not fill the void by providing an organizational structure to filter the highly politicized atmosphere. Although it is inaccurate to speak of a monolithic free-state party, the conservative free-state men lacked an effective political organization, allowing Charles Robinson and James Lane's more aggressive faction to dominate politics. Free-state activists believed the federal government's actions had led to an untenable local situation. "Kansas is now governed partly by a military despotism, partly by an outside oligarchy, under the form of the most unlimited democracy," one resident reported.[11] Yet on the other side, proslavery activists believed the free-state faction was equally despotic. Even moderate, free-state Democrats were deeply angered by the government's unwillingness to move decisively against the extralegal Topeka government. Within Kansas, both sides characterized themselves as patriotic—one faction cited its support of the federal government, the other its refusal to adhere to unjust and illegitimate laws at odds with the democratic foundations of the country.

Kansas and the Presidency

The presidential campaign of 1852 was marked by both major parties' commitment to withdrawing the slavery question from Congress. In the debate over the Kansas-Nebraska Bill, however, Representative Origen Seymour (CT) warned that "instead of transferring the subject of slavery from the Halls of Congress to the people of the Territories, [the bill] transferred it, in effect, to the President of the United States."[12] In embracing this legislation, Franklin Pierce made a calculated decision that the benefits derived from satisfying Southern demands outweighed the risks of eradicating the Missouri Compromise of 1820. Senator Stephen Douglas's (IL) argument that the bill merely codified decisions made in the Compromise of 1850 offered a tempting justification for this startling break with party and national policy. Yet because of the bill's unpopularity in the North and the devastating midterm electoral results, Pierce had to tread carefully to avoid the appearance that his Kansas policy was proslavery. Although his selection of the territorial teams for Nebraska and Kansas were intended to demonstrate impartiality, the perception grew that he favored establishing a slave state in the southernmost territory.

Pierce was elected as a compromise candidate without a genuine, national base, but his rapid decline in influence and popularity was startling. In an article published shortly before the midterm elections of 1854, *Putnam's Monthly* dismissed Franklin Pierce as a party machine Democrat, a "little man" whose election was possible only during a time of "comparative public indifference or reaction"; on the other hand, times of crises drew men of "lofty ambition or ability." With "little men" at the helm, the article posited, "public policy fluctuates between awkwardness of conscious incompetence and the blustering arrogance of bullyism. The possession of office becomes a badge, either of imbecility, or cunning or insolence."[13] Soon after this harsh disparagement of the president, a national crisis arose that provided Pierce with an opportunity to transform himself into a man of vision.

Caught between extremists, Pierce could not rehabilitate himself. As the situation worsened with the disastrous territorial elections and the organization of the free-state party in 1855, the president's indecision contributed to his problems with the territorial administration. Had Pierce acted sooner and dismissed Governor Andrew Reeder before the territorial legislature convened in 1855, a new governor might have prevented the slide into the Wakarusa War that winter and the violence of the following summer. Although Pierce finally removed Reeder, he miscalculated with his replacement. Wilson Shannon proved to be a resolute party man, but he was undone by his responsibilities as commander-in-chief of the militia. In fairness, the need to design a military policy against residents of an American territory was a new and unwelcome innovation and dismayed all concerned. By the time Pierce selected a competent governor in 1856, his political future had been decided.

Given his advocacy of the Kansas-Nebraska Bill, Pierce was tied to the success of popular sovereignty. However, the president allowed himself to become overidentified with slavery. His partiality was seen in his weak efforts to stabilize the territory. Not only did he fail to control his appointees, but he passed the responsibility for the territory back onto Congress and did so with an impolitic, public rebuke of abolitionists for causing the mayhem while entirely overlooking proslavery excesses. According to Congressman Samuel Brenton (IN), Pierce had forsaken neutrality in Kansas. "In his attempts to discuss the constitutional relations of slavery," Brenton argued, "I regret to find that the President, forgetful of the dignity of his position, has shown an intimate acquaintance with all the catch-words and cant phrases of the low demagogue. . . ."[14] Indeed, Pierce's lack of neutrality was critical as Governor John Geary demonstrated that a neutral mien and policy could effectively calm the territory. Just before he left office, Pierce discussed the "inviolability of the constitutional rights of the different sections of the Union." Critic Leonard Bacon dismissed his views as the "worst kind of nonsense," pointing out that states, not sections, retain rights.[15] However, this distinction was overlooked in Kansas as each section feared it would be materially damaged if it could not bring the future state into the Union on their side. Pierce ultimately lacked the wherewithal to control either his governors or the conflict, and his efforts to effectively govern Kansas failed.

By all accounts, Pierce's viability as a presidential candidate in 1856 ended with his endorsement of the Kansas-Nebraska Act. In truth, his chances for a second term had been slim to begin with, as his 1852 selection stemmed from circumstances unlikely to be duplicated four years later. Moreover, Pierce's patronage policies alienated crucial party members prior to the thirty-third Congress. Although he achieved a major legislative victory with the passage of the Kansas-Nebraska Act, the president's inability to adroitly manage the conflict—from the notoriously fraudulent elections to sporadic warfare—damaged his stature. The uproar in Kansas fed the growth of the Republican Party, and with its own numbers diminished in the midterm elections, the Democratic Party's failure to secure the House speakership in 1856 granted the opposition a formidable advantage in setting the legislative agenda. During this congressional session, Pierce wilted under a Republican onslaught. Although he forced Congress to appropriate funds for the Army despite concerns about a politicized military, the president had to convene a special session to do so. Moreover, the Howard Committee provided fodder for the presidential campaign and ensured that Pierce's Kansas decisions were discussed almost daily in chambers. The Committee generated unparalleled publicity focusing the public on Kansas.

After Pierce's well-advertised difficulties, the Democrats chose James Buchanan with his lengthy record of distinguished public service as their 1856 presidential candidate. Buchanan was nominated because he embodied qualities Pierce lacked—he was an experienced, national man untainted by the 1854 Kansas debate—but despite the party's optimism and his background, he too fell victim to the same problems Pierce encountered. Indeed, fears that Buchanan would be "just like Mr. Pierce, *only more so*" in the sense of being a proslavery, pro-Southern president despite Northern roots, proved prescient.[16]

Buchanan's problems in Kansas stemmed less from poor administrative appointments than from the policies he chose to implement. Pierce contended with a Topeka Constitution that was clearly illegitimate, and the desperation that antislavery advocates cited during congressional debates could not justify this status. The legitimacy of the Lecompton Constitution was a murkier question. Buchanan was correct in stating that it derived from a legally authorized convention, and while a significant portion of the populace disliked it, the free-state faction's refusal to participate in the electoral process contributed to the proslavery faction's ability to construct the constitution it wanted. Nonetheless, in a divided territory, the spirit of the law was equally as important as its form. As the incoming president, Buchanan entered office with a clean slate, but his decisions, especially regarding the legitimacy of territorial elections and the proslavery constitution, quickly mired his administration in controversy. Buchanan began auspiciously with the appointment of the well-regarded Robert Walker to the governorship of Kansas, but he faltered by failing to support him.

In addition, Buchanan was roundly criticized for continuing the trend of disappointing territorial appointments. Kansas delegate Marcus Parrott complained that the territory persisted under "a dreary despotism, imposed by foreign domination, and maintained by the direct intervention of the military arm of the Government," and disputed that the change in administration had helped Kansas. "Not only do the old offenders remain, but new appointments have been made, if possible, more insulting, intolerable, and outrageous, than the preceding ones. No other test of fitness has been sought for or applied, save a clear complicity with the crimes that have characterized the career of the Administration party in the Territory."[17] While Parrott's perspective was admittedly partisan, it was indicative of the tenor of the criticism lobbed against Buchanan.

The identification of the president as the embodiment of proslavery policies, begun under Pierce, seemed to have been completed during the Buchanan administration. "I regret the tendency of the Executive recommendation [on Lecompton], which, to my mind, is to place the President in a position of antagonism to the majority of Kansas," Congressman John Hickman (PA) complained. "It leads to an issue between power on the other hand, and the people on the other."[18] Free-state residents believed the national administration muffled the voice of the people, and Buchanan's advocacy of the Lecompton Constitution typified administration meddling on behalf of slavery in Kansas. The free-state faction came to believe that freedom could only be obtained in spite of the president. "*Thank God*, in this country the President is not absolute," one Kansan wrote. "His power is very limited. The Governmental power is in the *people* by universal theory and general practice. In the end, the *people* here will triumph against the slave power and all its hosts, including President, cabinet, and their long tail of office holders and seekers."[19] Resistance to administration policies, increasingly perceived as proslavery, continued until the free-state faction had grown sufficiently to risk participating in elections.

A mere two years into his administration, Buchanan suffered in comparison with his predecessor, an outcome difficult to foresee given Pierce's disgrace at the close of his term. "Those papers that are constantly asserting that Buchanan's Administration is on an equality with Pierce's, do the latter injustice," wrote the *Freedom's Champion*. "Pierce was merely a facile plaything in the hands of men who were his superiors, both in intellect and energy and in capacity for doing wrong. Buchanan is not carried away from the path of justice or right, by the pressure of party leaders; for the influential and talented men of his party . . . oppose him now. The Administration of Pierce was simply pitiable—that of Buchanan is infamous and disgraceful."[20] Entering office with territorial troubles in full flower, and in light of the high expectations that surrounded his nomination in 1856, Buchanan's policies disappointed many Democrats. Despite statements advocating territorial self-determination, Buchanan's support of the Lecompton Constitution diminished his reputation. While Pierce may have made mistakes, Buchanan's critics saw his Kansas policy as premeditated and therefore more reprehensible.

> We were told that the affairs of the country would be committed to firm and skillful hands—that Mr. Buchanan was a tried and disciplined statesman, whose patriotism had been tested during long service of the Republic—that his prudence was proverbial—that any deficiency in brilliancy of intellect which might exist, was compensated for in him by an unusual endowment of the more solid qualities of mind—that he did not seek a re-election, and would not be seduced from the path of duty by the dangerous desire for place—that he was an old man, and could have no other earthly object except to illustrate his declining years by reconciling unfortunate differences, and conferring a lasting peace upon a distracted country.[21]

The break with Robert Walker, Frederick Stanton, and Stephen Douglas over the Lecompton Constitution was especially damaging because it enabled his opponents to emphasize that it was not merely Republicans but prominent Democrats as well who disassociated themselves from the national administration over the president's unwillingness to allow "the people" to determine their own institutions.

For many free-state partisans, Buchanan's ideas for peace translated into distasteful, dough-faced policies. However, as historian Philip Auchampaugh contends, the president "looked to the material welfare of the country rather than upon any theory *per se*. . . . Buchanan was devoted to states rights as the best means of holding a diversified union together."[22] The outbreak of civil war immediately after his term made Buchanan, always sensitive to his place in the nation's pantheon, extremely sensitive about charges of culpability. Rare for politicians of the era, Buchanan wrote a memoir refuting responsibility for the nation's dissolution and adamantly maintained that his freedom of action was severely circumscribed by decisions made prior to his inauguration.

Kansas began and ended with too much executive activism, as both Pierce and Buchanan crossed the line from dispassionate support to proslavery advocacy. Both presidents suffered from their inability to adjust once it became evident their assumptions about territorial politics were incorrect. This was most evident in the drift of Democratic governors to the support of free-state views, or what is considered in diplomatic circles as "going native." As Representative Solomon G. Haven (NY) noted, "They want now to get this question settled, and well they may, for they are decimating their party, by sending governors to Kansas. Reeder, Geary, Walker and Stanton were all democrats when they went there, but somehow when they got among the people of Kansas they turned out something else."[23] Once the governors advocated greater sympathy for the free-state side, they were removed. James Denver did not suffer this disgrace because he kept his disagreements with Buchanan private. Only Wilson Shannon remained stalwart, and his incompetence forced his resignation. Despite ample evidence to the contrary, Pierce and Buchanan persistently believed that the vehement opposition in Kansas was limited to abolitionists and therefore unrepresentative. As such, they continued to actively press a proslavery agenda despite growing evidence that Kansans wanted a free state. Moreover, they did so in a manner that brought their neutrality into question. In sum, rather than support popular sovereignty as it was meant to be—neutral, fair, democratic—their Kansas policy was seen as driven by a desire for a slave state.

Both presidents were undermined by the difficulties of territorial administration; the novelty of extensive, partisan murder and mayhem disconcerted even those governors accustomed to frontier violence. In discussing the territorial governors' efficacy, one journalist assessed their difficulties:

> It did not make much difference whether the territorial governor was inclined to slavery or free state notions. He landed in trouble the day he took office and was haunted by it day and night, with seldom a moment of peace or ease.... Kansas was no place for a pacifist, either as a settler or as an official. Those governors who were sent to Kansas with orders to try to smooth out the difficulties in the new territory found themselves in hot water as soon as they landed. Some of them really tried to iron out some of the hardest of political situations. Most were thoroughly honest in their efforts and deeds in trying to give the territory decent government and protect the citizens and in trying to see that the elections were conducted fairly and honestly. But the situation called for men of iron nerve and large numbers of loyal cohorts of similar beliefs. Few of the territorial governors had sufficient courage and support of either side of the controversy to control the warring factions within the territory completely.[24]

Although this analysis sympathizes with the governors' plight, it does not address the culpability of Pierce and Buchanan in failing to provide sufficient, unbiased support to render "loyal cohorts" unnecessary.

Pierce's and Buchanan's presidential policies damaged their party, but as John Speer, a reporter for the *Kansas Tribune* and the *Kansas Free State* noted, men such as Lane, Pierce, Buchanan, and Douglas were all steeped in "what they all called the 'compromise of the constitution,'" and without them, there would have been no party.[25] The compromise of the constitution involved respecting the existence of slavery, but Pierce and Buchanan came to embody the slavocracy rather than merely, neutrally recognizing the South's right to perpetuate its peculiar institution. Neither man recognized that public opinion on the slavery question had changed and that abolitionism no longer adequately described antislavery advocates. In 1854 Stephen Douglas had predicted that the Kansas-Nebraska bill would be a positive force. "We shall pass the Nebraska bill in both Houses by decisive majorities," Douglas confided to a friend, "and the party will be stronger than ever for it will be united upon principle."[26] In the end, both Franklin Pierce's and James Buchanan's inability to deftly handle developing territorial problems weakened their respective presidencies and fragmented the Democratic Party upon Stephen Douglas's principle.

Kansas and Congress

In terms of organizing the frontier, national territorial policy had been characterized by a laissez-faire approach. As a result, there were no uniform policies to ameliorate the disorder either in the territory or in Congress when Kansas sent up successively problematic constitutions in advance of meeting population requirements for statehood. Throughout government, long-term planning on managing continental expansion was absent. Although the territories of Utah and New Mexico offered prototypes of popular sovereignty, their organization derived from postwar treaty considerations with Mexico. Cited in the organization of Nebraska and Kansas, popular sovereignty promised "a more perfect freedom,"[27] but this freedom was severely limited as territorial residents lost political freedom, such as selecting their governor, in relocating further west. Congress was ill-advised in selecting an underpopulated Kansas and Nebraska for an experiment in self-government so crucial in determining the ongoing, delicate balance between the sections in national politics.

On the Kansas issue, Congress could not forge a compromise, as the debate over slavery had degenerated too much to be withstood by a fractured legislative branch. In the days of the greatest compromises, the two-party system was at its strongest, and even the recent Compromise of 1850 had been forged by two clearly defined parties. By mid-decade, however, party politics had fragmented. While both major parties were hurt by the 1854 midterm elections, the Democrats held together while the Whigs disintegrated. Political parties were fluid in 1854 and 1855 as the Whigs and Americans transformed themselves. But while the Republicans began to coalesce into a significant party in late 1855, compromise requires parity, and it had not yet solidified sufficiently to add weight to a congressional compromise. More important, however, was the party's willingness to compromise on slavery. On the Kansas issue, the Republican Party rejected all solutions in favor of continued advocacy of immediate admission under the Topeka Constitution. And they had incentive to do so. Why compromise and help quiet the Kansas conflict when the brouhaha was expanding the party? Furthermore, in 1856 the White House beckoned, a tempting prize for the young party.

The Republicans were able to use Kansas as a party issue so effectively because the presidents' actions left them and their party vulnerable to charges of a proslavery bias. The perception that the national administration was in the wrong in Kansas was underscored by the presidents' inability to use executive appointments to provide stability. The problem was so perplexing that even fellow Democrats wondered why Kansas drained party loyalty from its gubernatorial appointments. "How does it happen that no man has yet been found with Democracy sound enough to bear up against the air of Kansas? Four Governors have been appointed in the space of about thirty months, from among the wisest and best of our party, and now the office is again vacant. How comes this?" asked Representative John Hickman (PA) in 1858. "It finds its solution in the fact that 'Democracy is morality,' and unable to countenance so gross and palpable a usurpation as has always existed there. Those four high officers have all returned to us, speaking the same language, uttering the same words—that sovereignty is crushed out there."[28] But despite concerns over Democratic policies in Kansas, Republicans were limited to propaganda, as their numbers were insufficient for policy formation. Disproportionately concentrated in the House, they depended on Democratic cooperation for legislative success. Without the defection of the Douglas Democrats, for instance, the Republican opposition was limited to creating nuisances like the Howard Committee or the Army appropriation bill, which drew attention to their cause, but they lacked the strength to pass the Topeka Constitution or to force Pierce to withdraw the military. In the end, Congress was too fragmented, disorganized, and ultimately disinterested to settle the conflict in the territory.

Pierce and Buchanan were more active in the slavery debate than their predecessors had been, and their active interest usurped Congress's traditional role. The Kansas crisis forced executive rather than legislative leadership on the issue as the development of territorial turmoil impinged on Congress's traditional role in setting the legislative agenda for the territories. Although the Kansas-Nebraska Bill was brought forward by the Senate, once Pierce embraced it as a party measure, presidential interference with the legislative branch on this topic increased. Just as Pierce had asked Congress to enable a constitutional convention to settle matters, Buchanan would push the Lecompton Constitution two years later. Moreover, under Buchanan, Governor Robert Walker implied that Congress would follow his lead by refusing to act unless certain strictures were met, that it would reject the constitution unless all Kansans voted on it.[29] At least one congressman was offended by the suggestion that Congress answered to the executive branch. "Who clothed Gov. Walker or anybody else with authority to say, either that she [Kansas] would not or ought not to be admitted into the Union?" Representative Alexander Stephens (GA) asked, declaring Walker's doctrine "too outrageous and monstrous to allow any such interference."[30] Yet the greatest legislative activity on Kansas came directly after presidential messages requesting congressional action, and as a body, Congress was extremely reactive.

After 1854, ample evidence exists of legislative resentment toward executive initiative on this issue. In the debate over the Lecompton Constitution, Senator William Seward (NY) stood in the upper chamber and flatly stated that he did not trust the president of the United States.[31] But Seward's statement was not atypical. Throughout the debates on Kansas, both Pierce and Buchanan were vilified as untrustworthy and overly tied to slavery's perpetuation. Moreover, the House of Representatives authorized two separate select committees to investigate executive action in Kansas. Both the Howard and Covode Committee reports were extraordinary documents indicting Pierce and Buchanan for their intervention in territorial affairs. Both had their genesis as fodder for upcoming presidential campaigns, and both extensively damaged the Democrats. While the Howard Committee was organized in 1856 to investigate the disturbances in Kansas, the Covode Committee was convened in 1860 to investigate whether Buchanan acted unethically in garnering votes for the Lecompton Constitution and had used corruption to bolster his administration. The Covode Report charged Buchanan with excessive interference for his attempt to use "forgeries, frauds, and force" to ensure Kansas's admission as a slave state.[32] The Howard Committee was a constant annoyance for Pierce, but the Covode Committee was potentially more damaging to Buchanan, who believed the House "pursued a course not merely at war with the constitutional rights of the Executive, but tending to degrade the presidential office itself to such a degree as to render it unworthy of the acceptance of any man of honor or principle." Buchanan charged the legislature with attempting to subvert the constitution; indeed, "one of the three massive columns on which the whole superstructure rests will be broken down. Instead of the Executive being a coordinate it will become a subordinate branch of the Government," he warned. "The presidential office will be dragged into the dust. The House of Representatives will then have rendered the Executive almost necessarily subservient to its wishes, instead of being independent. . . ."[33] Although neither the Howard nor Covode Committee reflected the entire legislative branch, their existence reveals unease with the increased activism of both Pierce and Buchanan.

Conclusion

The 1854 Kansas-Nebraska Act passed with overwhelming Southern support since the ability to compete freely for new territories was seen as critical to reasserting the South's political power in Congress. But the South became disenchanted with the actuality of popular sovereignty. In his famous composition, "The Kansas Emigrants," John G. Whittier described the aim of the Northern activists. "We go to rear a wall of men / On Freedom's southern line, / And plant beside the cotton tree / The rugged Northern pine! /. . . . / Upbearing, like the Ark of old, / The Bible in our van, / We go to test the truth of God / Against the fraud of man."[34] But the South came to believe the North was itself propagating that fraud and through the activities of the emigrant aid societies and the Topeka government, thwarting newly established rules of sectional competition for available territories. Believing they were backed by a sympathetic administration, proslavery partisans were frustrated by their lack of progress and assumed the governors sent by Pierce would be more cooperative than they proved to be. Only Shannon obliged, and his efficacy diminished as the violence grew. Hence, the proslavery faction felt stranded by the administration: "Unfortunately *our* friends are doing but little—Here, we are but few and poor—we have neither time or money to spare over what little we do contribute—we have not the aid of organized societies in the South—their counsel or advice—but we are a determined set. We have resolved that thus far and no farther shall the aggression of the North, come, so far or our lives. . . ." Their impatience was spurred by the sense that they were at a disadvantage due to Northern efforts, especially when both Reeder and John Geary, Shannon's replacement, proved susceptible to antislavery arguments.[35]

Had they been better able to compete, they might have felt different, but the failure of the Lecompton Constitution was disheartening. Many Southerners believed the question of admission was one of principle: would Congress accept a new slave state or not? There were differences of opinion among Southern members, but the central issue was undeniable. "The Constitution prescribes that Congress may admit new States, and the only proviso it has any concern with, is whether its Constitution is Republican. We want no more compromise," the *Charleston Mercury* warned. "We claim the pound of flesh in the case, and we should claim it at all hazards. The South united can and should insist on the naked question, divested of all adventitious influences."[36] The *Spirit of the South* (Eufaula, Alabama) concurred, for rejecting the Lecompton Constitution solely because it supported the South's institution "adds the insult of supposing we can be amused by the trick of giving us the words, 'admitting the State,' while they nullify the rights—the constitution with slavery."[37]

The Missouri Compromise had provided a foundation for sectional peace, and while there was some discontent over it, especially in the South, it also provided stability. But antislavery agitation was revived in 1854 because as one journal stated, "where society is divided on a principle, and that principle involves, besides its moral issues, vast practical interests, no parliamentary device of legislative expedient can put a stop to the discussion of it—no compromise or temporary adjustment of it can settle it forever."[38] Although it was expected the reaffirmation of the Compromise of 1850 would ensure stability, without the Missouri Compromise the freedom to compete in any territory merely heightened sectional competition. Located too far north, Nebraska was not in contention, but while the South was willing to cede Nebraska to freedom, the North was unwilling to cede Kansas to slavery. Moreover, with Southern expansion critical to slavery's growth, the South had to attain Kansas. Thus even though many Southerners believed slavery could not flourish in the area, the acceptance of a new slave state into the Union became a question of principle.

However, Kansas did not provide a true test of the viability of the new system. From the start, popular sovereignty was perverted by partisans' unwillingness to allow the territory to develop organically. The very nature of the Kansas-Nebraska Act changed the settlement process. When Congress overturned the Missouri Compromise, they set off a chain reaction. Southerners were pleased they could now compete for land that had been closed to slavery, by virtue of its latitude, in 1820. But Northerners felt betrayed that a region that had been intended to be free from slavery might not be. And so a race began and decisions that should have been made by territorial residents over many years as the territory matured would be made by ideologues descending on Kansas either to save it for freedom or secure it for slavery. Within six months, the territory's first elections were tainted by fraud that would split the territory. Proslavery partisans gained the delegate position and would secure the legislature in March 1855. In turn, antislavery partisans rejected these results and pursued a strategy that involved setting up an entire shadow government.

Within a year of the Kansas-Nebraska Act, the local government was being pressured by residents fighting for control of the processes of government. These failures on the ground were matched by failures in Washington. Both the legislative and executive branches failed to intervene after it became obvious that outsiders were contaminating the settlement process. In doing so, the nation accepted armed conflict as a substitute for debate and compromise. While there is no doubt that the years from 1854 to 1858 were sufficiently transformative in national politics to set the stage for war, territorial events in Kansas made civil war a possibility, not a certainty. The legislature's failure to respond when it became evident that popular sovereignty (which allowed Southerners to compete for Kansas) was not working allowed the conflict over slavery in the territories to undermine the republic. During the Lecompton debate, many critics of the constitution focused on Buchanan as a tool of the slave oligarchy and charged that Congress withered before a strengthened, partisan president. In speaking to one such gathering, Representative Haven stated, "You have come together because the country is misgoverned—because the fundamental principles of free government has been assailed—because the right of free men to self-government is withheld—because the power of Congress over the territories has been denied and the absolute powers of the Executive substituted and insisted upon in its place. . . ."[39] But while Haven only perceived a weak Congress, the years in which Kansas's future were shaped saw a catastrophic failure of leadership in both the executive and legislative branches. This failure resulted in territorial residents' alienation from the federal government and the questioning of what precisely government is for if not to protect "we the people." Kansans wanted a voice as is amply evident by their embrace of governance in all its forms. However, their inability to manage their own affairs and the government's incompetence in providing guidance or relief as needed was early evidence of the breakdown of the country's political mechanisms. The violence that erupted in 1856 heralded a future where finding a solution to managing expansion and its challenges proved harder than resorting to war.

Appendix A

Kansas-Nebraska Vote in the Senate
March 3, 1854

Party affiliation derived from the *Congressional Globe*:
Democrats are recorded in plain text, *Whigs are in italics*, and **Free Soilers are in bold**.

SENATOR	STATE	SECTION	PARTY	VOTE
Adams, Stephen	Mississippi	South	Democrat	Yes
Allen, Phillip	Rhode Island	North	Democrat	absent
Atchison, David	Missouri	South	Democrat	Yes
Badger, George E.	*North Carolina*	*South*	*Whig*	*Yes*
Bayard, James A.	Delaware	South	Democrat	Yes
Bell, John	*Tennessee*	*South*	*Whig*	*No*
Benjamin, Judah P.	*Louisiana*	*South*	*Whig*	*Yes*
Bright, Jesse D.	Indiana	North	Democrat	absent
Brodhead Jr., Richard	Pennsylvania	North	Democrat	Yes
Brown, Albert G.	Mississippi	South	Democrat	Yes
Butler, Andrew P.	South Carolina	South	Democrat	Yes
Cass, Lewis	Michigan	North	Democrat	Yes
Chase, Salmon P.	**Ohio**	**North**	**Free Soil**	**No**
Clay Jr., Clement C.	*Alabama*	*South*	*Democrat*	*Yes*
Clayton, John M.	*Delaware*	*South*	*Whig*	*absent*
Cooper, James	*Pennsylvania*	*North*	*Whig*	*absent*
Dawson, William C.	*Georgia*	*South*	*Whig*	*Yes*
Dixon, Archibald	*Kentucky*	*South*	*Whig*	*Yes*
Dodge, Augustus C.	Iowa	North	Democrat	Yes
Dodge, Henry	Wisconsin	North	Democrat	No
Douglas, Stephen	Illinois	North	Democrat	Yes
Evans, Josiah J.	South Carolina	South	Democrat	Yes
Everett, Edward	*Massachusetts*	*North*	*Whig*	*absent*
Fessenden, William Pitt	*Maine*	*North*	*Whig*	*No*
Fish, Hamilton	*New York*	*North*	*Whig*	*No*
Fitzpatrick, Benjamin	Alabama	South	Democrat	Yes
Foot, Solomon	*Vermont*	*North*	*Whig*	*No*
Geyer, Henry S.	*Missouri*	*South*	*Whig*	*Yes*
Gwin, William	California	North	Democrat	Yes
Hamlin, Hannibal	Maine	North	Democrat	No

Appendix A

SENATOR	STATE	SECTION	PARTY	VOTE
Houston, Sam	Texas	South	Democrat	No
Hunter, Robert M.T.	Virginia	South	Democrat	Yes
James, Charles T.	Rhode Island	North	Democrat	No
Johnson, Robert W.	Arkansas	South	Democrat	Yes
Jones, George W.	Iowa	North	Democrat	Yes
Jones, James C.	*Tennessee*	*South*	*Whig*	*Yes*
Mallory, Stephen	Florida	South	Democrat	Yes
Mason, James M.	Virginia	South	Democrat	Yes
Morton, Jackson	*Florida*	*South*	*Whig*	*Yes*
Norris Jr., Moses	New Hampshire	North	Democrat	Yes
Pearce, James Alfred	*Maryland*	*South*	*Whig*	*absent*
Pettit, John	Indiana	North	Democrat	Yes
Pratt, Thomas G.	*Maryland*	*South*	*Whig*	*Yes*
Rusk, Thomas J.	Texas	South	Democrat	Yes
Sebastian, William K.	Arkansas	South	Democrat	Yes
Seward, William H.	*New York*	*North*	*Whig*	*No*
Shields, James	Illinois	North	Democrat	Yes
Slidell, John	Louisiana	South	Democrat	Yes
Smith, Truman	*Connecticut*	*North*	*Whig*	*No*
Stuart, Charles E.	Michigan	North	Democrat	Yes
Sumner, Charles	**Massachusetts**	**North**	**Free Soil**	**No**
Thompson, John B.	*Kentucky*	*South*	*Whig*	*Yes*
Thomson, John R.	New Jersey	North	Democrat	Yes
Toombs, Robert	*Georgia*	*South*	*Whig*	*absent*
Toucey, Isaac	Connecticut	North	Democrat	Yes
Wade, Benjamin F.	Ohio	North	Whig	No
Walker, Isaac P.	Wisconsin	North	Democrat	No
Weller, John B.	California	North	Democrat	Yes
Williams, Jared W.	New Hampshire	North	Democrat	Yes
Wright, William	New Jersey	North	Democrat	absent
Vacancy	North Carolina			
Vacancy	Vermont			

Note: The Kansas-Nebraska Act passed the Senate on March 3, 1854, with 37 senators voting in favor of the bill and 14 voting against it.

Appendix B

Senate Results by Section and Party

Vote Count by Section

SECTION	FOR	AGAINST
North	14	12
South	23	2

Vote Count in North by Party

PARTY	FOR	AGAINST
Democrats	14	4
Whigs	0	6
Free Soil	0	2

Vote Count in South by Party

PARTY	FOR	AGAINST
Democrats	14	1
Whigs	9	1
Free Soil	not applicable	not applicable

Vote Count by Section and Party

SECTION AND PARTY	FOR	AGAINST
Northern Democrats	14	4
Southern Democrats	14	1
Northern Whigs	0	6
Southern Whigs	9	1
Northern Free Soil	0	2
Southern Free Soil	not applicable	not applicable

Appendix C

Final Kansas-Nebraska Vote in the House
May 22, 1854

Party affiliation derived from the *Congressional Globe*:
Democrats are recorded in plain text, *Whigs are in italics*, and **Free Soilers are in bold**.

REPRESENTATIVE	STATE	SECTION	PARTY	VOTE
Abercrombie, James	*Alabama*	*South*	*Whig*	*Yes*
Aiken, William	South Carolina	South	Democrat	absent
Allen, James C.	Illinois	North	Democrat	Yes
Allen, Willis	Illinois	North	Democrat	Yes
Appleton, William	*Massachusetts*	*North*	*Whig*	*absent*
Ashe, William S.	North Carolina	South	Democrat	Yes
Bailey, David J.	Georgia	South	Democrat	Yes
Ball, Edward	*Ohio*	*North*	*Whig*	*No*
Banks Jr., Nathaniel P.	Massachusetts	North	Democrat	No
Barksdale, William	Mississippi	South	Democrat	Yes
Barry, William S.	Mississippi	South	Democrat	Yes
Bayly, Thomas H.	Virginia	South	Democrat	Yes
Belcher, Nathan	Connecticut	North	Democrat	No
Bell, Peter H.	Texas	South	Democrat	Yes
Bennett, Henry	*New York*	*North*	*Whig*	*No*
Benson, Samuel P.	Maine	North	Democrat	No
Benton, Thomas H.	Missouri	South	Democrat	No
Bissell, William H.	Illinois	North	Democrat	absent
Bliss, George	Ohio	North	Democrat	absent
Bocock, Thomas S.	Virginia	South	Democrat	Yes
Boyce, William W.	South Carolina	South	Democrat	Yes
Boyd, Linn	Kentucky	South	Democrat	absent
Breckinridge, John C.	Kentucky	South	Democrat	Yes
Bridges, Samuel A.	Pennsylvania	North	Democrat	Yes
Brooks, Preston S.	South Carolina	South	Democrat	Yes
Bugg, Robert M.	*Tennessee*	*South*	*Whig*	*No*
Campbell, Brookins	Tennessee	South	Democrat	absent
Campbell, Lewis D.	**Ohio**	**North**	**Free Soil**	**No**

220 Appendix C

REPRESENTATIVE	STATE	SECTION	PARTY	VOTE
Carpenter, Davis	*New York*	*North*	*Whig*	*No*
Caruthers, Samuel	*Missouri*	*South*	*Whig*	*absent*
Caskie, John S.	Virginia	South	Democrat	Yes
Chamberlain, E.M.	Indiana	North	Democrat	absent
Chandler, Joseph R.	*Pennsylvania*	*North*	*Whig*	*No*
Chase, George W.	*New York*	*North*	*Whig*	*absent*
Chastain, E.W.	Georgia	South	Democrat	Yes
Chrisman, James S.	Kentucky	South	Democrat	Yes
Churchwell, William M.	Tennessee	South	Democrat	Yes
Clark, Samuel	Michigan	North	Democrat	Yes
Clingman, Thomas L.	North Carolina	South	Democrat	Yes
Cobb, Wilson R.W.	Alabama	South	Democrat	Yes
Colquitt, Alfred H.	Georgia	South	Democrat	Yes
Cook, John P.	*Iowa*	*North*	*Whig*	*absent*
Corwin, Moses B.	*Ohio*	*North*	*Whig*	*absent*
Cox, Leander M.	*Kentucky*	*South*	*Whig*	*Yes*
Craige, Burton	North Carolina	South	Democrat	Yes
Crocker, Samuel	*Massachusetts*	*North*	*Whig*	*No*
Cullom, William	*Tennessee*	*South*	*Whig*	*No*
Cumming, Thomas W.	New York	North	Democrat	Yes
Curtis, Carlton B.	Pennsylvania	North	Democrat	No
Cutting, Francis B.	New York	North	Democrat	Yes
Davis, John G.	Indiana	North	Democrat	Yes
Davis, Thomas	Rhode Island	North	Democrat	No
Dawson, John L.	Pennsylvania	North	Democrat	Yes
De Witt, Alexander	**Massachusetts**	**North**	**Free Soil**	**No**
Dean, Gilbert	New York	North	Democrat	No
Dent, William B.W.	Georgia	South	Democrat	absent
Dick, John	*Pennsylvania*	*North*	*Whig*	*No*
Dickinson, Edward	*Massachusetts*	*North*	*Whig*	*No*
Disney, David T.	Ohio	North	Democrat	Yes
Dowdell, James F.	Alabama	South	Democrat	Yes
Drum, Augustus	Pennsylvania	North	Democrat	No
Dunbar, William	Louisiana	South	Democrat	Yes
Dunham, Cyrus J.	Indiana	North	Democrat	Yes

Appendix C **221**

REPRESENTATIVE	STATE	SECTION	PARTY	VOTE
Eastman, Ben C.	Wisconsin	North	Democrat	No
Eddy, Norman	Indiana	North	Democrat	Yes
Edgerton, Alfred P.	Ohio	North	Democrat	No
Edmands, J. Wiley	*Massachusetts*	*North*	*Whig*	*No*
Edmundson, Henry A.	Virginia	South	Democrat	Yes
Eliott, John M.	Kentucky	South	Democrat	Yes
Elliot, Thomas D.	*Massachusetts*	*North*	*Whig*	*No*
Ellison, Andrew	Ohio	North	Democrat	No
English, William H.	Indiana	North	Democrat	Yes
Etheridge, Emerson	*Tennessee*	*South*	*Whig*	*No*
Everhart, William	*Pennsylvania*	*North*	*Whig*	*No*
Ewing, Presley	*Kentucky*	*South*	*Whig*	*absent*
Farley, E. Wilder	*Maine*	*North*	*Whig*	*No*
Faulkner, Charles J.	Virginia	South	Democrat	Yes
Fenton, Reuben E.	New York	North	Democrat	No
Flagler, Thomas S.	*New York*	*North*	*Whig*	*No*
Florence, Thomas B.	Pennsylvania	North	Democrat	Yes
Franklin, John R.	*Maryland*	*South*	*Whig*	*absent*
Fuller, Thomas J. D	*Maine*	*North*	*Democrat*	*No*
Gamble, James	*Pennsylvania*	*North*	*Democrat*	*No*
Giddings, Joshua R.	**Ohio**	**North**	**Free Soil**	**No**
Goode, William O.	Virginia	South	Democrat	Yes
Goodrich, John Z.	*Massachusetts*	*North*	*Whig*	*No*
Green, Frederick W.	Ohio	North	Democrat	Yes
Greenwood, Alfred B.	Arkansas	South	Democrat	Yes
Grey, Ben Edwards	*Kentucky*	*South*	*Whig*	*Yes*
Grow, Galusha A.	*Pennsylvania*	*North*	*Democrat*	*No*
Hamilton, William T.	Maryland	South	Democrat	Yes
Harlan, Aaron	*Ohio*	*North*	*Whig*	*No*
Harlan, Andrew	Indiana	North	Democrat	No
Harris, Sampson W.	Alabama	South	Democrat	Yes
Harris, Wiley P.	*Mississippi*	*South*	*Democrat*	*absent*
Harrison, John Scott	*Ohio*	*North*	*Whig*	*No*
Hastings, George	New York	North	Democrat	No
Haven, Solomon G.	*New York*	*North*	*Whig*	*No*

222   Appendix C

REPRESENTATIVE	STATE	SECTION	PARTY	VOTE
Heister, Isaac E.	*Pennsylvania*	*North*	*Whig*	*No*
Hendricks, Thomas A.	Indiana	North	Democrat	Yes
Henn, Bernhart	Iowa	North	Democrat	Yes
Hibbard, Harry	New Hampshire	North	Democrat	Yes
Hill, Clement S.	*Kentucky*	*South*	*Whig*	*Yes*
Hillyer, Junius	Georgia	South	Democrat	Yes
Houston, George S.	Alabama	South	Democrat	Yes
Howe, Thomas M.	*Pennsylvania*	*North*	*Whig*	*No*
Hughes, Charles	New York	North	Democrat	No
Hunt, Theodore G.	*Louisiana*	*South*	*Whig*	*No*
Ingersoll, Colin M.	Connecticut	North	Democrat	Yes
Johnson, Harvey H.	Ohio	North	Democrat	No
Jones, Daniel	New York	North	Democrat	No
Jones, George W.	Tennessee	South	Democrat	Yes
Jones, J. Glancy	Pennsylvania	North	Democrat	Yes
Jones, Roland	Louisiana	South	Democrat	Yes
Keitt, Lawrence M.	South Carolina	South	Democrat	absent
Kerr, John	*North Carolina*	*South*	*Whig*	*Yes*
Kidwell, Zedekiah	Virginia	South	Democrat	Yes
Kittredge, George W.	New Hampshire	North	Democrat	No
Knox, James	*Illinois*	*North*	*Whig*	*No*
Kurtz, William H.	Pennsylvania	North	Democrat	Yes
Lamb, Alfred W.	Missouri	South	Democrat	Yes
Lane, James H.	Indiana	North	Democrat	Yes
Latham, Milton	California	North	Democrat	Yes
Letcher, John	Virginia	South	Democrat	Yes
Lilly, Samuel	New Jersey	North	Democrat	Yes
Lindley, James J.	*Missouri*	*South*	*Whig*	*Yes*
Lindsay, William D.	Ohio	North	Democrat	No
Lyon, Caleb	New York	North	Democrat	No
Macdonald, Moses	Maine	North	Democrat	Yes
Mace, Daniel	Indiana	North	Democrat	No
Macy, John B.	Wisconsin	North	Democrat	absent
Matteson, Orsamus B.	*New York*	*North*	*Whig*	*No*
Maurice, James	New York	North	Democrat	absent

Appendix C **223**

REPRESENTATIVE	STATE	SECTION	PARTY	VOTE
Maxwell, Augustus E.	Florida	South	Democrat	Yes
May, Henry	Maryland	South	Democrat	Yes
Mayall, Samuel	Maine	North	Democrat	No
McCulloch, John	*Pennsylvania*	*North*	*Whig*	*No*
McDougal, James A.	California	North	Democrat	Yes
McMullin, Fayette	Virginia	South	Democrat	absent
McNair, John	Pennsylvania	North	Democrat	Yes
McQueen, John	South Carolina	South	Democrat	absent
Meacham, James	*Vermont*	*North*	*Whig*	*No*
Middleswarth, Ner	*Pennsylvania*	*North*	*Whig*	*No*
Miller, John G.	*Missouri*	*South*	*Whig*	*Yes*
Miller, Smith	Indiana	North	Democrat	Yes
Millson, John S.	Virginia	South	Democrat	No
Morgan, Edwin B.	*New York*	*North*	*Whig*	*No*
Morrison, George W.	New Hampshire	North	Democrat	No
Muhlenberg, Henry A.	Pennsylvania	North	Democrat	absent
Murray, William	New York	North	Democrat	No
Nichols, Matthias H.	Ohio	North	Democrat	No
Noble, David A.	Michigan	North	Democrat	No
Norton, John O.	*Illinois*	*North*	*Whig*	*No*
Olds, Edson B.	Ohio	North	Democrat	Yes
Oliver, Andrew	New York	North	Democrat	No
Oliver, Mordecai	*Missouri*	*South*	*Whig*	*Yes*
Orr, James L.	South Carolina	South	Democrat	Yes
Packer, Asa	Pennsylvania	North	Democrat	Yes
Parker, Samuel W.	*Indiana*	*North*	*Whig*	*No*
Peck, Jared V.	New York	North	Democrat	No
Peckham, Rufus W.	New York	North	Democrat	No
Pennington, Alexander C.	*New Jersey*	*North*	*Whig*	*No*
Perkins, Bishop	New York	North	Democrat	No
Perkins Jr., John E.	Louisiana	South	Democrat	Yes
Phelps, John S.	Missouri	South	Democrat	Yes
Phillips, Phillip	Alabama	South	Democrat	Yes
Powell, Paulus	Virginia	South	Democrat	Yes
Pratt, James T.	Connecticut	North	Democrat	No

Appendix C

REPRESENTATIVE	STATE	SECTION	PARTY	VOTE
Preston, William	*Kentucky*	*South*	*Whig*	*Yes*
Pringle, Benjamin	*New York*	*North*	*Whig*	*No*
Puryear, Richard C.	*North Carolina*	*South*	*Whig*	*No*
Ready, Charles	*Tennessee*	*South*	*Whig*	*Yes*
Reese, David A.	*Georgia*	*South*	*Whig*	*Yes*
Richardson, William A.	Illinois	North	Democrat	Yes
Riddle, George R.	Delaware	South	Democrat	Yes
Ritchey, Thomas	*Ohio*	*North*	*Democrat*	*No*
Ritchie, David	*Pennsylvania*	*North*	*Whig*	*No*
Robbins Jr., John	Pennsylvania	North	Democrat	Yes
Rogers, Sion H.	*North Carolina*	*South*	*Whig*	*No*
Rowe, Peter	New York	North	Democrat	Yes
Ruffin, Thomas	North Carolina	South	Democrat	Yes
Russell, Samuel L.	*Pennsylvania*	*North*	*Whig*	*No*
Sabin, Alvah	*Vermont*	*North*	*Whig*	*No*
Sage, Russel	*New York*	*North*	*Whig*	*No*
Sapp, William R.	*Ohio*	*North*	*Whig*	*No*
Scudder, Zeno	*Massachusetts*	*North*	*Whig*	*absent*
Seward, James L.	Georgia	South	Democrat	absent
Seymour, Origen S.	Connecticut	North	Democrat	No
Shannon, Wilson	Ohio	North	Democrat	Yes
Shaw, Henry M.	North Carolina	South	Democrat	Yes
Shower, Jacob	Maryland	South	Democrat	Yes
Simmons, George A.	*New York*	*North*	*Whig*	*No*
Singleton, Otho R.	Mississippi	South	Democrat	Yes
Skelton, Charles	New Jersey	North	Democrat	No
Smith, Gerrit	**New York**	**North**	**Free Soil**	**No**
Smith, Samuel A.	Tennessee	South	Democrat	Yes
Smith, William	Virginia	South	Democrat	Yes
Smith, William R.	Alabama	South	Democrat	Yes
Smyth, George W.	Texas	South	Democrat	Yes
Snodgrass, John F.	Virginia	South	Democrat	Yes
Sollers, Augustus R.	*Maryland*	*South*	*Whig*	*absent*
Stanton, Frederick P.	Tennessee	South	Democrat	Yes
Stanton, Richard H.	Kentucky	South	Democrat	Yes

Appendix C   **225**

REPRESENTATIVE	STATE	SECTION	PARTY	VOTE
Stephens, Alexander H.	*Georgia*	*South*	*Whig*	*Yes*
Stevens, Hestor L.	Michigan	North	Democrat	No
Stratton, Nathan T.	New Jersey	North	Democrat	No
Straub, Christian M.	Pennsylvania	North	Democrat	Yes
Stuart, Andrew	Ohio	North	Democrat	No
Stuart, David	Michigan	North	Democrat	Yes
Taylor, John J.	New York	North	Democrat	Yes
Taylor, John L.	*Ohio*	*North*	*Whig*	*No*
Taylor, Nathaniel G.	*Tennessee*	*South*	*Whig*	*No*
Thurston, Benjamin B.	Rhode Island	North	Democrat	No
Tracy, Andrew	*Vermont*	*North*	*Whig*	*No*
Trout, Michael C.	Pennsylvania	North	Democrat	No
Tweed, William M.	New York	North	Democrat	Yes
Upham, Charles W.	*Massachusetts*	*North*	*Whig*	*No*
Vail, George	New Jersey	North	Democrat	Yes
Vansant, Joshua	Maryland	South	Democrat	Yes
Wade, Edward	**Ohio**	**North**	**Free Soil**	**No**
Walbridge, Hiram	New York	North	Democrat	Yes
Walker, William A.	New York	North	Democrat	Yes
Walley, Samuel H.	*Massachusetts*	*North*	*Whig*	*No*
Walsh, Mike	New York	North	Democrat	Yes
Warren, Edward A.	Arkansas	South	Democrat	Yes
Washburn Jr., Israel	*Maine*	*North*	*Whig*	*No*
Washburne, Ellihu B.	*Illinois*	*North*	*Whig*	*No*
Wells Jr., Daniel	Wisconsin	North	Democrat	No
Wentworth, John	Illinois	North	Democrat	No
Wentworth, Tappan	*Massachusetts*	*North*	*Whig*	*No*
Westbrook, Theodoric R.	New York	North	Democrat	Yes
Wheeler, John	New York	North	Democrat	No
Witte, William H.	Pennsylvania	North	Democrat	Yes
Wright, Daniel B.	Mississippi	South	Democrat	Yes
Wright, Hendrick B.	Pennsylvania	North	Democrat	Yes
Yates, Richard	*Illinois*	*North*	*Whig*	*No*
Zollicoffer, Felix K.	*Tennessee*	*South*	*Whig*	*Yes*

The Kansas-Nebraska Act passed the House on May 22, 1854, with 113 representatives in favor and 100 representatives against it.

Appendix D

House Results by Section and Party

Vote Count by Section

SECTION	FOR	AGAINST
North	44	91
South	69	9
TOTALS	**113**	**100**

Vote Count in North by Party

PARTY	FOR	AGAINST
Democrats	44	44
Whigs	0	42
Free Soil	0	5
TOTALS	**44**	**91**

Vote Count in South by Party

PARTY	FOR	AGAINST
Democrats	56	2
Whigs	13	7
Free Soil	not applicable	not applicable
TOTALS	**69**	**9**

Vote Count by Section and Party

SECTION AND PARTY	FOR	AGAINST
Northern Democrats	44	44
Southern Democrats	56	2
Northern Whigs	0	42
Southern Whigs	13	7
Northern Free Soil	0	5
Southern Free Soil	not applicable	not applicable
TOTALS	**113**	**100**

Appendix E

House Results by State

Party affiliation derived from the *Congressional Globe*:
Democrats are recorded in plain text, *Whigs are in italics*, and **Free Soilers are in bold**.

Abercrombie, James	*Alabama*	*South*	*Whig*	*Yes*
Cobb, Wilson R.W.	Alabama	South	Democrat	Yes
Dowdell, James F.	Alabama	South	Democrat	Yes
Harris, Sampson W.	Alabama	South	Democrat	Yes
Houston, George S.	Alabama	South	Democrat	Yes
Phillips, Phillip	Alabama	South	Democrat	Yes
Smith, William R.	Alabama	South	Democrat	Yes
Greenwood, Alfred B.	Arkansas	South	Democrat	Yes
Warren, Edward A.	Arkansas	South	Democrat	Yes
Latham, Milton	California	North	Democrat	Yes
McDougal, James A.	California	North	Democrat	Yes
Belcher, Nathan	Connecticut	North	Democrat	No
Ingersoll, Colin M.	Connecticut	North	Democrat	Yes
Pratt, James T.	Connecticut	North	Democrat	No
Seymour, Origen S.	Connecticut	North	Democrat	No

Connecticut: Ingersoll is the only Democrat in state to break rank and vote in favor of the bill.

Riddle, George R.	Delaware	South	Democrat	Yes
Maxwell, Augustus E.	Florida	South	Democrat	Yes
Bailey, David J.	Georgia	South	Democrat	Yes
Chastain, E.W.	Georgia	South	Democrat	Yes
Colquitt, Alfred H.	Georgia	South	Democrat	Yes
Dent, William B.W.	Georgia	South	Democrat	absent
Hillyer, Junius	Georgia	South	Democrat	Yes

230   Appendix E

Reese, David A.	Georgia	South	Whig	Yes
Seward, James L.	Georgia	South	Democrat	absent
Stephens, Alexander H.	Georgia	South	Whig	Yes

Allen, James C.	Illinois	North	Democrat	Yes
Allen, Willis	Illinois	North	Democrat	Yes
Bissell, William H.	Illinois	North	Democrat	absent
Knox, James	Illinois	North	Whig	No
Norton, John O.	Illinois	North	Whig	No
Richardson, William A.	Illinois	North	Democrat	Yes
Washburne, Elihu B.	Illinois	North	Whig	No
Wentworth, John	Illinois	North	Democrat	No
Yates, Richard	Illinois	North	Whig	No

In Illinois, Wentworth abandons the Democrats and joins the state's Whigs in voting against the bill.

Chamberlain, E.M.	Indiana	North	Democrat	absent
Davis, John G.	Indiana	North	Democrat	Yes
Dunham, Cyrus J.	Indiana	North	Democrat	Yes
Eddy, Norman	Indiana	North	Democrat	Yes
English, William H.	Indiana	North	Democrat	Yes
Harlan, Andrew	Indiana	North	Democrat	No
Hendricks, Thomas A.	Indiana	North	Democrat	Yes
Lane, James H.	Indiana	North	Democrat	Yes
Mace, Daniel	Indiana	North	Democrat	No
Miller, Smith	Indiana	North	Democrat	Yes
Parker, Samuel W.	Indiana	North	Whig	No

In Indiana, Democrats Harlan and Mace join Whig Parker in voting against passage.

Cook, John P.	Iowa	North	Whig	absent
Henn, Bernhart	Iowa	North	Democrat	Yes

Boyd, Linn	Kentucky	South	Democrat	absent
Breckinridge, John C.	Kentucky	South	Democrat	Yes
Chrisman, James S.	Kentucky	South	Democrat	Yes
Cox, Leander M.	Kentucky	South	Whig	Yes

Eliott, John M.	Kentucky	South	Democrat	Yes
Ewing, Presley	*Kentucky*	*South*	*Whig*	*absent*
Grey, Ben Edwards	*Kentucky*	*South*	*Whig*	*Yes*
Hill, Clement S.	*Kentucky*	*South*	*Whig*	*Yes*
Preston, William	*Kentucky*	*South*	*Whig*	*Yes*
Stanton, Richard H.	Kentucky	South	Democrat	Yes
Dunbar, William	Louisiana	South	Democrat	Yes
Hunt, Theodore G.	*Louisiana*	*South*	*Whig*	*No*
Jones, Roland	Louisiana	South	Democrat	Yes
Perkins Jr., John E.	Louisiana	South	Democrat	Yes
Benson, Samuel P.	Maine	North	Democrat	No
Farley, E. Wilder	*Maine*	*North*	*Whig*	*No*
Fuller, Thomas J. D.	Maine	North	Democrat	No
Macdonald, Moses	Maine	North	Democrat	Yes
Mayall, Samuel	Maine	North	Democrat	No
Washburn Jr., Israel	*Maine*	*North*	*Whig*	*No*

In Maine, MacDonald is the only legislator in favor of the bill.

Franklin, John R.	*Maryland*	*South*	*Whig*	*absent*
Hamilton, William T.	Maryland	South	Democrat	Yes
May, Henry	Maryland	South	Democrat	Yes
Shower, Jacob	Maryland	South	Democrat	Yes
Sollers, Augustus R.	*Maryland*	*South*	*Whig*	*absent*
Vansant, Joshua	Maryland	South	Democrat	Yes
Appleton, William	*Massachusetts*	*North*	*Whig*	*absent*
Banks Jr., Nathaniel P.	Massachusetts	North	Democrat	No
Crocker, Samuel	*Massachusetts*	*North*	*Whig*	*No*
De Witt, Alexander	**Massachusetts**	**North**	**Free Soil**	**No**
Dickinson, Edward	*Massachusetts*	*North*	*Whig*	*No*
Edmands, J. Wiley	*Massachusetts*	*North*	*Whig*	*No*
Elliot, Thomas D.	*Massachusetts*	*North*	*Whig*	*No*
Goodrich, John Z.	*Massachusetts*	*North*	*Whig*	*No*
Scudder, Zeno	*Massachusetts*	*North*	*Whig*	*absent*

Appendix E

Upham, Charles W.	*Massachusetts*	*North*	*Whig*	*No*
Walley, Samuel H.	*Massachusetts*	*North*	*Whig*	*No*
Wentworth, Tappan	*Massachusetts*	*North*	*Whig*	*No*
Clark, Samuel	Michigan	North	Democrat	Yes
Noble, David A.	Michigan	North	Democrat	No
Stevens, Hestor L.	Michigan	North	Democrat	No
Stuart, David	Michigan	North	Democrat	Yes
Barksdale, William	Mississippi	South	Democrat	Yes
Barry, William S.	Mississippi	South	Democrat	Yes
Harris, Wiley P.	Mississippi	South	Democrat	absent
Singleton, Otho R.	Mississippi	South	Democrat	Yes
Wright, Daniel B.	Mississippi	South	Democrat	Yes
Benton, Thomas H.	Missouri	South	Democrat	No
Caruthers, Samuel	*Missouri*	*South*	*Whig*	*absent*
Lamb, Alfred W.	Missouri	South	Democrat	Yes
Lindley, James J.	*Missouri*	*South*	*Whig*	*Yes*
Miller, John G.	*Missouri*	*South*	*Whig*	*Yes*
Oliver, Mordecai	*Missouri*	*South*	*Whig*	*Yes*
Phelps, John S.	Missouri	South	Democrat	Yes

Benton is the sole hold-out in Missouri and one of only two Southern Democrats to vote against the bill.

Hibbard, Harry	New Hampshire	North	Democrat	Yes
Kittredge, George W.	New Hampshire	North	Democrat	No
Morrison, George W.	New Hampshire	North	Democrat	No

In New Hampshire, only Hibbard is in favor of the bill.

Lilly, Samuel	New Jersey	North	Democrat	Yes
Pennington, Alexander C.	*New Jersey*	*North*	*Whig*	*No*
Skelton, Charles	New Jersey	North	Democrat	No

Appendix E   **233**

| Stratton, Nathan T. | New Jersey | North | Democrat | No |
| Vail, George | New Jersey | North | Democrat | Yes |

Bennett, Henry	*New York*	*North*	*Whig*	*No*
Carpenter, Davis	*New York*	*North*	*Whig*	*No*
Chase, George W.	*New York*	*North*	*Whig*	*absent*
Cumming, Thomas W.	New York	North	Democrat	Yes
Cutting, Francis B.	New York	North	Democrat	Yes
Dean, Gilbert	New York	North	Democrat	No
Fenton, Reuben E.	New York	North	Democrat	No
Flagler, Thomas S.	*New York*	*North*	*Whig*	*No*
Hastings, George	New York	North	Democrat	No
Haven, Solomon G.	*New York*	*North*	*Whig*	*No*
Hughes, Charles	New York	North	Democrat	No
Jones, Daniel	New York	North	Democrat	No
Lyon, Caleb	New York	North	Democrat	No
Matteson, Orsamus B.	*New York*	*North*	*Whig*	*No*
Maurice, James	New York	North	Democrat	absent
Morgan, Edwin B.	*New York*	*North*	*Whig*	*No*
Murray, William	New York	North	Democrat	No
Oliver, Andrew	New York	North	Democrat	No
Peck, Jared V.	New York	North	Democrat	No
Peckham, Rufus W.	New York	North	Democrat	No
Perkins, Bishop	New York	North	Democrat	No
Pringle, Benjamin	*New York*	*North*	*Whig*	*No*
Rowe, Peter	New York	North	Democrat	Yes
Sage, Russel	*New York*	*North*	*Whig*	*No*
Simmons, George A.	*New York*	*North*	*Whig*	*No*
Smith, Gerrit	**New York**	**North**	**Free Soil**	**No**
Taylor, John J.	New York	North	Democrat	Yes
Tweed, William M.	New York	North	Democrat	Yes
Walbridge, Hiram	New York	North	Democrat	Yes
Walker, William A.	New York	North	Democrat	Yes
Walsh, Mike	New York	North	Democrat	Yes

Westbrook, Theodoric R.	New York	North	Democrat	Yes
Wheeler, John	New York	North	Democrat	No

In New York, 22 no votes (12 Democrat, 9 Whig, 1 Free Soil) and 9 yes votes (all Democrats).

Ashe, William S.	North Carolina	South	Democrat	Yes
Clingman, Thomas L.	North Carolina	South	Democrat	Yes
Craige, Burton	North Carolina	South	Democrat	Yes
Kerr, John	*North Carolina*	*South*	*Whig*	*Yes*
Puryear, Richard C.	*North Carolina*	*South*	*Whig*	*No*
Rogers, Sion H.	*North Carolina*	*South*	*Whig*	*No*
Ruffin, Thomas	North Carolina	South	Democrat	Yes
Shaw, Henry M.	North Carolina	South	Democrat	Yes

In North Carolina, Kerr breaks from the other two Whigs in the state and votes with the Democrats in favor of the bill.

Ball, Edward	*Ohio*	*North*	*Whig*	*No*
Bliss, George	Ohio	North	Democrat	absent
Campbell, Lewis D.	**Ohio**	**North**	**Free Soil**	**No**
Corwin, Moses B.	*Ohio*	*North*	*Whig*	*absent*
Disney, David T.	Ohio	North	Democrat	Yes
Edgerton, Alfred P.	Ohio	North	Democrat	No
Ellison, Andrew	Ohio	North	Democrat	No
Giddings, Joshua R.	**Ohio**	**North**	**Free Soil**	**No**
Green, Frederick W,	Ohio	North	Democrat	Yes
Harlan, Aaron	*Ohio*	*North*	*Whig*	*No*
Harrison, John Scott	*Ohio*	*North*	*Whig*	*No*
Johnson, Harvey H.	Ohio	North	Democrat	No
Lindsay, William D.	Ohio	North	Democrat	No
Nichols, Matthias H.	Ohio	North	Democrat	No
Olds, Edson B.	Ohio	North	Democrat	Yes
Ritchey, Thomas	Ohio	North	Democrat	No
Sapp, William R.	*Ohio*	*North*	*Whig*	*No*
Shannon, Wilson	Ohio	North	Democrat	Yes
Stuart, Andrew	Ohio	North	Democrat	No

| Taylor, John L. | Ohio | North | Whig | No |
| Wade, Edward | Ohio | North | Free Soil | No |

In Ohio, yes was the odd vote, with 4 in favor of it, all Democrats. Fifteen were against it (7 Democrats, 5 Whigs, and 3 Free Soil).

Bridges, Samuel A.	Pennsylvania	North	Democrat	Yes
Chandler, Joseph R.	Pennsylvania	North	Whig	No
Curtis, Carlton B.	Pennsylvania	North	Democrat	No
Dawson, John L.	Pennsylvania	North	Democrat	Yes
Dick, John	Pennsylvania	North	Whig	No
Drum, Augustus	Pennsylvania	North	Democrat	No
Everhart, William	Pennsylvania	North	Whig	No
Florence, Thomas B.	Pennsylvania	North	Democrat	Yes
Gamble, James	Pennsylvania	North	Democrat	No
Grow, Galusha A.	Pennsylvania	North	Democrat	No
Heister, Isaac E.	Pennsylvania	North	Whig	No
Howe, Thomas M.	Pennsylvania	North	Whig	No
Jones, J. Glancy	Pennsylvania	North	Democrat	Yes
Kurtz, William H.	Pennsylvania	North	Democrat	Yes
McCulloch, John	Pennsylvania	North	Whig	No
McNair, John	Pennsylvania	North	Democrat	Yes
Middleswarth, Ner	Pennsylvania	North	Whig	No
Muhlenberg, Henry A.	Pennsylvania	North	Democrat	absent
Packer, Asa	Pennsylvania	North	Democrat	Yes
Ritchie, David	Pennsylvania	North	Whig	No
Robbins Jr., John	Pennsylvania	North	Democrat	Yes
Russell, Samuel L.	Pennsylvania	North	Whig	No
Straub, Christian M.	Pennsylvania	North	Democrat	Yes
Trout, Michael C.	Pennsylvania	North	Democrat	No
Witte, William H.	Pennsylvania	North	Democrat	Yes
Wright, Hendrick B.	Pennsylvania	North	Democrat	Yes

Among Pennsylvania Democrats, no is the odd vote. Eleven Democrats were in favor of it, 5 against. Overall, 14 were against it (the five joined by 9 Whigs).

Davis, Thomas	Rhode Island	North	Democrat	No
Thurston, Benjamin B.	Rhode Island	North	Democrat	No
Aiken, William	South Carolina	South	Democrat	absent
Boyce, William W.	South Carolina	South	Democrat	Yes
Brooks, Preston S.	South Carolina	South	Democrat	Yes
Keitt, Lawrence M.	South Carolina	South	Democrat	absent
McQueen, John	South Carolina	South	Democrat	absent
Orr, James L.	South Carolina	South	Democrat	Yes
Bugg, Robert M.	*Tennessee*	*South*	*Whig*	*No*
Campbell, Brookins	Tennessee	South	Democrat	absent
Churchwell, William M.	Tennessee	South	Democrat	Yes
Cullom, William	*Tennessee*	*South*	*Whig*	*No*
Etheridge, Emerson	*Tennessee*	*South*	*Whig*	*No*
Jones, George W.	Tennessee	South	Democrat	Yes
Ready, Charles	*Tennessee*	*South*	*Whig*	*Yes*
Smith, Samuel A.	Tennessee	South	Democrat	Yes
Stanton, Frederick P.	Tennessee	South	Democrat	Yes
Taylor, Nathaniel G.	*Tennessee*	*South*	*Whig*	*No*
Zollicoffer, Felix K.	*Tennessee*	*South*	*Whig*	*Yes*

In Tennessee, Ready and Zollicoffer break with the state's Whigs and join the Democrats and vote in favor of the bill.

Bell, Peter H.	Texas	South	Democrat	Yes
Smyth, George W.	Texas	South	Democrat	Yes
Meacham, James	*Vermont*	*North*	*Whig*	*No*
Sabin, Alvah	*Vermont*	*North*	*Whig*	*No*
Tracy, Andrew	*Vermont*	*North*	*Whig*	*No*
Bayly, Thomas H.	Virginia	South	Democrat	Yes
Bocock, Thomas S.	Virginia	South	Democrat	Yes
Caskie, John S.	Virginia	South	Democrat	Yes
Edmundson, Henry A.	Virginia	South	Democrat	Yes

Faulkner, Charles J.	Virginia	South	Democrat	Yes
Goode, William O.	Virginia	South	Democrat	Yes
Kidwell, Zedekiah	Virginia	South	Democrat	Yes
Letcher, John	Virginia	South	Democrat	Yes
McMullin, Fayette	Virginia	South	Democrat	absent
Millson, John S.	Virginia	South	Democrat	No
Powell, Paulus	Virginia	South	Democrat	Yes
Smith, William	Virginia	South	Democrat	Yes
Snodgrass, John F.	Virginia	South	Democrat	Yes

Millson is the only Virginia Democrat to vote no and only one of two Southern Democrats to vote against the bill.

Eastman, Ben C.	Wisconsin	North	Democrat	No
Macy, John B.	Wisconsin	North	Democrat	absent
Wells Jr., Daniel	Wisconsin	North	Democrat	No

Appendix F

Kansas Contested Delegate Election:
Comparison of Vote to Oust Whitfield and to Seat Reeder (August 4, 1856) with Vote to Authorize a Special Investigating Committee, March 19, 1856*
Democrats are in plain text, *anti-Nebraska men in italics*, and **Whigs/Know-Nothings in bold**.

REPRESENTATIVE	STATE	PARTY	OUST WHITFIELD?	SEAT REEDER?	SPECIAL CMTE?
Aiken, William	S. Carolina	D	No	No	No
Albright, Charles J.	*Ohio*	*A-N*	*Yes*	*Yes*	*---*
Allison, John	*Penn.*	*A-N*	*Yes*	*Yes*	*Yes*
Ball, Edward	*Ohio*	*A-N*	*Yes*	*No*	*Yes*
Barbour, Lucian	*Indiana*	*A-N*	*Yes*	*Yes*	*Yes*
Barclay, David	Penn.	D	Yes	Yes	Yes
Barksdale, William	Miss.	D	No	No	---
Bell, Peter H.	*Texas*	*A-N*	*No*	*No*	*---*
Bennett, Hendley S.	Miss.	D	No	No	No
Bennett, Henry	*New York*	*A-N*	*Yes*	*Yes*	*Yes*
Benson, Samuel P.	*Maine*	*A-N*	*Yes*	*Yes*	*Yes*
Billinghurst, Charles	*Wisc.*	*A-N*	*Yes*	*Yes*	*Yes*
Bliss, Philemon	*Ohio*	*A-N*	*Yes*	*Yes*	*Yes*
Bobcock, Thomas	Virginia	D	No	No	No
Bowie, Thomas F.	Maryland	D	No	No	No
Boyce, William W.	S. Carolina	D	No	No	Yes
Bradshaw, Samuel	*Penn.*	*A-N*	*Yes*	*Yes*	*---*
Branch, Lawrence	N. Carolina	D	No	No	No
Brenton, Samuel	*Indiana*	*A-N*	*Yes*	*Yes*	*Yes*
Broom, Jacob	**Penn.**	**W**	**Yes**	**No**	**No**
Buffington, James	*Mass.*	*A-N*	*Yes*	*Yes*	*Yes*
Burnett, Henry C.	Kentucky	D	No	No	No
Cadwalader, John	Penn.	D	No	No	No
Campbell, James	*Penn.*	*A-N*	*Yes*	*Yes*	*Yes*
Campbell, John P.	**Kentucky**	**W**	**No**	**No**	**No**
Campbell, Lewis	*Ohio*	*A-N*	*Yes*	*No*	*---*
Carlile, John S.	**Virginia**	**W**	**No**	**No**	**No**
Caruthers, Sam.	**Missouri**	**W**	**No**	**No**	**No**
Caskie, John S.	Virginia	D	No	No	No
Chaffee, Calvin C.	*Mass.*	*A-N*	*Yes*	*Yes*	*Yes*

*With the parties in transition, party affiliation was extremely fluid during this session of Congress. For this table, affiliations were determined by *The Tribune Almanac and Political Register for 1856* (New York: New York Tribune, 1857).

Appendix F

REPRESENTATIVE	STATE	PARTY	OUST WHITFIELD?	SEAT REEDER?	SPECIAL CMTE?
Clark, Ezra	Conn.	A-N	Yes	Yes	Yes
Clawson, Isaiah D.	New Jersey	A-N	Yes	Yes	Yes
Cobb, Howell	Georgia	D	No	No	No
Cobb, W.R.W.	Alabama	D	No	No	No
Colfax, Schulyer	Indiana	A-N	Yes	Yes	Yes
Comins, Linus B.	Mass.	A-N	Yes	Yes	Yes
Covode, John	Penn.	A-N	Yes	Yes	Yes
Cox, Leander M.	**Kentucky**	**W**	**No**	**No**	**No**
Cragin, Aaron H.	NH	A-N	Yes	Yes	Yes
Craige, Burton	N. Carolina	D	No	No	No
Crawford, Martin J.	Georgia	D	No	No	No
Cullen, Elisha D.	**Delaware**	**W**	**No**	**No**	---
Cumback, William	Indiana	A-N	Yes	Yes	Yes
Damrell, William S.	Mass.	A-N	Yes	Yes	Yes
Davidson, Thomas	Louisiana	D	No	No	No
Davis, Henry W.	**Maryland**	**W**	**No**	**No**	**No**
Day, Timothy C.	Ohio	A-N	Yes	Yes	Yes
Dean, Sidney	Conn.	A-N	Yes	Yes	Yes
Denver, James W.	California	D	No	No	---
Dick, John	Penn.	A-N	Yes	Yes	Yes
Dickson, Samuel	New York	A-N	---	Yes	Yes
Dodd, Edward	New York	A-N	Yes	Yes	Yes
Dowdell, James F.	Alabama	D	No	No	No
Dunn, George G.	Indiana	A-N	Yes	No	Yes
Durfee, Nathaniel	Rhode Isl.	A-N	Yes	Yes	Yes
Edie, John R.	Penn.	A-N	Yes	Yes	Yes
Edmundson, Henry	Virginia	D	No	No	No
Edwards, Francis	New York	A-N	Yes	No	Yes
Emrie, J. Reece	Ohio	A-N	Yes	Yes	Yes
English, William H.	Indiana	D	No	No	No
Eustis Jr., George	**Louisiana**	**W**	**No**	**No**	**No**
Evans, Lemuel D.	**Texas**	**W**	**No**	**No**	**No**
Faulkner, Charles J.	Virginia	D	No	No	No
Flagler, Thomas S.	New York	A-N	Yes	Yes	Yes
Florence, Thomas	Penn.	D	No	No	No
Foster, Nathaniel	**Georgia**	**W**	**No**	**No**	---
Fuller, Henry M.	Penn.	A-N	Yes	No	---
Fuller, Thomas	Maine	D	No	No	No
Galloway, Samuel	Ohio	A-N	Yes	Yes	Yes

Appendix F   **241**

REPRESENTATIVE	STATE	PARTY	OUST WHITFIELD?	SEAT REEDER?	SPECIAL CMTE?
Giddings, Joshua	Ohio	A-N	Yes	Yes	Yes
Gilbert, William A.	New York	A-N	Yes	Yes	Yes
Goode, William O.	Virginia	D	No	No	No
Granger, Amos A.	New York	A-N	Yes	---	Yes
Greenwood, Alfred	Arkansas	D	No	No	---
Grow, Galusha A.	Penn.	A-N	Yes	Yes	Yes
Hall, Robert B.	Mass.	A-N	Yes	Yes	Yes
Harlan, Aaron	Ohio	A-N	Yes	Yes	Yes
Harris, J.M.	**Maryland**	W	No	No	No
Harris, Sampson	Alabama	D	No	No	No
Harris, Thomas L.	**Illinois**	W	No	No	No
Harrison, John	Ohio	A-N	Yes	No	Yes
Haven, Solomon	**New York**	Whig	Yes	No	Yes
Herbert, Philip T.	California	D	No	No	No
Hickman, John	Penn.	D	Yes	No	Yes
Hoffman, Henry	**Maryland**	W	No	No	No
Holloway, David P.	Indiana	A-N	Yes	Yes	---
Horton, Thomas R.	New York	A-N	Yes	Yes	Yes
Horton, Valentine	Ohio	A-N	Yes	No	Yes
Houston, George S.	Alabama	D	No	No	No
Hughston, Jonas A.	New York	A-N	Yes	Yes	Yes
Jones, George W.	Tennessee	D	No	No	No
Kelsey, William H.	New York	A-N	Yes	Yes	Yes
Kennett, Luther	**Missouri**	W	No	No	No
Kidwell, Zedekiah	Virginia	D	No	No	No
King, Rufus H.	New York	A-N	Yes	No	Yes
Knapp, Chauncey	Mass.	A-N	Yes	Yes	Yes
Knight, Jonathan	Penn.	A-N	Yes	Yes	Yes
Knowlton, Ebenezer	Maine	A-N	Yes	Yes	Yes
Knox, James	Illinois	A-N	Yes	Yes	Yes
Kunkel, John C.	Penn.	A-N	Yes	Yes	---
Lake, William A.	**Miss.**	W	No	No	No
Leiter, Benjamin F.	Ohio	A-N	Yes	Yes	Yes
Letcher, John	Virginia	D	No	No	No
Lindley, James J.	**Missouri**	W	No	No	No
Lumpkin, John H.	Georgia	D	No	No	No
Mace, Daniel	Indiana	A-N	Yes	Yes	Yes
Marshall, Alex.	**Kentucky**	W	No	No	No
Marshall, H.	**Kentucky**	W	No	No	No

Appendix F

REPRESENTATIVE	STATE	PARTY	OUST WHITFIELD?	SEAT REEDER?	SPECIAL CMTE?
Marshall, Samuel	Illinois	D	No	No	No
Matteson, Orsamus	*New York*	*A-N*	*Yes*	*Yes*	*Yes*
Maxwell, Augustus	Florida	D	No	No	No
McCarty, Andrew	*New York*	*A-N*	*Yes*	*Yes*	*Yes*
McMullin, Fayette	Virginia	D	No	No	No
Miller, Killian	*New York*	*A-N*	*Yes*	*Yes*	*Yes*
Miller, Smith	Indiana	D	No	No	No
Millson, John S.	Virginia	D	No	No	No
Moore, Oscar F.	*Ohio*	*A-N*	*Yes*	*No*	*Yes*
Morgan, Edwin B.	*New York*	*A-N*	*Yes*	*Yes*	*Yes*
Morrill, Justin S.	*Vermont*	*A-N*	*Yes*	*Yes*	*Yes*
Mott, Richard	*Ohio*	*A-N*	*Yes*	*Yes*	*Yes*
Nichols, Matthias	*Ohio*	*A-N*	*Yes*	*Yes*	*Yes*
Norton, Jesse O.	*Illinois*	*A-N*	*Yes*	*Yes*	*Yes*
Oliver, Andrew	*New York*	*A-N*	---	*Yes*	*Yes*
Oliver, Mordecai	**Missouri**	**W**	**No**	**No**	**No**
Orr, James L.	S. Carolina	D	No	No	No
Parker, John M.	*New York*	*A-N*	---	*Yes*	*Yes*
Peck, George W.	Michigan	D	No	No	No
Pelton, Guy R.	*New York*	*A-N*	---	*Yes*	---
Pennington, Alex.	*New Jersey*	*A-N*	*Yes*	*No*	---
Pettit, John U.	*Indiana*	*A-N*	---	*Yes*	*Yes*
Phelps, John S.	Missouri	D	No	No	No
Pike, Andrew	?	?	---	Yes	---
Pike, James	*NH*	*A-N*	*Yes*	---	*Yes*
Porter, Gilchrist	**Missouri**	**W**	**No**	**No**	**No**
Powell, Paulus	Virginia	D	No	No	No
Pringle, Benjamin	New York	A-N	Yes	Yes	Yes
Purviance, Samuel	Penn.	A-N	Yes	Yes	---
Puryear, Richard	**N.Carolina**	**W**	**No**	**No**	---
Quitman, John A.	Miss.	D	No	No	No
Reade, Edwin G.	**N.Carolina**	**W**	**No**	**No**	---
Ready, Charles	**Tennessee**	**W**	**No**	**No**	**No**
Ricaud, James B.	**Maryland**	**W**	**No**	**No**	**No**
Richardson, William	Illinois	D	No	No	No
Ritchie, David	*Penn.*	*A-N*	*Yes*	*No*	*Yes*
Rivers, Thomas	**Tennessee**	**W**	**No**	**No**	---
Robbins, George R.	*New Jersey*	*A-N*	*Yes*	*Yes*	*Yes*

Appendix F 243

REPRESENTATIVE	STATE	PARTY	OUST WHITFIELD?	SEAT REEDER?	SPECIAL CMTE?
Roberts, Anthony	*Penn.*	*A-N*	*Yes*	*Yes*	*Yes*
Ruffin, Thomas	N. Carolina	D	No	No	No
Rust, Albert	Arkansas	D	No	No	---
Sabin, Alvah	*Vermont*	*A-N*	*Yes*	*Yes*	---
Sage, Russel	*New York*	*A-N*	*Yes*	*Yes*	*Yes*
Sandidge, John M.	Louisiana	D	No	No	No
Sapp, William R.	*Ohio*	*A-N*	*Yes*	*Yes*	*Yes*
Savage, John H.	Tennessee	D	No	No	No
Scott, Harvey D.	*Indiana*	*A-N*	*Yes*	*No*	*Yes*
Seward, James L.	Georgia	D	No	No	No
Sherman, John	*Ohio*	*A-N*	*Yes*	*Yes*	*Yes*
Shorter, Eli S.	Alabama	D	No	No	No
Simmons, George	*New York*	*A-N*	*Yes*	*No*	*Yes*
Smith, Samuel A.	Tennessee	D	No	No	No
Smith, William	Virginia	D	No	No	No
Smith, William R.	**Alabama**	**W**	**No**	**No**	**No**
Sneed, William H.	**Tennessee**	**W**	**No**	---	**No**
Spinner, Francis E.	New York	D	Yes	Yes	Yes
Stephens, A.H.	*Georgia*	*D*	*No*	*No*	---
Stewart, James A.	Maryland	D	No	No	No
Stranahan, James	**New York**	**W**	**Yes**	**Yes**	**Yes**
Swope, Samuel F.	**Kentucky**	**W**	**No**	**No**	**No**
Talbott, Albert G.	Kentucky	D	No	No	No
Tappan, Mason D.	*NH*	*A-N*	*Yes*	*Yes*	---
Taylor, Miles	LA	D	No	No	No
Thorington, James	*Iowa*	*A-N*	*Yes*	*Yes*	*Yes*
Thurston, Benjamin	*Rhode Isl.*	*A-N*	*Yes*	*Yes*	---
Todd, Lemuel	*Penn.*	*A-N*	*Yes*	*Yes*	*Yes*
Trafton, Mark	*Mass.*	*A-N*	*Yes*	*Yes*	*Yes*
Trippe, Robert P.	**Georgia**	**W**	**No**	**No**	**No**
Tyson, Job R.	*Penn.*	*A-N*	*Yes*	*No*	*Yes*
Underwood, W.	**Kentucky**	**W**	**No**	**No**	**No**
Vail, George	New Jersey	D	No	No	No
Valk, William W.	**New York**	**W**	**Yes**	**No**	**No**
Wade, Edward	*Ohio*	*A-N*	*Yes*	*Yes*	*Yes*
Wakeman, Abram	*New York*	*A-N*	*Yes*	*Yes*	*Yes*
Walbridge, David	*Mich*	*A-N*	---	*Yes*	*Yes*
Walbridge, Hiram	*New York*	*A-N*	*Yes*	---	---

Appendix F

REPRESENTATIVE	STATE	PARTY	OUST WHITFIELD?	SEAT REEDER?	SPECIAL CMTE?
Waldron, Henry	*Michigan*	A-N	Yes	Yes	Yes
Walker, Percy	**Alabama**	**W**	**No**	**No**	**No**
Warner, Hiram	Georgia	D	No	No	No
Washburn Jr., Isr.	*Maine*	A-N	Yes	Yes	Yes
Washburne, C.C.	*Wisconsin.*	A-N	Yes	Yes	Yes
Washburne, Ellihu	*Illinois*	A-N	Yes	Yes	Yes
Watkins, Albert G.	Tennessee	D	No	No	No
Watson, Cooper K.	*Ohio*	A-N	Yes	Yes	Yes
Wells Jr., Daniel	Wisconsin	D	---	No	---
Welch, William W.	*Conn.*	A-N	Yes	Yes	Yes
Wells, Daniel	Wisconsin	D	Yes	---	---
Whitney, Thomas	**New York**	**W**	**Yes**	**No**	**No**
Williams, John	New York	D	Yes	No	---
Winslow, Warren	N. Carolina	D	No	No	No
Wood, John M.	*Maine*	A-N	Yes	Yes	---
Woodruff, John	*Conn.*	A-N	Yes	Yes	Yes
Woodworth, James	*Illinois*	A-N	Yes	Yes	Yes
Wright, Daniel B.	Miss.	D	No	No	---
Wright, John V.	Tennessee	D	No	No	No
Zollicoffer, Felix K.	*Tennessee*	W	No	No	No

Notes

Abbreviations

AHR	American Historical Review
CWH	Civil War History
DBR	De Bow's Review
ERCJ	The Edinburgh Review or Critical Journal
HNMM	Harper's New Monthly Magazine
HW	Harper's Weekly
JISHS	Journal of the Illinois State Historical Society
JSH	Journal of Southern History
KH	Kansas History
KHQ	The Kansas Historical Quarterly
KSHS	Kansas State Historical Society
MHS	Massachusetts Historical Society
MVHR	Mississippi Valley Historical Review
MWH	Magazine of Western History
NAR	The North American Review
NE	The New Englander
NEM	The New England Magazine
NQR	National Quarterly Review
OM	The Overland Monthly
PH	Pennsylvania History
PM	Putnam's Monthly: A Magazine of Literature, Science, and Art
SAQ	The South Atlantic Quarterly
TH	The Historian
USDR	The United States Democratic Review

Introduction

1. Alice Nichols, *Bleeding Kansas* (New York: Oxford University Press, 1954), 139.

2. Cecil [Sidney G. Fisher], *Kanzas and the Constitution* (Boston: Printed by Damrell & Moore, 1856), 4–5, Gilder Lehrman Collection 5116.17.

3. Thomas Corwin to William W. Corcoran, June 2, 1856, William W. Corcoran Papers, Library of Congress.

4. "An Appeal to the South from the Kansas Emigrant Society of Missouri," *Advertiser and Gazette* (Montgomery, AL), 1855, in Walter L. Fleming, "The Buford Expedition to Kansas," *AHR* 6, n. 1 (October 1900): 38–39.

5. Charles Whipple [Aaron D. Stevens] to Henry E. Stevens, August 28, 1856, Gilder Lehrman Collection 7231.04.

6. Robert Walker, *An Appeal for Union. Letter from the Hon. Robert J. Walker* (New York: John F. Trow, Steam Book and Job Printer, 1856), 10, Gilder Lehrman Collection, 267.203.

1

1. Donald Bruce Johnson, ed., *National Party Platforms, Volume I: 1840–1956*, rev. ed. (Urbana: University of Illinois Press, 1978), 17.
2. Nathaniel Hawthorne, *The Life of Franklin Pierce* (Boston: Ticknor, Reed, and Fields, 1852; New York: MSS Information Corporation, 1970), 112.
3. Franklin Pierce, quoted in Robert W. Johannsen, *Stephen A. Douglas (SAD)* (New York: Oxford University Press, 1973), 374–75; Johnson, *National Party Platforms*, 1:17.
4. Hawthorne, *The Life of Franklin Pierce*, 131.
5. Gerald W. Wolff, *The Kansas-Nebraska Bill: Party, Section, and the Coming of the Civil War* (New York: Revisionist Press, 1977), 6; Roy Franklin Nichols, *The Democratic Machine, 1850–1854* (New York: Columbia University Press, 1923), 187.
6. Nichols, *Democratic Machine*, 18–22, 192; Wolff, *Kansas-Nebraska Bill*, 10–11.
7. "Our New President," *PM*, 2, n. 9 (September 1853): 308.
8. Colin M. Ingersoll to Howell Cobb, January 20, 1854, Ulrich B. Phillips, ed., *Annual Report of the American Historical Association for the Year 1911, Vol. II: The Correspondence of Robert Toombs, Alexander H. Stephens, and Howell Cobb* (Washington: 1913), 339–40.
9. Quoted in Johannsen, *SAD*, 389.
10. *New York Herald*, January 2, 1854, quoted in William E. Parrish, *David Rice Atchison: Border Politician* (Columbia: University of Missouri Press, 1961), 141.
11. Wolff, *Kansas-Nebraska Bill*, 26; Roy Franklin Nichols, *Franklin Pierce: Young Hickory of the Granite Hill* (Philadelphia: University of Pennsylvania Press, 1931), 308.
12. Johnson, *National Party Platforms*, 1:21; Roy Franklin Nichols and Eugene H. Berwanger, *The Stakes of Power, 1845–1877* (New York: Hill and Wang, 1982, 1961), 43–44.
13. Johnson, *National Party Platforms*, 1:18.
14. Nichols and Berwanger, *Stakes of Power*, 23, 31–32; Nichols, *Franklin Pierce*, 362–64.
15. Douglas to Charles H. Lanphier, November 11, 1853, in Robert W. Johannsen, ed., *The Letters of Stephen A. Douglas (Letters of SAD)* (Urbana: University of Illinois Press, 1961), 267.
16. William Gienapp, *The Origins of the Republican Party, 1852–1856* (New York: Oxford University Press, 1987), 69.
17. Johannsen, *SAD*, 395.
18. Frederick Starr [Lynceus], *Letters for the People on the Present Crisis* (1853?), 30–43.
19. Johannsen, *SAD*, 389, 397; Parrish, *Atchison*, 143. In the House, the vote was equally lopsided: Southerners cast only 18 of the 98 affirmative votes (*Congr. Globe*, 33 Cong., 1st Sess., Appx., 425–26).
20. Roy Franklin Nichols, "The Kansas-Nebraska Act: A Century of Historiography," *MVHR*, XLIII, n. 2 (September 1956): 187–212; Gienapp, *Origins*, 70; Parrish, *Atchison*, 115–16.
21. Douglas to J.H. Crane, et al., December 17, 1853, in Johannsen, *Letters of SAD*, 268–70.
22. Stephen Douglas, "Mr. Douglas's Report, January 4, 1854," in *The Nebraska Question* (New York: J.S. Redfield, 1854), 35–36.
23. *Washington Union*, January 5, 8, and 12, 1854.
24. *Washington Sentinel*, January 14, 1854, quoted in Parrish, *Atchison*, 145.

25. Parrish, *Atchison*, 144.

26. "Mr. Douglas's Report," *Nebraska Question*, 36; Gienapp, *Origins*, 71; David M. Potter, *The Impending Crisis: 1848-1861* (New York: Harper & Row, 1976), 159; Johannsen, *SAD*, 408.

27. Gienapp, *Origins*, 70-71; Dixon to Henry S. Foote, 1858, cited in Parrish, *Atchison*, 145-46; *Congr. Globe*, 175, Appx., 165; William C. Davis, *Breckinridge: Statesman, Soldier, Symbol* (Baton Rouge: Louisiana State University Press, 1974), 104.

28. Willard Carl Klunder, *Lewis Cass and the Politics of Moderation* (Kent, OH: The Kent State University Press, 1996), 264-66; Salmon P. Chase to Edward S. Hamlin, January 23, 1854, in John Niven, ed., *The Salmon P. Chase Papers, vol. 2: Correspondence, 1823-1857* (Kent, OH: The Kent State University Press, 1993), 382.

29. *Washington Union*, January 20 and 21, 1854.

30. *Charleston Mercury*, January 20, 1854; Davis, *Breckinridge*, 105-6; Johannsen, *SAD*, 413.

31. Chase to Hamlin, *op. cit.*; Potter, *Impending Crisis*, 162; Davis, *Breckinridge*, 108-9; Lynda Lasswell Crist, ed., *The Papers of Jefferson Davis, vol. 6: 1856-1860* (Baton Rouge: Louisiana State University Press, 1989), 68n.

32. Gienapp, *Origins*, 71; Nichols and Berwanger, *Stakes of Power*, 50; Johannsen, *SAD*, 415-17.

33. *Washington Union*, January 24, 1854.

34. Salmon P. Chase, et al., *An Appeal of the Independent Democrats in Congress to the People of the United States: Shall Slavery be Permitted in Nebraska?* (Washington: Tower Printers, 1854), 1-4.

35. Ibid., 6-7; Johnson, *National Party Platforms*, 1:19. According to Potter, the *Appeal*'s novelty stems from its attack on slavery's defenders "not on the merits or demerits of their position, but on the grounds that they were vicious, dishonest, and evil." See Potter, *Impending Crisis*, 162-64.

36. Douglas, "Speech, Jan. 30, 1854," in *Nebraska Question*, 37-38, 45-46; *Washington Union*, January 31, 1854.

37. *Washington Union*, January 31, 1854.

38. Benjamin Wade, *Speech of the Hon. B.F. Wade, of Ohio, on the Nebraska and Kansas Bills, in the Senate, March 3, 1854* (Washington: Congressional Globe Office, 1854), 7.

39. Robert Toombs, *Speech of the Hon. Robert Toombs, of Georgia, in the Senate, February 23, 1854, on Nebraska and Kansas* (Washington: Sentinel Office, 1854), 8.

40. Douglas to the *Concord (New Hampshire) State Capitol Reporter*, February 16, 1854, in Johannsen, *Letters of SAD*, 284-89.

41. James Cooper, *Nebraska and Kansas: Speech of Hon. Jas. Cooper, of Pennsylvania, in the Senate, February 27, 1854* (Washington: Congressional Globe Office, 1854), 2.

42. Quoted in John Botts, *Letters of John Minor Botts, of Virginia, on the Nebraska Question* (Washington: John T. and Lem. Towers, Printers, 1853), 14.

43. Truman Smith, "Speech, February 9, 1854," in *Nebraska Question*, 80-81.

44. Klunder, *Lewis Cass*, 270.

45. *Congr. Globe*, 450-51; Douglas, *Nebraska Question*, 64. Also see Klunder, *Lewis Cass*, 266; Potter, *Impending Crisis*, 57-59.

46. Sam Houston, *Speech of Senator Houston, of Texas, on the Nebraska and Kansas Bill, Previous to the Final Passage of the Same by the Senate of the United States, in the Senate, March 3, 1854* (Washington: Congressional Globe Office, 1854), 6.

47. Wade, *Nebraska and Kansas Bills*, 7. William E. Gienapp argues the political system's stability was undermined by the "new generation of political leaders less fearful of sectional agitation and less willing to compromise." See "The Crisis of American Democracy: The Political System and the Coming of the War," in Gabor S. Boritt, ed., *Why the Civil War Came* (New York: Oxford University Press, 1996), 112.

48. Robert Russel, "The Issues in the Congressional Struggle over the Kansas-Nebraska Bill, 1854," *JSH* 29, n. 2 (May 1963): 188.

49. William Fessenden, *Speech of W.P. Fessenden, of Maine, against the Repeal of the Missouri Prohibition, North of 36° 30', in the Senate, March 3, 1854* (Washington: Congressional Globe Office, 1854), 13.

50. Toombs to W.W. Burwell, February 3, 1854, in *Correspondence*, 342; Joseph H. Parks, *John Bell of Tennessee* (Baton Rouge: Louisiana State University Press, 1950), 288.

51. Andrew Butler, *Nebraska and Kansas: Speech of Hon. A.P. Butler, of South Carolina, in the Senate, February 24 and 25, 1854* (Washington: Congressional Globe Office, 1854), 2, 11-12.

52. Robert Hunter, *Speech of the Hon. R.M.T. Hunter, of Virginia, in the Senate, February 24, 1854 on Nebraska and Kansas* (Washington: Sentinel Office, 1854), 5-6.

53. Butler, *Nebraska and Kansas*, 16.

54. Quoted in *Washington Union*, January 12, 1854.

55. Charles Sumner, "The Landmark of Freedom," *Nebraska Question*, 107-9.

56. Chase, "Maintain Plighted Faith," in ibid., 59. Douglas claimed legislators intended to supersede the Missouri Compromise in 1850. See Potter, *Impending Crisis*, 157-58.

57. Fessenden, *Repeal of the Missouri Prohibition*, 15.

58. Wade, *Nebraska Question*, 68.

59. Had the four Democrats and five Whigs who were absent all voted as expected, the count would have been 43 to 17, close to the 45 to 15 or 17 Douglas predicted in mid-February. Of those absent, Democrats Jesse Bright (IN), William Wright (NJ), and Stephen Mallory (FL) and Whigs John Clayton (DE), James Pearce (PA), and Robert Toombs (GA) favored the bill, while Whigs Edward Everett (MA), James Cooper (PA), and Democrat Stephen Allen (RI) did not. See *Washington Union*, March 7, 1854; Douglas to Lanphier, February 13, 1854, in Johannsen, *Letters of SAD*, 283.

60. William Cullen Bryant, "Backbones Wanted—A North," February 27, 1854, *New York Evening Post*, in William Cullen Bryant II, ed., *Power for Sanity: Selected Editorials of William Cullen Bryant, 1829-1861* (New York: Fordham University Press, 1994), 273-74.

61. Douglas protested Samuel Wolcott's "coarse and insulting epithets" while writing George Nicholas Sanders that the latter would experience "*more mortification and chagrine at having written your unkind letter to me than I did in reading it.*" See Douglas to Wolcott, April 24, 1854, and to Sanders, March 27, 1854, in Johannsen, *Letters of SAD*, 323, 299.

62. Klunder, *Lewis Cass*, 175. Douglas risked disappointing both sections. See Sumner to John Jay, January 22, 1854, in Beverly Wilson Palmer, ed., *The Selected Letters of Charles Sumner* (Boston: Northeastern University Press, 1990), 403.

63. Houston, *Nebraska and Kansas Bill*, 6.

64. For the Senate vote, see Appendix A (page 215) and Appendix B (page 217).

65. Houston, *Nebraska and Kansas Bill*, 4-6. Houston was also upset that it violated congressional pledges that Indian tribes would remain outside the territorial system (*Congr. Globe*, 1020). For others speaking on behalf of Indian tribes, see Alexander Pennington (NJ), *Congr. Globe*, 1234.

66. Parks, *John Bell*, 284–85, 288–89. Everett noted that the bill would have died in committee had Houston and Bell voted against it there (299n).

67. *Congr. Globe*, 294–98.

68. Stephen Douglas, *Letter of Senator Douglas, Vindicating his Character and his Position on the Nebraska Bill against the Assaults Contained in the Proceedings of a Public Meeting Comprised of Twenty-Five Clergymen of Chicago* (Washington: Printed at the Sentinel Office, 1854), 10–11.

69. G.A. Grow, *Nebraska and Kansas: Speech of Hon. G.A. Grow, of Pennsylvania, in the House of Representatives, May 10, 1854* (Washington: 1854?), 5.

70. Thomas Hart Benton, *Nebraska and Kansas: Speech of Mr. Benton, of Missouri, in the House of Representatives, April 25, 1854* (Washington: Congressional Globe Office, 1854), 6.

71. *Congr. Globe*, Appx., 166–67.

72. Ibid., Appx., 342–45, 587.

73. Ibid., Appx., 371–73.

74. Ibid., Appx., 726, 193–96, 166–68, 453–57, 467.

75. Ibid., Appx., 353–56, 154.

76. James Meacham, *Nebraska and Kansas: Speech of Mr. Meacham, of Vermont, in the House of Representatives, February 15, 1854, Against the Nebraska and Kansas Territorial Bill, and in favor of maintaining the Government faith with the Indian Tribes* (Washington: Congressional Globe Office, 1854), 6.

77. *Congr. Globe*, 1234.

78. Charles Skelton, *Speech of Mr. Skelton, of New Jersey, in the House of Representatives, February 14, 1854, against the Repeal of the Missouri Compromise* (Washington: Congressional Globe Office, 1854), 7.

79. Richard Yates, *Speech of Hon. Richard Yates, of Illinois, on the Bill to Organize Territorial Governments in Nebraska and Kansas, and Opposing the Repeal of the Missouri Compromise, in the House of Representatives, March 28, 1854* (Washington: Congressional Globe Office, 1854), 9; *Congr. Globe*, Appx., 452, 460–63.

80. *Congr. Globe*, 429, 122; *Congr. Globe*, Appx., 429–32.

81. Davis, *Breckinridge*, 111–12; Wolff, *Kansas-Nebraska Bill*, 41–42.

82. *Congr. Globe*, 702.

83. Wolff, *Kansas-Nebraska Bill*, 41–42; Davis, *Breckinridge*, 111–12; *Congr. Globe*, 701.

84. *Congr. Globe*, Appx., 419–21, 439–42, 463; Davis, *Breckinridge*, 117.

85. Houston, *Nebraska and Kansas Bill*, 1.

86. *Washington Union*, January 21, 1854.

87. Sumner to John Jay, January 12, 1854, *Letters of Charles Sumner*, 399.

88. *Congr. Globe*, 378, 625, 702.

89. Ibid., 482, 1380; Wolff, *Kansas-Nebraska Bill*, 229. Abraham Lincoln reported that only three of seventy Democrats supported the measure before Douglas's orders arrived. Lincoln to Joshua F. Speed, August 24, 1855, in *The Collected Works of Abraham Lincoln*, ed. Roy P. Basler (New Brunswick, NJ: Rutgers University Press, 1953), 2:322.

90. *Congr. Globe*, 678; *Washington Union*, March 29, 1854.

91. Quoted in Leverett Spring, "Kansas and the Abolition of Slavery," *MWH* 9, n. 1 (November 1888): 80.

92. Botts, *Letters of John Minor Botts*, 6–8. Botts complained that the *Richmond Enquirer* had been particularly abusive.

93. Reverend Edward B. Hall, in *Proceedings of a Public Meeting of the Citizens of Providence, Held in the Beneficent Congregational Church, March 7, 1854, to Protest against Slavery in Nebraska; with the Addresses of the Speakers* (Providence, RI: Knowles, Anthony, & Co., Printers, 1854), 10.

94. Francis Wayland, *Dr. Wayland on the Moral and Religious Aspects of the Nebraska Bill: Speech at Providence, RI, March 7, 1854* (Rochester, NY: William N. Sage, 1854), 5.

95. *Charleston Mercury*, cited in *Proceedings of a Public Meeting*, 28.

96. Botts, *Letters*, 12.

97. W.B. Davis, *Appeal in Behalf of the Republic, to Southern Rights Gentlemen and Republicans of the North* (Wilmington, NC, 1854), 1.

98. *Macon Telegraph*, in *Charleston Mercury*, March 16, 1854.

99. Chase, *Appeal*, 7.

100. *Congr. Globe*, 442.

101. Ibid., 625; Gienapp, *Origins*, 74.

102. Douglas to Twenty-five Chicago Clergymen, April 5, in Johannsen, *Letters of SAD*, 301-21. He charged the memorialists with desecrating their calling for "neglecting their flocks and bringing our holy religion into disrepute by violating its sacred principles. . . ." He denied these religious meetings' importance, dismissing the over five hundred sermons preached on a single day in New England by claiming these clergy profaned their profession for "political designs and schemes." See Leonard Bacon, "The Morality of the Nebraska Bill," reprinted from *NE* (May 1854): 26-27; *Congr. Globe*, Appx., 787.

103. Wayland, *Moral and Religious Aspects of the Nebraska Bill*, 2.

104. Heman Humphrey, *The Missouri Compromise: An Address Delivered before the Citizens of Pittsfield by Rev. Heman Humphrey, D.D., in The Baptist Church, on Sabbath Evening, February 26, 1854* (Pittsfield: Reed, Hull, and Pierson, 1854), 14, 22.

105. J. Nelson, *A Discourse on the Proposed Repeal of the Missouri Compromise; Delivered on Fast Day, April 6, 1854, in The First Congregational Church, in Leicester, Mass.* (Worcester, MA: Edward R. Fiske, 1854), 5, 8, 12.

106. Leonard Marsh, *A Bake-Pan for Dough-Faces. By One of Them* (Burlington, VT: C. Goodrich, 1854), 39.

107. Wayland, *Moral and Religious Aspects*, 3.

108. Nelson, *Discourse on the Proposed Repeal*, 12.

109. Davis, *Breckinridge*, 118.

110. Wolff, *Kansas-Nebraska Bill*, 65, 231n.

111. Ibid., 43, 220n.

112. *New Orleans Daily Picayune*, May 18, 1854.

113. *Congr. Globe*, 1209.

114. Wolff, *Kansas-Nebraska Bill*, 43-44, 220-21n. Tappan Wentworth of Illinois; Gilbert Dean and Charles Hughes of New York; Thomas Fuller and Samuel Mayall of Maine; George Kittredge and George Morrison of New Hampshire; Nathaniel Banks of Massachusetts; Origen Seymour of Connecticut; Michael Trout of Pennsylvania; Alfred Edgerton, Andrew Ellison, Harvey Johnson, William Lindsay, and Thomas Ritchey of Ohio; Andrew Harlan and Daniel Mace of Indiana; David Noble and Hestor Stevens of Michigan; and John Macy of Wisconsin changed their votes.

115. *Congr. Globe*, 1235-40.

116. Ibid., 1240-54; Wolff, *Kansas-Nebraska Bill*, 225.

117. *New Orleans Daily Picayune*, May 18. For a breakdown of the House votes, see Appendix C (page 219), Appendix D (page 227), and Appendix E (page 229).

118. Wolff, *Kansas-Nebraska Bill*, 74.
119. *The Territorial Slavery Question. Non-Intervention Principle. Position of the National Democracy* (1854?), 6.
120. Wolff, *Kansas-Nebraska Bill*, 72.
121. *Congr. Globe*, 1230.
122. Thomas Hart Benton, Dred Scott pamphlet, quoted in William M. Meigs, *The Life of Thomas Hart Benton* (Philadelphia and London: J.B. Lippincott, 1904), 426.
123. *Congr. Globe*, Appx., 426.
124. Alexander H. Stephens to J.W. Duncan, May 26, 1854, in *Correspondence*, 345.
125. Quoted in James Brewer Stewart, *Joshua R. Giddings and the Tactics of Radical Politics* (Cleveland and London: The Press of Case Western Reserve University, 1970), 225.
126. Fessenden, June 4, 1854, cited in Francis Fessenden, *Life and Public Services of William Pitt Fessenden*, vol. 1 (Boston and New York: Houghton, Mifflin and Company, 1907), 47–48.
127. *Congr. Globe*, Appx., 760–61, 769, 780.
128. Ibid., Appx., 755–65.
129. Douglas to Howell Cobb, April 2, 1854, *Correspondence*, 343.
130. *Congr. Globe*, Appx., 769.
131. Homer E. Socolofsky and Huber Self, *Historical Atlas of Kansas* (Norman: University of Oklahoma Press, 1972, 1988), sections 12, 16, 21.
132. Russel, "The Issues in the Congressional Struggle," 209–10. Russel concisely outlines the legislative issues.
133. Charles Upham, *Nebraska and Kansas: Speech of Hon. Charles W. Upham, of Massachusetts, in the House of Representatives, May 10, 1854* (Washington: 1854?), 6.
134. Quoted in Parks, *John Bell*, 295.
135. *Congr. Globe*, Appx., 1913; Isaac Toucey, *Speech of Mr. Toucey, of Connecticut, Defending Himself Against the Nebraska Resolutions of the Legislature of Connecticut* (Washington: printed at the Sentinel Office, 1854), 4–5, 7.
136. Smith, *Letter to his Constituents*, 2–5. Smith was under bitter attack from all sides.
137. Nichols and Berwanger, *Stakes of Power*, 52–53; Nichols, *Franklin Pierce*, 362–65; Gienapp, *Origins*, 160–62. Alexander Stephens believed these results stemmed from general administration policies that had bred a legion of malcontents rather than from the Nebraska bill. See *Congr. Globe*, 33 Cong., 2nd Sess., Appx., 36–37.
138. *The Whig Almanac 1855* in *The Tribune Almanac for the Years 1838 to 1868* (New York: 1868), 40–51. Many of the Massachusetts replacements were other anti-Nebraska men.
139. *Congr. Globe*, 33 Cong., 2nd Sess., Appx., 36.
140. *Charleston Mercury*, October 25, 1854.
141. Ibid.
142. Stephens to W.W. Burwell, June 26, 1854, in *Correspondence*, 346.
143. *The Whig Almanac 1855*, 5, 40.
144. Johannsen, *SAD*, 408.
145. Toombs, *Nebraska and Kansas*, 8.
146. Seward, "Freedom and Public Faith," in *The Nebraska Question*, 102.
147. *Lynchburg Virginian*, in *Charleston Mercury*, October 25, 1854. The *Virginian* noted that the bill brought ministers into politics: "Until the agitation of the Nebraska bill northern preachers kept within the proper sphere of their holy duties. . . . They preached

religion, not politics. But now the pulpit has become one of the main *conduits* through which flows the turbid and poisoned stream of treason and abolitionism...."

148. Howell Cobb to James Buchanan, December 5, 1854, in *Correspondence*, 348.

149. Hawthorne, *Life of Franklin Pierce*, 113.

2

1. Russell K. Hickman, "The Reeder Administration Inaugurated, Part II—The Census of Early 1855," *KHQ* 36, n. 4 (Winter 1970): 425. Soldiers and other government employees were not considered residents. By 1855, the territory had grown to 8,506 residents (445).

2. Ibid.

3. Frederic L. Paxton, *History of the American Frontier: 1763-1893* (Boston and New York: Houghton Mifflin, 1924), 435.

4. Paul Wallace Gates, *Fifty Million Acres: Conflicts over Kansas Land Policy, 1854-1890* (Ithaca, NY: Cornell University Press, 1954), 17. Most of the relevant treaties were ratified in July and August 1854; the Wyandot treaty was completed in early 1855.

5. Paxton, *American Frontier*, 432.

6. Gates, *Fifty Million Acres*, 3, 22, 49; Paxton, *American Frontier*, 432. The Pre-emption Act of 1841 allowed squatting, and if settlers made improvements, they could purchase the land at a minimum of $1.25 per acre before public auction. In 1844, a similar act was passed for town sites under 320 acres.

7. Clarence E. Carter, "Colonialism in Continental United States," *SAQ* 47 (1948): 24-26. Also see Carter, "The Territorial Papers of the United States," *MVHR* 42 (1955): 510-24. The War Department supervised Indian agents until the Department of the Interior was created in 1849; in 1873, it assumed supervision of territorial governors. See Carter, "Territorial Papers," 512; Earl S. Pomeroy, *The Territories and the United States: 1861-1890* (Philadelphia: University of Pennsylvania Press, 1947), 16.

8. Pomeroy, *The Territories*, 5.

9. Territorial officers were perpetually seeking office. See Earl S. Pomeroy, "The Territory as a Frontier Institution," *TH* 7, n. 1 (Autumn 1944): 38.

10. *New York Daily Tribune*, May 20, 1854, Thomas H. Webb Scrapbooks, vol. 1 (1854), KSHS.

11. Roy Franklin Nichols, *Franklin Pierce: Young Hickory of the Granite Hill* (Philadelphia: University of Pennsylvania Press, 1931), 407.

12. *New York Daily Tribune*, June 30, 1854, Webb Scrapbooks, vol. 1, KSHS. The other nominees were Daniel Woodson (VA), Secretary; Madison Brown (MO), Chief Justice; Rush Ellmon (AL), Associate Justice; Saunders W. Johnston (OH), Associate Justice; Andrew J. Isaacs (LA), District Attorney; J.B. Donaldson (IL), Marshal. Brown declined and was replaced by Samuel Lecompte from the same state. Donaldson is variously spelled Donalson or, more accurately, J.B. Donelson.

13. *Daily Advertiser* (Mobile, AL), December 22, 1854, Webb Scrapbooks, vol. 2 (Nov. 1854–Feb. 1855).

14. Homer E. Socolofsky, *Kansas Governors* (Lawrence: University of Kansas, 1990), 33; Gustaf Adolf Youngstrom, "The Official Career of Andrew Horatio Reeder in Kansas" (Master's thesis, Northwestern University, 1931), 2, 10. The *Washington Union* reported Reeder's views on slavery. See W.W. Admire, "A Fragment of Early Kansas History," *MWH* 11, n. 6 (April 1890): 591.

15. *Transactions of the Kansas State Historical Society* (Topeka: Kansas Publishing House, 1886), 3:198. Reeder's children prepared this biography in 1881.
16. Ralph Volney Harlow, "The Rise and Fall of the Kansas Aid Movement," *AHR* 41, n. 1 (October 1935): 1; William H. Carruth, "New England in Kansas," *NEM* 16, n. 1 (March 1897): 4.
17. Louise Barry, "The Emigrant Aid Company Parties of 1854," *KHQ* 12, n. 2 (May 1943): 123.
18. Quoted in Edward Everett Hale, *Kanzas and Nebraska* (Boston: Phillips, Sampson and Company, 1854; Freeport, NY: Books for Libraries Press, 1972), 228, 232.
19. Barry, "Parties of 1854," 116. Most contemporary accounts list 670 settlers, 579 of whom can be verified through existent rosters. By 1855, the renamed NEEAC sponsored 900 more emigrants although few remained in the territory. See Barry, "The Emigrant Aid Company Parties of 1855," 227.
20. Harlow, "Kansas Aid Movement," 3.
21. Alice Nichols, *Bleeding Kansas* (New York: Oxford University Press, 1954), 10. By summer, enough border men laid claims to establish proslavery towns in Leavenworth, Kickapoo, and Atchison (12).
22. Horace Greeley, *American Conflict*, 1:235, quoted in Admire, "A Fragment of Early Kansas History," 589–90. See also Nichols, *Bleeding Kansas*, 11.
23. Admire, "A Fragment of Early Kansas History," 590; W.H. Isley, "The Sharps Rifle Episode in Kansas History," *AHR* 12, n. 3 (April 1907): 550; Charles Robinson, *The Kansas Conflict* (Lawrence, KS: Journal Publishing Company, 1898; Freeport, NY: Books for Libraries Press, 1972), 76.
24. Carruth, "New England in Kansas," 4.
25. Benjamin F. Stringfellow, *Negro-Slavery, No Evil; or The North and the South* (St. Louis: M. Niedner & Co., 1854), collected in New England Emigrant Aid Company, *Information for the People: Two Tracts of the Times. The One Entitled "Negro Slavery, No Evil": by B.F. Stringfellow, of Missouri. The Other, An Answer to the Inquiry "Is it Expedient to Introduce Slavery into Kanzas?" by D.R. Goodloe, of North Carolina* (Boston: Alfred Mudge and Sons, 1855), 4, 6, 7, 8, 35.
26. Daniel R. Goodloe, *Is it Expedient to Introduce Slavery into Kansas? A Tract for the Times. Respectfully Inscribed to the People of Kansas* (Cincinnati: 1854 or 1855), collected in *Information for the People*, 43, 53.
27. Cora Dolbee, "The First Book on Kansas: The Story of Edward Everett Hale's 'Kansas and Nebraska,'" *KHQ* 2, n. 2 (May 1933): 140–41. Also see Carruth, "New England in Kansas," 3–4.
28. E.E. Hale, *How to Conquer Texas Before Texas Conquers Us* (Boston: Redding & Co., 1845), 5.
29. Samuel Wood to the *National Era*, August 20, 1854, in Richard W. Richmond, "A Free-Stater's 'Letters to the Editor,'" *KHQ* 23, n. 2 (Summer 1957): 189.
30. Edward Chapman, speaking at the Territorial Indignation Meeting, reprinted in the *Kansas Tribune*, quoted in Robinson, *Kansas Conflict*, 84.
31. Quoted in Nichols, *Bleeding Kansas*, 14–15. Also see Robinson, *Kansas Conflict*, 82–90.
32. Gunja SenGupta, *For God & Mammon: Evangelicals and Entrepreneurs, Masters and Slaves in Territorial Kansas, 1854–1860* (Athens: University of Georgia Press, 1996), 44–56.

33. Elmer LeRoy Craik, "Southern Interest in Territorial Kansas," in *Collections of the Kansas Historical Society* XV (1922), 426.

34. *Kansas Weekly Herald* (Leavenworth), October 13, 1854, quoted in Russell K. Hickman, "The Reeder Administration Inaugurated, Part I—The Delegate Election of November, 1854," *KHQ* 36, n. 3 (August 1970): 310.

35. "An Act to Organize the Territories of Nebraska and Kansas," *The State of the Union: Being a Complete Documentary History of the Public Affairs of the United States, Foreign and Domestic, for the Year 1854* (Washington: Taylor & Maury, 1855), 264.

36. Hickman, "Part I," 313; House of Representatives, 34th Cong., 1st Sess., *Report 200: Report of the Special Committee Appointed to Investigate the Troubles in Kansas; with the Views of the Minority of Said Committee* (Washington: Cornellius Wendell, Printer, 1856), 933, 934.

37. Ibid., 255.

38. *Platte Argus* (Missouri), November 6, 1854, quoted in Daniel Webster Wilder, *The Annals of Kansas* (Topeka: T. Dwight Thacher, Kansas Publishing House, 1886; New York: Arno Press, 1975), 52.

39. Admire, "Early Kansas History," 593.

40. A.H. Reeder to F. Gwinner et al., quoted in Robinson, *Kansas Conflict*, 108–9.

41. Benjamin Stringfellow, *Slavery in Kansas: Letter from B.F. Stringfellow, in reply to one addressed to him by the Hon. P.S. Brooks, Thomas Clingman, Wm. Smith, and John McQueen* (Washington: Printed at the Sentinel Office, 1855), 4.

42. See *House Report 200*.

43. See Wilder, *Annals of Kansas*, 53; Admire, "Early Kansas History," 594; Hickman, "Part I," 322.

44. Hickman, "Part I," 311, 316, 339. For the petition, see Robinson, *Kansas Conflict*, 98.

45. *Chicago Daily Journal*, December 29, 1854, Webb Scrapbooks, vol. 2.

46. Socolofsky, *Kansas Governors*, 36.

47. Quoted in John H. Gihon, *Geary and Kansas. Governor Geary's Administration in Kansas. With a Complete History of the Territory until June 1857* (Philadelphia: J.H.C. Whiting, 1857; Freeport, NY: Book for Libraries Press, 1971), 39.

48. *Kansas Herald*, March 28 or 29, 1855, quoted in Admire, "Early Kansas History," 602.

49. In the 1860 census, Kansas had 2 slaves and 625 free blacks, while more New Englanders had settled in Missouri than in the territory. See Hickman, "Part II," 445–46.

50. Sion H. Rodgers (NC), February 15, 1855, *Congr. Globe*, 33rd Cong., 2nd Sess., Appx., 168.

51. Socolofsky, *Kansas Governors*, 36. According to James C. Malin, this excessive zeal was a tactical error, as the first census showed settlers from slave states in the majority. See "Judge Lecompte and the 'Sack of Lawrence,'" *KHQ* 20, no. 7 (August 1953): 466.

52. *Kansas Herald*, 1855, quoted in Admire, "Early Kansas History," 602.

53. Robinson, *Kansas Conflict*, 104.

54. "People's Proclamation," April 9, 1855, *Transactions*, 3:200. Although territorial residents did not elect their governor, considerable resentment centered on this issue since it was incompatible with popular sovereignty.

55. Socolofsky, *Kansas Governors*, 36.

56. Reeder, in *House Report 200*, 935.

57. Craik, "Southern Interest in Territorial Kansas," 346.

58. "An Act to Organize the Territories of Nebraska and Kansas," *State of the Union*, 255.

59. Leverett Spring, "Kansas and the Abolition of Slavery," *MWH* 9, n. 1 (November 1888), 83.

60. Atchison to R.M.T. Hunter, April 4, 1855, quoted in James C. Malin, "The Proslavery Background of the Kansas Struggle," *MVHR* 10, n. 3 (December 1923): 288.

61. Atchison to Amos A. Lawrence, April 15, 1855, quoted in F.B. Sanborn, "Negro Slavery in Kansas and Missouri," *MHS* (March 1911): 508.

62. Isley, "The Sharps Rifle Episode," 551-52.

63. Vigilance Club, 1855, William Hutchison Papers, KSHS.

64. Quoted in Robinson, *Kansas Conflict*, 117.

65. Wilder, *Annals of Kansas*, 63; Socolofsky, *Kansas Governors*, 35; Youngstrom, "Official Career of Reeder," 50; *New York Tribune*, October 8, 1855, Kansas Territorial History, Clippings, vol. 3, KSHS.

66. Youngstrom, "Official Career of Reeder," 46.

67. Hickman, "Part I," 312.

68. Ibid., 312. For Reeder's interpretation of these events, see *House Report 200*, 936-42.

69. *House Report 200*, 938.

70. Youngstrom, "Official Career of Reeder," 47.

71. *House Report 200*, 941.

72. Franklin Pierce, c. 1855, "Draft of letter to be filled out and signed by Gov. Reeder of Kansas," *Franklin Pierce Papers*, Library of Congress (microfilm, Reel 2, document number 2033-2035). Although undated, the content suggests it was written after these May 1855 meetings.

73. Marcy to Reeder, June 11, 1855, in *Transactions* 5:227-28; Wilder, *Annals of Kansas*, 65. See also Hickman, "Part I," 312.

74. Socolofsky, *Kansas Governors*, 36.

75. *Transactions*, 3:200.

76. Wilder, *Annals of Kansas*, 51.

77. See Nichols, *Bleeding Kansas*, 34-35; Wilder, *Annals of Kansas*, 66-67; Gihon, *Geary and Kansas*, 40; Robinson, *Kansas Conflict*, 142-43, 148, 153-56.

78. "An Act to Organize the Territories of Nebraska and Kansas," 254-55.

79. Admire, "Early Kansas History," 590; Socolofsky, *Kansas Governors*, 36-37.

80. Gihon, *Geary and Kansas*, 42-43.

81. Socolofsky, *Kansas Governors*, 40-41. This faction began its movement against the "bogus" legislature this summer.

82. Wilder, *Annals of Kansas*, 68.

83. Youngstrom, "Official Career of Reeder," 39.

84. Wilder, *Annals of Kansas*, 69-70.

85. Socolofsky, *Kansas Governors*, 37.

86. Leonard Woolsey Bacon, "Buchanan on Kansas," *NE* (November 1857): 676. Bacon was a charter member of the New England Emigrant Aid Company. See Carruth, "New England in Kansas," 5.

87. *Transactions*, 3:199.

88. Ibid., 3:202.

89. Letter to the Editor, *Chicago Democratic Press*, August 18, 1855, William M. Snow Scrap-book, KSHS, 39.

90. Samuel A. Johnson, *The Battle Cry of Freedom: The New England Emigrant Aid Company in the Kansas Crusade* (Westport, CT: Greenwood Press, 1954), 134–35.

91. Leverett W. Spring, "The Career of a Kansas Politician," *AHR* 4, no. 1 (October 1898): 81–82. Until his death, Lane maintained that Douglas had sent him to Kansas. See [Reeder McCandless Fish,] *The Grim Chieftain of Kansas* (Cherryvale, KS: Clarion Book and Job Print, 1885), 48–49.

92. Malin, "The Topeka Statehood Movement," *Territorial Kansas: Studies Commemorating the Centennial* (Lawrence: University of Kansas Publications, Social Science Studies, 1954), 40.

93. Kansas Territory Delegate Convention, *Proceedings of the Territorial Delegate Convention, held at Big Springs, on the 5-6th of Sept., 1855* (Lawrence, K.T.: Herald of Freedom Print, 1855), 3.

94. Ibid., 3.

95. Ibid., 4–5. Also see Gihon, *Geary and Kansas*, 44.

96. Robinson to Amos Lawrence, November 1, 1855, in Robinson, *Kansas Conflict*, 160–61.

97. John Speer, *Life of Gen. James H. Lane, 'The Liberator of Kansas,' with Corroborative Incidents of Pioneer History* (Garden City, KS: John Speer, Printer, 1896), 43–44; *Kansas Tribune*, September 15, 1855, quoted in David W. Johnson, "Freesoilers for God: Kansas Newspaper Editors and the Antislavery Crusade," *KH* 2, n. 2 (Summer 1979), 79; Nichols, *Bleeding Kansas*, 43.

98. Kansas Territory Delegate Convention, *Big Springs*, 3.

99. Ibid.

100. *Herald of Freedom*, September 15, 1855, quoted in Johnson, "Freesoilers for God," 79.

101. See Letter to the Editor, *Herald of Freedom*, June 31, 1855, Snow Scrap-book, 48.

102. Garrison in *Liberator*, June 1, 1855, quoted in Eli Thayer, *The New England Emigrant Aid Company and its Influence, Through the Kansas Contest, Upon National History* (Worcester, MA: Franklin P. Rice, 1887), 35.

103. John Everett to Robert Everett Sr., January 25, 1856, John and Sarah Everett, "Letters of John and Sarah Everett," *KHQ* 8, n. 1 (February 1939): 25–26.

104. F.B. Sanborn, "Negro Slavery in Kansas and Missouri," 508.

105. James Lane to A. Doniphan and A. Boon, September 22, 1856, reprinted by the *New York Tribune*, October 3, 1856. Also see John James Ingalls, "Kansas: 1854–1891," *HNMM* 86, n. DXV (April 1893): 701; Robinson, *Kansas Conflict*, 161.

106. Stearn to Sumner, October 2, 1855, Miscellaneous Edward Lillis Pierce Manuscripts, KSHS.

107. Socolofsky, *Kansas Governors*, 44.

108. Ibid., 44.

109. George W. Clarke to John Quitman, January 29, 1856, Misc. Geo. W. Clarke Manuscripts, KSHS.

110. Thomas W. Thomas to Alexander H. Stephens, January 12, 1857, Ulrich B. Phillips, ed., *Annual Report of the American Historical Association for the Year 1911, Vol. II: The Correspondence of Robert Toombs, Alexander H. Stephens, and Howell Cobb* (Washington: 1913), 392.

111. Proceedings of the State Constitutional Convention, held at Topeka, Sept. 19–20, 1855, in Kansas Territory Delegate Convention, *Big Springs*, 12–16.

112. Wilder, *Annals of Kansas*, 79.
113. Letter, Thomas C. Wells to Thomas P. Wells, October 12, 1855, "Letters of a Kansas Pioneer," *KHQ* 5, no. 2 (May 1936): 158.
114. Stearn to Sumner, October 2, 1855, Misc. Edward Lillis Pierce Manuscripts, KSHS.
115. Whitfield to Reeder, October 17, 1855, *Congr. Globe*, 34th Cong., 1st Sess., 455.
116. Ibid., 91–106.
117. Speer, *James H. Lane*, 42.
118. Johnson, "Freesoilers for God," 80; Wilder, *Annals of Kansas*, 90–91.
119. Wilder, *Annals of Kansas*, 86–87.
120. Quoted in Nichols, *Bleeding Kansas*, 48.
121. *St. Louis Intelligencer*, August 1855, quoted in "The Kansas Question," *PM* 6, n. 4 (October 1855): 427.
122. Atchison to Friends, September 12, 1855, reprinted by the *New York Tribune*, November 2, 1855, in Isley, "The Sharps Rifle Episode," 546.
123. "An Appeal to the South from the Kansas Emigrant Society of Missouri," *Advertiser and Gazette* (Montgomery, AL), 1855, in Walter L. Fleming, "The Buford Expedition to Kansas," *AHR* 6, n. 1 (October 1900): 38–39.
124. Jefferson Buford, "Aid to Kansas: Col. Buford's Propositions," *Spirit of the South* (Eufaula, AL), November 26, 1855, in Fleming, "Buford Expedition," 39.
125. O.N. Merrill, *True History of the Kansas Wars, and their Origin, Progress and Incidents* (Cincinnati: J.R. Telfer, 1856), 14. On the common nature of preemption violence, see Johnson, *Battle Cry of Freedom*, 138.
126. Shannon to Strickler, November 27, 1855, *Transactions*, 3:292; Shannon to Pierce, November 28, 1855, ibid., 3:293.
127. Shannon to Jones, December 2, 1855, ibid., 3:295.
128. Shannon to Pierce, December 11, 1855, ibid., 3:299.
129. Shannon to Pierce, November 28, 1855, ibid., 3:293.
130. Ibid., 3:293–94.
131. Shannon, "Proclamation," November 29, 1855, *Transactions*, 3:294–95.
132. Socolofsky, *Kansas Governors*, 45; Shannon to George Douglas Brewerton, quoted in Nichols, *Bleeding Kansas*, 54.
133. Jones to Shannon, quoted in Gihon, *Geary and Kansas*, 61.
134. Sumner to Shannon, December 7, 1855, *Transactions*, 3:299.
135. Shannon to Pierce, December 11, 1856, ibid., 3:299.
136. Shannon to Pierce, December 11, 1856, *Transactions*, 3:300–1.
137. Wakarusa Treaty, reprinted in Robinson, *Kansas Conflict*, 202–3.
138. Ibid., 206; Gihon, *Geary and Kansas*, 64–65.
139. George W. Clarke to John Quitman, January 29, 1856, Misc. Geo. W. Clarke Manuscripts, KSHS.
140. Shannon to Pierce, December 11, 1856, *Transactions*, 3:301.
141. Socolofsky, *Kansas Governors*, 44–45.
142. Ibid.
143. John A. Bingham, *Kansas Contested Election: Speech of Hon. J.A. Bingham, of Ohio, in the House of Representatives, March 6, 1856, on the Resolution Reported from the Committee of Elections, in the Contested Election Case from the Territory of Kansas* (Washington: Buell & Blanchard, Printers, 1856), 6.

144. *New York Tribune*, October 8, 1855, in Kansas Territorial History, Clippings, vol. 3, KSHS.
145. Quoted in Nichols, *Bleeding Kansas*, 59.

3

1. Franklin Pierce, *Message of the President of the United States, Relative to Disturbances in the Territory of Kansas*, January 24, 1856, Senate, 34th Cong., 1st Sess., *Ex. Doc. No. 4*.
2. See Charles Robinson, *The Kansas Conflict* (Lawrence, KS: Journal Publishing Company, 1898; Freeport, New York: Books for Libraries Press, 1972), 225-26. See also Samuel A. Johnson, *The Battle Cry of Freedom: The New England Emigrant Aid Company in the Kansas Crusade* (Westport, CT: Greenwood Press, 1954), 148.
3. Reeder to Charles Robinson, February 16, 1856, Charles and Sara Robinson Papers, KSHS.
4. *New York Times*, February 15, 1856, Kansas Territorial History, Clippings, vol. 3, pt. 3, KSHS.
5. James Malin, *John Brown and the Legend of Fifty-Six* (Philadelphia: The American Philosophical Society, 1942), 520.
6. David R. Atchison to Jefferson Davis, February 26, 1856, in Lynda Lasswell Crist, ed., *The Papers of Jefferson Davis, vol. 6: 1856-1860* (Baton Rouge: Louisiana State University Press, 1989), 13.
7. Johnson, *Battle Cry of Freedom*, 154-55.
8. Henry Wilson, *Cong. Globe*, 34th Cong., 1st Sess., Appx., 94.
9. John P. Hale, *The Wrongs of Kansas: Speech of John P. Hale, of New Hampshire, in the United States Senate, February 26 and 28, 1856* (Washington: Buell & Blanchard, Printers, 1856), 2.
10. Reeder to Robinson, February 16, 1856, Charles and Sara Robinson Papers, KSHS.
11. Jonas W. Colburn to Peggy Colburn, February 17, 1856, Jonas Colburn Letters, KSHS.
12. Shannon to Marcy, April 11, 1856, *Transactions of the Kansas State Historical Society* (Topeka: Kansas Publishing House, 1890), 4:385; John H. Gihon, *Geary and Kansas. Governor Geary's Administration in Kansas* (Philadelphia: J.H.C. Whiting, 1857; Freeport, NY: Books for Libraries Press, 1971), 44; Johnson, *Battle Cry of Freedom*, 145-46; Daniel Webster Wilder, *The Annals of Kansas* (Topeka: T. Dwight Thacher, Kansas Publishing House, 1886; New York: Arno Press, 1975), 114.
13. U.S. House of Representatives, *Memorial of the Senators and Representatives [of the State of Kansas], and the Constitution of the State of Kansas; also, the Majority and Minority Reports of the Committee on Territories on the Said Constitution* (Washington: Cornelius Wendell, 1856), 4-5, 7, 9.
14. Quoted in Elmer LeRoy Craik, "Southern Interest in Territorial Kansas: 1854-1858," *Collections of the Kansas Historical Society* 15 (1922), 356.
15. George W. Clarke to John Quitman, January 29, 1856, Misc. Geo. W. Clarke Manuscripts, KSHS.
16. Ibid.
17. William A. Johnson, *The History of Anderson County* (Garnett, KS: Kauffman & Iler, 1877), 40.

18. Charles Robinson, "Governor Robinson's Message," April 4, 1856, reprinted in the *Herald of Freedom*, William M. Snow Scrap-book, KSHS, 62–64.

19. Shannon to Marcy, April 11, 1856, *Transactions*, 4:386.

20. William Heiskell to Shannon, April 30, 1856, ibid., 4:418–19.

21. Shannon to Marcy, April 27, 1856, ibid., 4:405–8.

22. Gihon, *Geary and Kansas*, 77.

23. The Howard Committee held hearings at the Free State Hotel in Lawrence through May 12 (with a session in Tecumseh from May 5 to 7), and then moved to Leavenworth from May 12 to 14, 1856.

24. O.N. Merrill, *True History of the Kansas Wars* (Cincinnati: J.R. Telfer, 1856), 40.

25. For insight into the Howard Committee, see John Sherman, *John Sherman's Recollections of Forty Years in the House, Senate and Cabinet* (Chicago: The Werner Company, 1895), 1:114–35.

26. Nichols, *Bleeding Kansas*, 103.

27. James C. Malin, "The Proslavery Background of the Kansas Struggle," *MVHR* 10, n. 3 (December 1923): 304; Malin, *John Brown*, 49–50.

28. Jonas Colburn to Peggy Colburn, May 23, 1856, James Colburn Letters, KSHS.

29. C.W. Topliff et al., to Sumner, May 11, Senate, 34th Cong., 1st Sess., *Ex. Doc. No. 97: Message of the President of the United States communicating a Report, in compliance with a resolution of the Senate of the 21st ultimo, calling for information relative to the instructions sent to military officers in Kansas* (Washington: 1856), 4.

30. Shannon to Topliff et al., May 12, 1856, quoted in U.S. House of Representatives, Committee on the Territories, *R.G. Elliott and Others, of Kansas, to Accompany Bill H.R. no. 810, February 7, 1857* (Washington: 1857), 3. See also Johnson, *Battle Cry of Freedom*, 158.

31. Sumner to Col. Samuel Cooper, Adjutant General, May 12, 1856, *Ex. Doc. No. 97*, 3. On May 23, before the news reached the capital, Davis clarified his orders, writing Sumner that "it matters not whether the subversion of the law arises from a denial of the existence of the government, or whether it proceed from a lawless disregard of the right to protection of person and property. . . ." See Davis to Sumner, May 23, 1856, *Ex. Doc. No. 97*, 5.

32. Sumner to Shannon, May 12, 1856, *Ex. Doc. No. 97*, 4.

33. Pierce to Shannon, May 23, 1856, *Transactions*, 4:414. His telegraphs arrived after the sack but before the news reached Washington.

34. McIntosh to Sumner, May 21, 1856, ibid., 4:435–36.

35. Donelson to Robert Morrow et al., May 15, 1856, in *Elliott Memorial*, 5–6.

36. Shannon to Pierce, May 31, 1856, *Transactions*, 4:415. After receiving Pierce's May 23 telegraphs, he assured him he had only authorized the posse Jones requested on April 20 and asked Sumner for troops to prevent civil war, seemingly unaware that his instructions allowed him to do so on his own authority. See Shannon to Pierce, May 31, 1856, *Transactions*, 4:415–16. Also see Wilder, *Annals of Kansas*, 118–20.

37. Malin, "Judge Lecompte," 466. In his lucid account, Malin argues that these events were the Republican Party's only unifying issue. Also see Malin, "The Proslavery Background," 304.

38. Shannon to Pierce, May 31, 1856, *Transactions*, 4:416. For the threat Sharps rifles posed, see Dale E. Watts, "Plows and Bibles, Rifles and Revolvers: Guns in Kansas Territory," *KH* 18, n. 2 (Spring 1998): 39, 44.

39. See Malin, *John Brown*, 50, and Malin, "Judge Lecompte," for a wider discussion of the territory's legal system.

40. Illinois Women's Kansas Aid and Liberty Association, *Constitution and By-Laws of the Illinois Woman's Kansas Aid and Liberty Association, Organized June 10, 1856* (Chicago: Daily Tribune Book and Job Office, 1856), 9–10.

41. Victims included James P. Doyle and sons William and Drury, legislator Allen Wilkinson, and William Sherman.

42. The *New York Times* devoted merely eleven lines to this story, with four disclaiming the source (the *St. Louis Republican*). See Nichols, *Bleeding Kansas*, 116–17.

43. Sumner to Cooper, May 28, 1856, *Transactions*, 4:437.

44. See Malin, *John Brown*, 643.

45. Shannon to Pierce, May 31, 1856, *Transactions*, 4:417.

46. George W. Brown to his mother, July 24, 1856, G.W. Brown Collection, KSHS.

47. Homer E. Socolofsky, *Kansas Governors* (Lawrence: University Press of Kansas, 1990), 45.

48. Shannon to Sumner, June 4, 1856, *Transactions*, 4:440–41.

49. Shannon, "Proclamation," June 4, 1856, *Transactions*, 4:442–43.

50. Socolofsky, *Kansas Governors*, 46.

51. Pierce to Shannon, June 6, 1856, *Transactions*, 4:421.

52. Davis to Smith, June 27, 1856, *Transactions*, 4:426. See also Eugene T. Wells, "Jefferson Davis and Kansas Territory," *KHQ* 22, n. 4 (Winter 1956): 356. Ill for much of this time, Smith left in February 1857 without playing an active role in Kansas. See Gihon, *Geary and Kansas*, 92.

53. John Everett to Robert Everett Sr., June 14?, 1856, John and Sarah Everett, "Letters of John and Sarah Everett," *KHQ* 8, n. 1 (February 1939): 32.

54. Sarah to Cynthia Everett, August 1, 1856, *KHQ* 8, n. 2 (May 1939): 146.

55. Shannon to Pierce, June 17, 1856, *Transactions*, 4:388.

56. Cooke to Cooper, June 18, 1856, *Transactions*, 4:444.

57. *Report of the Proceedings of a Convention of Delegates from Kansas Aid Societies, in Different States, Held at Cleveland, Ohio, on the 20th and 21st of June, 1856, and Adjourned and held at Buffalo, in the State of New York, on the 9th and 10th Days of July, 1856* (Cleveland?: 1856), 2, 5, 7.

58. Ibid., 12–13.

59. Ibid., 16.

60. Proceedings in Buffalo, July 9, 1856, ibid., 19.

61. John Everett to Cynthia Everett, July 24, 1856, "Letters of John and Sarah Everett," 144.

62. Roy Franklin Nichols, *Franklin Pierce: Young Hickory of the Granite Hill* (Philadelphia: University of Pennsylvania Press, 1931), 476.

63. Proceedings in Buffalo, *Convention of Delegates from Kansas Aid Societies*, 19.

64. Nichols, *Franklin Pierce*, 476.

65. George W. Smith et al., to The Friends of "Law and Order," July 1, 1856, Blood Collection, KSHS.

66. Colburn to Peggy Colburn, July 7, 1856, Jonas Colburn letters, KSHS.

67. Smith to The Friends of "Law and Order," July 1, 1856, Blood Collection, KSHS.

68. Jonas Colburn to Peggy Colburn, July 7, 1856, Jonas Colburn letters, KSHS.

69. Thomas H. Webb to William Barnes, August 2, 1856, William Barnes Collection, KSHS.

70. C. Robinson to Allen, Blood, W. Hutchison and Others, August 16, 1856, Wil-

liam Hutchison Papers, KSHS. Hutchison was a correspondent for the *New York Times*.

71. Thomas C. Wells to G.H. Wells, June 21, 1856, Thomas C. Wells, "Letters of a Kansas Pioneer," *KHQ* 5, n. 2 (May 1936): 170. See also Thomas H. Webb to William Barnes, June 27, 1856, William Barnes Collection, KSHS.

72. Dale E. Watts, "How Bloody Was Bleeding Kansas? Political Killings in Kansas Territory, 1854-1861," *KH* 18, n. 2 (Summer 1995): 117.

73. See Johnson, *Battle Cry of Freedom*, 202. Gihon describes these terms as "humiliating" and "degrading" for Shannon. See Gihon, *Geary and Kansas*, 96.

74. Shannon to Pierce, August 18, 1856, *Transactions*, 4:403.

75. Socolofsky, *Kansas Governors*, 40-41; Woodson, "Proclamation," August 25, 1856, *Transactions*, 4:471. Woodson had one of the longest tenures of territorial officials, serving from September 28, 1854, until July 7, 1857.

76. Woodson to Cooke, September 1, 1856, and Cooke to Woodson, September 2, 1856, *Transactions*, 4:479-80.

77. Acting Governor Daniel Woodson to William Hutchinson and H. Miles Moore, "On Behalf of the Kansas State Central Committee," September 3, 1856, William I.R. Blackman Collection, KSHS.

78. Alabama Democratic and Anti-Know-Nothing State Convention, *Official Proceedings of the Democratic and Anti-Know-Nothing State Convention of Alabama* (Montgomery, AL: Advertiser and Gazette Book and Job Office, 1856), 10.

79. Smith to Cooper, August 29, 1856, *Transactions*, 4:468-70.

80. Smith to Cooper, September 10, 1856, ibid., 4:471.

81. See Gilman M. Ostrander, "Emerson, Thoreau, and John Brown," *MVHR* 39, n. 4 (March 1953): 713-26.

82. *Kansas Chief* (White Cloud), February 11, 1858, quoted in Watts, "How Bloody Was Bleeding Kansas?," 123.

83. Ibid., 123-25. California's population was much larger than Kansas's in the 1850s. Although determining which deaths are political is difficult, Watts calculated that of the 157 violent deaths in the territory, 56 were political. Of these, 30 were proslavery, 24 antislavery, 1 neutral United States soldier, and 1 claimed by both sides. Of the remaining 101 deaths, 52 stemmed from personal conflicts; 17 derived from land disputes; 11 were lynched; 5 died during robberies; and 16 could not be determined.

84. Johnson, *Battle Cry of Freedom*, 181.

85. Anna Ella Carroll, *Review of Pierce's Administration; Showing its only Popular Measures to Have Originated with the Executive of Millard Fillmore* (Boston: James French & Company; New York: Miller, Orton & Mulligan, 1856), 106.

86. "The Dispute with America," July 1856, 116.

87. Anson Burlingame, *Defence of Massachusetts: Speech of Hon. Anson Burlingame, of Massachusetts in the United States House of Representatives, June 21, 1856* (Boston: John P. Jewett and Company, 1856), 17.

88. Antislavery congressmen wanted to prevent Pierce from using the Army to enforce laws they considered illegitimate. After a lengthy fight, the Army appropriations bill passed in late August. Afterwards Preston Brooks told the *Carolina Times* that he wished it had failed for "then the army would have been withdrawn from Kansas, and *leave the people of the South free to go there and cut the throats of* Lane and his abolition companions." Quoted in *The Reign of Terror in Kanzas* (Boston: Charles W. Briggs, 1856), 12.

89. Quoted in Gihon, *Geary and Kansas*, 130.

90. Socolofsky, *Kansas Governors*, 49; Nichols, *Franklin Pierce*, 401–2, 408–9; John White Geary, "John White Geary: Biography and Papers," KSHS.
91. Geary to Marcy, September 9, 1856, *Transactions*, 4:522.
92. Ibid.
93. Geary, Inaugural Address, "John White Geary: Executive Minutes Diary of Kansas Territory," KSHS; Frank W. Blackmar, *Kansas: A Cyclopedia of State History*, 2 volumes (Chicago: 1912), 1:720, in Socolofsky, *Kansas Governors*, 50.
94. Geary, Inaugural Address, September 11, 1856, "Executive Minutes Diary," 4, 5, 7.
95. Marcy to Geary, September 9, "Executive Minutes Diary," 25. Given Smith's August 22 report, Davis authorized more troops, directing him to ask the governors of Illinois and Kentucky for troops if needed to suppress insurrections. See Davis to Smith, September 3, 1856, *Transactions*, 4:426–27.
96. Geary to the Council and the House of Representatives, January 12, 1857, "Messages of the Governors of Kansas, 1857–1877," 16, KSHS.
97. Geary, Proclamation 1 and Proclamation 2, September 11, 1856, in "Executive Minutes Diary," 8–9.
98. Geary to Donelson, September 27, 1856, quoted in Gihon, *Geary and Kansas*, 185.
99. Marcy to Geary, September 23, 1856, "Executive Minutes Diary," 121.
100. George W. Brown to John White Geary, September 1, 1856, John White Geary Papers, Beinecke Library.
101. Geary to Marcy, September 22, 1856, *Transactions*, 4:553.
102. For instance, Whitfield won 4,252 votes in an October election for delegate after the House vacated the position in July 1856. In December the free-state faction again protested his election but success was more elusive. Democrats defeated efforts to eject Whitfield because the chamber's mood had changed by then, reflecting the territory's overall calm.
103. Geary to Marcy, November 7, 1856, "Executive Minutes Diary," 198.
104. Geary to Marcy, November 22, 1856, ibid., 239.
105. Geary to Price, September 20, 1856, ibid., 45.
106. Ibid., 46.
107. Geary, "Executive Minutes Diary," 106–9; Gihon, *Geary and Kansas*, 194.
108. Geary to Murphy, October 1, 1856, "Executive Minutes Diary," 105.
109. Murphy to Geary, October 3, 1856, "Executive Minutes Diary," 124.
110. Ibid., 124, 127.
111. Geary to General Persifor Smith, September 23, 1856, ibid., 66. Also see Geary to Smith, October 4, 1856, *Transactions*, 4:507.
112. Geary to Pate, September 26, 1856, "Executive Minutes Diary," 84.
113. Geary to Marcy, September 30, 1856, *Transactions*, 4:572; Thomas Wentworth Higginson, a *New York Tribune* correspondent, quoted in Bernard A. Weisberger, "The Newspaper Reporter and the Kansas Imbroglio," *MVHR* 36, n. 4 (March 1950): 639.
114. Smith to Samuel Cooper, November 11, 1856, *Transactions*, 4:517–18.
115. Geary to Marcy, October 15, 1856, "Executive Minutes Diary," 171.
116. Louise Barry, "The Emigrant Aid Company Parties of 1855," *KHQ* 12, n. 2 (August 1943): 227.
117. Note by Territorial Secretary, October 1, 1856, "Executive Minutes Diary," 110–11.

118. William Preston to Geary, October 12, 1856, ibid., 140–41.
119. Deputy U.S. Marshal William T. Preston, Note of Arms Taken, October 12, 1856, ibid., 142.
120. Geary to Cato and Lecompte, September 23, 1856, ibid., 67. Reeder described Lecompte as "a man of frivolous mind, little ability, less integrity, great perversity and indolence, and limited knowledge of the law, [and had] neither property, practice, nor reputation at home." His description was typical of how the antislavery faction viewed Lecompte. See *Transactions*, 3:203.
121. Geary to Cato and Lecompte, September 23, 1856, "Executive Minutes Diary," 67.
122. Lecompte to Geary, October 6, 1856, ibid., 147, 155.
123. Geary to Marcy, November 22, 1856, ibid., 243. His increasing frustration was due to David Buffum's case. Buffum was found assaulted on the road, and Geary accompanied Cato to take his affidavit before he died. After Charles Hay was arrested for murder, Lecompte released him on bail, and then Geary issued a warrant to rearrest Hays. See Geary to Buchanan, February 20, 1857, *State Department Territorial Papers, Kansas, 1854–1861, Roll 1: Official Correspondence, May 30, 1854–April 30, 1861* (Washington: National Archives and Record Service, 1953), Microfilm Publications, Microcopy No. 218, 7.
124. Colburn to Peggy Colburn, November 13, 1856, Jonas Colburn Letters, KSHS.
125. Pierce to Geary, December 12, 1856, Gilder Lehrman Collection.
126. A. Hoole to Elizabeth Euphrasia Hoole, January 4, 1857, in William Stanley Hoole, ed., "A Southerner's Viewpoint of the Kansas Situation," *KHQ* 3, n. 2 (May 1934): 154.
127. John Everett to Robert Everett Sr., January 28, 1857, John and Sarah Everett, "Letters of John and Sarah Everett," 162.
128. Socolofsky, *Kansas Governors*, 51.
129. See Nichols, *Bleeding Kansas*, 175.
130. Geary to Pierce, December 22, 1856, Franklin Pierce Papers, Library of Congress, 1959, document no. 847–849, 1.
131. Ibid., 2–3.
132. Ibid., 3.
133. Ibid., 1.
134. Ibid.
135. William Cumback, *Politics of the Country: Speech of Hon. Will. Cumback of Indiana, in the House of Representatives, December 17, 1856* (Washington: Buell & Blanchard, Printers, 1857), 3.
136. See Gihon, *Geary and Kansas*, 175.
137. Robert Toombs to Thomas W. Thomas, February 5, 1857, Ulrich B. Phillips, ed., *Annual Report of the American Historical Association for the Year 1911, vol. II: The Correspondence of Robert Toombs, Alexander H. Stephens, and Howell Cobb* (Washington: 1913), 394.
138. Geary to Edward Geary, February 25, 1857, "JWG: Biography and Letters."
139. William Bigler to John White Geary, November 14, 1856, John White Geary Papers, Beinecke Library.
140. John Geary to the Council and the House of Representatives, January 12, 1857, "Messages of the Governors of Kansas, 1857–1877," 15–22. The legislature repealed the test oath but refused to amend the slave or voting laws.
141. Geary to Pierce, January, 12, 1857, in "Documents: Some Papers of Franklin Pierce, 1852–1862, II," *AHR* 10, n. 2 (January 1905): 353–54.

142. Geary to Edward Geary, January 21, 1857, "JWG: Biography and Letters."
143. Gihon, *Geary and Kansas*, 216.
144. Ibid., 254, 257. This was a popular ruse: according to Robinson, he agreed to push for admission under the Topeka Constitution in exchange for the governorship of the new state, but it is not verifiable from any other source. See Nichols, *Bleeding Kansas*, 175; Robinson, *Kansas Conflict*, 339.
145. Gihon, *Geary and Kansas*, 266-68.
146. Quoted in Wilder, *Annals in Kansas*, 155. Also see Robert W. Johannsen, "The Lecompton Constitutional Convention," *KHQ* 23, n. 3 (Autumn 1957): 226-27. Johannsen dismisses the first two rationales, arguing that smaller territories had done so (although population requirements for a representative were also smaller) and that they had already asked Congress for admission.
147. Johannsen, "The Lecompton Constitutional Convention," 226.
148. Buchanan, "Speech at Wheatland," November 6, 1856, John Bassett Moore, *The Works of James Buchanan, Comprising his Speeches, State Papers, and Private Correspondence* (Philadelphia & London: J.B. Lippincott Company, 1910), 10:97.
149. Geary to Buchanan, February 20, 1857, State Department Territorial Papers, 3-4.
150. Ibid., 5-7, 27-28.
151. Socolofsky, *Kansas Governors*, 52.
152. For health concerns (lung hemorrhages), see Geary to Woodson, March 10, 1857, *Transactions*, 4:742. Geary's financial situation was also precarious. See John White Geary Papers, Beinecke Library.
153. "Geary's Farewell Address," reprinted by the *St. Louis Republican*, March 17, 1857, "Executive Minutes Diary," 2:3.
154. Geary, "Executive Minutes Diary," 2:63.
155. Leonard Woolsey Bacon, "Buchanan on Kansas," *NE* 15, n. 4 (November 1857): 677.
156. Transactions, 4:282.
157. *Ex. Doc. No. 97*, 2.
158. Wells, "Jefferson Davis and Kansas Territory," 357.
159. Ibid., 356.
160. Nichols, *Bleeding Kansas*, 139.
161. Persifor Smith to John White Geary, September 28, 1856, John White Geary Papers, Beinecke Library.
162. Geary to Marcy, October 10, 1856, "Executive Minutes Diary," 134.
163. Geary to Edward Geary, February 25, 1857, "JWG: Biography and Letters."
164. Marcy to Geary, September 27, 1856, *Transactions*, 4:573.
165. For instance, Malin denounced Geary as a dictator. See Malin, *John Brown*, 175, 642.

4

1. Earl S. Pomeroy, *The Territories and the United States: 1861-1890* (Philadelphia: University of Pennsylvania Press, 1947), 4.
2. Clarence Carter, "Colonialism in Continental United States," *SAQ* 47 (1948): 26.
3. U.S. Senate, *Report of the Committee on Territories, to Whom was Referred so Much of the Annual Message of the President of the United States as Relates to Territorial Affairs*,

Together with his Special Message on the 24th Day of January, 1856, in Regard to Kansas Territory, and his Message of the 18th of February, in Compliance with the Resolution of the Senate of the 4th of February, 1856, Requesting Transcripts of Certain Papers Relative to the Affairs of the Territory Kansas (Washington: 1856), 7.

4. Charles Sumner, *The Slave Oligarchy and its Usurpations: Speech of Hon. Charles Sumner, November 2, 1855, in Faneuil Hall, Boston* (Washington: Buell & Blanchard, Printers, 1855), 8.

5. Hall to Sumner, January 27, 1856, Misc. Edward Lillis Pierce Manuscripts, KSHS.

6. William H. Seward, "The Contest and the Crisis," *Speeches of William H. Seward, Delivered at Albany and at Buffalo, in October, 1855* (Washington: The Republican Association, 1855), 13.

7. Roy Franklin Nichols, *Franklin Pierce: Young Hickory of the Granite Hill* (Philadelphia: University of Pennsylvania Press, 1931), 426-29, 441-43. The *Congressional Globe* omitted affiliations, but Temple R. Hollcroft suggests the new House included 79 administration Democrats, 117 Anti-Nebraska Congressman widely dispersed among opposition parties (with newly elected Republicans forming the core of the group), and 37 Whigs. See Temple R. Hollcroft, ed., "A Congressman's Letters on the Speaker Election in the Thirty-Fourth Congress," *MVHR* 43, n. 3 (December 1956): 444-45. Democrats made the Kansas-Nebraska Act a central issue by selecting William A. Richardson, who steered the bill through the House, as their candidate for speaker. Given the strong anti-Nebraska membership in the House, this was a poor choice. See William Gienapp, *The Origins of the Republican Party, 1852-1856* (New York: Oxford University Press, 1987), 240-48.

8. Theodore Parker to Nathaniel P. Banks, February 10, 1856, Gilder Lehrman Collection.

9. U.S. Senate, 34th Cong., 1st Sess., *Ex. Doc. No. 4: Message of the President of the United States, Relative to Disturbances in the Territory of Kansas*, January 24, 1856 (Washington: 1856), 2-3.

10. Ibid., 4-8.

11. Jo Tice Bloom, "Early Delegates in the House of Representatives," in John Porter Bloom, ed., *The American Territorial System* (Athens: Ohio University Press, 1973), 65-69.

12. *Congr. Globe*, 353. Unless otherwise indicated, all citations of the *Congr. Globe* are from the 34th Congr., 1st Sess.

13. The committee included six members from free states: Israel Washburn (ME), Francis E. Spinner (NY), John Hickman (PA), Schuyler Colfax (IN), Cooper K. Watson (OH), and John A. Bingham (OH), as well as three members from slave-holding states: Alexander H. Stephens (GA), Mordecai Oliver (MO), and William R. Smith (AL). As the Speaker appoints committees and both Washburn and Colfax had been key managers in his election, Banks had arranged the committee to exploit the Kansas issue.

14. U.S. House of Representatives, *Memorial of the Senators and Representatives [of the State of Kansas], and the Constitution of the State of Kansas; also, the Majority and Minority Reports of the Committee on Territories on the Said Constitution* (Washington: Cornellius Wendell, 1856), 4-5.

15. *Congr. Globe*, 455. Reeder recognized the legislature before its relocation to Pawnee.

16. *Congr. Globe*, 451-53. Also see Stephens, *Congr. Globe*, Appx., 182.

17. Campbell, *Congr. Globe*, 458; Davis, *Congr. Globe*, Appx., 230; Lake, *Congr. Globe*, Appx., 217.

18. *Congr. Globe*, Appx., 120-21.

266   Notes to Pages 104-7

19. *Congr. Globe*, 451-52. William R. Smith argued that territorial legislatures were creatures of convenience or informality and related the story of Alabama's first territorial legislature whose Senate included only one man. Although a senate implies more than one person, Alabama's laws had never been rendered invalid. See *Congr. Globe*, Appx., 157.

20. *Congr. Globe*, 458.

21. Percy Walker (AL), *Congr. Globe*, 613. See Martin Crawford (GA), John Wright (TN), and W. Smith (AL), *Congr. Globe*, Appx., 136, 142, 157. George A. Simmons (NY) also argued that since Reeder was not a contestant, the House ought to just vacate the seat if necessary. See *Congr. Globe*, Appx., 189.

22. *Congr. Globe*, Appx., 228.

23. Crawford, ibid., 136; William W. Valk (NY), ibid., 174; A. Stephens, ibid., 180.

24. Ibid., 280.

25. Ibid., 155. As further evidence, Harris noted that the *New York Times* had written "Delegate from Kansas: A.H. Reeder, *disputed by John W. Whitfield*" when it listed newly elected members and delegates. Thus, abolitionists intended to "mislead the judgments and corrupt the minds of the people upon this question, and to prepare them for the ready reception as truth of whatever may be said by the friends of Reeder in the contest going on here" (156).

26. Ibid., 181-82. Also see Boyce, ibid., 121; Wright, ibid., 144; Oliver, ibid., 169; Miles Taylor (CA), ibid., 186; William H. English (IN), ibid., 289-90.

27. Ibid., 142-43. Reeder was naturally seen as self-interested: "Removed from his office, chagrined, mortified, and vexed, he moodily determines on revenge; but not the revenge of the noble-minded and generous heart; rather call it the studied effort of a deep design, born and nurtured in the dark corners of the mind, and here exposed to the full light of open day." See Valk, ibid., 175.

28. Wright, March 11, 1856, ibid., 137.

29. *Congr. Globe*, 674-75; Harris (IL), *Congr. Globe*, Appx., 156; George Dunn (IN), *Congr. Globe*, Appx., 206.

30. *Congr. Globe*, Appx., 166.

31. Ibid., 118.

32. Ibid., 160-61.

33. *Congr. Globe*, 674-75.

34. *Congr. Globe*, Appx., 228. In the Senate, John Crittenden (KY) echoed these sentiments: "it is our duty, and our only business, to remedy the existing evil, leaving to the proper tribunals whatever criminal jurisdiction it may be proper for them to exercise over individuals who have committed crimes." See *Congr. Globe*, 1381.

35. *Congr. Globe*, Appx., 193; John C. Kunkel (PA) and D.F. Robinson (PA), 153, 199; James H. Campbell (PA), 164.

36. Ibid., 210.

37. John A. Bingham, *Kansas Contested Election: Speech of Hon. J.A. Bingham, of Ohio, in the House of Representatives, March 6, 1856, on the Resolution Reported from the Committee of Elections, in the Contested Election Case from the Territory of Kansas* (Washington: Buell & Blanchard, Printers, 1856), 3-4.

38. *Congr. Globe*, 1009.

39. W. Damrell, *Kansas Contested Election: Speech of Hon. W.S. Damrell, of Massachusetts, in the House of Representatives, March 18, 1856, on the Resolution Reported from the Committee of Elections, in the Contested Election Case from the Territory of Kansas* (Washington: Buell & Blanchard, Printers, 1856), 1.

40. *Congr. Globe*, Appx., 213.

41. Ibid., 129. The importance of "truth" was a common theme: see Samuel Purviance and J.H. Campbell of Pennsylvania, ibid., 163–64.

42. Ibid., 207. This debate occurred as Congress was considering admitting Kansas under the Topeka Constitution on March 4, 1856 (discussed below). See Robert W. Johannsen, ed., "A Footnote to the Pottawatomie Massacre, 1856" *KHQ* 22, n. 3 (Autumn 1956): 236–41.

43. John Everett to Robert Everett Sr., June 27, 1856, John and Sarah Everett, "Letters of John and Sarah Everett," *KHQ* 8, n. 9 (February 1939): 34.

44. O.N. Merrill, *True History of the Kansas Wars, and their Origin, Progress, and Incidents* (Cincinnati: J.R. Telfer, 1856), 40.

45. House of Representatives, 34th Cong., 1st Sess., *Report 200: Report of the Special Committee Appointed to Investigate the Troubles in Kansas; with the Views of the Minority of Said Committee* (Washington: Cornellius Wendell, Printer, 1856), 1–3, 8–9, 21, 35. Illegal voting benefiting the free-state side occurred as well, as ineligible Fort Riley soldiers and employees also voted. See Russell K. Hickman, "The Reeder Administration Inaugurated, Part I–The Delegate Election of November, 1854," *KHQ* 36, n. 3 (August 1970): 327–28.

46. *House Report 200*, 45, 46, 57. A pamphlet entitled *Subduing Freedom in Kansas. Report of the Congressional Committee, Presented in the House of Representatives on Tuesday, July 1, 1856*, printed by the *New York Tribune*, transcribes this line as "[t]hese elections whether they were conducted in pursuance of law or not, were not illegal" (23).

47. *House Report 200*, 36–44.

48. Ibid., 67.

49. Ibid., 68. Oliver also accused Sherman and Howard of violating House rules that forbade committee members from working separately. He complained that they had deposed witnesses in Lexington, St. Louis, and New York without his knowledge and prepared the majority report without his input, only informing him of its salient points when he arrived in Washington. See *Congr. Globe*, 1528.

50. *House Report 200*, 73, 104.

51. Ibid., 72–75, 81.

52. Ibid., 81–83.

53. Ibid., 72, 90.

54. Ibid., 109. A biography of Reeder prepared by his children contends that he received 2,849 votes to Whitfield's 2,721. Of course, genuine comparisons are difficult given that they were cast at different elections. See *Transactions of the Kansas State Historical Society* (Topeka: Kansas State Publishing House, 1886), 3:202.

55. *Congr. Globe*, 1857. As Washburn noted in reading the committee's report into the record, fair elections could not be held in Kansas without vast changes including a new census, impartial judges, and federal troops. In fact, Whitfield was returned to Congress the following winter, and the free-state party again tried to force his ouster. However, this time, success eluded them.

56. *Congr. Globe*, 1863, 1868.

57. Ibid., 1868, 1872.

58. Homer E. Socolofsky, *Kansas Governors* (Lawrence: University of Kansas Press, 1990), 45; *Congr. Globe*, 1873.

59. See Appendix F (page 239).

60. These included two members from Pennsylvania, Jacob Broom and Henry Fuller, and one from New York, Thomas Whitney.

61. All 21 members were Northerners. The members who switched positions came from 6 states: 7 were from New York (Francis Edwards, Solomon Haven, Rufus King, George Simmons, William Valk, Thomas Whitney, and John Williams); 5 from Pennsylvania (Jacob Broom, Henry Fuller, John Hickman, David Ritchie, and Job Tyson); 5 from Ohio (Edward Ball, Lewis D. Campbell, John Harrison, Valentine Horton, and Oscar Moore); 2 from Indiana (George Dunn and Harvey Scott); 1 from Wisconsin (Daniel Wells); and 1 from New Jersey (Alexander Pennington).

62. A core group of members continued to be sympathetic, and Reeder was granted a per diem and mileage from the House Contingent Fund on August 11, 1856 (103 to 82 votes against). *Congr. Globe*, 1984.

63. "The Political Aspect," *PM* 8 (July 1856): 90–93. The article referred to Federalist No. 40.

64. Grow, Majority Report, *Memorial ... and the Constitution of the State of Kansas*, 40.

65. Stephen Douglas, *Report of the Committee on Territories*, 5–6.

66. Ibid., 7.

67. *Congr. Globe*, 178.

68. W.Y. Roberts, in *Memorial ... and Constitution of the State of Kansas*, 5–7, 9.

69. Grow, Majority Report, ibid., 47, 40, 42–43.

70. Zollicoffer, Minority Report, *Memorial ... and Constitution of the State of Kansas*, 51.

71. Ibid., 52.

72. Roberts, *Memorial ... and Constitution of the State of Kansas*, 9.

73. Zollicoffer, Minority Report, 53.

74. *Congr. Globe*, 1541.

75. Ibid., 553.

76. Hale, *Congr. Globe*, 1519; Wilson, *Congr. Globe*, Appx., 773; Wade, *Congr. Globe*, Appx., 756. Bell argues that admission would not help since discord would continue throughout the presidential election (*Congr. Globe*, Appx., 781–82).

77. *Congr. Globe*, Appx., 789–90.

78. Ibid., 794.

79. Ibid., 792.

80. *Congr. Globe*, 1304, 1369–1375.

81. *Congr. Globe*, 1375.

82. Ibid., 1439.

83. Little could Douglas foresee that debate would extend into a special August session (see *Congr. Globe*, 1506). For more on the Toombs Bill, see Nichols, *Franklin Pierce*, 475.

84. *Congr. Globe*, Appx., 730.

85. Ibid., 795, 804.

86. *Congr. Globe*, 1539.

87. Joseph C. Lovejoy, *The True Democracy: A Speech delivered at East Cambridge, September 29, 1856* (Cambridge, MA, 1856), 8–9.

88. Zollicoffer, Minority Report, *Memorial ... and Constitution of the State of Kansas*, 54.

89. Paul Wallace Gates, *Fifty Million Acres: Conflicts over Kansas Land Policy, 1854–1890* (Ithaca, NY: Cornell University Press, 1954), 20.

90. Nichols, *Franklin Pierce*, 474–75.

91. *Congr. Globe*, 1381–82.

92. *Congr. Globe*, 1388.

93. *Congr. Globe*, 1395.
94. Ibid., 1388. Also see Stephen Mallory (FL), ibid., 1389.
95. Anna Ella Carroll, *The Union of the States* (Boston: James French & Company; New York: Miller, Orton, & Mulligan, 1856), 53–54.
96. Nichols, *Franklin Pierce*, 475.
97. Johnson, *Battle Cry of Freedom*, 188. While Sumner's subsequent removal dampened criticism, it predated the uproar, as Persifor Smith was sent to the territory in June (189).
98. Davis to the Adjutant General, June 21, 1856, Senate, 34th Cong., 1856, 1st Sess., *Ex. Doc. No. 97, Message of the President of the United States communicating a Report, in compliance with a resolution of the Senate of the 21st ultimo, calling for information relative to the instructions sent to military officers in Kansas*, 5–6.
99. Davis to Pierce, July 30, 1856, *Ex. Doc. No. 97*, 1.
100. Nichols, *Franklin Pierce*, 479.
101. Schulyer Colfax, *The "Laws" of Kansas: Speech of Schuyler Colfax, of Indiana, in the House of Representatives, June 21, 1856* (Washington: Buell & Blanchard, Printers, 1856), 1. See also Lucian Barbour (IN), *Congr. Globe*, 1751–52.
102. *Congr. Globe*, 1754.
103. Ibid., 1790.
104. Ibid., 1752.
105. Lewis D. Campbell, *Supremacy of the Constitution and Laws: Speech of Hon. Lewis D. Campbell, of Ohio, in the House of Representatives, in Reply to his Colleague, Mr. J.R. Giddings, the Senate's Amendments to the Deficiency Bill being under Consideration* (Washington: Buell & Blanchard, 1856), 6. Campbell was unmoved by arguments that the territorial laws were "unconstitutional or inexpedient," stating that it was not within his purview to deny funds to the president to prevent him from executing laws (5). See also John Phelps (MO), *Congr. Globe*, 1752.
106. *Congr. Globe*, 1756. Stephens agreed that Congress lacked the power to control the executive in this manner but preferred that the troops be recalled nonetheless (1753–54).
107. Smith, ibid., 1792.
108. Persifor Smith to Cooper, September 10, 1856, *Transactions*, 4:473.
109. Pierce, Proclamation, August 18, 1856, *Congr. Globe*, 1.
110. Pierce, Message to Fellow-citizens of the Senate and House of Representatives, August 21, 1856, *Congr. Globe*, 34th Cong., 2nd Sess., 5. The British were also a potential problem as they considered the American navy "feeble" and believed they would quickly win any war with the United States; the embarrassing failure to pass the Army bill just underscored the country's feebleness. See James Buchanan to Marcy, January 18, 1856, in John Bassett Moore, *The Works of James Buchanan, Comprising his Speeches, State Papers, and Private Correspondence* (Philadelphia & London: J.B. Lippincott Company, 1910), 10:10. Also see, Buchanan to Marcy, February 5, 1856, 10:34.
111. *Congr. Globe*, 34th Cong., 2nd Sess., 8, 6, 51.
112. Ibid., 65–66, 69.
113. Nichols, *Franklin Pierce*, 480. Pierce's weaknesses were further demonstrated when Congress passed five internal improvement bills over his veto that summer.
114. *Congr. Globe*, 34th Cong., 2nd Sess., 83.
115. Michael W. Cluskey, *Buchanan and Breckinridge. The Democratic Hand-Book, Compiled by Mich. W. Cluskey, of Washington City, D.C. Recommended by the Democratic*

National Committee. The Success of the Democracy essential for the preservation of the Union and the protection of the integrity of the Constitution (Washington: R.A. Waters, 1856), 19. Democratic presidential nominee James Buchanan disapproved of Republican tactics in Congress: "I should have been sorely tempted, had I been the President, to let the Black Republicans bear the consequences of their own outrageous conduct in refusing to pass the Army Bill without the proviso. This would beyond question have decided the fate of the Presidential election in our favor, and thus have prevented the danger to the constitution and the Union which would exist should Fremont be elected." Buchanan to Marcy, August 27, 1856, in *Works of James Buchanan*, 10:90.

116. *Congr. Globe*, Appx., 137. The tremendous sympathy for the free-state party was negated somewhat by news of the Pottawatomie Massacre that same month. See Johnson, *The Battle Cry of Freedom*, 185.

117. "The Political Crisis in the United States," *ERCJ*, American edition, 45, n. 2 (October 1856): 298. As historian William Gienapp explains, the caning motivated Northerners because "the deliberate attack on a senator for words spoken in debate seemed an attack on the Constitution, and as such it was much more ominous and threatening than events in a distant, sparsely settled territory." See Gienapp, *Origins*, 299–303.

118. J. Watson Webb, "Slavery and its Tendencies: A Letter from General J. Watson Webb to the New York *Courier* and *Enquirer*," May 24, 1856, in J. Watson Webb, *Speech of General J. Watson Webb, at the Great Mass Meeting on the Battle Ground of Tippecanoe, 60,000 Freemen in Council* (New York: 1856), 84.

119. Cluskey, *Buchanan and Breckinridge*, 21. See also Lovejoy, *The True Democracy*, 8.

120. William H. Seward, "The Contest and the Crisis," in *Speeches of William H. Seward, Delivered at Albany and at Buffalo, in October, 1855* (Washington: The Republican Association, 1855), 14.

5

1. William H. Seward, "Dangers of Extending Slavery," in *Speeches of William H. Seward, Delivered at Albany and at Buffalo, in October, 1855* (Washington: The Republican Association, 1855), 1.

2. Ibid., 7.

3. Seward, "The Contest and the Crisis," ibid., 13.

4. Bill Cecil-Fronsman, "'Advocate the Freedom of White Men, As Well As That of Negroes': The *Kansas Free State* and Antislavery Westerners in Territorial Kansas," *KH* 20, n. 2 (Summer 1997): 108–9.

5. Letter to the Editor, *Chicago Democratic Press*, August 18, 1855, William M. Snow Scrap-book, 39, KSHS.

6. Charles Sumner, *The Slave Oligarchy and its Usurpations: Speech of Hon. Charles Sumner, November 2, 1855, in Faneuil Hall, Boston* (Washington: Buell & Blanchard, Printers, 1855), 8–9.

7. Calhoun to Stephen Douglas, November 27, 1855, in Donald Eugene Day, "A Life of Wilson Shannon, Governor of Ohio, Diplomat, Territorial Governor of Kansas" (Ph.D. diss., Ohio State University, 1978), 215.

8. Atchison, quoted in the *Daily Missouri Democrat*, December 25, 1855, ibid., 229.

9. Roy Franklin Nichols, *Franklin Pierce: Young Hickory of the Granite Hill* (Philadelphia: University of Pennsylvania Press, 1931), 426.

10. *Charleston Mercury*, December 8, 1855.
11. Sumner to Theodore Parker, January 20, 1856, in Beverly Wilson Palmer, ed., *The Selected Letters of Charles Sumner* (Boston: Northeastern University Press, 1990), 441.
12. Charles Sumner to Samuel Gridley Howe, December 28, 1855, ibid., 438.
13. Franklin Pierce, Proclamation, February 11, 1856, *Transactions of the Kansas State Historical Society* (Topeka: Kansas Publishing House, 1896), 5:259.
14. Reeder, January 25, 1856, reprinted in *Herald of Freedom*, February 16, 1856, ibid., 5:257–58.
15. Joseph C. Lovejoy, *The True Democracy: A Speech delivered at East Cambridge, September 29, 1856* (Cambridge?: 1856), 8.
16. Ibid., 11.
17. James A. Pearce, public letter, July 31, 1856, in James Raymond, *Political: or, The Spirit of Democracy in '56* (Baltimore: John W. Woods, Printer, 1857), 42–43.
18. Michael W. Cluskey, *Buchanan and Breckinridge. The Democratic Hand-Book* (Washington: R.A. Waters, 1856), 19.
19. Lovejoy, *The True Democracy*, 8.
20. Raymond, *The Spirit of Democracy in '56*, 67.
21. Lovejoy, *The True Democracy*, 8–9.
22. "The War Against the South," *DBR* 21 (1856): 272.
23. Nicholas Hill, in New York State Democratic Party, *Proceedings and Address, of the Democratic State Convention, held at Syracuse, January Tenth and Eleventh, 1856* (Albany: 1856), 21, 17, 20.
24. *Proceedings of the Pennsylvania Democratic Convention, Held at Harrisburg, March 4th, 1856. Reported by James B. Sheridan.* (Philadelphia: Wm. Rice, Pennsylvanian Office, Printer, 1856), 21, 33.
25. Thomas to Alexander H. Stephens, February 25, 1856, Ulrich B. Phillips, ed., *Annual Report of the American Historical Association for the Year 1911, vol. II: The Correspondence of Robert Toombs, Alexander H. Stephens, and Howell Cobb* (Washington: 1913), 362.
26. Hamlin to A.M. Robinson, January 10, 1856, in Charles Eugene Hamlin, *The Life and Times of Hannibal Hamlin* (Cambridge: Riverside Press, 1899), 283.
27. Stephens to Thomas W. Thomas, June 16, 1856, in Phillips, *Correspondence*, 367. For Pierce's patronage decisions, see Nichols, *Franklin Pierce,* and Nichols, *The Democratic Machine, 1850–1854* (New York: Columbia University Press, 1923).
28. Thomas Drew, compiler, *The Campaign of 1856: Frémont Songs. For the People, Original and Selected* (Boston: John P. Jewett and Company; Cleveland, OH: Jewett, Proctor, and Worthington; New York: Sheldon, Blackeman and Company, 1856), 36–37. The Gilder Lehrman Collection.
29. John M. Read, *Speech of Hon. John M. Read, on the Power of Congress over the Territories, in Favor of Free Kansas, Free Labor, and of Frémont and Dayton, at the Eighth Ward Mass Meeting, Held in the Assembly Buildings, on Tuesday Evening, September 30, 1856* (Philadelphia: C. Sherman & Son, 1856), 43.
30. *Cincinnati Commercial*, June 8, 1856, William B. Hesseltine and Rex G. Fisher, eds., *Trimmers, Trucklers & Temporizers: Notes of Murat Halstead from the Political Conventions of 1856* (Madison: The State Historical Society of Wisconsin, 1961), 63.
31. Hon. William Montgomery, in *Pennsylvania Democratic Convention*, 51, and Hon. William H. Welsh, in ibid., 67.
32. Buchanan, "Memoir of James Buchanan, of Pennsylvania," ibid., 72, 77.

33. *Cincinnati Commercial*, May 29, 1856, in Hesseltine and Fisher, *Trimmers, Trucklers & Temporizers*, 24.

34. Howell Cobb to James Buchanan, December 5, 1854, in Phillips, *Correspondence*, 348–49.

35. *Justice to "Buck": Papers Containing Several Reasons why James Buchanan Should Receive the Distinguished Consideration of the People, by One Who Knows Him Well* (Philadelphia: Alex C. Bryson, 1856), 4.

36. Buchanan to John Ward et al., June 16, 1856, National Democratic Convention, *Official Proceedings of the National Democratic Convention, Held in Cincinnati, June 2–6, 1856. Published by Order of the Convention* (Cincinnati: Enquirer Company Steam Printing Establishment, 1856), 77.

37. Donald Bruce Johnson, ed., *National Party Platforms, Volume I: 1840–1956*, rev. ed. (Urbana: University of Illinois Press, 1978), 24–27.

38. William C. Davis, *Breckinridge: Statesman, Soldier, Symbol* (Baton Rouge: Louisiana State University Press, 1974), 150–55, 160. This trip was critical because neither Pierce nor his cabinet publicly exerted themselves for Buchanan (although Pierce contributed by removing Shannon and granting his replacement considerable leeway, which allowed for some measure of calm in the territory). See Howell Cobb to James Buchanan, July 14, 1856, and August 3, 1856, in Phillips, *Correspondence*, 374–79.

39. *New York Journal of Commerce*, cited in *Conspiracy Disclosed!! Kansas Affairs* (Washington: Granite State Club of Washington, 1856), 3.

40. W.O. Duvall, letter, in ibid., 2.

41. Ibid., 9, 13–14.

42. Sumner to Theodore Parker, February 25, 1856, Palmer, *Selected Letters*, 446. The *Congressional Globe* did not record the vote, but the *Kansas Weekly Herald* and the *New York Tribune* reported it as 50 to 12. See Day, "A Life of Wilson Shannon," 254.

43. Sumner to Henry J. Raymond, March 2, 1856, Palmer, ed., *Selected Letters*, 449.

44. Hesseltine and Fisher, eds., *Trimmers, Trucklers & Temporizers*, 13.

45. Johnson, *National Party Platforms*, 1:27–28.

46. Sumner to Theodore Parker, March 26, 1856, in Palmer, ed., *Selected Letters*, 454.

47. *New York Tribune*, September 3, 1856.

48. H.G., *New York Tribune*, April 4, 1856, Snow Scrap-book, 58.

49. Frémont to Robinson, March 17, 1856, *New York Tribune*, April 4, 1856, ibid., 58.

50. *New York Tribune*, October 24, 1856.

51. Bryant, "What May Happen in the Next Four Years," October 31, 1856, in William Cullen Bryant II, ed., *Power for Sanity: Selected Editorials of William Cullen Bryant, 1829–1861* (New York: Fordham University Press, 1994), 301.

52. Henry H. Williams, July 31, 1856, and August 2, 1856, Nathan Smith, ed., "Letters of a Free-State Man in Kansas, 1856," *KHQ* 21, n. 3 (Autumn 1954): 168, 170.

53. G.W. Brown to his mother, July 24, 1856, G.W. Brown Collection, KSHS.

54. W. Stiff Robinson Jr., "The Role of the Military in Territorial Kansas," *Territorial Kansas: Studies Commemorating the Centennial* (Lawrence: University of Kansas Publications, Social Science Studies, 1954), 97.

55. *The Reign of Terror in Kanzas* (Boston: Charles W. Briggs, 1856), 12–13.

56. *South Side Democrat*, in Read, *Speech of Hon. John M. Read*, 40–41.

57. Drew, *The Campaign of 1856: Frémont Songs*, 7–8.

58. Ibid., 14.

59. Eugene Batchelder, *A New Fremont Song, Respectfully Dedicated to the Cambridge Fremont Club No. 2, and the Fremont Men of the Country* (n.p., 1856) 1.

60. Bryant, "The Outrage on Mr. Sumner," May 23, 1856, Bryant II, *Power for Sanity*, 289 and 291. Just as Republicans charged Democrats were brutes, Democrats often depicted their opponents as weaklings. Robert Toombs, for instance, wrote that "Sumner takes a beating badly. He is said to be ill, tho' I don't believe it." See Toombs to George W. Crawford, May 30, 1856, in Phillips, *Correspondence*, 365.

61. The *Charleston Mercury* described Sumner's speech as "coarse and malignant" and defended Brooks because it was "time for freedom of speech and freedom of the cudgel to go together." See *Charleston Mercury*, May 28, 1856. Occasionally a Northern newspaper took exception to Sumner's speech as well. The *Boston Courier* editorialized that the portion that offended Brooks was "excessively insulting and provoking, and not only highly indiscreet in sentiment and language, but unjustifiable. . . ." Reprinted in *Charleston Mercury*, May 29, 1856.

62. J. Watson Webb, for instance, was unprepared to defend Sumner's language, but argued his comments were retaliatory. See "Slavery and its Tendencies: A Letter from General J. Watson Webb to the *New York Courier and Enquirer*," May 24, 1856, in J. Watson Webb, *Speech of General J. Watson Webb, at the Great Mass Meeting on the Battle Ground of Tippecanoe, 60,000 Freemen in Council* (New York: 1856), 94. For a Southerner who found Brooks's actions reprehensible and deserving of expulsion, see Gazaway B. Lamar to Howell Cobb, May 31, 1856, in Phillips, *Correspondence*, 366.

63. Hamlin to Fessenden, May 28, 1856, in Hamlin, *The Life and Times*, 284.

64. Preston S. Brooks, *National Politics: Speech of Hon. P.S. Brooks, of South Carolina, on Resigning his Seat in Congress, Delivered in the House of Representatives, July 14, 1856* (Washington, 1856), 2–3.

65. J. Watson Webb, *Speech of General J. Watson Webb*, 37–38, 8.

66. "The War Against the South," *DBR* 21 (1856): 273.

67. Sarah to Cynthia Everett, August 1, 1856, John and Sarah Everett, "Letters of John and Sarah Everett," *KHQ* 8, n. 2 (May 1939): 146.

68. Theodore Parker to Horace Mann, June 27, 1856, in Henry Steele Commager, ed., *Theodore Parker: An Anthology* (Boston: Beacon Press, 1960), 295.

69. C.A. Adams, *Letter from a Kansas Settler, Formerly of Concord, Mass., to his Brother [W. Henry Adams]*, broadside, dated August 24, 1856 (Lawrence, K.T.?: 1856).

70. Jonas Colburn to Peggy Colburn, November 13, 1856, Jonas W. Colburn Letters, KSHS.

71. *Cincinnati Commercial*, February 25, 1856, Hesseltine and Fisher, *Trimmers, Trucklers & Temporizers*, 4.

72. Ibid., ix–x.

73. Johnson, *National Party Platforms*, 1:22–23.

74. Anna Ella Carroll, *Review of Pierce's Administration; Showing its only Popular Measures to Have Originated with the Executive of Millard Fillmore* (Boston: James French & Company; New York: Miller, Orton & Mulligan, 1856), 107–8.

75. Samuel A. Johnson, *The Battle Cry of Freedom: The New England Emigrant Aid Company in the Kansas Crusade* (Westport, CT: Greenwood Press, 1954), 227.

76. *Republican Scrap Book; Containing the Platforms, and a Choice Selection of Extracts, Setting Forth the Real Questions in Issue, the Opinions of the Candidates, the Nature and Design of the Slave Oligarchy, as Shown by Their Own Writers, and the Opinions of Clay,*

Webster, Josiah Quincy, and Other Patriots, on Slavery and Its Extensions (Boston: John P. Jewett & Co., 1856), 3. Vanderbilt Special Collections.

77. Jesse D. Bright to William W. Corcoran, October 12, 1856, William W. Corcoran Papers, Library of Congress.

78. Andrew H. Reeder, *A Letter from Governor Reeder on the Approaching Election of the President and the Candidates* (New York: John W. Oliver, Steam Printer, 1856), 1–2.

79. Walt Whitman, *The Eighteenth Presidency! A Critical Text* edited by Edward F. Grier (Lawrence: University of Kansas Press, 1956), 29. He wrote the book between mid-June and mid-September 1856, although it was not published until March 1926.

80. Ibid., 26, 6–7.

81. Johnson, *National Party Platforms*, 1:22.

82. Bryant, "The Election of Yesterday," November 5, 1856, in *Power for Sanity*, 303.

83. John Everett to Robert Everett Sr., November 20, 1856, "Letters of John and Sarah Everett," 150–51.

84. Bryant, "The Duty of the Republican party," November 7, 1856, *Power for Sanity*, 307.

85. William Cumback, *Politics of the Country: Speech of Hon. Will. Cumback of Indiana, in the House of Representatives, December 17, 1856* (Washington: Buell & Blanchard, Printers, 1857), 3.

86. *Charleston Mercury*, November 7, 1856.

87. On the day following the election, the *New York Evening Post* expressed its satisfaction with the "immense strides towards the ascendancy" of their principles. See *Charleston Mercury*, November 14, 1856.

6

1. James Buchanan to John Ward et al., June 16, 1856, National Democratic Convention, *Official Proceedings of the National Democratic Convention, Held in Cincinnati, June 2–6, 1856* (Cincinnati, OH: Enquirer Company Steam Printing Establishment, 1856), 77.

2. James Buchanan, *Inaugural Address of the President of the United States on the Fourth of March, 1857* (Washington: A.O.P. Nicholson, Printer, 1857), 3–4.

3. James Buchanan, "Speech at Wheatland," November 6, 1856, in John Bassett Moore, ed., *The Works of James Buchanan, Comprising his Speeches, State Papers, and Private Correspondence* (Philadelphia & London: J.B. Lippincott Company, 1910), 10:97–98.

4. Lewis Cass to Robert J. Walker, March 30, 1857, paraphrasing Buchanan's directives, in *Transactions of the Kansas State Historical Society* (Topeka: Kansas Publishing House, 1896), 5:323.

5. James Buchanan, *Mr. Buchanan's Administration on the Eve of the Rebellion* (New York: D. Appleton and Company, 1866), 29.

6. Ibid., 50. The Supreme Court unexpectedly ruled on the constitutionality of Congress's restriction on slavery. Because it would seem too political for a Southern majority to declare the Missouri Compromise unconstitutional, Justice John Catron of Tennessee asked Buchanan to influence Justice Robert Grier of Pennsylvania by dropping him "a line, saying how necessary it is . . . to settle agitation by an affirmative decision of the Supreme Court, the one way or the other." The Court found that Scott was not a citizen and thus could not sue in federal court. In his decision, Chief Justice Roger Taney expounded on territorial aspects not germane to the case. See Kenneth M. Stampp, *America in 1857: A*

Nation on the Brink (New York: Oxford University Press, 1990), 90–93.

7. Buchanan to Jeremiah Black, September 16, 1859, quoted in Philip G. Auchampaugh, "The Buchanan-Douglas Feud," *JISHS* 25 (April 1932–January 1933): 28.

8. Buchanan, *Mr. Buchanan's Administration*, 30.

9. John L. Madden, "The Financing of a New Territory: The Kansas Territorial Tax Structure, 1854–1861," *KHQ* 35, n. 2 (Summer 1969): 157–58. The 1860 census revealed Kansas's population had exploded to 107,206 residents, an average increase of 20,000 settlers per year since 1855. Critics of admission could not have guessed the territory would exceed population requirements for a representative so rapidly.

10. Ibid., 157, 161–62. Territorial expenses are listed according to outlay. The poll tax was unpopular, but realism outweighed idealism as it was retained in the 1858 and 1860 revenue acts precisely because solvency required it. Financial stability would change this reallocation; by 1861, 95 percent of total tax revenue came from property taxes. For the rest of the United States, the per capita income was $149.

11. Homer E. Socolofsky, *Kansas Governors* (Lawrence: University Press of Kansas, 1990), 59. The fate of Kansas's governors was an oft-mined source of humor: when Buchanan requested four regiments to serve in Utah, one newspaper suggested he "form one of them of the *ci-devant* Governors of Kansas." See *Freedom's Champion* (Atchison, K.T.), February 20, 1858.

12. Robert Walker, *An Appeal for the Union. Letter from the Hon. Robert J. Walker* (1856), bound pamphlets, Robert John Walker Papers, Library of Congress (LOC).

13. House of Representatives, 36th Cong., 1st Sess., *House Report 648: Select Committee on Alleged Corruptions in Government: The Covode Investigation* (Washington: 1860), 105. According to Walker, Buchanan had stated "that the safety of the union may depend upon the selection of the individual to whom shall be assigned the task of settling the difficulties which again surround the Kansas question. . . ." See Walker to Buchanan, March 26, 1857, *Transactions*, 5:290.

14. "Documentary History: Kansas Governors Biographies," *Transactions*, 5:158. Despite his Mississippi political service, he lived in the North until he was 25 and married into the politically prominent Pennsylvania Bache family. See "The New Governor of Kansas," *HW* (April 11, 1857): 230.

15. J.H. St. Matthew, "Walker's Administration in Kansas," *OM* 5, n. 6 (December 1870): 544. *Harper's Weekly* described the Kansas governorship as "the post of honor and the post of danger," promising both great risk and great reward: if Walker pacified the territory, "what reward would be too high for such a man?" See "The New Governor of Kansas," 229–30.

16. Schulyer Colfax to Charles Robinson, April 18, 1857, Charles Robinson, Correspondence/Misc., KSHS. In 1860, S.M. Johnson, who became editor of the *Washington Union* in January 1857, testified that Buchanan had agreed to "support and carry out certain principles" and that Walker "should be entirely unrestricted and unencumbered by any further instructions from the government." See S.M. Johnson, May 7, 1860, *House Report 648*, 154.

17. Socolofsky, *Kansas Governors*, 59; Walker to Buchanan, March 26, 1857, *Transactions*, 5:290. According to Walker, he had explicitly stated that any constitution had to be submitted to the people, and Buchanan had modified only one sentence of his inaugural. See *House Report 648*, 105–7.

18. Robert John Walker to Martha Walker Cook, April 6, 1857, Robert John Walker Papers, LOC.

19. Cass to Walker, March 30, 1857, Robert John Walker Papers, LOC.
20. *New York Daily Tribune*, April 1, 1857.
21. Colfax to Robinson, April 18, 1857, Robinson Correspondence, KSHS.
22. John to Robert Everett Sr., April 2, 1857, "Letters of John and Sarah Everett," *KHQ* 8, n. 2 (May 1939): 169.
23. Colfax to Robinson, April 18, 1857, Robinson Correspondence, KSHS.
24. Ibid.
25. Cass to Stanton, March 31, 1857, Robert John Walker Papers, LOC, "Documentary History," *Transactions*, 5:159; St. Matthew, "Walker's Administration," 544.
26. *New York Tribune*, April 8, 1857.
27. Stanton to Cass, April 17, 1857, and "Address of Acting Governor Stanton," April 17, 1857, *Transactions*, 5:324–26. On May 6, Cass responded that this suggestion was under consideration. See Cass to Stanton, May 6, 1857, ibid., 5:326.
28. *New York Tribune*, May 5, 1857, quoted in Wilder, *Annals of Kansas* (Topeka: T. Dwight Thacher, Kansas Publishing House, 1886; New York: Arno Press, 1975), 161; John Speer, *Life of Gen. James H. Lane* (Garden City, KS: John Speer, Printer, 1896), 135. Stanton later regretted being "betrayed into some rash and indiscreet expressions." See Frederick P. Stanton, "Address of Ex-Governor Frederick P. Stanton, September 2, 1884," in *Publications of the Kansas State Historical Society* (Topeka: T.D. Thacher, State Printer, 1886), 1:148.
29. Walker to Stanton, May 6, 1857, Robert John Walker Papers, LOC.
30. *Chicago Tribune*, reprinted in Charles Robinson, *The Kansas Conflict* (Lawrence, KS: Journal Publishing Company, 1898; Freeport, New York: Books for Libraries Press, 1972), 345–50.
31. Robinson et al., to Stanton, April 25, 1857, *Transactions*, 5:434; Wilder, *Annals of Kansas*, 161.
32. Stanton to Robinson et al., April 30, 1857, *Transactions*, 5:435–36.
33. Stanton, "Message of the Acting Governor," December 8, 1857, *Transactions*, 5:415; Robert W. Johannsen, "The Lecompton Constitutional Convention," *KHQ* 23, n. 3 (Autumn 1957): 227–28; William Frank Zornow, *Kansas: A History of the Jayhawk State* (Norman: University of Oklahoma Press, 1957), 76; Philip Shriver Klein, *President James Buchanan* (University Park: Pennsylvania State University Press, 1962), 296; John Hickman, *Popular Sovereignty—The Will of the Majority against the Rule of a Minority: Speech of Hon. J. Hickman, of Pennsylvania, in the House of Representatives, January 28, 1858* (Washington: Congressional Globe Office, 1858), 5.
34. Wilder, *Annals of Kansas*, 165–66; *The New York Tribune*, May 9, 1857.
35. Stanton, "September 2, 1884," *Publications*, 1:149.
36. John to Robert Everett Sr., May 28, 1857, "Letters of John and Sarah Everett," 279.
37. Quoted in the *New York Tribune*, May 19, 1857. The *New York Tribune* criticized Walker's and Stanton's acceptance of the census, arguing it showed them to be "a pair of snakes in the grass, such as might have been expected to creep out from under the Cincinnati Platform and from the recesses of [Buchanan's] Cabinet...." See the *New York Tribune*, June 5, 1857.
38. Robert J. Walker, *Inaugural Address of Hon. Robert J. Walker, Governor of Kansas Territory: Delivered in Lecompton, May 27, 1857* (Lawrence, KS: Herald of Freedom Steam Press Print, 1857), 1–3.
39. Ibid., 2.
40. Ibid., 10–12.

41. Quoted in George W. Brown, *Reminiscences of Gov. R.J. Walker* (Rockford, IL: G.W. Brown, 1881, 1902; Freeport, NY: Books for Libraries Press, 1972), 41. Walker also wrote Cass about this positive reception. See Walker to Cass, June 2, 1857, in *Transactions*, 5:327.

42. J.H. St. Matthew, "Walker's Administration," 547.

43. Howell Cobb to Alexander Stephens, June 17 and June 18, 1857, Ulrich B. Phillips, ed., *Annual Report of the American Historical Association for the Year 1911, vol. II: The Correspondence of Robert Toombs, Alexander H. Stephens, and Howell Cobb* (Washington: 1913), 402. Walker claimed Buchanan had approved a version of his inaugural address which, while incomplete, did include the pivotal section on submission. Most historians accept that he gave Walker unconditional support, but in the context of the entire inaugural, Buchanan and Walker likely differed in their understanding of what submission meant. See Walker, *House Report 648*, 106; David M. Potter, *The Impending Crisis: 1848-1861* (New York: Harper & Row, Publishers, 1976), 298-99; Allan Nevins, *The Emergence of Lincoln: Douglas, Buchanan, and Party Chaos, 1857-1859* (New York: Charles Scribner's Sons, 1950), 1:144-47; Stampp, *America in 1857*, 158-60.

44. Robert Toombs to W.W. Burwell, July 11, 1857, in Phillips, *Correspondence*, 403.

45. St. Matthew, "Walker's Administration," 545.

46. A.J. Hoole to Elizabeth Euphrasia Hoole, July 5, 1857, in William Hoole, ed., "A Southerner's Viewpoint of the Kansas Situation," *KHQ* 3, n. 2 (May 1934): 165. After Senator Henry Wilson (MA) visited Kansas in mid-1857, the *New York Times* reported that "he thinks, as we do, that, whatever a few hot-heads may insist on, the wily leaders of the Pro-Slavery party in Kansas must by this time be satisfied that it is no longer possible to make her a *bona fide* Slave State—that the only result of earnestly persisting in that game will be to make her a more zealous and determined Free State." See *New York Tribune*, June 5, 1857.

47. Walker to Jacob A. Marcell and Walker to J.H. Pritchett, May 30, 1857, Robert John Walker Papers, LOC.

48. Robert J. Walker, "Address of Governor Walker at Topeka," June 6, 1857, transcribed in *Herald of Freedom*, June 20, *Transactions*, 5:293.

49. Wilder, *Annals of Kansas*, 169; Johannsen, "Lecompton Constitutional Convention," 227-28.

50. *Herald of Freedom*, July 4, 1857, quoted in Brown, *Reminiscences*, 48-50. Nonetheless, on August 9, the free-state party elected officers, and the Topeka Constitution garnered 7,257 votes (34 against) in a referendum. While it was doubtful that admission under this constitution was possible, this vote reflected the depth of the free-state commitment to this path. See Wilder, *Annals of Kansas*, 174.

51. Walker to Cass, July 15, 7, 13, 1857, State Department Territorial Papers, Kansas, 1854-1861, Roll 1: Official Correspondence, May 30, 1854-April 30, 1861 (Washington: The National Archives and Records Service, 1953; National Archives Microfilm Publications, Microcopy No. 218); Robinson, *Kansas Conflict*, 355.

52. J. Blood et al., "To the People," *Transactions*, 5:354.

53. Wilder, *Annals of Kansas*, 170.

54. Walker, "To the people of Lawrence—Proclamation," July 15, 1857, *Transactions*, 5:356-58.

55. Judge John McLean to Lewis Cass, July 25, 1857, Gilder Lehrman Collection.

56. St. Matthew, "Walker's Administration," 548-49.

57. Walker, "To the People of Kansas," September 10, 1857, *Leavenworth Journal*, *Transactions*, 5:399.

58. Walker to Cass, July 20, 1857, *Transactions*, 5:358-59. The following week, he asked for two thousand troops to be sent at once. See Walker to Cass, July 27, 1857, State Department Territorial Papers.

59. Cass to Walker, September 1, 1857, *Transactions*, 5:382.

60. John H. Gihon, *Geary and Kansas. Governor Geary's Administration in Kansas* (Philadelphia: J.H.C. Whiting, 1857; Freeport, NY: Books for Libraries Press, 1971), 307.

61. Quoted in James Shenton, *Robert John Walker: A Politician from Jackson to Lincoln* (New York: Columbia University Press, 1961), 165-66.

62. Howell Cobb to D.C. Lamar, July 27, 1857, Robert J. Walker Papers, New-York Historical Society.

63. Walker to Cass, July 20, 1857, *Transactions*, 5:359. For more on Walker's perception of how Southerners affected local views, see Walker to Cass, July 27, ibid., 5:377-78.

64. Quoted in Wilder, *Annals of Kansas*, 175.

65. Douglas to Walker, July 21, 1857, Misc. S.A. Douglas Manuscripts, KSHS.

66. Walker to Cass, July 20, 1857, *Transactions*, 5:359-60.

67. Walker to Buchanan, June 28, 1857, *House Report 648*, 115-19. His letter is so self-congratulatory that it supports Cobb's complaint that Walker was consumed with his own consequence. As Charles Robinson stated on June 11, 1857, not all readers were as enamored of the governor's climate doctrine: "There is indeed an 'isothermal line' . . . but there is unhappily no 'law of the thermometer' to prevent infatuated slavery propagandists from attempting to establish the institution, where wise policy says it should never be." See *The New York Tribune*, June 22, 1857.

68. William Frederick Worner, "Letters of James Buchanan," in *Papers Read Before the Lancaster County Historical Society* 36, n. 12 (1932): 313-14.

69. Thompson to Black, July 4, 1857, quoted in Shenton, *Robert John Walker*, 164-65.

70. Nathaniel Taylor, et al., *The New Haven Memorial to the President, Protesting against the use of the United-States Army to Enforce the Bogus Laws of Kansas; The Answer of President Buchanan; and the Reply of the Memorialists* (Boston: John Wilson and Son, 1858), 2. The memorialists, understandably, found much approbation among free-state advocates. Leonard Bacon, for instance, criticized Buchanan's response, arguing that his Kansas failure stemmed from refusing to repudiate his predecessor. See Leonard Woolsey Bacon, "Buchanan on Kansas," *NE* 15, n. 4 (November 1857): 690-94.

71. Buchanan, *Mr. Buchanan's Administration*, 31.

72. Ibid., 31-32.

73. Taylor, et al., *New Haven Memorial to the President*, 6-9.

74. Quoted in Kendall E. Bailes, *Rider on the Wind: Jim Lane and Kansas* (Shawnee Mission, KS: The Wagon Wheel Press, 1962), 95.

75. Grasshopper Falls Platform, quoted in Wilder, *Annals of Kansas*, 176.

76. Johannsen, "The Lecompton Constitutional Convention," 233-42.

77. Ibid., 229.

78. Walker to Cass, July 27, 1857, *Transactions*, 5:376-77.

79. Cass to Walker, September 2, 1857, Robert John Walker Papers, LOC.

80. Walker, "To the People of Kansas," *Transactions*, 5:388-400.

81. Walker to Cass, September 26, 1857, State Department Territorial Papers.

82. Brown, *Reminiscences*, 90.

83. Nevins, *Emergence of Lincoln*, 1:172-73.
84. George H. Hildt, October 16, 1857, Martha B. Caldwell, "The Diary of George H. Hildt," *KHQ* 10, n. 3 (August 1941): 294.
85. Stanton, "Address of Hon. F.P. Stanton, of Tennessee, January 29, 1858," in *Democratic Protests against the Lecompton Fraud* (Philadelphia: 1858), 2.
86. Bailes, *Rider on the Wind*, 98.
87. Walker, "Proclamation to the People of Kansas," October 19, 1857, and "Proclamation to the People of Kansas," October 22, 1857, *Transactions*, 5:404-5, 406-7.
88. *House Report 648*, 109. See G.W. Smith et al., "Election Protest," October 14, 1857, regarding Oxford; and R. Gilpatrick et al., "Election Protest," October 20, 1857, regarding McGee, *Transactions*, 5:316-18.
89. Walker to Cass, November 3, 1857, *Transactions*, 5:402.
90. Walker received permission on October 21 to take a leave of absence after the convention ended. Stanton had resigned effective December 31, but on November 11, he wrote Buchanan about rumors of a reprimand. If true, he asked to withdraw his resignation so he could defend himself. See Stanton to Buchanan, November 11, 1857, *Transactions*, 5:411.
91. Stanton, "September 2, 1884," *Publications*, 1:153-54.
92. Wilder, *Annals of Kansas*, 192, 195; Johannsen, "Lecompton Constitutional Convention," 229.
93. Wilder, *Annals of Kansas*, 196. According to other reports, Jones pulled a gun on Stanton. Whatever his choice of weapon and target, Jones was clearly livid over the denial. See Alice Nichols, *Bleeding Kansas* (New York: Oxford University Press, 1954), 198.
94. Sterling Cato to Walker et al., October 23, 1857, *Transactions*, 5:408; Walker and Stanton to Cato, October 23, 1857, *Transactions*, 5:408-10. Also see H. Martin, in *House Report 648*, 162.
95. John Everett to Robert Everett Sr., April 2, 1857, "Letters of John and Sarah Everett," 169.
96. *Freedom's Champion*, February 20, 1858.
97. Walker, in *House Report 648*, 109-11, 114. According to Walker, Buchanan denied this charge.
98. Martin, ibid., 158-60.
99. Thompson, ibid., 315-16.
100. Martin, ibid., 162-63.
101. Johannsen, "Lecompton Constitutional Convention," 243.
102. Wilder, *Annals of Kansas*, 187. The Lecompton Constitution is reprinted on 177-91.
103. These provisions are quoted in James Buchanan, "First Annual Message, December 8, 1857," in John B. Moore, ed., *Works of James Buchanan*, 10:150.
104. Stanton, "September 2, 1884," *Publications*, 1:154.
105. Gunja SenGupta, *For God & Mammon: Evangelicals and Entrepreneurs, Masters and Slaves in Territorial Kansas, 1854-1860* (Athens: University of Georgia Press, 1996), 123. SenGupta is less skeptical about slavery's potential. Although roughly 2.2 percent of Kansas's population were slaves in 1855 (186 slaves), SenGupta points out that the number doubled during 1856 and 1857 with the approximately 400-500 slaves divided among roughly 50 slaveholders. SenGupta believes this indicates a growing plantation system (see chapter 6).
106. Quoted in Shenton, *Robert John Walker*, 174; Black to Van Dyke, November 15,

1856, quoted on 162–63; 257, fn. 28.

107. Stanton, "September 2, 1884," *Publications*, 1:155.

108. Cass to Stanton, November 30 and December 2, 1857, and Stanton to Cass, December 9, 1857, *Transactions*, 5:412–14.

109. Quoted in Wendell Holmes Stephenson, "The Political Career of General James H. Lane," *Publications of the Kansas State Historical Society* (Topeka: Kansas State Printing Plant, 1930), 3:91.

110. Stanton, "Acting Governor Stanton's Proclamation Convening the Legislature in Extra Session," December 1, 1857, *Transactions*, 5:318; Socolofsky, *Kansas Governors*, 56; Wilder, *Annals of Kansas*, 201; Klein, *Presidency of James Buchanan*, 302. In informing Denver of his appointment, Cass confided that Stanton had been fired for calling the special session and throwing "a new element of discord among the excited people of Kansas, and is directly at war, therefore, with the peaceful policy of the administration." See Cass to James W. Denver, December 11, 1857, *Transactions*, 5:419–20.

111. Thomas Ewing, "The Struggle for Freedom in Kansas," *The Cosmopolitan* 17, n. 1 (May 1894): 78.

112. Quoted in Stephenson, "General James H. Lane," 91.

113. "The Diary of George H. Hildt," December 2, 1857, 297.

114. Buchanan, *Mr. Buchanan's Administration*, 37.

115. James Buchanan, "First Annual Message," December 8, 1857, in Moore, *Works of James Buchanan*, 10:148–49. At this point, Buchanan still hoped that the free-state party would participate in the December 21 vote.

116. Buchanan, "First Annual Message," in Moore, *Works of James Buchanan*, 10:146–51.

117. Stanton, "Acting Governor Fred Stanton to Fellow Citizens of the Council and House of Representatives, December 8, 1857," 11–13; "Messages of the Governors of Kansas, 1857–1877," KSHS. Despite administration displeasure that legislators had been called into special session before their terms began, Cass instructed Stanton's replacement that "its rightful action must also be respected." See Cass to Denver, December 11, 1857, *Transactions*, 5:420.

118. Stanton, "Message of the Acting Governor," December 8, 1857, *Transactions*, 5:416–18.

119. Stanton to Walker, January 5, 1858, Robert J. Walker Papers, New-York Historical Society.

120. Wilder, *Annals of Kansas*, 201.

121. Stephenson, "James H. Lane," *Publications*, 3: 93.

122. Wilder, *Annals of Kansas*, 200–201.

123. *Freedom's Champion* (Atchison, KS), February 27, 1858; Wilder, *Annals of Kansas*, 203.

124. Wilder, *Annals of Kansas*, 206–8; Buchanan, "Message on the Constitution of Kansas," February 2, 1858, in Moore, *Works of James Buchanan*, 10:188; Ewing, "The Struggle for Freedom in Kansas," 80, 82–84.

125. *Squatter Sovereign*, February 10, 1857, quoted in Bill Cecil-Fronsman, "'Death to All Yankees and Traitors in Kansas': The *Squatter Sovereign* and the Defense of Slavery in Kansas," *KH* 16, n. 1 (Spring 1993): 33.

126. *New York Herald*, December 2, 1857, Kansas Territorial History, Clippings, vol. 3, pt. 3, KSHS.

127. Shenton, *Robert John Walker*, 174.

128. Walker to Cass, December 15, 1857, State Department Territorial Papers, 2, 4.
129. Ibid., 24.
130. Socolofsky, *Kansas Governors*, 62.
131. Cass to Walker, December 18, 1857, *Transactions*, 5:431.
132. Shenton, *Robert John Walker*, 163.
133. Quoted in Shenton, *Robert John Walker*, 169–70. For instance, Postmaster General Aaron Brown noted, "Your inaugural was well received here and read with general approbation. Not so however some of your *speeches* particularly the Topeka one." Brown to Walker, July 8, 1857, quoted in Shenton, *Robert John Walker*, 253, fn. 4.
134. Stanton, "September 2, 1884," *Publications*, 1:150–51.
135. *New York Tribune*, June 22, 1857.
136. Walker, *Inaugural Address*, 2.
137. Worner, "Letters of James Buchanan," 313–14.

7

1. James Buchanan, "First Annual Message," December 8, 1857, in John Bassett Moore, ed., *The Works of James Buchanan* (Philadelphia & London: J.B. Lippincott Company, 1910), 10:151.
2. John Speer, *Life of Gen. James H. Lane* (Garden City, KS: John Speer, Printer, 1896), 175. Speer's tally includes acting governors.
3. "Documentary History: Kansas Governor Biographies," *Transactions of the Kansas State Historical Society* (Topeka: Kansas Publishing House, 1896), 5:160.
4. J. [or T.] Lykins to J.W. Denver, December 17, 1857, James William Denver Papers, KSHS.
5. James W. Denver, "Address of Ex-Governor James W. Denver, September 3, 1884," *Publications of the Kansas State Historical Society* (Topeka, KS: T.D. Thacher, State Printer, 1886), 1:167–68.
6. Buchanan's instructions as reported by Cass, December 11, 1857, quoted in Denver, "Address to the People of Kansas," *Transactions*, 5:466–67.
7. Denver, "Address to the People of Kansas," ibid., 5:465, 467–68.
8. "Proclamation by Governor James W. Denver," December 26, 1857, ibid., 5:468–69.
9. Denver to Dennis, January 1 and January 2, 1858, ibid., 5:471.
10. Denver to Dennis, January 9, 1858, ibid., 5:472.
11. Denver to Mrs. Denver, January 4, 1858, Denver Papers, KSHS.
12. Denver to Buchanan, January 11, 1858, in George C. Barns, *Denver, the Man: The Life, Letters and Public Papers of the Lawyer, Soldier and Statesman* (Wilmington, OH: Shenandoah Publishing House, 1949), 155.
13. Ibid., 155–56; E. Duane Elbert, "The English Bill: An Attempt to Compromise the Lecompton Dilemma," *KH* (Winter 1978): 221, fn. 13.
14. Barns, *Denver, the Man*, 159–61.
15. Denver, "Address of Ex-Governor James W. Denver," *Publications of the Kansas State Historical Society*, 1:169.
16. Lane, quoted in the *Quindaro Chindowan*, March 20, 1858, Wendell Holmes Stephenson, "The Political Career of General James H. Lane," *Publications of the Kansas State Historical Society* (Topeka: Kansas State Printing Plant, 1930), 3:94. Even though they

controlled the official legislature, the Topeka legislature continued to meet to act as an emergency backup, and the stubbornness with which they clung to the Topeka government made working with them difficult.

17. Denver, "Acting Governor Denver to the Council of the Legislative Assembly," February 6, 1858, Records of the Territorial Executive Department: Kansas Territory (RTED), KSHS.

18. Among his many reasons for refusing to relocate, Denver cited the fishing to be found at Lecompton. See Denver, "Address of Ex-Governor James W. Denver," *Publications of the Kansas State Historical Society*, 1:169.

19. Ibid., 1:170-71; Jeremiah Black, "Opinion of Attorney General J.S. Black to Secretary Cass," March 10, 1858, RTED; Alice Nichols, *Bleeding Kansas* (New York: Oxford University Press, 1954), 216-18; Charles Robinson, *The Kansas Conflict* (Lawrence, KS: Journal Publishing Company, 1898; Freeport, NY: Books for Libraries Press, 1972), 381-82.

20. Buchanan to Joseph Baker, January 11, 1858, in *Works of James Buchanan*, 10:177.

21. James W. Davidson, June 14, 1860, House of Representatives, 36th Cong., 1st Sess., *House Report 648: Select Committee on Alleged Corruptions in Government: The Covode Investigation* (Washington: 1860), 323.

22. *National Intelligencer*, February 15, 1858.

23. James Buchanan, *Mr. Buchanan's Administration on the Eve of the Rebellion* (New York: D. Appleton and Company, 1866), 40.

24. Ibid., 42.

25. Buchanan, "Message on the Constitution of Kansas," *Works of James Buchanan*, 10:180, 186.

26. Ibid., 10:186-88, 189-92.

27. McClernand to Douglas, February 17, 1858, quoted in Robert W. Johannsen, ed., *The Letters of Stephen A. Douglas* (Urbana: University of Illinois Press, 1961), 417, fn. 2.

28. Thomas C. Wells to Mrs. Thomas P. Wells, February 27, 1858, Thomas C. Wells, "Letters of a Kansas Pioneer," *KHQ* 5, n. 4 (November 1936): 384.

29. *Charleston Mercury*, February 26, 1858.

30. Quoted in Philip G. Auchampaugh, "The Buchanan-Douglas Feud," *JISHS* 25 (April 1932-January 1933): 7.

31. Philip Shriver Klein, *President James Buchanan* (University Park: Pennsylvania State University Press, 1962), 301-2.

32. See Reinhard H. Luthin, "The Democratic Split During Buchanan's Administration," *PH* 11, n. 1 (January 1944): 16; Richard R. Stenberg, "An Unnoted Factor in the Buchanan-Douglas Feud," *JISHS* 25, n. 4 (January 1933): 275, 280-81; Douglas to Treat, February 28, 1858, *Letters of Stephen A. Douglas*, 418. For a view that downplays patronage, see David E. Meerse, "Origins of the Douglas-Buchanan Feud Reconsidered," *JISHS* 67 (April 1974): 154-74.

33. Douglas to Forney et al., February 6, 1858, *Letters of Stephen A. Douglas*, 409.

34. Stanton, "Address of Ex-Governor Frederick P. Stanton, September 2, 1884," *Publications of the Kansas State Historical Society*, 1:159.

35. Stanton, "Address of Hon. F.P. Stanton, of Tennessee, January 29, 1858," *Democratic Protests against the Lecompton Fraud* (Philadelphia: 1858), 2.

36. Walker to the Indiana Anti-Lecompton Democratic Convention, February 20, 1858, reprinted in *National Intelligencer*, March 1.

37. Buchanan, "Message on the Constitution of Kansas," *Works of James Buchanan*,

10:180-83.

38. Buchanan, *Mr. Buchanan's Administration*, 43.

39. William B. Maclay, *Letters from the Hon. William B. Maclay, Member of Congress from Fifth District of New York, on the Admission of Kansas under the Lecompton Constitution* (New York?: 1858?), 2, 3-4, 6-10.

40. Conrad Swackhamer, ed., "The Admission of Kansas," *USDR* 41, n. 3 (March 1858): 177-81. The Lecompton Constitution prohibited amendment until 1865.

41. Klein, *President James Buchanan*, 303, 310.

42. Elbert, "The English Bill," 219-20.

43. Douglas to Samuel Treat, February 28, 1858, *Letters of Stephen A. Douglas*, 418.

44. J. Collamer and B. Wade, February 18, 1858, *Views of the Minority on the Constitution of Kansas* (Washington: 1858), 6-7.

45. Stephen A. Douglas, in U.S. Senate Committee on Territories [Minority Report], *Report of Senator Douglas, of Illinois, on the Kansas-Lecompton Constitution, February 18, 1858* (Washington: Lemuel Towers, 1858), 1, 16.

46. James H. Hammond, *Kansas-Lecompton Constitution: Speech of Hon. James H. Hammond, of South Carolina, on the Admission of Kansas, Delivered in the Senate of the United States, March 4, 1858* (Washington: 1858?), 4, 7, 9.

47. Lafayette Sabine Foster, *Speech of Hon. L.F.S. Foster, of Connecticut, on the Lecompton Constitution; Delivered in the Senate of the United States, March 8 and 19, 1858* (Washington: Congressional Globe, 1858), 14-15.

48. Auchampaugh, "Buchanan-Douglas Feud," 17.

49. *New York Times*'s Washington correspondent, January 14, 1858, *Freedom's Champion*, February 20.

50. Conrad Swackhamer, ed., "Kansas Congressional Record," *USDR* 41, n. 6 (June 1858): 446; Klein, *President James Buchanan*, 310.

51. Swackhamer, ed., "Kansas Congressional Record," 447-48; Klein, *President James Buchanan*, 310; Daniel Webster Wilder, *The Annals of Kansas* (Topeka: T. Dwight Thacher, Kansas Publishing House, 1886; New York: Arno Press, 1975), 215; Elbert, "The English Bill," 221.

52. Buchanan to Denver, March 27, 1858, *Works of James Buchanan*, 10:201-02. For a similar view, see R.S. Stevens to Denver, April 25, 1858, Denver Papers.

53. Quoted in Barns, *Denver, the Man*, 171-72.

54. Henry S. Foote, *War of the Rebellion*, quoted in Stenberg, "Unnoted Factor," 274.

55. Elbert, "The English Bill," 221, fn. 16.

56. Harris to J. Forney et al, "February 5, 1858," in *Democratic Protests*, 5-6.

57. Samuel S. Cox, *Lecompton Constitution of Kansas: Speech of Hon. Samuel S. Cox, of Ohio, on the President's Message, Delivered in the House of Representatives, December 16, 1857* (Washington: Lemuel Towers, 1857), 2.

58. Marcus J. Parrott, *Kansas—the Lecompton Constitution: Speech of Hon. Marcus J. Parrott, Delegate from Kansas, Delivered in the House of Representatives, March 31, 1858* (Washington: 1858), 5, 8.

59. James F. Dowdell, *The Kansas Issue: Remarks of Hon. James F. Dowdell, of Alabama, in the House of Representatives, March 10, 1858, Advocating the Necessity of Additional Guarantees for the Protection of Southern Rights* (Washington: Congressional Globe Office, 1858), 1, 5, 6.

60. A.G. Bradford to J.W. Denver, March 18, 1858, Denver Papers.

61. Cox, *Lecompton Constitution of Kansas*, 9. Klein notes that each section's traditions played a role. The 33 states had formed 63 constitutions, with 20 submitted to a popular vote and 33 accepted by constitutional conventions. In the South, the people voted on only 9 of 30 constitutions, while in the West 11 of 14 were put to a popular vote. The Northeast and Mid-Atlantic states were more evenly divided, with 10 of 19 subjected to a vote. See Klein, *President James Buchanan*, 305.

62. Elbert, "The English Bill," 222.

63. Daniel W. Gooch, *The Lecompton Constitution, and the Admission of Kansas into the Union: Speech of Hon. D.W. Gooch, of Mass., delivered in the House of Representatives, March 29, 1858* (N.p., 1858), 7.

64. Wilder, *Annals of Kansas*, 215.

65. *Leavenworth Ledger*, April 19, 1858, reprinted in *National Intelligencer*, April 27, 1858.

66. Frank Heywood Hodder, "Some Aspects of the English Bill for the Admission of Kansas," *Annual Report of the American Historical Association for the Year 1906*, vol. 1 (1908), 203–4. Kansas requested more than 23 million acres. See Nichols, *Bleeding Kansas*, 211.

67. Cox, May 31, 1860, *House Report 648*, 229–30.

68. Cox, *House Report 648*, 290. Of the House's 53 Northern Democrats, 26 consistently supported the administration, 11 consistently voted against both the constitution and the English bill, and 16 switched their position, mostly in favor of the administration. These 16 included 8 from Ohio, 3 from Indiana, 3 from Pennsylvania, and 1 each from New York and New Jersey. See David E. Meerse, "The Northern Democratic Party and the Congressional Elections of 1858," *CWH* 19, n. 2 (June 1973): 124–25.

69. *The Tribune Almanac for 1859*, 31, in *The Tribune Almanac for the Years 1838 to 1868* (New York: The New York Tribune, 1868).

70. Wilder, *Annals of Kansas*, 234.

71. Buchanan to William Reed, July 31, 1858, *Works of James Buchanan*, 10:225.

72. *Washington Union*, May 2, 1858, quoted in Philemon Bliss, *Success of the Absolutists. Their Idealism; What and Whence is it? Speech of Hon. Philemon Bliss, of Ohio, in the House of Representatives, May 24, 1858* (Washington: Buell & Blanchard, 1858), 6. The South saw the English Bill "generally as a satisfactory settlement." The *New Orleans Daily Picayune*, for instance, thought its conditions might momentarily provoke dissension, but would "die away into insignificance and ridicule when the condition is examined. . . ." See *New Orleans Daily Picayune*, May 2 and May 7, 1858.

73. *Freedom's Champion*, May 8, 1858.

74. Geary to Pierce, December 15, 1856, John Geary, "John White Geary: Letters and Papers, 1855–1871, Executive Minutes Diary of Kansas Territory," 290, KSHS.

75. Paul Wallace Gates, *Fifty Million Acres: Conflicts over Kansas Land Policy, 1854–1890* (Ithaca, NY: Cornell University Press, 1954), 4. Also see James C. Malin, *John Brown and the Legend of Fifty-Six* (Philadelphia: The American Philosophical Society, 1942), 507–8.

76. Gates, *Fifty Million Acres*, 5.

77. Ibid., 77.

78. Ibid., 93.

79. John to Everett Family, May 28, 1858, John and Sarah Everett, "Letters of John and Sarah Everett," *KHQ* 8, n. 3 (August 1939): 298. Buchanan's decision was widely assailed as motivated by revenge. See *Freedom's Champion*, April 3, 1858. On the scarcity of

Notes to Pages 189-95   **285**

funds, see Julia Louisa Lovejoy to the *Independent Democrat* (Concord, MA), September 10, 1858, Julia Louisa Lovejoy, "Letters of Julia Louisa Lovejoy," *KHQ* 15, n. 4 (November 1947): 393.

80. See Denver to Buchanan, August 26, 1858, *Transactions*, 5:543.

81. Cass to Denver, May 7, 1858, Kansas Territory, Executive Department Correspondence (EDC), KSHS.

82. John S. Cummings to Stanton, December 13, 1857, *Transactions*, 5:318-19.

83. Denver to Cass, June 23, 1858, ibid., 5:534, 532.

84. Ibid., 5:532-33.

85. J.P. Jones and Ben. J. Newsom to Denver, June 3, 1858, ibid., 5:526-28.

86. Denver to Cass, June 7, 1858, ibid., 5:528-30.

87. Ibid., 5:530.

88. John Hamilton, T.R. Robert, and J.W. Denver, "Resolution at Mass-Meeting of the Citizens of Bourbon county," June 15, 1858, ibid., 5:494-95.

89. Sherman to Denver, June 28, 1858, ibid., 5:537; Denver to Sherman, June 29, 1858, ibid., 5:538.

90. Denver to Cass, August 24, 1858, ibid., 5:540-42; Floyd to Cass, September 16, 1858, ibid., 5:544.

91. Thompson to Denver, June 21, 1858, quoted in Barns, *Denver, the Man*, 183.

92. Barns, *Denver, the Man*, 183.

93. *Richmond South*, September 27, 1858, quoted in *Freedom's Champion*, October 23, 1858.

94. *New Orleans Daily Picayune*, August 20, 1858.

95. Elbert, "The English Bill," 232.

96. Black to James W. Davidson, August 1?, 1858, *House Report 648*, 323-24.

97. Cobb to Alexander Stephens, September 8, 1858, in Phillips, *Correspondence*, 443.

98. Denver to Buchanan, August 26, 1858, *Transactions*, 5:543; Denver to Cass, September 1, ibid., 5:544.

99. Thompson to Denver, October 10, 1858, Denver Papers.

100. Denver, "Proclamation Issued Upon His Resignation," October 9, 1858.

101. Denver, "Address of Ex-Governor James W. Denver," *Publications*, 1:168.

102. Homer E. Socolofsky, *Kansas Governors* (Lawrence: University Press of Kansas, 1990), 67.

103. Quoted in J.H. St. Matthew, "Walker's Administration in Kansas," *OM* 5, n. 6 (December 1870): 556.

104. Denver to his wife, May 9, 1858, quoted in Barns, *Denver, the Man*, 208.

105. Denver to Cass, September 1, 1858, *Transactions*, 5:544.

106. *St. Louis Republican*, March 29, 1858, in *Denver, the Man*, 176.

107. See Medary, in *House Report 648*, 135-36.

108. Wilder, *Annals of Kansas*, 244.

109. Only 1,425 voted against another attempt. See Wilder, *Annals of Kansas*, 253.

110. William Frank Zornow, *Kansas: A History of the Jayhawk State* (Norman: University of Oklahoma Press, 1957), 80-83; Socolofsky, *Kansas Governors*, 72.

111. Zornow, *Kansas*, 86.

112. Ibid., 84, 86.

113. Lovejoy, Letter to the Editor, *Zion's Herald* (Boston), October 6, 1859, "Letters

of Julia Louisa Lovejoy," *KHQ* 16, n. 1 (February 1948): 70.

114. Wilder, *Annals of Kansas*, 295.

115. Zornow, *Kansas*, 88.

116. Buchanan, *Mr. Buchanan's Administration*, 46.

117. *Freedom's Champion*, May 15, 1858. Also see *Charleston Mercury*, July 27, 1858.

118. Bruce W. Collins, "The Democrats' Electoral Fortunes during the Lecompton Crisis," *CWH* 24, n. 4 (December 1978): 314–31. Congressmen in Pennsylvania, New York, New Jersey, Ohio, Indiana, and the Northeast who voted for the English Bill were defeated. See Klein, *Presidency of James Buchanan*, 330.

119. Collins, "The Democrats' Electoral Fortunes," 328. For the divisions in New York and Pennsylvania, see Klein, *Presidency of James Buchanan*, 220, 262. Democrats were seen as weak because of incumbents' alleged inability to be renominated. Among 26 administration friends, 21 were renominated, 1 declined to run, and 2 were denied renomination for other reasons. Of the 16 who switched positions, 3 did not seek renomination (2 were from districts with one-term traditions), and 11 of the 13 who did seek it achieved it. On the other hand, of the 11 consistent administration opponents, 4 did not seek it and 4 were defeated in convention. Meerse points out that Republicans also had difficulties: 8 of 11 in Massachusetts, 13 of 21 in New York, and 6 of 10 in Pennsylvania were not renominated. See Meerse, "The Congressional Elections of 1858," 125–26.

120. Luthin, "Democratic Split," 17.

121. Buchanan to Harriet Lane, October, 15, 1858, in *Works of James Buchanan*, 10:229–30.

122. Buchanan, "Second Annual Message," December 6, 1858, in *Works of James Buchanan*, 10:237–38.

123. Ibid., 10:241.

124. Buchanan, *Mr. Buchanan's Administration*, 55.

125. Ibid., 56.

126. Ibid., 50–51.

127. Howell Cobb to D.C. Lamar, July 27, 1857, Robert J. Walker Papers, New-York Historical Society.

128. R.G. Horton, *The Life and Public Services of James Buchanan* (New York: Derby & Jackson, 1856), 397, 428, 403–4.

129. Gates, *Fifty Million Acres*, 104.

Conclusion

1. Historian Kenneth Owens argues that territorial settlement is characterized by chaotic factionalism and a disorderly style of politics endemic to western development. The meager population and the minute number of politically active individuals within territories exacerbate residents' unfamiliarity with one another and the surrounding environment. See Owens, "Pattern and Structure in Western Territorial Politics," in John Porter Bloom, ed., *The American Territorial System* (Athens: Ohio University Press, 1973), 164–65.

2. Geary to William Marcy, November 22, 1856, "John White Geary: Executive Minutes Diary," 245, KSHS.

3. Clarence E. Carter, "The Territorial Papers of the United States: A Review and

Commentary," *MVHR* 42 (1955): 515-16.

4. James W. Denver to Mrs. Denver, January 4, 1858, James William Denver Papers, KSHS.

5. Homer E. Socolofsky, *Kansas Governors* (Lawrence: University Press of Kansas, 1990), 2. Socolofsky tallied Acting Governors as separate executive terms regardless of the length or reason for appointment.

6. John H. Gihon, *Geary and Kansas. Governor Geary's Administration in Kansas. With a Complete History of the Territory until June 1857* (Philadelphia: J.H.C. Whiting, 1857; Freeport, NY: Books for Libraries Press, 1971), 163.

7. Bernard A. Weisberger, "The Newspaper Reporter and the Kansas Imbroglio," *MVHR* 36, n. 4 (March 1950): 633-56.

8. Ibid., 633-37.

9. Don W. Wilson, "Barbed Words on the Frontier: Early Kansas Newspaper Editors," *KH* 1, n. 3 (Autumn 1978): 147.

10. Earl S. Pomeroy, "The Territory as a Frontier Institution," *TH* 7, n. 1 (Autumn 1944): 37.

11. John to Robert Everett Sr., May 28, 1857, John and Sarah Everett, "Letters of John and Sarah Everett, 1854-1864: Miami County Pioneers," *KHQ* 8, n. 3 (August 1939): 279.

12. *Congressional Globe*, 33rd Congr., 1st Sess., 1234.

13. "Our Parties and Politics," *PM* 4, n. 21 (September 1854): 239.

14. Samuel Brenton, March 20, 1856, *Congressional Globe*, 34th Cong., 1st Sess. Appx., 196.

15. Leonard Woolsey Bacon, "The President's Message," *NE* 15, n. 1 (February 1857): 17.

16. "The Political Crisis in the United States," *ERCJ*, American edition, 45, n. 2 (October 1856): 304.

17. Marcus J. Parrott, *Kansas—the Lecompton Constitution: Speech of Hon. Marcus J. Parrott, Delegate from Kansas, Delivered in the House of Representatives, March 31, 1858* (Washington: 1858), 1, 3.

18. John Hickman, *Popular Sovereignty—The Will of the Majority against the Rule of a Minority: Speech of Hon. J. Hickman, of Pennsylvania, in the House of Representatives, January 28, 1858* (Washington: Congressional Globe Office, 1858), 1.

19. John to Robert Everett Sr., May 14, 1857, "Everett Letters," *KHQ* 8, n. 2 (May 1939): 174.

20. *Freedom's Champion*, March 6, 1858.

21. William Dorsheimer, in *Proceedings of the Union Anti-Lecompton Mass Meeting of the Citizens of Erie County, N.Y. Opposed to the Policy of the National Administration, Held at St. James Hall, Buffalo, Thursday, May 27th, 1858* (Buffalo: Commercial Advertiser Steam Press, 1858), 20-21.

22. Philip G. Auchampaugh, "James Buchanan, The Conservatives' Choice, 1856: A Political Portrait," *TH* 7, n. 2 (Spring 1945): 86-87.

23. Solomon Haven, in Union Anti-Lecompton Mass Meeting, *Proceedings*, 14.

24. Cecil Howes, "The Lot of the Territorial Governor in Kansas Was Not an Enviable One," *Kansas City Star*, December 11, 1935, Governors of Kansas: Clippings, vol. 2, 1925-1940, KSHS.

25. John Speer, *Life of Gen. James H. Lane, 'The Liberator of Kansas,' with Corroborative Incidents of Pioneer History* (Garden City, KS: John Speer, Printer, 1896), 13.

26. Douglas to Charles Lanphier, February 13, 1854, Misc. Stephen A. Douglas Manuscripts, KSHS.

27. William H. Seward, *Freedom in Kansas: Speech of William H. Seward, in the Senate of the United States, March 3, 1858* (Washington: Buell & Blanchard, Printers, 1858?), 6.

28. Hickman, *Popular Sovereignty*, 5.

29. Robert J. Walker, *Inaugural Address of Hon. Robert J. Walker, Governor of Kansas Territory: Delivered in Lecompton, May 27, 1857* (Lawrence, KS: Herald of Freedom Steam Press Print, 1857), 3.

30. Alexander H. Stephens to the Voters of the Eighth Congressional District of Georgia, August 14, 1857, in Ulrich B. Phillips, ed., *Annual Report of the American Historical Association for the Year 1911, vol. II: The Correspondence of Robert Toombs, Alexander H. Stephens, and Howell Cobb* (Washington: 1913), 417–18.

31. Seward, *Freedom in Kansas*, 9.

32. House of Representatives, 36th Cong., 1st Sess., *House Report 648: Select Committee on Alleged Corruptions in Government: The Covode Investigation* (Washington: 1860), 6.

33. James Buchanan, "Message on the Covode Investigation," June 22, 1860, in John Bassett Moore, *The Works of James Buchanan, Comprising his Speeches, State Papers, and Private Correspondence* (Philadelphia & London: J.B. Lippincott Co., 1910), 10:436, 439–41.

34. J.G. Whittier, "The Kansas Emigrants," quoted in William A. Johnson, *The History of Anderson County, Kansas, From its First Settlement to the Fourth of July, 1876* (Garnett, KS: Kauffman & Iler, 1877), 20–21.

35. George Clarke to John Quitman, January 29, 1856, Miscellaneous Geo. W. Clarke Manuscripts, KSHS.

36. *Charleston Mercury*, March 9, 1858.

37. Reprinted in *Charleston Mercury*, April 17, 1858. Also see the *Mobile Register* (Alabama), reprinted in the same issue.

38. "The Kansas Question," *PM* 6, n. 4 (October 1855): 426.

39. Union Anti-Lecompton Mass Meeting, *Proceedings*, 12.

Bibliography

I. Primary Sources
A. Archival Material

Beinecke Rare Book & Manuscript Library, New Haven, Connecticut
    John White Geary Papers
Center for American History, Austin, Texas
Gilder Lehrman Collection, New York City, New York
    Charles Whipple [Aaron D. Stevens] Letters
    Pierce to Geary, December 12, 1856
    Theodore Parker to Nathaniel P. Banks, February 10, 1856
    Judge John McLean to Lewis Cass, July 25, 1857
Historical Society of Pennyslvania, Philadelphia, Pennsylvania
Kansas State Historical Society, Topeka, Kansas
    William Barnes Collection
    William I.R. Blackman Collection
    Blood Collection
    G.W. Brown Collection
    Governors of Kansas: Clippings, vol. 2, 1925–1940
    Misc. Geo. W. Clarke Manuscripts
    Jonas Colburn Letters
    James William Denver Papers
    Misc. S.A. Douglas Manuscripts
    Miscellaneous Stephen A. Douglas Manuscripts
    John White Geary: Biography and Letters (originals in the Oregon Historical Society)
    John White Geary: Biography and Papers
    John White Geary: Executive Minutes Diary of Kansas Territory
    William Hutchison Papers
    Kansas Territorial History, Clippings
    Kansas Territory: Executive Department Correspondence
    Messages of the Governors of Kansas, 1857–1877
    Miscellaneous Edward Lillis Pierce Manuscripts
    Records of the Territorial Executive Department: Kansas Territory
    Charles and Sara Robinson Papers
    Charles Robinson, Correspondence/Misc.
    William M. Snow Scrap-book
    Thomas H. Webb Scrapbooks
Kenneth Spencer Research Collection, Lawrence, Kansas
Lancaster County Historical Society, Lancaster, Pennsylvania
Library and Research Center, Missouri History Museum, St. Louis, Missouri
Library of Congress, Washington, D.C.

William W. Corcoran Papers
Franklin Pierce Papers
Robert John Walker Papers
Louisiana State Museum, New Orleans, Louisiana
New-York Historical Society, New York City, New York
Robert J. Walker Papers
St. Louis Mercantile Library, St. Louis, Missouri
Special Collections and University Archives, Wichita State University, Wichita, Kansas
Tennessee State Library and Archives, Nashville, Tennessee
Tulane Special Collections, New Orleans, Louisiana
Vanderbilt Special Collections, Nashville, Tennessee
Western Historical Manuscript Collection, St. Louis, Missouri
Williams Research Center, New Orleans, Louisiana

B. Congressional Speeches and Government Documents

Allen, Jason. *Speech of Hon. Jas. C. Allen, of Illinois, on the Slavery Question and the Missouri Compromise. Delivered in the House of Representatives, February 21, 1854.* Washington: Printed at the Congressional Globe Office, 1854.

Benton, Thomas Hart. *Nebraska and Kansas: Speech of Mr. Benton, of Missouri, in the House of Representatives, April 25, 1854.* Washington: Congressional Globe Office, 1854.

Bingham, John A. *Kansas Contested Election: Speech of Hon. J.A. Bingham, of Ohio, in the House of Representatives, March 6, 1856, on the Resolution Reported from the Committee of Elections, in the Contested Election Case from the Territory of Kansas.* Washington: Buell & Blanchard, Printers, 1856.

Bliss, Philemon. *Success of the Absolutists. Their Idealism; What and Whence is it? Speech of Hon. Philemon Bliss, of Ohio, in the House of Representatives, May 24, 1858.* Washington: Buell & Blanchard, 1858.

Botts, John Minor. *Letters of John Minor Botts, of Virginia, on the Nebraska Question.* Washington: John T. and Lem. Towers, Printers, 1853.

Brooks, Preston S. *National Politics: Speech of Hon. P.S. Brooks, of South Carolina, on Resigning his Seat in Congress, Delivered in the House of Representatives, July 14, 1856.* Washington, 1856.

Broom, Jacob. *Defense of Americanism: Speech of Hon. Jacob Broom, of Pennsylvania, delivered in the House of Representatives, August 4, 1856.* Washington: Congressional Globe Office, 1856.

Burlingame, Anson. *An Appeal to Patriots against Fraud and Disunion: Speech of Hon. Anson Burlingame, of Massachusetts, Delivered in the U.S. House of Representatives, March 31, 1858.* Washington: Buell & Blanchard, Printers, 1858.

———. *Defence of Massachusetts: Speech of Hon. Anson Burlingame, of Massachusetts in the United States House of Representatives, June 21, 1856.* Boston: John P. Jewett and Company, 1856.

Butler, Andrew P. *Nebraska and Kansas: Speech of Hon. A.P. Butler, of South Carolina, in the Senate, February 24 and 25, 1854.* Washington: Congressional Globe Office, 1854.

Campbell, Lewis D. *Supremacy of the Constitution and Laws: Speech of Hon. Lewis D. Campbell, of Ohio, in the House of Representatives, in Reply to his Colleague, Mr. J.R. Giddings, the Senate's Amendments to the Deficiency Bill being under Consideration.*

Washington: Buell & Blanchard, 1856.

Cass, Lewis. *Kansas—The Territories: Speech of Hon. Lewis Cass, of Michigan, delivered in the Senate, May 13, 1856.* Washington: Congressional Globe Office, 1856.

———. *Nebraska and Kansas: Speech of Mr. Cass, of Michigan, on the Powers of the Government over Slavery in the Territories, in the Senate, February 20, 1854.* Washington: Congressional Globe Office, 1854.

———. *Speech of Lewis Cass, of Michigan, on the Nebraska and Kansas Bill. Delivered in the Senate of the United States, May 25, 1854.* N.p: Towers, Printers, 1854.

Chandler, Joseph R. *Sanctity of National Pledges: Speech of Hon. Joseph R. Chandler, on the Bill to Organize Territorial Government in Nebraska, in the House of Representatives, April 5, 1854.* Washington: Congressional Globe Office, 1854.

Clingman, Thomas L. *Speech of Hon. Thomas L. Clingman, of North Carolina, on the Resolutions Reported by the Select Committee to Investigate the Alleged Assault upon Senator Sumner by Mr. Brooks, delivered in the House of Representatives, July 9, 1856.* Washington: Congressional Globe Office, 1856.

Colfax, Schuyler. *The "Laws" of Kansas: Speech of Schuyler Colfax, of Indiana, in the House of Representatives, June 21, 1856.* Washington: Buell & Blanchard, Printers, 1856.

Collamer, James, and Benjamin Wade. *Views of the Minority on the Constitution of Kansas.* Washington: 1858.

Congressional Globe. 33rd to 36th Congresses. Washington: Office of John C. Rives, Printer, 1854–1860.

Cooper, James. *Nebraska and Kansas: Speech of Hon. Jas. Cooper, of Pennsylvania, in the Senate, February 27, 1854.* Washington: Congressional Globe Office, 1854.

Cox, Samuel S. *Lecompton Constitution of Kansas: Speech of Hon. Samuel S. Cox, of Ohio, on the President's Message, Delivered in the House of Representatives, December 16, 1857.* Washington: Lemuel Towers, 1857.

Cullom, William. *Speech of Hon. Wm. Cullom, of Tennessee, on the Nebraska and Kansas Bill, in the House of Representatives, April 11, 1854.* Washington: Congressional Globe Office, 1854.

Cumback, William. *Politics of the Country: Speech of Hon. Will. Cumback of Indiana, in the House of Representatives, December 17, 1856.* Washington: Buell & Blanchard, Printers, 1857.

Damrell, William S. *Kansas Contested Election: Speech of Hon. W.S. Damrell, of Massachusetts, in the House of Representatives, March 18, 1856, on the Resolution Reported from the Committee of Elections, in the Contested Election Case from the Territory of Kansas.* Washington: Buell & Blanchard, Printers, 1856.

Douglas, Stephen A. *Non-Intervention—Popular Sovereignty: Speech of Hon. S.A. Douglas, of Illinois, in the Senate of the United States, February 23, 1859, . . .* Washington: Lemuel Towers, 1859.

Dowdell, James F. *The Kansas Issue: Remarks of Hon. James F. Dowdell, of Alabama, in the House of Representatives, March 10, 1858, Advocating the Necessity of Additional Guarantees for the Protection of Southern Rights.* Washington: Congressional Globe Office, 1858.

Edmands, J. Wiley. *Speech of J. Wiley Edmands, of Massachusetts, Delivered in the House of Representatives, May 20, 1854, on the Nebraska and Kansas Territorial Bill.* Washington: Buell & Blanchard, Printers, 1854.

Eliot, Thomas D. *Nebraska and Kansas: Speech of Hon. T.D. Eliot, of Massachusetts, in the*

House of Representatives, May 10, 1854. Washington: 1854.
Fessenden, William P. *Speech of W.P. Fessenden, of Maine, against the Repeal of the Missouri Prohibition, North of 36°30', in the Senate, March 3, 1854.* Washington: Congressional Globe Office, 1854.
Foster, Lafayette Sabine. *Speech of Hon. L.F.S. Foster, of Connecticut, on the Lecompton Constitution; Delivered in the Senate of the United States, March 8 and 19, 1858.* Washington: Congressional Globe, 1858.
Gooch, Daniel W. *The Lecompton Constitution, and the Admission of Kansas into the Union: Speech of Hon. D.W. Gooch, of Mass., delivered in the House of Representatives, March 29, 1858.* N.p. 1858.
Goodrich, John Z. *Speech of Hon. John Z. Goodrich, of Mass., Delivered in the House of Representatives, May 20, 1854.* Washington: Congressional Globe Office, 1854.
Grow, Galusha Aaron. *Nebraska and Kansas: Speech of Hon. G.A. Grow, of Pennsylvania, in the House of Representatives, May 10, 1854.* Washington: 1854 (?).
Hale, John Parker. *The Wrongs of Kansas: Speech of John P. Hale, of New Hampshire, in the United States Senate, February 26 and 28, 1856.* Washington: Buell & Blanchard, Printers, 1856.
Hammond, James H. *Kansas-Lecompton Constitution: Speech of Hon. James H. Hammond, of South Carolina, on the Admission of Kansas, Delivered in the Senate of the United States, March 4, 1858.* Washington: 1858 (?).
Hickman, John. *Popular Sovereignty—The Will of the Majority against the Rule of a Minority: Speech of Hon. J. Hickman, of Pennsylvania, in the House of Representatives, January 28, 1858.* Washington: Congressional Globe Office, 1858.
Houston, Samuel. *Nebraska Bill—Indian Tribes: Speech of Hon. Sam Houston, of Texas, in the Senate, February 14 and 15, 1854, in Favor of Maintaining the Public Faith with the Indian Tribes.* Washington: Congressional Globe Office, 1854.
———. *Speech of Senator Houston, of Texas, on the Nebraska and Kansas Bill, Previous to the Final Passage of the Same by the Senate of the United States, in the Senate, March 3, 1854.* Washington: Congressional Globe Office, 1854.
Howard, William A., and John Sherman. *Subduing Freedom in Kansas. Report of the Congressional Committee, Presented in the House of Representatives on Tuesday, July 1, 1856.* New York: Office of the New York Tribune, 1856.
Hunt, Theodore G. *Good Faith and Union: Speech of Hon. T.G. Hunt, of Louisiana, in the House of Representatives, March 23, 1854, on the Bill to establish the Nebraska and Kansas Territories, and to repeal the Missouri Compromise.* Washington: Congressional Globe Office, 1854.
Hunter, Robert Mercer Taliaferro. *Speech of the Hon. R.M.T. Hunter, of Virginia, in the Senate, February 24, 1854 on Nebraska and Kansas.* Washington: Sentinel Office, 1854.
Meacham, James. *Nebraska and Kansas: Speech of Mr. Meacham, of Vermont, in the House of Representatives, February 15, 1854, Against the Nebraska and Kansas Territorial Bill, and in favor of maintaining the Government faith with the Indian Tribes.* Washington: Congressional Globe Office, 1854.
The Nebraska Question Comprising Speeches in the United States Senate by Mr. Douglas, Mr. Chase, Mr. Smith, Mr. Everett, Mr. Wade, Mr. Badger, Mr. Seward, and Mr. Sumner, Together with The History of the Missouri Compromise, Daniel Webster's Memorial in Regard to it—History of the Annexation of Texas—The Organization of Oregon Territory—and the Compromises of 1950. New York: J.S. Redfield, 1854.

Parrott, Marcus J. *Kansas—The Lecompton Constitution: Speech of Hon. Marcus J. Parrott, Delegate from Kansas, Delivered in the House of Representatives, March 31, 1858.* Washington: n.p., 1858.

Pugh, George E. *Kansas Affairs. Speech of Hon. George E. Pugh, of Ohio, Delivered in the Senate of the United States, July 2, 1856.* Washington: Congressional Globe Office, 1856.

Ritchie, David. *Power of Congress over the Territories: Speech of Hon. David Ritchie, of Pennsylvania, in the House of Representatives, April 24, 1856.* Washington: Buell & Blanchard, Printers, 1856.

Seward, William H. *Freedom in Kansas: Closing Speech of William H. Seward, in the Senate of the United States, April 30, 1858.* Washington: Buell & Blanchard, 1858.

———. *Freedom in Kansas: Speech of William H. Seward, in the Senate of the United States, March 3, 1858.* Washington: Buell & Blanchard, Printers, 1858 (?).

———. *The Usurpations of Slavery: Speech of William H. Seward, in the Senate of the United States, on the Bill to Protect Officers of the United States, February 23, 1855.* Washington: Buell & Blanchard, Printers, 1855.

Skelton, Charles. *Speech of Mr. Skelton, of New Jersey, in the House of Representatives, February 14, 1854, against the Repeal of the Missouri Compromise.* Washington: Congressional Globe Office, 1854.

Smith, Gerrit. *Speeches of Gerrit Smith in Congress.* New York: Mason Brothers, 1855.

———. *Speeches of Gerrit Smith. In Congress, 1853-'4.* Washington: Buell and Blanchard, Printers, 1854.

Smith, Samuel A. *Speech of Hon. S.A. Smith, of Tennessee, on the State of Affairs in Kansas, Delivered in the House of Representatives, June 25, 1856.* N.p., 1856.

Speeches and other Proceedings at the Anti-Nebraska Meetings Held in New Haven, Connecticut, March 18th and 10th, 1854. New Haven: John H. Austin, 1854.

Speeches of Messrs. Weller, Orr, Lane, and Cobb, Delivered in Phoenix and Depot Halls, Concord, N.H., at a Mass Meeting of the Democratic Party of Merrimac County. N.p., 1856.

Stephens, Alexander H. *Speech of Hon. Alexander H. Stephens, of Georgia, on the Report of the Kansas Investigating Committee, in the Case of Reeder against Whitfield. Delivered in the House of Representatives, July 31, 1856.* Washington: Congressional Globe Office, 1856.

Sumner, Charles. *The Crime Against Kansas: Speech of Hon. Charles Sumner, of Massachusetts, in the Senate of the United States, May 19, 1856.* New York: Office of the Tribune, 1856.

Tappan, Mason W. *Modern "Democracy," The Ally of Slavery, Speech of Hon. M.W. Tappan, of New Hampshire, in the House of Representatives, July 29, 1856.* Washington: Buell & Blanchard, Printers, 1856.

Toombs, Robert. *Speech of the Hon. Robert Toombs, of Georgia, in the Senate, February 23, 1854, on Nebraska and Kansas.* Washington: Sentinel Office, 1854.

Toucey, Isaac. *Speech of Mr. Toucey, of Connecticut, Defending Himself Against the Nebraska Resolutions of the Legislature of Connecticut.* Washington: Printed at the Sentinel Office, 1854.

U.S. House of Representatives. *Memorial of the Senators and Representatives [of the State of Kansas], and the Constitution of the State of Kansas; also, the Majority and Minority Reports of the Committee on Territories on the Said Constitution.* Washington: Cornelius Wendell, 1856.

U.S. House of Representatives Committee on the Territories. *R.G. Elliott and Others, of Kansas, to Accompany Bill H.R. no. 810, February 7, 1857; Mr. Grow, from the Committee on Territories, Made the Following Report, the Committee on Territories, to Whom was Referred the Memorial of R.G. Elliott and Others, Citizens of the Territory of Kansas, Praying Compensation for Property Destroyed in Said Territory, Having Had the Same Under Consideration, Beg Leave to Submit the Following Report.* Washington (?): 1857.

U.S. House of Representatives. 34th Congress, 1st Session. *Report 200: Report of the Special Committee Appointed to Investigate the Troubles in Kansas; with the Views of the Minority of Said Committee.* Washington: Cornelius Wendell, Printer, 1856.

U.S. House of Representatives. 36th Congress, 1st Session. *Report 648: Select Committee on Alleged Corruptions in Government: The Covode Investigation.* Washington: 1860.

U.S. Senate Committee of Territories [Minority Report]. *Report of Senator Douglas, of Illinois, on the Kansas-Lecompton Constitution, February 18, 1858.* Washington: Lemuel Towers, 1858.

U.S. Senate. 34th Congress, 1st Session. *Ex. Doc. No. 4: Message of the President of the United States, Relative to Disturbances in the Territory of Kansas, January 24, 1856.* Washington: 1856.

U.S. Senate. 34th Congress, 1st Session. *Ex. Doc. No. 97: Message of the President of the United States communicating a Report, in compliance with a resolution of the Senate of the 21st ultimo, calling for information relative to the instructions sent to military officers in Kansas.* Washington: 1856.

U.S. Senate Committee on Territories and Insular Affairs. *Report of the Committee on Territories, to Whom was Referred so Much of the Annual Message of the President of the United States as Relates to Territorial Affairs, Together with his Special Message on the 24th Day of January, 1856, in Regard to Kansas Territory, and his Message of the 18th of February, in Compliance with the Resolution of the Senate of the 4th of February, 1856, Requesting Transcripts of Certain Papers Relative to the Affairs of the Territory of Kansas.* Washington: 1856.

U.S. State Department. *State Department Territorial Papers, Kansas, 1854–1861, Roll 1: Official Correspondence, May 30, 1854–April 30, 1861.* Washington: National Archives and Record Service, 1953.

Upham, Charles W. *Nebraska and Kansas: Speech of Hon. Charles W. Upham, of Massachusetts, in the House of Representatives, May 10, 1854.* Washington: 1854 (?).

Wade, Benjamin F. *Property in the Territories: Speech of the Hon. Benjamin F. Wade, of Ohio, Delivered in the Senate of the United States, March 7, 1860.* Washington: Buell & Blanchard, Printers, 1860.

———. *Speech of the Hon. B.F. Wade, of Ohio, on the Nebraska and Kansas Bills, in the Senate, March 3, 1854.* Washington: Congressional Globe Office, 1854.

Walley, Samuel H. *Speech of Hon. S.H. Walley, of Massachusetts, on the Nebraska & Kansas Territorial Bill, Delivered in the House of Representatives, May 9, 1854.* Washington: John T. and Lem. Towers, 1854.

Washburn Jr., Israel. *Speech of Hon. I. Washburn, Jr., of Maine, on the Bill to Organize Territorial Governments in Nebraska and Kansas, and against the Abrogation of the Missouri Compromise in the House of Representatives, April 7, 1854.* Washington: Congressional Globe Office, 1854.

Yates, Richard. *Speech of Hon. Richard Yates, of Illinois, on the Bill to Organize Territorial Governments in Nebraska and Kansas, and Opposing the Repeal of the Missouri Compromise, in the House of Representatives, March 28, 1854. Washington: Congressional Globe Office, 1854.

Zollicoffer, Felix K. *Organization of the House: Remarks of Mr. Zollicoffer, of Tennessee, delivered in the House of Representatives, December 20, 1855, on the election of Speaker and the organization of the House of Representatives, and in answer to a question of Mr. McMullin, why the party with which Mr. Zollicoffer acted would not vote for the Democratic nominee?* Washington: Congressional Globe Office, 1855.

C. Newspapers

Charleston Mercury
[Atchison, Kansas] *Freedom's Champion*
National Intelligencer
New Orleans Daily Picayune
New York Tribune
Washington Union

D. Pamphlets, Books, and Articles

Adams, C.A. *Letter from a Kansas Settler, Formerly of Concord, Mass., to his Brother [W. Henry Adams]*. Lawrence, K.T.(?): 1856.

Admire, W.W. "A Fragment of Early Kansas History." *MWH* 11, n. 6 (April 1890): 588–610.

An Adopted Catholic. *Letter of An Adopted Catholic, Addressed to the President of the Kentucky Democratic Association of Washington City, on Temporal allegiance to the Pope, and the relations of the Catholic Church and Catholics, both native and adopted, to the system of Domestic Slavery and its Agitation in the United States.* Washington: 1856.

Alabama Democratic and Anti-Know-Nothing State Convention. *Official Proceedings of the Democratic and Anti-Know-Nothing State Convention of Alabama, Held in the City of Montgomery, January 8th and 9th, 1856.* Montgomery: Advertiser and Gazette Book and Job Office, 1856.

American Abolition Society. *The Kansas Struggle of 1856, in Congress and in the Presidential Campaign; with Suggestions for the Future.* New York: John A. Gray, Printer, 1857.

Bacon, Leonard. *The Morality of the Nebraska Bill.* [Reprinted from *NE*, May 1854.]

Bacon, Leonard Woolsey. "Buchanan on Kansas." *NE* 15, n. 4 (November 1857): 675–700.

———. "The Moral of Harper's Ferry." *NE* (November 1859): 1066–78.

———. "The President's Message." *NE* 15, n. 1 (February 1857): 1–38.

Batchelder, Eugene. *A New Fremont Song, Respectfully Dedicated to the Cambridge Fremont Club No. 2, and the Fremont Men of the Country.* N.p., 1856.

Bell, John. *Speech of the Hon. John Bell, Delivered at a Mass Meeting of the American Party, Held at Knoxville, Tenn., September 22, 1855.* N.p., 1855.

Blair, Francis P. *General Jackson and James Buchanan: Letter from Francis P. Blair to the Public.* N.p., 1856.

Brown, George W. *Reminiscences of Gov. R.J. Walker.* [*Reminiscences of Gov. R.J. Walker; with the True Story of the Rescue of Kansas from Slavery.*] Rockford, IL: G.W. Brown, 1881, 1902; Freeport, NY: Books for Libraries Press, 1972.

Bryant, William Cullen. *Power for Sanity: Selected Editorials of William Cullen Bryant,*

1829-1861. Edited by William Cullen Bryant II. New York: Fordham University Press, 1994.

Buchanan, James. *Inaugural Address of the President of the United States on the Fourth of March, 1857*. Washington: A.O.P. Nicholson, Printer, 1857.

———. *Mr. Buchanan's Administration on the Eve of the Rebellion*. New York: D. Appleton and Company, 1866.

———. *The Works of James Buchanan, Comprising his Speeches, State Papers, and Private Correspondence*. Edited by John Bassett Moore. Philadelphia & London: J.B. Lippincott Company, 1908-1911. Twelve volumes.

Caldwell, Martha B., ed. "The Diary of George H. Hildt, June to December, 1857: Pioneer of Johnson Country." *KHQ* 10, n. 3 (August 1941): 260-98.

Carroll, Anna Ella. *Review of Pierce's Administration; Showing its only Popular Measures to Have Originated with the Executive of Millard Fillmore*. Boston: James French & Company; New York: Miller, Orton & Mulligan, 1856.

———. *The Union of the States*. Boston: James French & Company; New York: Miller, Orton & Mulligan, 1856.

Carruth, William H. "New England in Kansas." *NEM* 16, n. 1 (March 1897), 3-21.

Cecil [Sidney G. Fisher]. *Kanzas and the Constitution*. Boston: Printed by Damrell & Moore, 1856.

Chase, Salmon P., et al. *An Appeal of the Independent Democrats in Congress to the People of the United States: Shall Slavery be Permitted in Nebraska?* Washington: Tower Printers, 1854.

———. *The Salmon P. Chase Papers, volume 1: Journals, 1829-1872*. Edited by John Niven. Kent, OH: Kent State University Press, 1993.

———. *The Salmon P. Chase Papers, volume 2: Correspondence, 1823-1857*. Edited by John Niven. Kent, OH: Kent State University Press, 1993.

Choate, Rufus, and George T. Curtis. *The Old-Line Whigs for Buchanan! Letters of Rufus Choate and George T. Curtis of Massachusetts*. Boston: Boston Courier, 1856.

A Citizen of Vermont. *A Letter to the House of Representatives in Congress Assembled, and to the Citizens of the United States, on the Nebraska Bill*. N.p., 1854 (?).

Cluskey, Michael W. *Buchanan and Breckinridge. The Democratic Hand-Book, Compiled by Mich. W. Cluskey, of Washington City, D.C. Recommended by the Democratic National Committee. The Success of the Democracy essential for the preservation of the Union and the protection of the integrity of the Constitution*. Washington: R.A. Waters, 1856.

Comments on the Nebraska Bill, with Views on Slavery in Contrast with Freedom. Respectfully Addressed to the Free States, by one Acquainted with Southern Institutions. Second edition. Albany, NY: J. Munsell, 1854.

Connelley, William E., ed. "A Visit to Kansas in 1857." *MVHR* 13, n. 4 (March 1927): 541-44.

Conspiracy Disclosed!! Kansas Affairs. Washington: Granite State Club of Washington, 1856.

Convention of Delegates from Kansas Aid Societies. *Report of the Proceedings of a Convention of Delegates from Kansas Aid Societies, in Different States, Held at Cleveland, Ohio, on the 20th and 21st of June, 1856, and Adjourned and held at Buffalo, in the State of New York, on the 9th and 10th Days of July, 1856*. Cleveland (?): 1856.

Conway, Thomas. *Letters of Thomas Conway from the Kansas Territory in 1857 to Mrs. Conway*. Topeka: Kansas State Historical Society, 1958.

Davis, Jefferson. *The Papers of Jefferson Davis, vol. 6: 1856-1860*. Edited by Lynda Lasswell Crist. Baton Rouge: Louisiana State University Press, 1989.

Davis, W.B. *Appeal in Behalf of the Republic, to Southern Rights Gentlemen and Republicans of the North.* Wilmington, NC: 1854.
Democratic National Committee. *The Issue Fairly Presented. The Senate Bill for the Admission of Kansas as a State. Democracy, Law, Order, and the Will of the Majority of the Whole People of the Territory, against Black Republicanism, Usurpation, Revolution, Anarchy, and the Will of a Meagre Minority.* Washington: Printed at the Union Office, 1856.
Democratic Protests against the Lecompton Fraud. Philadelphia: 1858.
"The Dispute with America," [N.p. (July 1856), 111–26]. Edinburgh: William Blackwood and Sons, 1856.
Dixon, James [Chairman]. *Report of the Joint Select Committee on Federal Relations [of the Connecticut General Assembly] on the Kansas and Nebraska Territorial Bill, May, 1854.* New Haven: Babcock & Wildman, State Printers, 1854.
"Documents: Anglo-American Relations, 1853–57: British Statesmen on the Clayton-Bulwer Treaty and American Expansionism." *AHR* 42, n. 3 (April 1937): 491–500.
"Documents: Some Papers of Franklin Pierce, 1852–1862, I." *AHR* 10, n. 1 (October 1904): 110–27.
"Documents: Some Papers of Franklin Pierce, 1852–1862, II." *AHR* 10, n. 2 (January 1905): 350–70.
Douglas, Stephen A. *Letter of Senator Douglas, Vindicating his Character and his Position on the Nebraska Bill against the Assaults Contained in the Proceedings of a Public Meeting Comprised of Twenty-Five Clergymen of Chicago.* Washington: Printed at the Sentinel Office, 1854.
———. *The Letters of Stephen A. Douglas.* Edited by Robert Johannsen. Urbana: University of Illinois Press, 1961.
———. *Popular Sovereignty in the Territories: The Dividing Line between Federal and Local Authority* [reprinted from *Harper's Magazine*, September 1859]. New York: Harper & Brothers, Publishers, 1859.
———. *Popular Sovereignty in the Territories: Judge Douglas in Reply to Judge Black.* Washington: 1859.
Drew, Thomas, compiler. *The Campaign of 1856: Frémont Songs. For the People, Original and Selected.* Boston: John P. Jewett and Company; Cleveland, OH: Jewett, Proctor, and Worthington; New York: Sheldon, Blackeman and Company, 1856.
Eckloff, Christian F. *Memoirs of a Senate Page (1855–1859), edited by Percival G. Melbourne.* New York: Broadway Publishing Company, 1909.
Emerson, Ralph Waldo. *Letters and Social Aims.* Boston: Houghton, Mifflin and Company, 1899; Cambridge: The Riverside Press, 1899.
———. *Society and Solitude: Twelve Chapters.* Boston: Houghton, Mifflin and Company, 1898; Cambridge: The Riverside Press, 1899.
Everett, John and Sarah. "Letters of John and Sarah Everett, 1854–1864: Miami County Pioneers." *KHQ* 8, n. 1 (February 1939): 3–34; n. 2 (May 1939): 143–74; n. 3 (August 1939): 279–310; n. 4 (November 1939): 350–83.
Ewing, Thomas. "The Struggle for Freedom in Kansas." *The Cosmopolitan* 17, n. 1 (May 1894): 76–86.
Fish, Hamilton, and James A. Hamilton. *Frémont the Conservative Candidate: Correspondence between Hon. Hamilton Fish, U.S. Senator from New York, and Hon. James A. Hamilton, Son of Alexander Hamilton.* N.p., 1856.

[Fish, Reeder McCandless.] *The Grim Chieftain of Kansas, and Other Free-State Men in Their Struggles against Slavery. Some Political Seances, Incidents, Inside Political Views and Movements in their Career. By One Who Knows.* Cherryvale, KS: Clarion Book and Job Print, 1885.

Forbes, William T. *In Memoriam: John White Geary.* Philadelphia: W.W. Bates & Co., 1873.

Fremont's Romanism Established; Acknowledged by Archbishop Hughes; How Fremont's Nomination Was Brought About; Hughes, Seward, Fremont, and the Foreigners—a Most Foul Coalition. N.p., 1856.

Gazzam, Edward D., et al. *Report of the Minority of the Select Committee, Relative to the Admission of Kansas into the Union, Made to the Senate of Pennsylvania, March 17, 1858.* Harrisburg: A. Boyd Hamilton, State Printer, 1858.

Gibbens, V.E., ed. "Letters on the War in Kansas in 1856." *KHQ* 10, n. 4 (November 1941): 369–79.

Gihon, John H. *Geary and Kansas: Governor Geary's Administration of Kansas. With a Complete History of the Territory until June 1857.* Philadelphia: J.H.C. Whiting, 1857; Freeport, NY: Books for Libraries Press, 1971.

Gregg, Maxcy. *An Appeal to the State Rights Party of South Carolina in Several Letters on the Present Condition of Public Affairs.* Columbia, SC: Printed at the Office of the Southern Guardian, 1858.

Hale, E.E. *How to Conquer Texas Before Texas Conquers Us.* Boston: Redding & Co., 1845.

Hale, Edward Everett. *Kanzas and Nebraska: The History, Geographical and Physical Characteristics, and Political Position of those Territories; an Account of the Emigrant Aid Companies, and Directions to Emigrants.* Boston: Phillips, Sampson and Company, 1854; Freeport, NY: Books for Libraries Press, 1972.

Hammond, James H. *Speech of Hon. James H. Hammond Delivered at Barnwell Court House, October 29, 1858.* Washington: Henry Polkinhorn, Printer, 1858.

Hanna, Archibald, curator. *Western Americana: Frontier History of the Trans-Mississippi West, 1550-1900.* New Haven, CT: Research Publications, Inc., 1975.

Hawthorne, Nathaniel. *The Life of Franklin Pierce.* Boston: Ticknor, Reed, and Fields, 1852; New York: MSS Information Corporation, 1970.

Hesseltine, William B., and Rex G. Fisher, eds. *Trimmers, Trucklers & Temporizers: Notes of Murat Halstead from the Political Conventions of 1856.* Madison: The State Historical Society of Wisconsin, 1961.

Hollcroft, Temple R., ed. "A Congressman's Letters on the Speaker Election in the Thirty-Fourth Congress." *MVHR* 43, n. 3 (December 1956): 444–58.

Hoole, William Stanley, ed. "A Southerner's Viewpoint of the Kansas Situation, 1856–1857: The Letters of Lieut. Col. A.J. Hoole, C.S.A." *KHQ* 3, n. 1 (February 1934): 43–68; n. 2 (May 1934): 145–71.

Horton, R.G. *The Life and Public Services of James Buchanan.* New York: Derby & Jackson, 1856.

Humphrey, Heman. *The Missouri Compromise: An Address Delivered before the Citizens of Pittsfield by Rev. Heman Humphrey, D.D., in The Baptist Church, on Sabbath Evening, February 26, 1854.* Pittsfield: Reed, Hull, and Pierson, 1854.

Illinois Women's Kansas Aid and Liberty Association. *Constitution and By-Laws of the Illinois Woman's Kansas Aid and Liberty Association, Organized June 10, 1856.* Chicago: Daily Tribune Book and Job Office, 1856.

John Charles Fremont: A California Statement of his Connexion with Palmer, Cook & Co,

Together with a Brief Review of his Military and Financial Career, from the Record. N.p., 1856 (?).
Johnson, Donald Bruce, ed. *National Party Platforms, Volume I: 1840-1956.* Revised edition. Urbana: University of Illinois Press, 1978.
Johnson, William A. *The History of Anderson County, Kansas, from its First Settlement to the Fourth of July, 1876.* Garnett, Kansas: Kauffman & Iler, 1877.
Justice to "Buck": Papers Containing Several Reasons why James Buchanan Should Receive the Distinguished Consideration of the People, by One Who Knows Him Well. Philadelphia: Alex C. Bryson, 1856.
"Kansas A Slave State." *DBR* 20 (1856): 741-44.
"Kansas Matters—Appeal to the South." *DBR* 20 (1856): 635-39.
"The Kansas Question." *PM* 6, n. 4 (October 1855): 425-33.
Kansas Territory Delegate Convention. *Proceedings of the Territorial Delegate Convention, held at Big Springs, on the 5-6th of Sept., 1855.* Lawrence, K.T.: Herald of Freedom Print, 1855.
Langsdorf, Edgar, ed. "The Letters of Joseph H. Trego, 1857-1864, Linn Country Pioneer: Part One, 1857, 1858." *KHQ* 19, n. 2 (May 1951): 113-32.
Laurens, J. Wayne. *The Crisis: or, the Enemies of America Unmasked.* Philadelphia: G.D. Miller, Publisher, 1855.
Lincoln, Abraham. *The Collected Works of Abraham Lincoln.* Edited by Roy P. Basler. New Brunswick, NJ: Rutgers University Press, 1953.
Longstreet, A.B. *Know Nothingism Unveiled: Letter of Judge A.B. Longstreet, of Mississippi, Addressed to Rev. William Winans, in Reply to a Communication Published by Him in the Natchez (Mississippi) Courier, and addressed to Judge Longstreet, on the subject of Know Nothingism.* Washington: Printed at the Office of the Congressional Globe, 1855.
Lovejoy, Joseph C. *The True Democracy: A Speech delivered at East Cambridge, September 29, 1856.* Cambridge (?), 1856.
Lovejoy, Julia Louisa. "Letters for Kanzas." *KHQ* 11, n. 1 (February 1942): 29-44.
———. "Letters of Julia Louisa Lovejoy, 1856-1864: Part One, 1856." *KHQ* 15, n. 2 (May 1947): 127-42; "Part Two, 1857," n. 3 (August 1947): 277-319; "Part Three, 1858," n. 4 (November 1947): 368-403; "Part Four, 1859," 16, n. 1 (February 1948): 40-75; "Part Five, 1960-1964," n. 2 (May 1948): 175-211.
Maclay, William B. *Letters from the Hon. William B. Maclay, Member of Congress from Fifth District of New York, on the Admission of Kansas under the Lecompton Constitution.* New York (?): 1858 (?).
Marsh, Leonard. *A Bake-Pan for Dough-Faces. By One of Them.* Burlington, VT: C. Goodrich, 1854.
Martin, George W. *The First Two Years of Kansas, or Where, When and How the Missouri Bushwhacker, the Missouri Train and Bank Robber, and Those Who Stole Themselves Rich in the Name of Liberty, were Sired and Reared.* Topeka: State Printing Office, 1907.
Martineau, Harriet. *Harriet Martineau in the London Daily News: Selected Contributions, 1852-1866.* Edited by Elisabeth Sanders Arbuckle. New York & London: Garland Publishing, Inc., 1994.
Massachusetts Republican Convention. *Republican Campaign Documents, for the People to Read.* Boston: A.J. Wright, Printer, 1855.

Memorial Addresses on the Death of Gov. John W. Geary, Delivered in the Senate and House of Representatives of the Commonwealth of Pennsylvania and Attendant Obsequies, February, 1873. Harrisburg: Benjamin Singerly, State Printer, 1873.
Merrill, O.N. *True History of the Kansas Wars, and their Origin, Progress and Incidents*. Cincinnati: J.R. Telfer, 1856.
Moore, Hugh M. "Letters of Hugh M. Moore, 1856–1860." *KHQ* 10, n. 2 (May 1941): 115–23.
Morton, John A. "The Progress of Kansas." *NAR* 142, n. 352 (April 1886): 348–55.
National Democratic Convention. *Official Proceedings of the National Democratic Convention, Held in Cincinnati, June 2–6, 1856. Published by Order of the Convention*. Cincinnati: Enquirer Company Steam Printing Establishment, 1856.
Nelson, J. *A Discourse on the Proposed Repeal of the Missouri Compromise; Delivered on Fast Day, April 6, 1854, in the First Congregational Church, in Leicester, Mass*. Worcester, MA: Edward R. Fiske, 1854.
New England Emigrant Aid Company. *Information for the People: Two Tracts of the Times. The One Entitled "Negro-Slavery, No Evil": by B.F. Stringfellow, of Missouri. The Other, An Answer to the Inquiry "Is it Expedient to Introduce Slavery into Kanzas?" by D.R. Goodloe, of North Carolina*. Boston: Alfred Mudge and Son, Printers, 1855.
"The New Governor of Kansas." *HW* (April 11, 1857), 229–30.
New York State Democratic Party. *Proceedings and Address, of the Democratic State Convention, held at Syracuse, January Tenth and Eleventh, 1856*. Albany: 1856.
"Our New President." *PM* 2, n. 9 (September 1853): 301–10.
"Our New President: Editor's Note." *PM* 2, n. 10 (October 1853): 445.
"Our Parties and Politics." *PM* 4, n. 21 (September 1854): 233–46.
Palfrey, John Gorham. *Letter to a Whig Neighbor, on the Approaching State Election, by an Old Conservative*. Boston: Crosby, Nichols, and Company, 1855.
Parker, John A. "The Secret History of the Kansas-Nebraska Bill." *NQR* 7, n. 13, of second series (July 1880): 105–18.
Parker, Theodore. *Theodore Parker: An Anthology*. Edited by Henry Steele Commager. Boston: Beacon Press, 1960.
Pennsylvania State Democratic Party. *Proceedings of the Pennsylvania Democratic Convention, Held at Harrisburg, March 4th, 1856. Reported by James B. Sheridan*. Philadelphia: Wm. Rice, Pennsylvanian Office, Printer, 1856.
Phillips, Ulrich B., ed. *Annual Report of the American Historical Association for the Year 1911, Vol. II: The Correspondence of Robert Toombs, Alexander H. Stephens, and Howell Cobb*. Washington: 1913.
Pierce, Franklin. *Franklin Pierce Papers, 1820–1869*. Washington: Library of Congress Photoduplication Service, 1960.
"The Political Aspect." *PM* 8 (July 1856): 85–94.
"The Political Crisis in the United States." *ERCJ*, American edition, 45, n. 2 (October 1856): 289–307.
Proceedings of a Public Meeting of the Citizens of Providence, Held in the Beneficent Congregational Church, March 7, 1854, to Protest against Slavery in Nebraska; with the Addresses of the Speakers. Providence, RI: Knowles, Anthony & Co., Printers, 1854.
Publications of the Kansas State Historical Society. Volume 1. Topeka, KS: T.D. Thacher, State Printer, 1886.
Raymond, James. *Political: or, the Spirit of Democracy in '56*. Baltimore: John W. Woods, Printer, 1857.

Read, John M. *Speech of Hon. John M. Read, on the Power of Congress over the Territories, in Favor of Free Kansas, Free Labor, and of Fremont and Dayton, at the Eighth Ward Mass Meeting, Held in the Assembly Buildings, on Tuesday Evening, September 30, 1856.* Philadelphia: C. Sherman & Son, 1856.

Reed, William B. *The Appeal to Pennsylvania: A Speech by William B. Reed, Delivered at a Meeting of the Friends of Buchanan and Breckenridge, at Somerset, PA., September 24, 1856.* Philadelphia: 1856.

Reeder, Andrew H. *A Letter from Governor Reeder on the Approaching Election of the President and the Candidates.* New York: John W. Oliver, Steam Printer, 1856.

The Reign of Terror in Kanzas: By Which Men Have been Murdered and Scalped; Ministers of the Gospel Tarred and Feathered; Women Dragged from their Homes and Violated; Printing Offices and Private Houses Burned; Citizens Robbed, &c., by Border Ruffians. Boston: Charles W. Briggs, 1856.

Republican Scrap Book; Containing the Platforms, and a Choice Selection of Extracts, Setting Forth the Real Questions in Issue, the Opinions of the Candidates, the Nature and Design of the Slave Oligarchy, as Shown by Their Own Writers, and the Opinions of Clay, Webster, Josiah Quincy, and Other Patriots, on Slavery and Its Extensions. Boston: John P. Jewett & Co., 1856.

Rice, Harvey Dwight. *Reminiscences: Read Before the Congregational Pioneer Society of Topeka.* Topeka?, Kansas: n.p., 189_ (?).

Richmond, Richard W. "A Free-Stater's 'Letters to the Editor': Samuel N. Wood's Letters to Eastern Newspapers, 1854." *KHQ* 23, n. 2 (Summer 1957): 181-91.

Robinson, Charles. *The Kansas Conflict.* Lawrence, KS: Journal Publishing Company, 1898; Freeport, NY: Books for Libraries Press, 1972.

Rogers, Elymas Payson. *The Repeal of the Missouri Compromise Considered.* Newark, NJ: A. Stephen Holbrook, Printer, 1856.

Ryland, Robert. *The American Union: An Address, Delivered before the Alumni Association of the Columbian College, D.C., June 23, 1857.* Richmond, VA: H.K. Ellyson, 1857.

St. Matthew, J.H. "Walker's Administration in Kansas." *OM* 5, n. 6 (December 1870): 544-56.

Sanborn, F.B. "Negro Slavery in Kansas and Missouri." *MHS* (March 1911): 505-18.

Schoonover, Ebba, and Thomas Schoonover. "Documents: Bleeding Kansas and Spanish Cuba in 1857, A Postscript." *KH* 11, n. 4 (Winter 1988-1989): 240-42.

Seward, William H. *Speeches of William H. Seward, Delivered at Albany and at Buffalo, in October, 1855.* Washington: The Republican Association, 1855.

Sherman, John. *John Sherman's Recollections of Forty Years in the House, Senate and Cabinet. An Autobiography.* Volume 1. Chicago: The Werner Company, 1895.

Smith, Nathan, ed. "Letters of a Free-State Man in Kansas, 1856." *KHQ* 21, n. 3 (Autumn 1954): 166-72.

Socolofsky, Homer E., and Huber Self. *Historical Atlas of Kansas.* 2nd ed. Norman: University of Oklahoma Press, 1972, 1988.

A Southern Citizen [Reverdy Johnson]. *Remarks on Popular Sovereignty, as Maintained and Denied Respectively by Judge Douglas, and Attorney-General Black.* Baltimore: Murphy & Co. Printers and Publishers, 1859.

Southern Commercial Convention. *Proceedings of the Southern Commercial Convention, held in The City of New Orleans, on the 8th, 9th, 10th, 11th, 12th, 13th and 15th of January, 1855; embracing Resolutions, Speeches, General Transactions, etc. etc. etc.,*

Especially Reported for the New Orleans Daily Crescent. New Orleans: Office of the Crescent, 1855.
"Southern Development of Kansas." *DBR* 21 (1856): 95–97.
Speer, John. *Life of Gen. James H. Lane, "The Liberator of Kansas," with Corroborative Incidents of Pioneer History.* Garden City, KS: John Speer, Printer, 1896.
Sperber, Hans, and Travis Trittschuh. *American Political Terms: An Historical Dictionary.* Detroit: Wayne State University Press, 1962.
Spring, Leverett W. "The Career of a Kansas Politician." *AHR* 4, n. 1 (October 1898): 80–104.
———. "Kansas and the Abolition of Slavery." *MWH* 9, n. 1 (November 1888): 78–95.
Starr, Rev. Frederick [writing as Lynceus]. *Letters for the People on the Present Crisis.* New York, 1853.
The State of the Union: Being a Complete Documentary History of the Public Affairs of the United States, Foreign and Domestic, for the Year 1854. Washington: Taylor & Maury, 1855.
Stringfellow, Benjamin. *Slavery in Kansas: Letter from B.F. Stringfellow, in reply to one addressed to him by the Hon. P.S. Brooks, Thomas Clingman, Wm. Smith, and John McQueen.* Washington: Printed at the Sentinel Office, 1855.
Sumner, Charles. *The Selected Letters of Charles Sumner.* Edited by Beverly Wilson Palmer. Boston: Northeastern University Press, 1990.
———. *The Slave Oligarchy and its Usurpations: Speech of Hon. Charles Sumner, November 2, 1855, in Faneuil Hall, Boston.* Washington: Buell & Blanchard, Printers, 1855.
Swackhamer, Conrad, ed. "The Admission of Kansas." *USDR* 41, n. 3 (March 1858): 175–86.
———. "Kansas Congressional Record." *USDR* 41, n. 6 (June 1858): 440–65.
———. "Republican Inconsistency." *USDR* 41, n. 6 (June 1858): 438–40.
Taylor, Nathaniel, et al. *The New Haven Memorial to the President, Protesting against the use of the United-States Army to Enforce the Bogus Laws of Kansas; The Answer of President Buchanan; and the Reply of the Memorialists.* Boston: John Wilson and Son, 1858.
The Territorial Slavery Question. Non-Intervention Principle. Position of the National Democracy. N.p., n.d., 1854 (?).
Thayer, Eli. *The New England Emigrant Aid Company and its Influence, Through the Kansas Contest, Upon National History.* Worcester, MA: Franklin P. Rice, 1887.
Tomlinson, William P. *Kansas in Eighteen Fifty-eight: Being Chiefly a History of the Recent Troubles in that Territory.* New York: H. Dayton, 1859.
Transactions of the Kansas State Historical Society. Volumes 3–5. Topeka: Kansas Publishing House, 1886–1896.
The Tribune Almanac for the Years 1838 to 1868, Inclusive; Comprehending The Politician's Register and The Whig Almanac. Volume 2. New York: The New York Tribune, 1868.
Twining, Alexander C. *The Nebraska Bill, and its Results.* [*NE*, May 1854].
[Underhill, Edward F.] *The Life and Public Services of Hon. James Buchanan, of Pennsylvania.* New York: Livermore & Rudd, 1856.
Union Anti-Lecompton Mass Meeting. *Proceedings of the Union Anti-Lecompton Mass Meeting of the Citizens of Erie County, N.Y. Opposed to the Policy of the National Administration, Held at St. James Hall, Buffalo, Thursday, May 27th, 1858.* Buffalo: Commercial Advertiser Steam Press, 1858.
"The Voice of Kansas—Let the South Respond." *DBR* 21 (1856): 187–94.

Walker, Robert J. *An Appeal for Union. Letter from the Hon. Robert J. Walker.* New York: Steam Book and Job Printer, 1856.

———. *Inaugural Address of Hon. Robert J. Walker, Governor of Kansas Territory: Delivered in Lecompton, May 27, 1857.* Lawrence, KS: Herald of Freedom Steam Press Print, 1857.

"The War Against the South." *DBR* 21 (1856): 271–77.

Wayland, Francis. *Dr. Wayland on the Moral and Religious Aspects of the Nebraska Bill: Speech at Providence, RI, March 7, 1854.* Rochester, NY: William N. Sage, 1854.

Webb, J. Watson. *Speech of General J. Watson Webb, at the Great Mass Meeting on the Battle Ground of Tippecanoe, 60,000 Freemen in Council.* New York: 1856.

Wells, Eugene T. "Jefferson Davis and Kansas Territory." *KHQ* 22, n. 4 (Winter 1956): 354–57.

Whitman, Walt. *The Eighteenth Presidency! A Critical Text edited by Edward F. Grier.* Lawrence: University Press of Kansas, 1956.

Wilder, Daniel Webster. *The Annals of Kansas.* Topeka: T. Dwight Thacher, Kansas Publishing House, 1886; New York: Arno Press, 1975.

Willey, Waitman T. *Lecture on Liberty and Union! Delivered in Wheeling, Jan. 17, 1854 by Waitman T. Willey, Esq., of Monongalia County, Virginia.* Wheeling, VA: J.E. Wharton, 1854.

Wise, Henry A. *Territorial Government, and the Admission of New States into the Union: A Historical and Constitutional Treatise by Henry A. Wise, Governor of Virginia.* Richmond (?): 1859.

Worner, William Frederick. "Letters of James Buchanan." In *Papers Read Before the Lancaster County Historical Society* 36, n. 12 (1932).

II. Secondary Sources

A. Books and Articles

Auchampaugh, Philip G. "The Buchanan-Douglas Feud." *JISHS* 25 (April 1932–January 1933): 5–48.

———. "James Buchanan, The Conservatives' Choice, 1856: A Political Portrait." *TH* 7, n. 2 (Spring 1945): 77–90.

Bailes, Kendall E. *Rider on the Wind: Jim Lane and Kansas.* Shawnee Mission, KS: The Wagon Wheel Press, 1962.

Barns, George C. *Denver, the Man: The Life, Letters and Public Papers of the Lawyer, Soldier and Statesman.* Wilmington, OH: Shenandoah Publishing House, 1949.

Barry, Louise. "The Emigrant Aid Company Parties of 1854." *KHQ* 12, n. 2 (May 1943): 115–56.

———. "The Emigrant Aid Company Parties of 1855." *KHQ* 12, n. 3 (August 1943): 227–68.

Bloom, John Porter, ed. *The American Territorial System.* Athens: Ohio University Press, 1973.

Boritt, Gabor S., ed. *Why the Civil War Came.* New York: Oxford University Press, 1996.

Carter, Clarence E. "Colonialism in Continental United States." *SAQ* 47 (1948): 16–28.

———. "The Territorial Papers of the United States: A Review and Commentary." *MVHR* 42 (1955): 510–24.

Cecil-Fronsman, Bill. "'Advocate the Freedom of White Men, As Well As That of Negroes':

The *Kansas Free State* and Antislavery Westerners in Territorial Kansas." *KH* 20, n. 2 (Summer 1997): 102–15.

———. "'Death to All Yankees and Traitors in Kansas': The *Squatter Sovereign* and the Defense of Slavery in Kansas." *KH* 16, n. 1 (Spring 1993): 22–33.

Collins, Bruce W. "The Democrats' Electoral Fortunes during the Lecompton Crisis." *CWH* 24, n. 4 (December 1978): 314–31.

Craik, Elmer LeRoy. "Southern Interest in Territorial Kansas: 1854–1858." *Collections of the Kansas Historical Society* 15 (1922): 334–450.

Davis, William C. *Breckinridge: Statesman, Soldier, Symbol.* Baton Rouge: Louisiana State University Press, 1974.

Dodd, William Edward. *Robert J. Walker, Imperialist.* Gloucester, MA: Peter Smith, 1967; Chicago: The Lakeside Press, R.R. Donnelley & Sons Co., 1914.

Dolbee, Cora. "The First Book on Kansas: The Story of Edward Everett Hale's 'Kansas and Nebraska.'" *KHQ* 2, n. 2 (May 1933): 139–81.

Elbert, E. Duane. "The English Bill: An Attempt to Compromise the Lecompton Dilemma." *KH* 1, n. 4 (Winter 1978): 219–34.

Etcheson, Nicole. *Bleeding Kansas: Contested Liberty in the Civil War Era.* Lawrence: University Press of Kansas, 2004.

———. "'Labouring for the Freedom of This Territory': Free-State Kansas Women in the 1850s." *KH* 21, n. 2 (Summer 1998): 68–87.

———. "Novelists Revisit Territorial Kansas: A Review Essay." *KH* 21, n. 4 (Winter 1998–1999): 276–82.

Fessenden, Francis. *Life and Public Services of William Pitt Fessenden, volume one.* Boston and New York: Houghton, Mifflin and Company, 1907.

Fleming, Walter L. "The Buford Expedition to Kansas." *AHR* 6, n. 1 (October 1900): 38–48.

Franz, Joe B. "The Forty-Eighth Annual Meeting of the Mississippi Valley Historical Association." *MVHR* 42, n. 2 (September 1955): 288–309.

Gaeddert, G. Raymond. "First Newspapers in Kansas Counties: 1854–1864." *KHQ* 10, n. 1 (February 1941): 3–33.

Gates, Paul Wallace. *Fifty Million Acres: Conflicts over Kansas Land Policy, 1854–1890.* Ithaca, NY: Cornell University Press, 1954.

Gienapp, William E. *The Origins of the Republican Party, 1852–1856.* New York: Oxford University Press, 1987.

Gittinger, Roy. "The Separation of Nebraska and Kansas from the Indian Territory." *MVHR* 3, n. 4 (March 1917): 442–61.

Hamlin, Charles Eugene. *The Life and Times of Hannibal Hamlin.* Cambridge: Riverside Press, 1899.

Harlow, Ralph Volney. "The Rise and Fall of the Kansas Aid Movement." *AHR* 41, n. 1 (October 1935): 1–25.

Harrington, Fred Harvey, ed. "A Note on the Ray Explanation of the Origin of the Kansas-Nebraska Act." *MVHR* 25, n. 1 (June 1938): 79–81.

Hart, Charles Desmont. "The National Limits of Slavery Expansion, Kansas-Nebraska, 1854." *KHQ* 34, n. 1 (Spring 1968): 32–50.

Haynes, George H. "The Causes of Know-Nothing Success in Massachusetts." *AHR* 3, n. 1 (October 1897): 67–82.

Hickman, Russell K. "Lewis Bodwell, Frontier Preacher; The Early Years." *KHQ* 12, n. 3 (August 1943): 269–99; 12, n. 4 (November 1943): 349–65.

———. "The Reeder Administration Inaugurated, Part I—The Delegate Election of November, 1854." *KHQ* 36, n. 3 (August 1970): 305-40.
———. "The Reeder Administration Inaugurated, Part II—The Census of Early 1855." *KHQ* 36, n. 4 (Winter 1970): 424-55.
Hodder, Frank Heywood. "Genesis of the Kansas-Nebraska Act." *Wisconsin Historical Society, Proceedings* (1912), 69-86.
———. "The Railroad Background of the Kansas-Nebraska Act." *MVHR* 12, n. 1 (June 1925): 3-22.
———. "Some Aspects of the English Bill for the Admission of Kansas." *Annual Report of the American Historical Association for the Year 1906*, vol. 1 (Washington: Government Printing Office, 1908), 201-10.
Ingalls, John James. "Kansas: 1854-1891." *HNMM* 86, n. 515 (April 1893): 696-713.
Isley, W.H. "The Sharps Rifle Episode in Kansas History." *AHR* 12, n. 3 (April 1907): 546-66.
Johannsen, Robert W. *Frontier Politics and the Sectional Conflict: The Pacific Northwest on the Eve of the Civil War.* Seattle: University of Washington Press, 1955.
———. "James C. Malin: An Appreciation." *KHQ* 38, n. 4 (Winter 1972): 457-66.
———. "The Lecompton Constitutional Convention: An Analysis of Its Membership." *KHQ* 23, n. 3 (Autumn 1957): 225-43.
———. *Stephen A. Douglas.* New York: Oxford University Press, 1973.
———. "Stephen A. Douglas, 'Harper's Magazine,' and Popular Sovereignty." *MVHR* 45, n. 4 (March 1959): 606-31.
———, ed. "A Footnote to the Pottawatomie Massacre, 1856." *KHQ* 22, n. 3 (Autumn 1956): 236-41.
Johnson, David W. "Freesoilers for God: Kansas Newspaper Editors and the Antislavery Crusade." *KH* 2, n. 2 (Summer 1979): 74-85.
Johnson, Samuel A. *The Battle Cry of Freedom: The New England Emigrant Aid Company in the Kansas Crusade.* Westport, CT: Greenwood Press, 1954.
Klein, Philip Shriver. *President James Buchanan: A Biography.* University Park: Pennsylvania State University Press, 1962.
Klunder, Willard Carl. *Lewis Cass and the Politics of Moderation.* Kent, OH: Kent State University Press, 1996.
Lathin, Reinhard H. "Salmon P. Chase's Political Career before the Civil War." *MVHR* 29, n. 4 (March 1943): 517-40.
Learned, Henry Barret. "The Relation of Philip Phillips to the Repeal of the Missouri Compromise in 1854." *MVHR* 8, n. 4 (March 1922): 303-17.
Luthin, Reinhard H. "The Democratic Split During Buchanan's Administration." *PH* 11, n. 1 (January 1944): 13-35.
Madden, John L. "The Financing of a New Territory: The Kansas Territorial Tax Structure, 1854-1861." *KHQ* 35, n. 2 (Summer 1969): 155-64.
Malin, James C. *John Brown and the Legend of Fifty-Six.* Philadelphia: The American Philosophical Society, 1942.
———. "Judge Lecompte and the 'Sack of Lawrence,' May 21, 1856." *KHQ* 20, n. 7 (August 1953): 465-94; 20, n. 8 (November 1953): 553-97.
———. "The Motives of Stephen A. Douglas in the Organization of Nebraska Territory: A Letter Dated December 17, 1853." *KHQ* 19, n. 4 (November 1951): 321-53.
———. "Notes on the Writing of General Histories of Kansas." *KHQ* 21, n. 3 (Autumn 1954): 184-223; n. 4 (Winter 1954): 264-87; n. 5 (Spring 1955): 331-78; n. 6 (Sum-

mer 1955), 407–44; n. 8 (Winter 1955), 598–643.
———. "The Proslavery Background of the Kansas Struggle." *MVHR* 10, n. 3 (December 1923): 284–305.
Meerse, David E. "The 1857 Kansas Territorial Delegate Election Contest." *KH* 4, n. 2 (Summer 1981): 96–113.
———. "The Northern Democratic Party and the Congressional Elections of 1858." *CWH* 19, n. 2 (June 1973): 119–37.
———. "Origins of the Douglas-Buchanan Feud Reconsidered." *JISHS* 67 (April 1974): 154–74.
Meigs, William M. *The Life of Thomas Hart Benton*. Philadelphia and London: J.B. Lippincott Company, 1904.
Miller, Nyle H., Edgar Langsdorf, and Robert W. Richmond. *Kansas in Newspapers*. Topeka: Kansas State Historical Society, 1963.
Morrison, Michael A. *Slavery and the American West: The Eclipse of Manifest Destiny and the Coming of the Civil War*. Chapel Hill: University of North Carolina Press, 1997.
Mullis, Tony. *Peacekeeping on the Plains: Army Operations in Bleeding Kansas*. Columbia: University of Missouri Press, 2004.
Neely, Jeremy. *The Border between Them: Violence and Reconciliation on the Kansas-Missouri Line*. Columbia: University of Missouri Press, 2007.
Nevins, Allan. *The Emergence of Lincoln: Douglas, Buchanan, and Party Chaos, 1857–1859*. New York: Charles Scribner's Sons, 1950.
Nichols, Alice. *Bleeding Kansas*. New York: Oxford University Press, 1954.
Nichols, Roy Franklin. *The Democratic Machine, 1850–1854*. New York: Columbia University Press, 1923.
———. *Franklin Pierce: Young Hickory of the Granite Hill*. Philadelphia: University of Pennsylvania Press, 1931.
———. "The Kansas-Nebraska Act: A Century of Historiography." *MVHR* 43, n. 2 (September 1956): 189–212.
Nichols, Roy Franklin, and Eugene H. Berwanger. *The Stakes of Power, 1845–1877*. Revised edition. New York: Hill and Wang, 1961, 1982.
O'Connor, Thomas H. "Cotton Whigs in Kansas." *KHQ* 26, n. 1 (Spring 1960): 34–58.
Oertel, Kristen Tegtmeier. *Bleeding Borders: Race, Gender, and Violence in Pre–Civil War Kansas*. Baton Rouge: Louisiana State University Press, 2009.
Ostrander, Gilman M. "Emerson, Thoreau, and John Brown." *MVHR* 39, n. 4 (March 1953): 713–26.
Parks, Joseph Howard. *John Bell of Tennessee*. Baton Rouge: Louisiana State University Press, 1950.
———. "The Tennessee Whigs and the Kansas-Nebraska Bill." *JSH* 10, n. 3 (August 1944): 308–30.
Parrish, William E. *David Rice Atchison: Border Politician*. Columbia: University of Missouri Press, 1961.
Paxton, Frederic L. *History of the American Frontier: 1763–1893*. Boston and New York: Houghton Mifflin Company, 1924.
Pomeroy, Earl S. *The Territories and the United States: 1861–1890*. Philadelphia: University of Pennsylvania Press, 1947.
———. "The Territory as a Frontier Institution." *TH* 7, n. 1 (Autumn 1944): 29–41.
———. "Toward a Reorientation of Western History: Continuity and Environment." *MVHR* 41 (March 1955): 579–600.
Potter, David M. *The Impending Crisis: 1848–1861*. New York: Harper & Row, 1976.

Russel, Robert R. "The Issues in the Congressional Struggle over the Kansas-Nebraska Bill, 1854." *JSH* 29, n. 2 (May 1963): 187–210.

———. "The Pacific Railway Issue in Politics Prior to the Civil War." *MVHR* 12, n. 2 (September 1925): 187–201.

Seiler, William H. "Magazine Writers Look at Kansas, 1854–1904." *KHQ* 38, n. 1 (Spring 1972): 1–24.

SenGupta, Gunja. *For God & Mammon: Evangelicals and Entrepreneurs, Masters and Slaves in Territorial Kansas, 1854–1860*. Athens: University of Georgia Press, 1996.

Shenton, James P. *Robert John Walker: A Politician from Jackson to Lincoln*. New York: Columbia University Press, 1961.

Socolofsky, Homer E. *Kansas Governors*. Lawrence: University Press of Kansas, 1990.

Stampp, Kenneth M. *America in 1857: A Nation on the Brink*. New York: Oxford University Press, 1990.

Stenberg, Richard R. "An Unnoted Factor in the Buchanan-Douglas Feud." *JISHS* 25, n. 4 (January 1933): 271–84.

Stephenson, Wendell Holmes. "The Political Career of General James H. Lane." *Publications of the Kansas State Historical Society* (Topeka: Kansas State Printing Plant, 1930), 3:1–196.

Stewart, James Brewer. *Joshua R. Giddings and the Tactics of Radical Politics*. Cleveland and London: The Press of Case Western Reserve University, 1970.

Sutherland, Keith. "Congress and the Kansas Issue in 1860." *KHQ* 35, n. 1 (Spring 1969): 17–29.

Territorial Kansas: Studies Commemorating the Centennial. Lawrence: University of Kansas Publications, Social Science Studies, 1954.

Tinkcom, Harry Marlin. *John White Geary: Soldier-Statesman, 1819–1873*. Philadelphia: University of Pennsylvania Press, 1940.

Watts, Dale E. "How Bloody Was Bleeding Kansas? Political Killings in Kansas Territory, 1854–1861." *KH* 18, n. 2 (Summer 1995): 116–29.

———. "Plows and Bibles, Rifles and Revolvers: Guns in Kansas Territory." *KH* 21, n. 1 (Spring 1998): 31–45.

Weisberger, Bernard A. "The Newspaper Reporter and the Kansas Imbroglio." *MVHR* 36, n. 4 (March 1950): 633–56.

Wells, Thomas C. "Letters of a Kansas Pioneer: 1855–1860." *KHQ* 5, n. 2 (May 1936): 143–79; n. 3 (August 1936): 282–324; n. 4 (November 1936): 381–418.

Wilson, Don W. "Barbed Words on the Frontier: Early Kansas Newspaper Editors." *KH* 1, n. 3 (Autumn 1978): 147–54.

Wolff, Gerald W. *The Kansas-Nebraska Bill: Party, Section, and the Coming of the Civil War*. New York: Revisionist Press, 1977.

Zornow, William Frank. *Kansas: A History of the Jayhawk State*. Norman: University of Oklahoma Press, 1957.

B. Unpublished Material

Day, Donald Eugene. "A Life of Wilson Shannon, Governor of Ohio, Diplomat, Territorial Governor of Kansas." PhD. diss., Ohio State University, 1978.

Youngstrom, Gustaf Adolph. "The Official Career of Andrew Horatio Reeder in Kansas." Master's thesis, Northwestern University, 1931.

Index

abolitionists, 17, 23, 25, 33–34, 37, 41–43, 48, 54–55, 75, 80, 92, 111, 114, 122, 134–35, 141, 155, 158–59, 169, 174, 203, 206
Adams, Stephen, 28, 121
African Americans: enslaved in Kansas: 42, 46, 51, 54, 57, 155, 164, 166, 179, 252n49, 277n105; free in Kansas: 46, 57, 252n49; enslaved in Missouri, 13, 42
American Indians: affected by Kansas-Nebraska Act, 30, 34, 39, 57; tribes in Kansas, 39, 46, 48, 104; American policy towards, 38, 40, 96, 120, 123, 125, 246
American (Know-Nothing) Party, 7, 35–36, 100, 128, 132, 144–45, 182, 186, 200, 208
anti-Lecompton movement, 180–82, 186
anti-Nebraska movement, 20, 25–29, 30, 32, 35–36, 57. *See also* Appendix F
antislavery, 7, 33, 43, 46, 52, 77, 83, 101, 115, 149, 151, 155–56, 158, 160, 166, 182, 208; in Kansas, 3, 41, 43, 52–55, 88–89, 92, 105, 108, 116, 126, 151, 155, 164, 167, 204, 212. *See also* abolitionists; Republican Party; Topeka Government
Appeal of the Independent Democrats, 16–17, 21, 27
Atchison, David, 13, 17, 44–45, 47, 52, 54–56, 58, 74, 75, 85, 119, 131, 141, 195. *See also* border ruffians

Banks, Nathaniel, 77, 101, 108, 132, 138, 139
Bell, John, 21, 32–34
Benton, Thomas Hart, 22, 32
Big Springs convention, 53, 56, 111
Bigler, William, 93, 118, 135
Bingham, John, 61, 107
Black, Jeremiah, 160, 167, 171, 179, 184, 192

Bleeding Kansas, 3, 85, 97, 119, 195, 200. *See also* Chapters 3 and 5
border ruffians, 48, 56, 74, 80, 87, 105, 112–13, 123, 131, 141, 143, 145, 151–52, 161
Boyce, William, 104, 106
Branson, Jacob, 59–60, 77
Breckinridge, John, 15, 25, 29, 137–38, 147, 197
Brooks, Preston, 22, 113, 127, 136, 141–43, 259n 88, 271nn61 & 62
Brown, George, 78, 88, 141, 162
Brown, John, 80, 85, 113
Bryant, William Cullen, 142, 146
Buchanan, James, 5, 6, 71, 91, 95, 158, 165, 167–68, 176, 188–89, 195, 197, 199, 206–7, 209–10, 213; and election of 1856, 136–37, 140, 142–47, 203–4; views on Kansas troubles, 95, 148–50, 154–55, 170, 179, 186, 195–97; relationship with Robert Walker, 150, 154–55, 159–60, 181–82, 185; on the Lecompton Constitution, 159–60, 164–65, 168, 170–76, 179–80, 182, 184–88, 192, 195–97, 204–5; break with Stephen Douglas, 181, 185, 192, 206
Buford, James, 8, 58, 200
Butler, Andrew, 13, 19, 28, 142
Butler, Pardee, 110

Calhoun, John, 58, 86, 92, 131, 155, 159, 164–65
Campbell, Lewis, 30, 102, 124
Cass, Lewis, 15, 17–19, 32, 117; as Secretary of State, 151–52, 157–59, 161–63, 167, 171–72, 182, 185, 189–91, 193
Cato, Sterling, 90–91, 164, 166
Chapman, John Butler, 48–49
Charleston Mercury, 15, 27, 36, 132, 147, 158, 180, 211
Chase, Salmon, 16, 17, 20, 25, 29–30, 34, 54, 163

Clarke, George, 55, 61, 75–76
Clayton, John, 19
Clayton Amendment to Kansas-Nebraska bill, 20, 22, 24, 33
clergy, 21, 27–29, 37, 58, 141, 248n102, 249n147
Cobb, Howell, 34, 38, 137, 155, 158, 165, 171, 185, 187, 192, 196
Colburn, Jonas, 78, 91, 144
Coleman, Franklin, 59
Colfax, Schulyer, 123, 151
Compromise of 1820. *See* Missouri Compromise
Compromise of 1850, 7, 9, 11–16, 18–19, 99, 120, 128, 137, 144, 202, 208, 212
Congress: and territorial policy, 4, 40, 76, 99–102, 117, 119–20, 149–50, 186, 211; actions regarding Kansas, 6, 46, 73, 132, 161, 187, 189, 194–95, 208–10. *See also* Chapters 1, 4, and 7
Cooke, Philip, 82, 84, 96
Cooper, Samuel, 80, 124
Covode Committee, 163, 165, 210
Cox, Samuel, 185–87
Crittenden, John, 117, 121, 184
Crittenden Resolution, 120–29, 184, 186, 187
Cumback, William, 93, 107–8, 123, 146–47
Cushing, Caleb, 15, 49
Cutting, Francis, 24–26

Davis, Jefferson, 48, 50, 74, 81, 96, 120, 122, 123
Deitzler, George W., 78
Democratic Party: divisions within, 9–12, 25, 31, 34, 36, 38, 196, 207, 209 (*see also* the Lecompton Constitution); damaged by Kansas issue, 5–7, 35, 38, 52, 55, 80, 86, 113, 127–28, 130, 132, 134, 178, 183, 188, 195, 197, 208–10 (*see also* Chapter 5); in Kansas, 53, 55, 63, 86, 89, 91–95, 118, 131, 159, 164, 166, 169, 192, 194–95; drift of Democrats to opposition, 55, 69, 97, 206, 208–9; and Kansas-Nebraska Act, 16, 40, 127 (*see also* Chapter 1)
Denver, James, 176–79, 184–85, 189–94, 206

Dixon, Archibald, 14–15, 19–21
Donelson, Israel, 77–79, 88, 91–92
Douglas, Stephen, 53, 99, 115, 118–19, 125–26, 159, 185–86, 207; and Kansas-Nebraska Act, 12–18, 20–22, 24, 28–29, 34, 36–38, 202, 207; presidential ambitions of, 12, 18, 136–37, 185; and the Lecompton Constitution, 159–60, 181–84; break with Buchanan, 181, 183, 192, 206
Douglas Democrats, 186, 192, 196, 209
Dow, Charles, 59
Dred Scott decision, 149, 196–97

elections, local
—for delegate: 1854, 3–4, 44–46; 1855, 56–57, 73, 100, 102–14; 1857, 161–66, 173. *See* Appendix F. *See also* Reeder, Andrew; Whitfield, John
—for territorial legislature: 1855, 3–4, 46–47, 50–51, 56–58, 73, 100, 131; 1857, 157, 161–64, 166, 170
—alternative elections organized by Topeka Government, 52, 56, 73, 75, 169, 179. *See also* Topeka Government
—residency requirements, 4, 44, 47, 162, 177
—fraud in, 3–5, 44, 46–47, 50, 57, 63, 75–76, 89, 94, 101, 105–6, 130, 132, 139, 146, 149, 150–51, 154, 162–64, 169, 170, 173, 177, 183, 197, 203, 211–12
—referenda on Lecompton Constitution, 167, 169–70, 177, 180
—referendum on the English Bill, 192
—for constitutional convention delegates. *See* Leavenworth Constitution; Lecompton Constitution; Topeka Constitution; Wyandotte Constitution
elections, national
—for president: 1852, 9–11, 38, 122, 201, 203; 1856, 7, 38, 91–93, 95–96, 119, 122, 126, 128–29, 148; 1860, 96, 175, 184, 192, 195; 1864, 197. *See also* Chapter 5
—midterm elections: 1854, 23, 35–38, 57, 132, 202, 208; 1858, 195–96
Elmore, Rush, 48–49
Emigrant Aid Company, 41, 62, 74, 109, 115

Index   311

emigrant aid societies, 29, 41–42, 48, 49, 73–74, 76, 82–83, 90, 111, 138, 198, 211. *See also* Emigrant Aid Company; New England Emigrant Aid Company
English, William, 22, 187
English Bill, 187–89, 191–92, 195–96
Everett, Edward, 18, 43, 48
Everett, John, 54, 81, 146, 189
Everett, Sarah, 143

Fain, W.P., 78–79
Fenton, Reuben, 23, 35
Fessenden, William Pitt, 19–20, 33, 143
Fillmore, Millard, 122, 144–46
Floyd, John, 191
Forney, John, 41, 181
forts in Kansas: Fort Leavenworth, 39, 50, 60, 74, 81, 190, 191; Fort Riley, 48, 50, 82; Fort Scott, 190, 191
Free Soil Party, 10–11, 16, 24, 54–55, 91, 135, 143
Freedom's Champion (Kansas), 188, 195, 205
Frémont, John, 119, 128, 133, 140, 142, 144–46, 151, 170
Fugitive Slave Law (1850), 9, 12, 131

Garrison, William Lloyd, 46, 54
Geary, John, 87–95, 97–98, 114, 146, 150, 169, 178, 188–89, 198–99, 203, 206, 211
Giddings, Joshua, 16, 30, 33, 138
Goodloe, Daniel, 42
Grasshopper Falls meeting, 157, 161
Greeley, Horace, 119, 170, 200
Green, James, 183–84, 187
Grow, Galusha, 22, 102, 114, 116

Hale, Edward Everett, 43, 48
Hale, John, 74, 119
Hamilton, Charles, 190
Hamlin, Hannibal, 21, 33, 135, 143
Hammond, James, 183, 186
Harney, William, 120, 123, 158
Harris, Thomas, 105, 185
Haven, Solomon, 83, 206, 213
Herald of Freedom (Kansas), 54, 78, 88, 98, 141, 155, 157, 162

Hickman, John, 103, 204, 209
Houston, Samuel, 19, 21, 25, 184
Howard, William, 68, 77–78, 108, 110, 187. *See also* Howard Committee
Howard Committee, 77, 86, 108, 113, 115, 119, 121, 123, 129, 161, 183, 203, 209, 210
Hunt, Theodore, 23, 33
Hunter, Robert, 13–14, 19, 47, 187

Illinois state politics, 24, 26, 181

Jenkins, Gaius, 78
Johnson, Samuel, 86, 122
Johnston, Saunders, 48–49
Jones, Samuel, 59–61, 63, 77–79, 81, 97, 164

Kansas Free State, 53, 78, 207
Kansas-Nebraska Act: 4, 7, 39–41, 44, 49, 53, 55, 62, 104, 108, 111–12, 127, 132–33, 135–36, 144, 162, 184, 198–99, 201–3, 207, 209–10, 212. *See also* Chapter 1; Appendixes A–E
Kansas territorial constitutions. *See* Leavenworth Constitution;, Lecompton Constitution; Topeka Constitution; Wyandotte Constitution
Kansas territorial elections. *See* elections, local
Kansas territorial government, 40, 66, 75–77, 81, 85, 90, 103–4, 111, 118, 127, 149–50, 157, 160–61, 168, 179, 199, 207; judiciary, 41, 48–49, 90, 93, 98, 104, 109, 164, 199 (*see also* Samuel Lecompte); executive teams, 3, 5, 40–41, 82, 86, 96–97, 100, 164, 166, 169, 174, 181, 193, 199, 202, 204, 207 (*see also* Andrew Reeder, Wilson Shannon, Daniel Woodson, John Geary, Robert Walker, Frederick Stanton, James Denver, Samuel Medary, and Hugh Walsh); territorial legislature, 3, 4, 49–51, 56, 62, 73, 76, 93–96, 109, 123, 149–50, 154, 161–70, 176, 179, 194, 202, 212; perceived by antislavery activists, 3, 53, 56, 61, 75–76, 83, 100, 103, 109–10, 116, 161 (*see also* Topeka Government)
Kansas territorial militia, 59, 61, 63, 80–81, 85, 88, 94, 96–97, 101, 114, 123, 158, 169, 179, 189, 199, 202

Kansas Tribune, 43, 54, 207
Kerr, John, 22, 32
Know-Nothing Party. *See* American Party

Lane, James, 53, 55, 61–63, 75, 78, 83, 84, 87, 90, 126, 161, 164, 169, 179, 189, 194, 201, 207
Law and Order Party, 58, 63, 89, 94, 106, 159
Lawrence, Amos, 47, 74, 83, 145
Lawrence, Kansas Territory, 47, 50, 60–61, 68, 77–84, 87, 89, 113, 140–41, 152, 157–58. *See also* sack of Lawrence
Leavenworth Constitution, 5, 194
Lecompte, Samuel, 58, 77, 90–93, 98, 109, 261n120
Lecompton, Kansas Territory, 59, 70, 78–80, 85, 89, 95, 164
Lecompton convention, 148–49, 151, 154, 161, 164–65, 183
Lecompton Constitution, 5, 72, 157, 159, 161–73, 175–84, 197, 204–6, 209–11, 213. *See also* Chapter 7
Liberty Party, 11

Mace, Daniel, 30, 35, 111
Maclay, William, 182
Manypenny, George, 18, 39, 49, 51, 120
Marais des Cygnes massacre, 190, 194
Marcy, William, 15, 49, 76–77, 87–88, 93, 97–98
Martin, Henry, 165–66
McIntosh, James, 77, 79
Medary, Samuel, 194
Mexican-American War, 6–7, 11, 14, 81, 122
Millson, John, 32, 106
Missouri: and Kansas elections, 3, 44, 46–47, 75, 103, 161, 163; settlers in Kansas, 4, 12–13, 43, 46–47, 199; pro-slavery activism in, 41–42, 46, 48–49, 52–53, 58, 60, 81, 83, 85, 88–89, 92, 106–12, 115–16, 118, 131, 143, 147, 152, 190, 201. *See also* Atchison, David; border ruffians
Missouri Compromise, 7, 9, 13, 27, 37, 202, 211–12; overturned by the Kansas-Nebraska Act, 4, 6, 15–16, 19, 23–25, 28–29, 32, 36, 92, 140, 144

Montgomery, James, 189–91, 194
Murphy, William, 89

Nebraska, 4, 7, 42–44, 46, 53, 57, 62, 86, 92, 99, 101, 103, 118, 132, 137–38, 144, 191, 202, 208, 212. *See also* Chapter 1; Kansas-Nebraska Act
New England Emigrant Aid Company, 41, 42, 47, 74, 83, 199, 201, 251
New Orleans Picayune, 30–31, 192
New York Evening Post, 20, 29, 140, 142, 145
New York state politics, 10, 24, 31–32, 35, 134, 195
New York Times, 74, 153
New York Tribune, 14, 40–41, 48, 62, 127, 133, 139, 140, 151–53, 173
Northern Democrats, 21, 30–32, 89, 182, 185–87, 282n68. *See* Appendixes B and D. *See also* Democratic Party
Northern Whigs, 11, 21, 30, 31, 33, 34, 36. *See* Appendixes B and D. *See also* Whig Party

Oliver, Mordecai, 68, 77, 106, 108, 110–11. *See also* Howard Committee

Pacific railroad, 12, 13, 30
Packer, Asa, 35, 41
Parrott, Marcus, 170, 186, 204
Pearce, James, 93, 133
Pennsylvania state politics, 26, 31, 35, 91, 132, 135, 136, 138, 195
Pierce, Franklin, 5–6, 9–12, 21, 35, 40, 52–53, 62, 66, 76, 79–81, 83, 86, 117, 119–25, 147, 202–6, 208, 210–11; and Kansas-Nebraska Act, 15, 17, 21, 24, 29, 31–32, 34, 38, 40, 127, 201–2, 209; proclamations on Kansas, 73–74, 76, 101–2, 105, 107, 115, 118, 132, 134, 209; and Andrew Reeder, 41, 45, 47–49, 51, 62, 74, 101, 133, 171, 202; and Wilson Shannon, 51, 55–56, 59, 61, 63, 79, 81–82, 84, 87, 96, 100, 124; and John Geary, 87, 91–95, 97, 188, 198; and election of 1856, 122, 130–32, 135–37, 139, 141–44, 146, 203

Pomeroy, Samuel, 92
popular sovereignty: 4, 6, 7, 9, 14–15, 17–18, 22, 27, 32, 34, 36, 39, 41, 44, 63, 73, 87, 97, 99, 101, 102, 106–7, 114–15, 118–19, 126, 152, 181–82, 189, 197, 199, 200–203, 206, 208, 211–12
Pottawatomie massacre, 80, 85, 110, 113, 140, 194
Price, Sterling, 88–89
proslavery, 52, 74, 142, 176, 204–6, 208; activists in Kansas, 3, 45–52, 54–55, 58, 62, 75–76, 79–81, 84–86, 88–89, 92–95, 113, 130–31, 141, 155–57, 159, 162, 164, 169, 170, 174, 201, 203, 211–12. *See also* border ruffians; Law and Order Party; Missouri
Putnam's Monthly, 10, 202

Reeder, Andrew: as territorial governor, 41, 43–52, 62, 63, 66; claim to be territorial delegate, 102–13, 115, 129; relationship with Franklin Pierce, 49, 73–74, 101, 130, 132–33, 202; as antislavery activist, 52, 55–57, 75, 77–79, 82, 131, 145, 206. *See also* Appendix F
Republican Party: and use of Kansas issue, 7, 79, 86, 96, 106, 119, 125, 128, 183–84, 200, 204, 208; in Kansas, 45, 153, 159, 163–64, 170, 178, 192, 194–95; legislative agenda, 93, 104–12, 124, 126; as opposition, 100, 128, 151, 178, 184, 186, 206, 208, 209. *See also* Howard Committee; Chapter 5
Richardson, William, 22, 24–25, 29–30
Richardson, William P., 59–60, 108
Richmond South, 158, 192
Robinson, Charles, 43, 46, 48, 52, 55, 61, 63, 74–80, 83–84, 92, 140, 151–53, 164, 199, 201. *See also* Topeka Government

sack of Lawrence, 68, 79, 80, 83, 85–86, 113, 140, 141. *See also* Bleeding Kansas
St. Louis Republican, 89, 194
Scott, Winfield, 11, 121, 122, 129
secret societies in Kansas, 48, 110, 200
Seward, William, 11, 27, 33–34, 36–37, 100, 117, 121, 124, 128, 130, 170, 183, 187, 210

Shannon, Wilson, 3, 51, 55–56, 58–61, 63, 73–74, 76–82, 84, 86–89, 93, 96–97, 100, 102, 114, 120, 122, 124, 131, 139, 193, 201–2, 206, 211
Shawnee Mission, 42, 47, 50, 51, 73, 75, 104, 177
Sherman, John, 68, 77–78, 107–8, 110, 123. *See also* Howard Committee
Sherman, Thomas, 191
slavery: 3, 7, 9, 12, 16–18, 20, 34, 37, 47–48, 54, 58, 75, 108, 134, 146–57, 202, 207–9; in the territories, 13–14, 16, 19, 22–23, 30, 34, 138, 213; and popular sovereignty, 4, 6, 7, 14, 22, 23, 25, 34, 97, 126; as a national question, 3, 6, 9, 11, 13–14, 26, 43, 63, 118, 126, 128, 137–38, 144, 180, 182, 200–201; at issue in Kansas, 3–5, 8, 12, 42, 57, 72, 76, 94–95, 97, 109, 115, 139, 148–49, 151, 155, 157, 164–65, 172, 175–76, 178, 183, 188, 192, 194, 205, 212 (*see also* the Lecompton Constitution). *See also* abolitionists; antislavery; proslavery
slaves, 4, 13, 14, 22, 25, 42, 11, 16, 21, 46, 57, 60, 115, 142, 143, 151; in Kansas, 42, 46, 51, 54, 155, 164, 166, 179, 252n 49, 277n105
Smith, George, 78, 83, 170
Smith, Gerrit, 16, 35, 138
Smith, Persifor, 81, 85, 87, 90, 95–97, 122, 124, 126
Southern Democrats, 15, 21, 23, 32, 147, 185. *See* Appendixes B and D. *See also* Democratic Party
Southern Whigs, 11, 32, 33, 36. *See* Appendixes B and D. *See also* Whig Party
Special Committee to Investigate the Troubles in Kansas. *See* Howard Committee
Speer, John, 53–54, 57, 207
Squatter Sovereign (Kansas), 48, 141, 170
Stanton, Frederick, 152, 153, 162–64, 166–70, 172–73, 176, 179, 181–83, 206
Starr, Frederick ("Lynceus"), 12–13
Stearn, Charles, 56–57
Stephens, Alexander, 23, 30–31, 33, 36, 103, 105, 123, 135, 187, 209
Strickler, Hiram, 59–60

Stringfellow, Benjamin, 42, 47, 76, 119
Stringfellow, John, 48–50, 56
Sumner, Edwin, 60, 63, 74, 78–81, 83–84, 96, 122, 140
Sumner, Charles, 16–17, 20, 25–26, 34, 54, 56, 100, 113, 127, 131, 132, 139, 142–43, 200

territorial warfare, 5, 12, 37, 59, 73, 80, 82, 84–86, 113–14, 140, 190–91, 194, 199, 203. *See also* Bleeding Kansas
Thayer, Eli, 41–42, 48
Thompson, Jacob, 160, 165, 171, 178–79, 192–93
Toombs, Robert, 17, 19, 37, 93, 118, 156, 184
Toombs Bill, 82–83, 118–20, 129, 134
Topeka, Kansas Territory, 55–56, 83–86, 88, 94, 114, 122, 138, 156–57, 172
Topeka Constitution, 5, 56–57, 73, 75, 86, 92, 102, 109, 114–20, 128–29, 133–34, 139, 149, 155, 157, 166, 169, 179, 182, 186, 204, 208–9
Topeka Government, 4, 53, 74–77, 83, 85, 100–101, 103–4, 106, 110–11, 113, 115–16, 119, 133, 140, 149, 156, 158, 180, 182, 201, 211
Toucey, Isaac, 35, 121
Trumbull, Lyman, 118

Upham, Charles, 34–35

Wade, Benjamin, 117, 119, 183
Wade, Edward, 16, 17, 20, 33, 34, 54
Walker, Robert, 8, 72, 150–67, 169, 176, 186, 204, 206, 209; break with Buchanan over Lecompton, 170–74, 181–85
Walley, Samuel, 30, 35
Walsh, Hugh, 191
Washburn, Israel, 106, 111–12
Washburne, Elihu, 24
Washington Union, 14–17, 25, 167, 171, 181
Wheeler, John, 24, 26, 32
Whitfield, John, 45, 56–58, 70, 86, 102–15, 128–29, 141. *See also* Appendix F
Whig Party, 6–7, 11, 18, 21, 25, 27, 30–36, 38, 53, 100, 128, 130–31, 136, 144, 146, 208
Wilson, Henry, 74, 119, 139
Wood, Samuel, 43, 77–78
Woodson, Daniel, 58, 84–87, 92, 97, 114, 124, 152
Wright, John, 105, 127
Wyandotte Constitution, 5, 194–95

Young, Brigham, 87, 123

Zollicoffer, Felix, 32, 116–17

www.ingramcontent.com/pod-product-compliance
Lightning Source LLC
Chambersburg PA
CBHW031326230426
43670CB00006B/248